A CHRISTIAN GUIDE TO MENTAL ILLNESS

VOLUME 1

RECOGNIZING MENTAL ILLNESS IN THE CHURCH AND SCHOOL

STEPHEN M. SAUNDERS, PH.D.

NORTHWESTERN PUBLISHING HOUSE
Milwaukee, Wisconsin

Art Director: Karen Knutson
Design Team: Diane Cook, Pamela Dunn

Northwestern Publishing House
1250 N. 113th St., Milwaukee, WI 53226-3284
www.nph.net

Published 2016
Printed in the United States of America
ISBN 978-0-8100-2706-0
ISBN 978-0-8100-2707-7 (e-book)

Contents

Preface

"Preach the Word; be prepared in season and out of season; correct, rebuke and encourage—with great patience and careful instruction."
(2 Timothy 4:2)

By the end of my second meeting with the Howards, I was concerned. Mrs. Howard was furiously angry with her husband and could not put it aside in order to have a productive discussion about their problems. Despite his protestations and entreaties, she was certain he was having an affair. He vehemently denied this. He did admit that he was "really tired" of dealing with her accusations and bad moods. It had been going on so long and had gotten so bad that he wasn't sure he could do anything to make things right. He didn't want to leave her, but he could not live like this. They had four children, and the children were also starting to suffer from their mother's rages.

I was convinced that Mr. Howard had truly done nothing wrong. I was increasingly alarmed that Mrs. Howard might have a fairly serious mental health problem. Her glare seemed to curdle the air in the office. She scoffed every time her husband insisted that he loved her. They were on the same small couch, but she sat as far away as possible, leaning against the side of the couch. She was unreasonable and unrelenting in her accusations of infidelity, whereas Mr. Howard simply looked miserable. He said, "I don't dare get home late from work or she starts a fight and ends up crying. On the other hand, if I come home early, she says I don't trust her with the kids."

At one point, Mrs. Howard blurted out that she was both ugly and terrible. She confessed, "I can't really blame him for wanting to leave me," at which point she started weeping. I thought this might be a good moment to address the issue of a possible mental illness. I said, "Have either of you ever been concerned that you may have an emotional problem, such as depression or . . . ?" I was not able to complete the question.

Mrs. Howard had stopped crying and had stood up. She looked at me and, for a panicky moment, I thought she was going to strike me. She snarled, "You're just like him! You think this is all my fault!" It took ten minutes to persuade her not to walk out of my office. Finally, she sat down again. I thought, "Now what do I do?"

Why Write This Book?

I have written this book to help you answer the question "What do I do?" when you meet someone in your church who appears to have a mental illness or a mental health problem. There are many reasons to do this, but they come down to the following issues:

- First, mental illness and mental health problems are extraordinarily common. You have met and you will meet again many, many people who struggle with these. It is simply inevitable.
- Second, there is intense stigma associated with mental illness and mental health problems. The stigma hinders and even prevents people from seeking help. People are ashamed to talk about mental illness and mental health problems either they or those they love are experiencing.
- Third, if someone in your church has a mental illness or mental health problems, and if she does seek help, she will most likely seek *your* help. Ministers and other church workers are at the front lines in the fight against mental illness. People with broken limbs and infections don't turn first to their pastor, but people with mental illness do. The reasons for this are obvious. You represent the church, and the church is at the center of the most meaningful events in people's lives. You comfort them in their grief. You preside over their marriages. You baptize their children. You deliver God's message of forgiveness and salvation. You are a special and unique person in their lives. Of course they turn to you when facing the confusing, sad, and sometimes desperate issue of mental illness.

- Fourth, you are in a position to help even if they do not seek it out. Ministers and church workers know their parishioners and their families and, often, many of the details of their lives. You are "shepherds of God's flock that is under your care, watching over them—not because you must, but because you are willing, as God wants you to be" (1 Peter 5:2). As shepherds, you have a duty to help people even when they do not know they need it. This includes gently confronting them about mental illness and mental health problems that they may be experiencing. (It will usually go better than my experience with Mrs. Howard!)
- Finally, you can help. Most obviously, you can help by reminding them of God's love for them. As Mary sitting at the feet of Christ, you can thus give them all that is needful. However, this book is not written to direct or assist you in that regard.

Instead, this book is written to assist you in understanding mental illness and mental health problems from a Christian perspective. From that understanding, you can help them realize that suffering from a mental illness or mental health problem is not a sign of either weakness or badness. This book is also written to help you understand mental illness and mental health problems from a professional perspective. You will hopefully gain a better understanding of the mental health service system, which comprises psychiatrists, psychologists, clinics, and hospitals that provide inpatient, outpatient, and medication treatment for mental illness. Such understanding will help you help them obtain the professional help that is needed.

Helping You to Help

This book is written to assist you in helping your parishioners overcome mental illness. This can be quite challenging.

One minister described his first call as one of two assistant pastors to a large church in the Northeast. He did a lot of counseling under the supervision of the head pastor. He fairly quickly established a reputation as a good listener, as someone who would listen before speaking, and as someone who seemed to understand the stress of present-day life. His most memorable counseling experience was with a parishioner who was widowed a decade prior. She would allow him to visit but would not invite him inside her home. Indeed, she would not even open the door when he visited. He would speak with her through the door. At the end of every conversation, she would tell him that she hoped he would come back the next week. He didn't reply that he hoped it didn't snow the next week, but he often thought it.

Another minister described Matt to me. At age 18, Matt tried to kill himself. Matt never received treatment following the emergency hospitalization, despite the pastor's encouragement to the family that he do so. The only counseling Matt received after the suicide attempt was with this pastor, and that amounted to brief conversations and an occasional phone call initiated by the pastor. He still wonders about Matt, who moved to a different state with his mother and stepfather about a year later.

These examples illustrate a small portion of the issues and questions most people have about mental illness and mental health problems. These questions are addressed in this book:

- How can you determine whether someone has a mental illness or not?
- What are the defining features of the different mental illnesses?
- What are the effects of mental illness on the person and on the person's family?
- What causes mental illness?
- How do you talk to someone about your concern or belief that he or she may have a mental illness?
- How do you address the common concern that developing a mental illness is a sign that someone has too little faith?
- When should you refer someone to a mental health professional, such as a psychologist, psychiatrist, or counselor? When does a referral become not merely a good idea but a necessity?
- How can you find a good psychologist, psychiatrist, or counselor for your parishioners who may need one? Even more important, how can you be sure that the mental health professional will be respectful of your church's teachings?
- If you do decide you need to refer someone to a mental health professional, how do you convince him or her to accept it?
- After you have made a referral, should you stay involved? The short answer is "YES!" You need to stay involved to be sure that the treatment is progressing as it should (which will be described in this book) or to get the parishioner to another pro-

fessional if it is not. You should stay involved because the mental health professional should not address issues of faith and forgiveness, and your parishioner will need to hear those words of comfort from you.

Preview of Volume 1

This book will be a two-volume set. This first volume is intended to help pastors and other church workers to identify and understand mental illness. (The second volume is previewed at the end of chapter 21.) It comprises three parts.

Part 1 covers the basics of mental illness. Chapter 1 begins the journey by addressing the importance of distinguishing between mental illness and mental health, and chapter 2 provides an overview of mental health functioning, whether healthy or unhealthy. The formal definition of mental illness used by mental health professionals is presented in chapter 3. Chapter 4 discusses the prevalence of mental illnesses to show that it is *inevitable* that churches and schools (and businesses and everything and everyone else) will encounter mental illness. Chapter 5 reviews the devastating effects mental illness has on individuals, couples, families, and society in general.

Part 2 details the various types of mental illness. Depression and the anxiety-related disorders are reviewed in chapters 6 and 7, whereas the psychotic disorders (such as schizophrenia) are covered in chapter 8. Bipolar disorder is covered in chapter 9, and chapter 10 covers the stress-induced disorders, such as post-traumatic stress disorder. Chapter 11 reviews the substance use disorders, eating disorders, and disorders related to impulse control problems. Chapter 12 covers less common mental illnesses, including the somatization, tic, sleep, and sexual disorders. In chapter 13, three of the most common personality disorders are discussed. Chapter 14 reviews the mental illnesses that primarily affect children, and chapter 15 covers the issues of child abuse and neglect. Chapter 16 reviews those illnesses that primarily affect the elderly. Chapter 17 discusses domestic abuse, also known as spousal abuse or "intimate partner violence." Chapter 18 reviews the many issues related to suicide, which is more common among persons with mental illness.

Part 3 discusses the essential role of the church in the understanding, care, and treatment of persons with mental illness and their loved ones. Chapter 19 reviews commonplace ways that mental illness is misunderstood, both within general society and within the church. Chapter 20 reviews the proper understanding of mental illness from the perspective of the Bible and by reference to various Christian pastors throughout history, including St. Paul and Martin Luther. Chapter 21 discusses the central role that the church and its workers have in helping persons with mental illness, focusing on issues specific to Christians who need mental health treatment, including stigma and shame.

Postscript

After Mrs. Howard sat down again, with a glare for both me and her husband that, for some reason, made me think of Medusa, I decided to try a different approach. Clearly Mrs. Howard was having nothing to do with the suggestion that she might have a mental illness.

I acknowledged the distress in the room, demonstrating that I was listening and that I understood how they were feeling. "This situation is very distressing to both of you. You're both feeling upset and miserable. And although you didn't say it, I'm guessing you're both worried about the kids as well." That helped her to see that I realized she wanted things to be different and that she was a caring, concerned mother. I showed that I did not see her as a bad person.

I then offered a contrast between where they were and where they wanted to be. "You're both unhappy and your family isn't what you want it to be. You want to be able to trust each other, and you want to be trusted. The reason you married is because you love each other and you want to feel that love again. This situation has to change." Again, this was to show both of them, but her in particular, that I thought they were good people who were in a bad situation.

I then tried to instill some hope that things could change. "This won't be quick or easy, but if you stick with this, it can help." Unless someone has this hope, they won't bother returning for another meeting.

Finally, I asked them for their patience, noting that the problem had developed over a long period of time and might take more than one meeting to resolve. I then asked them to return, with the intention of getting them to a point where change was actually possible.

ONE

PART 1

BASIC INFORMATION ABOUT MENTAL ILLNESS

WHAT IS IT? HOW COMMON IS IT? HOW BAD IS IT?

Preview of Part 1

The first part of this volume provides basic information about mental illness, including what it is, how common it is, and the varieties of misery that it causes.

This basic information will hopefully clarify areas of confusion. A common source of confusion is the difference between mental illness and normality, which is covered in chapters 1 through 3. Perhaps the reader has heard, thought about, or even asked these questions:

- How do you tell the difference between sadness and depression?
- She's always been very shy around people, but could this actually be an anxiety problem?
- How do you know if you have a drinking problem?

Another commonly held misconception is that mental illness is very rare. As chapter 4 demonstrates, anyone who knows more than four people likely knows someone who is presently experiencing a mental illness. It is not rare at all.

Some claim that mental illness is really not that bad. "My aunt Betty supposedly had depression, but we all figured she was just seeking the attention of others. How bad is it really?" Here's a short preview of chapter 5, which addresses this issue—it's bad.

These first three chapters address commonly held beliefs about mental illness, which are a conglomeration of "It's not real," "It's not that common," and "It's not that bad." These beliefs are inspired by the commonly held *hope* that only bad or weak people will be stricken with mental illness. Christians sometimes adopt a particularly virulent and condemnatory notion that mental illness only happens to those of weak faith. I consolidate these notions into what I call the weakness-badness theory of mental illness. The effect of such notions, which are widely held, is that persons suffering with mental illness feel incredibly ashamed. As a result, they may be very reluctant to admit that they or someone they love may have a mental illness. They are reluctant to admit this even to themselves, but are especially reluctant to admit it to others. If they are too ashamed to admit as much, they are unlikely to get help for the mental illness.

This issue of stigma is almost entirely unique to mental illness. When I broke my arm because I tried to walk downstairs while drinking hot coffee and talking on my cell phone, I laughed about it with my friends. I was not ashamed of the cause of my injury. However, people whom God afflicts with mental illness almost always do feel shame, as if, somehow, they should have been able to avoid its cause. The third part of this volume addresses this issue in greater detail.

My prayer is that proper education about the reality of mental illness, the commonness of mental illness, and the misery that mental illness causes will diminish the weakness-badness theory. If you and I do not hold stigmatizing attitudes towards mental illness, we are much more capable of helping those suffering from it.

Chapter 1

The Importance of Distinguishing Mental Health and Mental Illness

"Stop judging by mere appearances, but instead judge correctly."
(John 7:24)

The most basic question regarding mental illness is "What is it?" This is a surprisingly challenging question. It can be difficult to decide whether someone's feelings, thoughts, and behavior are an indication of something abnormal. But making the distinction between normal and abnormal is absolutely essential. Consider Jenny and Richard.

Jenny the First Grader

Mrs. Wilson teaches first grade at Our Redeemer Grade School. She and Mr. Peters, the principal, ask for a meeting with Jenny's parents because they have some concerns. Jenny has missed almost three weeks of school in total, and it is only early November. When she is at school, Jenny seems anxious and fearful. She often asks to go to the office because her stomach is upset or she has a headache. During the meeting, Mom admits that some mornings she gives in to Jenny's pleas and crying and allows her to stay home.

On the one hand, school can be a scary place for any child, and first grade can be especially scary. On the other hand, teachers and schools know this and go out of their way to ease the fears of children. Most children are not so fearful that they beg to stay home. Missing school because of fear is not normal.

Should Jenny be referred to a psychologist? She is exhibiting at least some of the signs of separation anxiety disorder, which means that a child experiences extreme anxiety when separated from her parents. Perhaps a referral to a psychologist would be appropriate. On the other hand, perhaps mom should be referred to a psychologist. Perhaps Mom is somehow encouraging Jenny, her only child, to resist going to school. Jenny needing to stay home and be near her mom might make Mom feel better about herself.

However, Jenny's fears and refusal to go to school might be both normal and understandable. Perhaps Jenny is being teased and bullied by some of the other kids in her class. It might be the case that Jenny is being mistreated by her teacher. In these cases, there is a problem (i.e., the way Jenny is being treated at school), but it has nothing to do with Jenny or her family.

If the teacher and principal cannot tell whether Jenny's thoughts, feelings, and behaviors are normal or abnormal, they cannot know whether they are seeing a problem with Jenny (or her mom) or a problem situation that needs to be resolved. The difference is important.

Richard the Salesman

Richard sells commercials for a nationally broadcast radio program, and he is very good at it. He has won sales awards. He was offered a promotion to management several times, but he kept declining because he could make more from commissions than he would from being a supervisor.

Richard has not worked in several months. His employer put him on unofficial sabbatical, and his office waits empty in hopes of his return. When Richard didn't show up for a major out-of-town sales appointment, his boss called to find out why. Richard was home, as he had missed his flight. He was also intoxicated. He insulted his boss repeatedly, made disparaging remarks about the radio program, started crying, and hung up. He hasn't been back to the office since.

Does Richard need to be referred to a substance abuse counselor? He is exhibiting signs of an alcohol problem. He is drinking too much, and the drinking is causing some problems. (Missing appointments, skipping work, and insulting one's boss are almost always bad for one's career.)

If Richard's behavior is abnormal, we might conclude that he needs to be referred to a mental health professional. With the details just provided, it seems that this might be the case. But distinguishing normal and abnormal requires that we know all of the details about someone's situation.

Two weeks before Richard missed his flight, his eldest son, Robbie, had been killed in a plane crash. Richard had taught Robbie to fly. They loved to fly together, and Richard had helped Robbie buy his first plane. Richard's last view of his son's plane was of it crumpled off the side of the runway, surrounded by emergency vehicles. Ten days after his son's funeral, Richard sat in the waiting area at the airport, staring at the tunnel leading to the plane. He watched the other passengers board, heard his name called, heard the name of the standby passenger who took his seat, and watched the plane pull away. After several more hours, he went home and got drunk.

Perhaps it now seems clear that Richard does not need a substance abuse counselor. His reaction and his behavior seem more normal, and we may think he simply needs some more time to grieve and that he may benefit from a group that allows parents to talk about the exquisite pain felt when one loses a child. On the other hand, if we learn that Richard is a recovering alcoholic and has had a relapse due to Robbie's death, then his behavior is once again perceived as problematic. Distinguishing normal and abnormal can be difficult.

Abnormal or Normal? A Difficult But Important Distinction

Does Jenny need treatment? Or does her mom? Or does neither? If Jenny or her mom have a mental illness, then treatment would be beneficial. But if neither has a mental illness, treatment would be unnecessary and even potentially harmful. Imagine telling Jenny, who is being bullied, that she needs treatment because there is something abnormal about how she is feeling!

What about Richard? Distinguishing normal and abnormal is the difference between telling Richard who is grieving and Richard who is a lapsing alcoholic that there is something wrong. The difference is the difference between savage cruelty and steadfast kindness.

Does Someone Need Treatment?

Distinguishing the difference between normal and abnormal is thus very important for knowing who should be referred for treatment and who should not. It is similarly important for knowing when treatment is no longer necessary. Psychological and psychiatric treatment should discontinue when a person is no longer mentally ill and no longer needs it. Although some persons stay on psychiatric medications essentially forever in order to maintain mental health, most individuals who obtain treatment are helped enough that they eventually stop.

Research

Knowing the difference between normal and abnormal is essential for research. Research informs us about the causes of mental illness, as well as what works to treat it. To do research, researchers need to agree on what they are studying. This is why scientists distinguish frogs from toads, crickets from grasshoppers, and moths from butterflies. It is impossible to know anything about any thing unless there is agreement on what that thing is. This might be why the first task given to Adam was to name the creatures. When Adam told Abel to gather some goats, Abel needed to know the difference between the goats and the gorillas. Likewise, mental health researchers need an agreed-upon definition of mental illness so that we are all studying the same thing.

Mental health professionals need to distinguish mental health and mental illness. It seems like it should be easy, but it is not. This is because mental health, mental health problems, and mental illness lie on a continuum.

The Mental Health—Mental Health Problems—Mental Illness Continuum

There are no bright, bold lines of demarcation separating normal from deviant. That is, there is no definitive way of knowing that the way someone is feeling, acting, or thinking is indicative of abnormality.

For this reason, it is best to consider mental health and mental illness as points on a continuum, such as is shown in Figure 1. At one end is good mental health, at the other end is mental illness, and in between are mental health problems. Few people will go all of life with uninterrupted good mental health. Instead, most people will go back and forth along the continuum. Even those in good mental health will occasionally experience mild or moderate mental health problems, such as an episode of prolonged extreme sadness or anxiety. Some of these people will actually develop a diagnosable mental illness at some point, but the illness will be time-limited. Still others will develop a mental illness that never goes away.

Mental health, mental health problems, and mental illness are defined more thoroughly in the next two chapters.

Figure 1

Mental Health	Mental Health Problems	Mental Illness
Feel well Think well of self and others Infrequent feelings of sadness, anxiety, anger, etc. Able to do things much the way you want Successfully fulfill roles (as spouse, worker, friend, etc.) Able to establish and maintain relationships	Intermittent feelings of sadness, anger, anxiety, etc. Occasional unhealthy or inappropriate behavior Sporadic problems with roles and relationships, but usually able to work them out	Serious and persistent distress, including intensely negative self-perception Persistent negative feelings, such as depression, anxiety, anger, etc. Behavior that is unhealthy or inappropriate or that puts one at risk Serious problems fulfilling roles, including problems in relationships

Postscript

Should you refer Jenny and Richard to a mental health professional? Yes, you probably should. You should because you are concerned that the person *may* have a mental illness, and that is enough reason to do so. This book is intended to help you determine, to some extent, whether or not a person has a mental illness and needs referral to a mental health professional, but the distinction can be quite difficult. Reading this book might not be enough to help you make it.

If you are uncertain, make a referral. Mental health professionals are specially trained (thus the term *professional*) to distinguish between abnormal and normal reactions to the crises, events, and traumas that life throws at people. Of course, that means that some of the time the mental health professional should say to Jenny, Richard, or whomever he or she is evaluating, "No, this is not something that needs to be treated. Go home." Other times they may say, "While this is not mental illness, I can help you deal with this terrible situation, if you are willing to enter treatment."

We talk about how to make a referral in the second volume, including how to approach the person about your concerns and about your hope that he or she seek treatment, and also how to identify mental health professionals who are qualified to help.

Chapter 2

Defining Mental Health

"Therefore do not worry about tomorrow,
for tomorrow will worry about itself."
(Matthew 6:34)

The Components of Human Behavior

Mental health functioning constitutes the ABCs of our two Rs.

Within each of us, there exist the ABCs. **A**ffect is the way we feel both moment-to-moment and over long periods. **B**ehaviors are the way we act, either spontaneously (e.g., "I'm tired and will get myself a cup of coffee") or in reaction to something else (e.g., "I'm meeting Dave for coffee"). **C**ognitions are any thoughts we have, including considerations, memories, and plans.

The two Rs of life are *roles* and *relationships.* Roles include the things we are, such as a worker or student. Many of our roles involve relationships, such as being a parent, a spouse, a brother, or a friend.

Our ABCs affect our Rs. That is, the way we feel, act, and think influences how we function in our roles and in our relationships.

ABCs and the Two Rs

Affect is the way we feel, both at the present and over the long term (long-term affect is called mood).

Behavior is what we do, how we act, or how we behave.

Cognition is any mental activity, such as our perceptions, memories, expectations, reasoning, and thinking.

Relationships with others are the most central and essential aspect of our lives and include family, friends, acquaintances, and people at work.

Roles define our life's tasks, such as our role as a student, parent, son or daughter, wife or husband, or employee.

Affect (and Mood)

Emotions are such an integral part of mental health that mental illnesses are often referred to as emotional disorders.

Short-lived emotions are *affect.* Affect changes fairly quickly. During a conversation with a friend, we may feel sad at one moment (hearing about her brother's cancer), outraged in another (hearing about what the insurance company did), and happy at the end (hearing that the brother is okay now). While watching a half-hour news program, we can feel aggravated about a report on the economy, excited about the way our sports team performed, irritated at the weather prediction, and amused by a story about little kids at the zoo. Affect changes according to situation.

Mood is how we describe someone's emotional state over an extended period of time. Someone in a bad mood feels irritable for hours or even a whole day. The bad mood may slowly lift when he is doing something enjoyable. Likewise, someone may experience a good mood all morning, feeling cheerful and positive, but then the mood might get soured in the afternoon by an unpleasant interaction or task. Moods are feelings that last. Similar to affect, mood is usually changeable.

Thus, mood can be thought of as our baseline emotion, that is, the way we generally feel. Affect is how we feel moment to moment, and it usually returns to the emotional state congruent with our mood. For example, "I was in a really bad mood all day, except when I had lunch with Dan and cheered up for a while," or "Despite getting in a bad argument with Denise, I was in a really good mood today."

A mental health professional will evaluate both mood and affect when trying to determine whether someone has a mental illness or not. With regard to mood, a chronically bad or sad mood may indicate a mood disorder, such as depression. Regarding affect, displaying unusual affect, such as becoming intensely angry for no apparent reason, can be an indication of serious mental illness.

Behavior

Behavior is the way we act. Getting up in the morning, taking care of our hygiene (showering, brushing our teeth, dressing appropriately), taking care of children, getting ourselves to work or school, doing the tasks of work or school, meeting with friends, talking and interacting with others—these are a small sampling of the behaviors that make up many of our days.

In trying to determine whether a person has a mental illness, a mental health professional will evaluate how well someone's behaviors match with the expectations and demands of her roles and relationships. For example, the behavior of drunken driving violates the societal demand of being a good, safe driver who does not endanger others. Drunken driving while one's children are in the backseat would be evaluated as even more pathological.

Cognition

Cognition is any mental activity related to present, past, and future events. That is, cognition includes thoughts, memories, and plans.

Cognitions include what we currently think about ourselves and others. Many of my students think, during lecture, "Does he actually prepare for class?" and "How did he get a degree?" After a compliment, you may think, "My boss seems to like me."

Cognitions are anything we remember from the past. Memories are either event-based or informational. Event memories concern things we experienced. Many of us have memories of where we were on September 11, 2001, including who we were with and what we were doing. Other memories are informative, such as remembering Bible verses, people's names, directions to locations, and how to bake bread.

Cognitions are often future oriented. Cognitions include what we are planning for the future, which may be either short- or long-term ("I plan to leave work by 5:30" or "We are planning a trip to Spain this coming fall") and either vague or specific ("We are going out to eat tonight" or "We are going to Joe's Bar and Grill so that I can get their chicken wings").

Mental health professionals evaluate a person's cognitions in great detail in order to determine whether someone may have a mental illness. For example, someone who cannot remember information from the past may be diagnosed with mental retardation, a learning disability, alcoholism, or Alzheimer's disease. Someone who exhibits negative cognitions about himself (e.g., "I am a loser") may be diagnosed with depression. If he engages in cognitions that are frightening (e.g., "My racing heart is going to kill me"), he may be diagnosed with panic disorder.

The Interplay of the ABCs

Our thoughts, feelings, and behaviors influence one another (see image below). Let's go through these influences in turn.

How we feel influences how we act. If we do not care (a lack of feeling) about a performance (behavior), we might not do as well as we could. Feeling nervous before a presentation is a good thing, since it motivates us to prepare for it, which leads to a better performance. Alternatively, feelings can interfere with behavior. When hitting a golf ball by myself on the driving range (behavior), I do pretty well. When I play with friends, however, the nervous feeling caused by others watching me causes my performance to suffer.

How we feel influences what we think. If we feel badly about an experience or tragic event, we may not be able to stop thinking about it. This is the primary symptom of post-traumatic stress disorder (PTSD). Many years back, I treated a young man who saw fighting in the Iraq War. His Marine platoon came under sniper fire, and his best friend was killed. Two years later, he could not stop thinking about the horrifying incident, which also invaded his dreams every night.

The Interplay Between Thoughts, Feelings, and Actions

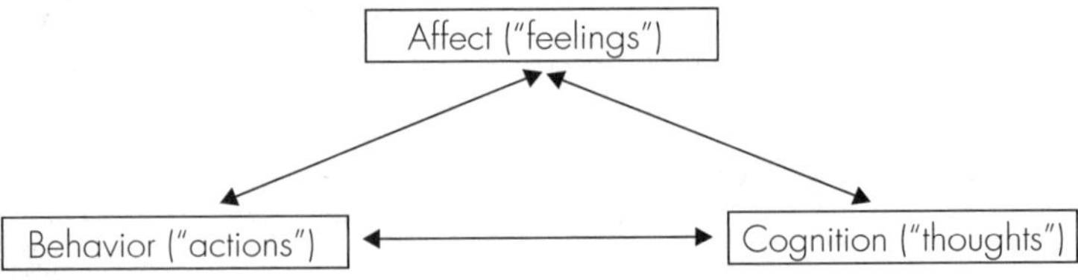

Our behavior influences how we feel. This fact leads to the expression, "All work and no play makes Jack a dull boy." If someone spends weeks doing nothing enjoyable, he will become bored and sad. The young marine in the previous paragraph withdrew from friends and family, and this behavior made his depression worse.

The effect of behavior on thinking is perhaps obvious. Most people have done things they have regretted, making them think over and over, "Why did I do that? What was I thinking?" Likewise, preparing for that presentation influences how we think about it ("I'm ready for this!"), which in turn will affect how we feel (less nervous).

Mental health professionals have long known *the important influence of thinking on how we feel.* If you think the car you purchased is a lemon, you will feel upset. Many persons spend much of every day reminding themselves that they are unworthy and unlovable, which leads them to develop depression. I had a patient who was convinced that his boss did not like him. During daily interactions with her, he would feel quite anxious. I instructed him to observe how she acted with other workers. Fairly quickly, he realized that she was rude towards everyone. He changed his thinking to "She is not nice to anyone, including me." This did not make him look forward to interacting with her, obviously, but the new way of thinking made him feel less anxious.

Examples of the ways that *thinking influences behavior* are also easy to generate. If you think that reading this book is worthwhile, then you are likely to keep reading it. If you think that this car is a better deal than that car, you will purchase accordingly. If you think that Jim would make a better president than Joe, you will vote accordingly. Everyone knows how school children behave if they think that a teacher will not follow through on threats of discipline. On the other hand, if students expect that a teacher will send home a note if they misbehave or if homework is not turned in, then they are more likely to behave and do that homework.

Paul recognized the importance of how we think. He admonished the Romans to "not think of yourself more highly than you ought, but rather think of yourself with sober judgment" (12:3). He advised the Philippians, "Whatever is true, whatever is noble, whatever is right, whatever is pure, whatever is lovely, whatever is admirable—if anything is excellent or praiseworthy—think about such things" (4:8).

More Examples of the Interplay of the ABCs

- John has a conversation over the phone with his wife and she abruptly ends the conversation. He *thinks* that his wife hung up because she was angry with him, and he then *feels* angry and *acts* defensively when he sees her later that night. The way John thinks, not reality, influences his feelings and behavior. In reality, she was abrupt on the phone not because she was angry but because she suddenly realized she was late for a meeting.
- Sally *feels* depressed and *thinks* others don't want to see her. As a result, she stops *doing* things she enjoys, such as attending church or going out with friends. This lack of activity in enjoyable behaviors will worsen her feelings of depression. This worsened depression will cause her to become more isolated and have even more depressing thoughts, and so it goes. In this manner, depression begets depression.
- The association between thoughts, behaviors, and feelings is the basis of the most common and effective psychotherapy ever developed. Cognitive behavior therapy, or CBT, focuses on changing *both* cognitions and behaviors so that the person feels better. For example, a CBT therapist will instruct a depressed patient to engage in enjoyable behaviors as often as possible (although she doesn't *feel* like doing so). As therapy progresses, they will focus on changing the negative, self-critical thoughts the patient continues to have.

Roles and Relationships (The Two Rs)

Sigmund Freud said, "Love and work are the cornerstones to our humanness". He may have been wrong about much, but he was right about that.

Our emotions, actions, and cognitions influence one another. They also influence how well we fulfill our roles and how well we function in relationships. To fulfill one's roles in life is one of the most essential aspects of being mentally healthy. This includes being productive at work or school, meeting our obligations and responsibilities to friends and loved ones, and taking care of ourselves. A mentally healthy person does not resent, resist, or neglect obligations to others but rather seeks to fulfill them to the best of his or her ability.

Roles and relationships are closely intertwined. Indeed, most roles are defined by relationships, such as being a husband or wife, a father or mother, a sister or brother, a son or daughter, a friend, a colleague, a boss, or an employee. Being a good spouse means fulfilling your obligations and responsibilities in that relationship by making your spouse feel loved, respected, and appreciated. Christian parents meet their obligation to their children by teaching them God's Word and by taking them to church. They meet their children's emotional and physical needs by accepting the responsibility to feed, clothe, love, support, discipline, and protect them. By fulfilling role obligations, the mentally healthy person is able to make and keep mutually satisfying relationships.

Mental Health

These components of human behavior (thoughts, feelings, behaviors, roles, and relationships) can be used to define mental health and mental illness. As indicated in the previous chapter, mental health and mental illness are most appropriately conceptualized as lying on a continuum rather than as being clearly and easily distinguished. (Mental illness is defined in the next chapter.)

To be mentally healthy means that a person *feels* much the way he or she wants, is in control of his or her *actions,* and *thinks* both realistically and optimistically. Because one's ABCs are healthy, one is able to fulfill *obligations* to others and is able to make and keep important *relationships.*

To be mentally healthy means to demonstrate generally positive and appropriate affect. It means, for the most part, feeling good about who you are and what you are doing and the direction that your life is heading. Healthy affective reactions towards the normal, everyday stress at work and in relationships mean not resenting the demands of work and of others, not becoming angry or abusive, and not withdrawing into fear and depression. Healthy affective reactions allow one to approach roles and relationships with love, calmness, purpose, and a generally pleasant demeanor.

Mentally healthy people demonstrate self-control and the capacity to change their behavior in order to maximize their success at work, school, or in relationships. Being mentally healthy means not losing self-control in outbursts of inappropriate behavior, such as temper tantrums or excessive alcohol use. A mentally healthy person is able to initiate, continue, and complete assignments and tasks. Mental health entails engaging in basic self-care behaviors, such as eating normally and at least somewhat nutritiously, being able to sleep well enough to feel rested for the most part, and participating in exercise appropriately.

A mentally healthy person will not have difficulty doing things he wants to do, such as engaging in hobbies, exercising, reading, or taking care of his family.

A mentally healthy person thinks about herself in a generally positive light. She will mostly like herself and what she does, even as she realizes that some improvements are possible or needed. A mentally healthy person will perceive his faults for what they are (i.e., an inevitable aspect of being a sinful, imperfect human being) and accept them. A mentally healthy person realizes he is loveable despite being flawed, and he likewise loves other people even though they too have flaws. Being mentally healthy entails thinking realistically and not setting expectations excessively high for either yourself or others.

To be in good mental health means that one is able to anticipate the future and make plans for improving it. Mental health entails being able to see yourself in the future, evaluating what you see, and formulating strategies for change if needed or desirable.

A mentally healthy person has an adequate memory. She is able to learn new material, to retain material that is necessary and useful, and to use information appropriately. She remembers meetings she needs to attend and people with whom she associates. A well-functioning memory enables her to adopt new behaviors to adapt to the challenges of a new situation, such as learning to use a new computer program at work.

In summary, healthy affect, behavior, and cognitions enable us to have productive lives full of satisfying relationships. As we will now see, having a mental illness means having difficulty with affect, behavior, and cognitions that leads to problems in roles and relationships.

Chapter 3

The Formal Definition of Mental Illness

"Have mercy on me, my God, have mercy on me, for in you I take refuge. I will take refuge in the shadow of your wings until the disaster has passed."
(Psalm 57:1)

In 1952, the American Psychiatric Association published the *Diagnostic and Statistical Manual of Mental Disorders* (DSM). It was an attempt to distinguish mental illness from mental health in a formal way that would be adopted and used by all psychiatrists belonging to the organization. The great needs of military men and women returning from service in the recent world wars were a major impetus for formalizing the definition. In fact, the two world wars greatly advanced the mental health profession in general.

The Effect of the World Wars on Psychiatry and Clinical Psychology

Numerous examples of the psychological effects of trauma existed long before the 20th century, including the biblical account of King Saul (1 Samuel 9–31) and works by Shakespeare *(Henry IV,* Lady Macbeth in *Macbeth)* and Stephen Crane *(The Red Badge of Courage).* Early in the 1900s, the nascent fields of neurology and psychiatry had celebrities, such as Sigmund Freud, who argued persuasively that psychological trauma could cause immense and long-term harm. The general population admired Freud, partly because he wrote beautifully, evidenced by his winning the 1930 Goethe Prize for literature. However, despite the many historical examples and despite Freud, the medical community did not believe in the notion of psychological trauma.

Most medical doctors and many psychiatrists were skeptical that psychological events, regardless of how traumatic, could cause mental illness. Most soldiers returning from combat did not experience mental illness as a result of that experience, so there must have been something flawed in the character of the soldiers who did. It was likewise easy to dismiss mental health professionals as self-serving: "Of course they believe that! It's good for their business!"

The early 1900s was also the heyday of the disease model of illness, which contends that all illness is due to some biological disease. Recent proofs that killing bacteria healed infections and that inoculations slowed the spread of viral illnesses convinced medical doctors that all illnesses could be attributed to biological causes. Mental illness, like biological illness, must therefore have a biological cause (the second volume will provide a more detailed history of this perspective). Just because the biological cause could not be seen did not mean it did not exist. They could not see bacteria or viruses until the invention of the microscope, but they were still there, causing infection and illness.

The world wars revealed the flaws in the disease model, especially with regard to mental illness.

World War I and Psychiatry

The level, breadth, and depth of destruction wrought on the battlefields of Europe during the Great War (World War I) were unprecedented. Tanks, machine guns, warplanes, and battleships were invented and improved. Bombs got bigger and bigger, and yet were lobbed farther and farther. During the early years of the war, the dazed, disoriented, fearful state of some soldiers recently at the front was usually (and somewhat correctly) attributed to temporary brain damage caused by exploding shells, leading to the term *shell shock.*

The ongoing war allowed doctors to continue to observe and document. Many reported the observation that not all soldiers exposed to explosions developed shell shock. Also, there was usually no physical evidence of injury in those soldiers who had developed it. Finally, some soldiers developed the symptoms of shell shock without exposure to explosions. These observations led, at first, to the conclusion that complaints associated with shell shock were actually evidence of either cowardice or malingering. The military therefore commanded that soldiers suffering from shell shock be punished and returned to duty as soon as possible.

As the war progressed, however, more and more soldiers and commanders, including decorated heroes, were found to exhibit shell shock. As a result, the idea that shell shock, or battle fatigue, was due to cowardice and shirking lost plausibility. Also influential in changing this perspective were military psychiatrists, whose views were gaining credibility because of their success treating cases of shell shock. By the end of the war, most medical doctors had become convinced that shell shock was actually due to emotional trauma. By then the term *shell shock* had been largely replaced by a different term: *battle fatigue.*

Progress had thus been made, but it was incomplete. Based on the observation that not all soldiers who had the same experience (e.g., fought in the same battle) developed battle fatigue, it was reasoned that some soldiers were psychologically weaker than others and were thus predisposed to develop it. This standpoint was consistent with Freudian notions of psychosexual development, so psychiatrists promoted this idea. This led to efforts to identify the capacity of military conscripts, which opened the door for a greater role for the developing field of professional psychology.

World War I and Clinical Psychology

In the early 1900s, being a psychologist usually meant being involved in research. The relatively few professional psychologists were mostly conducting educational assessments for states and schools. When the United States entered the Great War, professional psychologists were hurriedly engaged to develop a way of testing the troops being brought into the military. The testing was primarily vocational and educational in nature. The military wanted information about what role (e.g., soldier or sergeant, cook or gunner) a recruit would be capable of fulfilling. With regard to educational assessment, recall that in the United States in the early 1900s, relatively few citizens had completed much formal schooling, and many were foreign born and were not fluent in English. Using their established expertise in testing, psychologists quickly developed tests that could be administered to large groups of recruits.

In less than two years, psychologists had overseen the testing of more than 1.5 million soldiers. The military did not actually use the test results, but it was very impressed by the huge amount of information provided, and the assessment program was considered a great success. The reputation of psychology rose accordingly.

The "war to end all wars" in fact did not. World War II also added to the prestige of the professions of psychiatry and psychology.

World War II and Clinical Psychology

By the end of the Great War, psychiatry had convinced the military that war caused emotional trauma to soldiers who were psychologically vulnerable and psychology had convinced the military that it knew how to test and categorize human beings. Accordingly, as it geared up to enter World War II, the US government approached the American Psychological Association and asked it to apply its testing expertise to predict which recruits would develop trauma-related mental illness. Over the course of the war, 14 million soldiers were tested, and nearly two million were deemed unfit for duty due to "neuropsychiatric disorders."

World War II and Psychiatry

Based on experiences during the previous war, psychiatrists during World War II developed simple but effective means of dealing with psychological casualties in the field. They realized that the closer to the battle lines the intervention occurred, the better the outcome. Psychiatrists found that supportive counseling (listening sympathetically, providing reassurance) enabled over half of the soldiers who had been traumatized to the point of incapacity to return to duty within a few days.

Because of their success, in 1944 psychiatry was placed on an equal organizational level within the military as medicine and surgery. The psychiatrist William C. Menninger achieved the rank of brigadier general. The war confirmed the idea that stress, not just genetics, could contribute to emotional disorders, and that relatively simple, purposeful interventions could relieve or eliminate those same problems.

Psychiatry at the Battlefront

In the marvelous biography about WWII paratroopers called *Band of Brothers*, author Stephen Ambrose relates the following incident: Private Blithe was at an aid station because he had been blinded. When asked by Lieutenant Winters what happened, Blithe reported, "Everything just went black, sir. I can't see a thing. I'm sorry." Winters patted the soldier on the shoulder and reassured him that he would be okay. As he was walking away, the soldier called out, "Lieutenant, I can see. It's okay. I can see. I think I'll be all right." Incidents like that did and do happen during combat.

World War II and Clinical Psychology, Part 2

WWII helped clinical psychology enter the realm of treatment, which previously both the American Psychiatric Association and the American Medical Association had fought tooth and nail to prevent.

Based on its experience during the first war, the government realized that it had to prepare for large-scale psychological trauma both during the war and after it. The government realized that the need would far outstrip the number of psychiatrists capable of providing mental health services. This shortfall had actually been exacerbated by the large number of psychiatrists who were retrained as trauma surgeons during the war.

So, the federal government made an arrangement with departments of psychology around the country. If the departments provided the scientific training of students, the Veterans Affairs (VA) system would subsequently provide those students with clinical training. The hope (and ultimate reality) was that many of the newly created clinical psychologists would work for the overtaxed VA system. To this day, VA medical facilities are a major training ground and source of employment for clinical psychologists.

The Need for a Diagnostic System for Mental Illness

Prior to World War II, there was some agreement among mental health professionals about the distinction between mental health and mental illness. However, the distinction was more important to researchers than it was to clinicians. It enabled researchers to count, via the federal census, the number of persons who had a mental illness (i.e., who were in a psychiatric institution). In contrast, diagnoses had little impact on the assessment and treatment of actual patients. Practicing psychiatrists believed that mental illness was always unique to the person suffering it. If the manifestations of mental illness were unique, then treatment had to be individualized to the patient. No two patients were alike, so no two treatments should be alike.

World War II exposed the absurdity of this notion. Thousands of veterans had returned from Europe and Asia having had similar traumatic experiences, and they were exhibiting similar mental health problems. In addition were the positive results obtained by psychiatry during the war. The same relatively simple, brief treatment was given to all traumatized soldiers, and it was found to be effective in many instances.

At the same time, military psychiatrists and psychologists realized that not all soldiers had trauma-based disorders. Some exhibited substance use problems, others were suffering from depression, and still others were displaying extremely odd behaviors. There were a variety of disorders, but none had yet been properly categorized or named. For the appropriate treatment to be implemented, the disorder needed to be identified.

Thus emerged the need for a diagnostic system. As it tends to do when it needs something, when the military needed a classification system, it created one. Following the war, the VA system borrowed extensively from the military to create its own classification system of mental illnesses. These two systems formed the basis of the first DSM, which was published by the American Psychiatric Association.

The DSM (and the ICD)

In 1952, the *Diagnostic and Statistical Manual of Mental Disorders* (DSM) was published. (Many wonder why the term *statistical* is in the manual's title. It has to do with one of its original purposes, which was to provide psychiatrists a tally of the number of persons who needed their care.)At the time of this writing, the fifth edition has just been published. The vast majority of mental health professionals in the United States use the DSM. In contrast, medical doctors in the United States and both medical and mental health professionals outside of the United States use the *International Classification of Diseases* (ICD). The fifth chapter of the ICD covers mental illnesses. The DSM and ICD are nearly identical in their classification of mental illnesses. Currently there is a push to adopt the ICD system.

The DSM takes a "descriptive phenomenological approach" to diagnosing mental illnesses. Using the DSM, a person will be diagnosed as having a mental illness based on his or her *subjective* (i.e., phenomenological) experience of feelings, thoughts, and behaviors. A mental health professional would diagnose a person with a depressive disorder, for example, based on her subjective experience. That is, she may be diagnosed with depression if she describes herself as feeling sad, thinking badly about herself, withdrawing from friends, and so forth.

Important, to diagnose someone with a mental illness does not require that the mental health professional know what caused the disorder to develop. Contrast this to medical diagnoses, which often require a discovery of the cause of the symptoms. For example, diabetes is diagnosed when there are chronic, excessive levels of glucose in the blood, which is fairly easily measured. Likewise, reported pain, weight loss, and general sickness are attributed to cancer if and only if the cancer is discovered using X-rays, blood tests, CT scans, or other means.

Mental Illness Defined

According to the DSM, mental illness should be diagnosed if a person exhibits or experiences a clinically significant behavioral or psychological syndrome or pattern that is associated with present distress or disability.

Behavioral or Psychological Syndrome

Problems that are aspects of mental illness may be behavioral or psychological or both. Behavioral problems involve actions or things we do. These may include a person drinking too much, a person avoiding social events, or a student getting out of his seat repeatedly during class. Psychological problems may involve either feelings or cognitions. These may include feeling sad, thinking badly about oneself, having memory problems, or believing that the neighbors are plotting to destroy you. In other words, mental illness entails serious, unremitting problems in feelings (affect), actions (behavior), or thinking (cognition).

Some mental illnesses are primarily problems in only one of these. For example, a person with a substance use problem such as alcohol dependence has, by definition, a problem with his *behavior,* even if his thought processes and feelings are generally normal. Other mental illnesses are characterized by problems in two areas, and some entail problems in all three. For example, an autism spectrum disorder is primarily defined by impaired cognitive capacity that interferes with the ability to engage in appropriate social behavior. In the case of depression, the problem of feeling unremittingly sad is obvious, but there are also usually cognitive problems, including low self-esteem and problems concentrating, as well as behavioral problems, such as sleeping too little, eating too much, and becoming socially isolated. Thus, mental illness is usually a group of problems or symptoms, which the DSM definition calls a "syndrome or pattern."

Associated With Distress and/or Disability

Most mental illnesses cause profound *distress.* Indeed, the depressive and anxiety disorders are, for all practical purposes, problems of distress. The defining feature of depression is sad affect. The anxiety disorders are defined by severe and uncomfortable worry, fear, and anxiety, and such feelings essentially define distress. A young woman with the eating disorder bulimia nervosa will be very unhappy with or distressed by her behavior, which she perceives as out of control.

However, not all mental illnesses are accompanied by distress. Indeed, many are remarkable for its absence. For example, in contrast to the example of bulimia nervosa, a young woman with the eating disorder anorexia nervosa is usually not at all distressed by her behavior. The young woman with anorexia nervosa is preoccupied with her weight and shape, and she will engage in extraordinary and dangerous behaviors to lose weight. However, she will not see her behavior as a problem. Not eating to the point of starvation and death is simply not a big deal.

A mental health professional will diagnose someone with anorexia nervosa as having a mental illness because problems with affect, behaviors, and cognitions lead to *disability.* Disability is impairment in functioning, which means problems in roles and relationships or in self-care. Roles may include worker, parent, spouse, or church member. Relationships involve friends, family, and other loved ones. Self-care is the behavior of maintaining one's health. Impairment in any of these may indicate a mental illness.

For example, all have probably observed a person with an alcohol problem. He may not feel distress about his drinking behavior, but the excessive drinking will probably eventually cause problems with his functioning. Problem drinking causes people to show up late, do poorly on tasks, or miss work altogether. Problem drinking angers spouses and horrifies children. Problem drinking damages one's health. If drinking behavior has impaired one's role as an employee, husband, or father, or if it has damaged relationships with friends or family or has caused health problems, then a diagnosis of mental illness is warranted. In other words, if someone's drinking is causing problems, then more than likely the person has a drinking problem.

Distress, Impairment, and Willingness to Seek Treatment

Whether someone is experiencing distress or exhibiting impairment has a significant influence on whether or not he or she voluntarily seeks treatment. Distress motivates people to seek treatment. Feeling constantly anxious or depressed is very upsetting, as is being unable to sleep or feeling out of control of one's behavior. After a period of time, if a problem causing distress doesn't go away on its own, many people will seek help.

In contrast, not being distressed makes it unlikely a person will voluntarily seek help. A young woman with anorexia nervosa will likely have to be forced into treatment by her parents or others who are concerned that her behavior is going to kill her (which it does for about 5% of all women with the disorder). Likewise, an alcoholic will enter treatment at the behest or insistence of others, such as a boss or spouse.

In the same way, distress motivates a person to participate in treatment that he or she has entered, rather than be resistant to it.

One of the themes of the chapters to follow, which discuss the mental illnesses in detail, is encouraging people to seek treatment. When doing so it helps to highlight the effectiveness of treatment in resolving mental illness, including the associated distress and impairment. Another important aspect of encouraging the seeking of treatment is, ironically, to enhance the person's sense of distress about the problem. Many people are unbothered by their own dangerous, inappropriate, and maladaptive behavior. They are simply able to ignore the role and relationship problems that are occurring. Enhancing distress is possible by highlighting such impairment.

So, with a young woman with anorexia nervosa, the concern and distress of her parents may be emphasized in order to cause her to be distressed about their situation, which may motivate her to get better. Chapter 11 reviews in detail an effective way to encourage someone with an alcohol or drug use problem to seek treatment, which is to emphasize the drastic difference between what he wants his life to be like (happy marriage, happy family, good job) and what the alcohol or drugs have done to his life. This enhancement of distress, in combination with assertions about the effectiveness of treatment and hope for the future, has been shown to increase the motivation for treatment and change of persons with these problems.

Applying the Definition of Mental Illness

To review, a mental illness is diagnosed when a person has a group of symptoms (behavioral or psychological problems) that are accompanied by either subjective distress or impairment in roles and relationships (or both distress and impairment). Let's see how these rules apply to some people who have consulted with me over the last year. In each example, the question is whether or not the person likely meets criteria for a mental illness.

Mary and the Dress Shop

Mary described being quite upset about a situation that came up recently at the clothing store where she works as a salesperson. Three weeks ago she endured an angry disagreement with Emma, a coworker whom she considered a friend. Mary felt bad about the disagreement and was planning on talking with Emma to clear the air when they next worked together. Before she could, however, Mary learned that Emma had been telling lies about her to her boss. She learned this because the boss had confronted Mary about one of her supposed offenses, and Mary was forced to defend herself.

Mary used to enjoy her job. She still does it well, but now she dreads going to work. She's lost many nights of sleep over the situation, and last week she actually called in sick. She doesn't want to quit her job, but she is unsure how she should handle the situation. She doesn't want to complain to her boss about Emma, but she also does not want to have another argument with Emma or to have to defend herself again to her boss. Her relationships with her husband and her two children are still going well, and she still enjoys the company of other friends.

Is Mary exhibiting a mental illness? Given what we know about her symptoms, her distress, and her functioning, we would probably conclude that she is not. First, Mary does not seem to be experiencing an assortment of symptoms related to feeling, behaving, and thinking (ABCs). Her feelings seem fairly normal. She's upset, but not out of proportion to the situation. She does not seem to be paranoid (unless it turns out that she is making these stories up), and she is not particularly anxious, except about her job situation. She does not report that she is particularly depressed. Her behavior is generally normal, even though she skipped work once, and her thinking seems to be pretty accurate (e.g., "This is an unfair situation"). Mary is distressed, but it seems limited to the difficult work situation. Her home life and her social life are unaffected. Likewise, she is not exhibiting any impairment at work, as she is still doing well in her sales position.

Mary is probably not experiencing a mental illness. While she is facing a very difficult situation, we expect she will eventually be able to resolve it. Not every bad situation that causes distress indicates mental illness.

When Mary consulted me, we had two meetings during which we problem solved how she could handle the situation at work. We role-played discussions with Emma and with her boss, and I offered advice about how to minimize the likelihood that the other person would become defensive or angry. I also offered encouragement about her capacity for handling herself. When she left after the second session, I reminded her to call for another appointment if she felt it necessary. She never did.

John's Deconstruction

John has also been having troubles at work. His wife, Jill, accompanied him when he first came to see me. He would not have come in by himself, and she had to force the issue. It seems that John has not been himself lately. For the last two months, he has had to force himself to get out of bed, whereas he is usually quite enthusiastic about starting the day. His wife related, "Usually he drives me crazy in the morning, with his cheerfulness and his chatter." Lately, though, he seems apathetic about going to work and often leaves the house late.

John works as a carpenter. His long-time site supervisor, Dave, is also quite concerned about him. Dave is also married, and the two couples have gone out together. Indeed, Dave's wife called Jill to tell her about Dave's growing concerns. John has always been an exemplary worker, was the go-to guy whom Dan asked to train new workers, and was the acting supervisor while Dave was off-site. Lately, John has been in a fog. He is forgetting things, working too slowly, and making mistakes. Dave has asked John if everything was okay at home, and John replied that things were fine.

Things at home have not been particularly okay, however. Jill has noticed that John's mood has been quite poor lately. He seems both distracted and listless. The couple married five years ago and have a four-year-old son. Normally, he is a devoted and involved father, but lately he has been quite irritable when his son wants attention. He complains that he doesn't sleep well, and he is often fatigued. He has also been having frequent headaches. Two days ago, Jill confronted him with her concerns, worried that she had done something wrong. He was surprised to realize how poorly he had been behaving lately, and he admitted that he has been feeling either quite sad or nothing at all since the previous summer. He promised to try to do better, but the following day he was withdrawn and morose again. She insisted that they see a mental health professional.

Is John experiencing a mental illness? Let's review his ABCs. Concerning affect, John looks and reports feeling sad. Concerning behavior, at work, he is slow and mistake-prone. At home, he is not his usual self with either his wife or his young son. Concerning cognitions, he is distracted and forgetful. He admits to fatigue, sleep problems, and feeling in a fog. With regard to the two Rs, John is clearly exhibiting substantial impairment in both his work role and his home roles and relationships.

Given these symptoms and impairment, it appears that John is experiencing a mental illness. Notice, however, that his distress is not that great. He is more apathetic than distressed. Don't be fooled. Remember, John is a guy. Like many men, John is not especially insightful concerning his own emotional well-being and functioning. He is surprised to realize that his wife has noticed that he is acting differently.

When John and Jill consulted me, details about John's family history emerged. Some of the information came as a surprise to Jill, who was only somewhat familiar with it. It emerged that John's father had experienced fairly significant depressions his entire life, although the "black demon," as his father later called it, was expressed through heavy drinking and abusive behavior towards his wife and three sons. Jill was aware of the drinking and the abuse, but not of the depression history.

I referred John to a psychiatrist for an evaluation of the potential usefulness of antidepressant medications. An antidepressant was prescribed, but John quickly realized that it interfered with his love life, so he did not continue taking it. Instead, he and Jill came for several months of couple's therapy, which helped quite a lot. They were able to identify warning signs that he was becoming depressed, for which she especially would be on the lookout. (Again, John has never been well attuned to his own emotional functioning.) They also created a long list of activities that helped when he was depressed. It was particularly helpful to reassure John that he was not his father, even though he sometimes felt as if he was becoming him. Finally, it was helpful to Jill to realize that John's behavior towards her was due to the depression and not to something she was doing.

That Kid in the Back Row

Billy was Pastor Aaron's least favorite confirmation student. As Pastor told me, he wanted to like Billy and felt bad that he didn't, but it was awfully difficult to like him.

Every Saturday at 10 A.M., Billy seemed to delight in distracting other kids. He showed up every week, but he never seemed to know what was going on in the class. He sometimes blurted out guesses to questions, despite admonitions to raise his hand and wait to be called. Even worse, Billy engaged in seemingly endless commentary during the classes, more often than not about anything but the lesson. Billy seemed desperate to get other students to laugh. Pastor had scolded Billy during class about his behavior and had talked to him after class as well, but the behavior continued. Billy was a problem, but Pastor was concerned about an even bigger problem. The entire class was reacting to the situation and becoming unmanageable. The other kids, noticing that Billy was allowed to disrupt the classroom environment, seemed to be losing respect and losing interest.

As before, the question is, Does Billy have a mental illness? To meet criteria for a mental illness, a person must exhibit a group of psychological and/or behavioral symptoms and the person must also exhibit either distress or impairment. Billy is clearly exhibiting some behavioral problems. He seems to have difficulty paying attention, sitting still, and being cooperative. Although Billy is not exhibiting distress, the behaviors are causing Billy to be impaired in Pastor's classroom, in that they are interfering with his relationship with Pastor and in his role as student. However, we need much more information in order to conclude anything. Indeed, we need information to which Pastor does not have access.

When he consulted me, I advised the pastor to discuss the situation with Billy's mother. She told him that a psychologist had first diagnosed Billy with attention deficit hyperactivity disorder (ADHD) in first grade. He had a prescription for medications from a psychiatrist, but he did not take them over the weekend so that he could have a regular "drug holiday" to decrease the chances that he would have negative reactions to them. Unfortunately, confirmation class was on Saturdays. She offered to have him take the medication on Saturdays also, but her reluctance was obvious. Instead, she and Pastor talked about some strategies that Pastor might use in the classroom.

Chapter 4

The Prevalence of Mental Illness

"He went down with them and stood on a level place.
A large crowd of his disciples was there and a great number of people
from all over Judea, from Jerusalem, and from the coastal region
around Tyre and Sidon, who had come to hear him
and to be healed of their diseases."
(Luke 6:17,18)

The church is the place where your members seek comfort as they cope with life's terrible hardships, such as divorce, job loss, treatment for cancer, or the death of a loved one. It is good that the church can provide such comfort, for many members of the church experience mental illness and mental health problems.

Of course, most pastors and church workers know firsthand that there are many people in the church who suffer from various and sometimes-severe degrees of depression, anxiety, and behavioral problems. But even more common are church members who are dealing with mental illness in their family, such as a spouse with an alcohol or drug problem, a parent with Alzheimer's disease, a child with autism, or a sibling who has attempted suicide. This brief chapter reviews the science of epidemiology to show that in fact both will inevitably be seen in the church.

The Science of Epidemiology

To discover how many people experience a mental illness in a given year, mental health professionals and public health scientists have conducted epidemiologic studies. *Epidemiology* comes from the Greek words *epidemia* (the prevalence of disease) and *ology* (a subject of study). Epidemiology is the scientific field that studies the prevalence of diseases in the general population. Epidemiological studies show, for example, how many people contract the flu, develop cancer, or die in motor vehicle accidents. The current concern in the United States about increasing rates of obesity (with attendant increases in diabetes, heart disease, and other problems caused by obesity) comes from epidemiologic research.

Epidemiologists have studied the prevalence of mental illnesses. Two of the best such studies are the "Epidemiologic Catchment Area Survey," which was conducted during the 1980s, and the "National Comorbidity Survey," which was conducted in the early 1990s.

Epidemiological Studies of Mental Illness

To conduct the "Epidemiologic Catchment Area Survey" (ECA), researchers conducted face-to-face interviews in kitchens, living rooms, and screened-in porches with over 20,000 adult Americans in the early 1980s. Respondents were recruited from the "catchment areas" that surrounded the universities hired to conduct the study (Yale, Johns Hopkins, Washington University, Duke, and UCLA). The "National Comorbidity Survey" (NCS) also did face-to-face interviews with over 8,000 people, but these were randomly selected from across the entire United States (versus from catchment areas). The NCS was conducted to gather information about what mental illnesses tended to occur together, or tended to be "comorbid."

Both surveys comprised several *hundred* questions about how the respondent had been feeling and doing over the last year, including specific questions about depression, anxiety, drinking behavior, problems with anger, and so forth. Some example questions from the surveys are shown in the box. Both surveys defined mental illness according to the then-current edition of the DSM (see previous chapter), which lists the criteria for each of the mental illnesses. Based on the answers given, the researchers decided whether the survey respondent met criteria for a diagnosis of mental illness, either within the last month or within the last year. Recall that the "S" in DSM stands for "statistical" and that one of the first purposes of a diagnostic classification system was to generate a count or census of the number of persons with mental illness.

Sample Questions From the Epidemiologic Surveys

The following are similar to the questions interviewers asked respondents. In these questions, the interviewer is asking about the experience of depressive symptoms.

- In the last month, have you had periods of time when you felt excessively blue, down, sad, or depressed?
- (If respondent answered "Yes") During that period . . .
  - Did you find that you derived less enjoyment from activities or hobbies that you used to enjoy?
  - Did you have less energy than normal?
  - Did you have problems with your appetite?
  - Did you have difficulty sleeping?
  - Did you have difficulty concentrating or making decisions?
  - Did you feel very bad about yourself (have low self-esteem)?

The table (see following box) shows the results of the ECA and NCS surveys. This information is taken from the 1999 Surgeon General's report entitled, *Mental Health: A Report of the Surgeon General.* It is available for download from the Department of Health and Human Services.

The results of the ECA and NCS surveys were remarkably consistent. Both indicated that about *one out of five* adults in the United States will experience a mental illness during any given year. Generalizing to the general population of the United States, this amounts to almost 60 million adults. Most of these, about 40 million, will have a mental disorder only. Another 13 million will have a substance use disorder only. The remaining 7 million will have comorbid mental and substance use disorders. Comorbidity of the other disorders is quite common also. For example, it is quite common to have both a depressive and anxiety disorder at the same time.

The table (see following box) shows that the most common type of disorder is an anxiety disorder, of which the most common is some version of extreme fear (phobia) of certain things, social circumstances, or leaving home (agoraphobia or "fear of the marketplace"). Next most frequent are the mood disorders, of which the most common is major depression.

Best Estimate of 1-Year Prevalence Rates of Mental Illness
Based on ECA and NCS Results (Adults ages 18–54)

	ECA Prevalence (%)	NCS Prevalence (%)	Best Estimate (%)
Any Disorder	19.5	23.4	21.0
Any Anxiety Disorder	13.1	18.7	16.4
Simple Phobia	8.3	8.6	8.3
Social Phobia	2.0	7.4	2.0
Agoraphobia	4.9	3.7	4.9
Generalized Anxiety Disorder	NA	3.4	3.4
Panic Disorder	1.6	2.2	1.6
Obsessive-Compulsive Disorder	2.4	NA	2.4
Post-Traumatic Stress Disorder	NA	3.6	3.6
Any Mood Disorder	7.1	11.1	7.1
Major Depression	6.5	10.1	6.5
Dysthymic Disorder	1.6	2.5	1.6
Bipolar Disorder I or II	1.7	1.5	1.7
Alcohol or Drug Use Disorder	9.5	NA	NA
Schizophrenia	1.3	NA	1.3
Somatization Disorder	0.2	NA	0.2
Anorexia Nervosa	0.1	NA	0.1
Severe Cognitive Impairment	1.2	NA	1.2

NA = not asked in survey

Source: US Department of Health and Human Services. *Mental Health: A Report of the Surgeon General—Executive Summary.* Rockville, MD: US Department of Health and Human Services, Substance Abuse and Mental Health Services Administration, Center for Mental Health Services, National Institutes of Health, National Institute of Mental Health, 1999, p. 228.

Next most common are the substance use disorders, which are most frequently an alcohol problem. Finally, it can be seen that schizophrenia and mental retardation (severe cognitive impairment) each affect about 1 in 100 persons, which makes them much less commonplace than anxiety or depression. Nonetheless, there are millions of persons with each of these disorders in the United States.

Other epidemiological research conducted on children and adolescents indicates that mental illness is equally prevalent in children (persons under age 18). Such studies are much more difficult to conduct, since children cannot participate in a study without their parents' permission. As a result, there are fewer studies with fewer respondents. Nonetheless, high quality studies have been conducted. In a study of over 1,200 children and adolescents between the ages of 9 and 17, researchers interviewed both youths and their caretakers. Like the ECA and NCS studies, the surveys were done using standardized interviews that ascertained whether or not the children were experiencing or exhibiting certain problems over the last year. The results indicated that the rates of mental illness were almost identical to those of adults. Over 20% of the children and adolescents met criteria for mental illness in the last year. As you might expect, the specific disorders that children and adolescents experience are different than those of adults. For example, children have higher rates of attention deficit hyperactivity disorder (ADHD), and a common anxiety disorder in children concerns being separated from parents. For obvious reasons, children have much lower rates of alcohol and drug use disorders. They also have lower rates of schizophrenia, which tends to emerge in early adulthood.

The National Institute of Mental Health

The congressional mandate to the National Institute of Mental Health (NIMH) is to educate the populace about mental illness. The NIMH website contains a great deal of information about mental illness and its treatment (www.nimh.nih.gov/statistics/index.shtml).

Scrutinizing the Numbers

What do these figures mean? Given the prevalence of mental illness, it is inevitable that clergy and other church workers will be confronted by mental illness in their ministry. If you are in contact with more than five people, chances are that you will meet someone—whether you realize it or not—experiencing a mental illness. (Presumably your church has more than five members.) If a church has 500 members, then a pastor should expect that in any given year 100 members will experience a mental illness. In a church of any size, it is statistically probable that at least half of the families will have a member (or two or three) with a mental illness.

Let us suppose that your church has 1,000 members. That means that there are about 65 members who are suffering from major depression. Some will get treatment. Robert was lucky that his pastor knew him fairly well and fortunate to have a wife who was willing to call the pastor about her concerns for her husband. On the other hand, some members of your church who are suffering from major depression may not make it to church at all. Others may sit quietly, looking sad, and leave without saying much. They may be confused about what they are experiencing, and they might not know that treatment is both readily available and highly effective. These are the ones for whom you are reading this book.

If you don't know who in your church is experiencing a mental illness, either personally or through a family member, it is not because your church is somehow lucky or healthy or better than others. It might be that those families have felt unwelcome and have found another place to worship. It might be that the ill individual has stopped going to church altogether. Mental illness causes people to experience profound shame, and many reason that God has stopped loving them or that they don't deserve God's love. Or, it might be that they simply have not told you. In summary, if you don't know who in your church is affected by mental illness, it is simply because you don't know, not because it is not there.

All mental illnesses are serious and should be addressed, but some are more serious than others. Some persons will have a serious and persistent mental illness (SPMI) such as mental retardation, schizophrenia, or bipolar disorder. However, most will be one of the anxiety, depression, or substance use disorders that, while less severe and probably more short-lived (especially if they get professional treatment), are still seriously impairing and distressing. The varieties of mental illness that you will encounter are described in more detail in the next section.

Let's not forget about the mental health problems, however. As described earlier, many persons suffer emotional and psychological distress without meeting the official criteria for mental illness. They are distressed due to overwhelmingly stressful situations that overpower their capacity to cope.

That is, in addition to the millions of Americans who experience a mental illness every year, there are as many who are overwhelmed by stressful situations but don't qualify for a diagnosis of mental illness. These individuals nonetheless call on mental health professionals, quite appropriately, for help dealing with stress and the difficult situations they confront. They are couples who love each other, but bicker so constantly that they can't stand to be in the same room after ten minutes. They are men who are despondent about finding another job. They are women who are exhausted by working and raising a family alone. These individuals don't make the "official count" of mental illness, but they will seek your help.

Bad News, Good News, and More Bad News

The bad news is that mental illness is extremely common and that there are many people in your church who either have a mental illness themselves or have a family member with one. The next chapter expands on the bad news to describe the immense burdens of mental illness.

However, there is good news. Mental illnesses respond well to treatment. Researchers have created, developed, and disseminated effective treatments for all of the mental illnesses. Likewise, there are many competent mental health professionals, and more are being trained every year. The United States has created one of the best mental health treatment systems in the world. People facing or experiencing mental illness have dozens of effective biological and psychological therapies from which to choose. There are specific treatments for particularly difficult problems, such as severe depression and schizophrenia. Disorder-specific treatments abound, including treatments designed for alcohol-related problems, sexual problems, misbehaving teenagers, college adjustment struggles, and practically everything else that may affect mental health. There are specially designed treatments for specific populations, such as the elderly and young children. There exist effective treatments for couples and families. Of course, many of these treatments are designed to manage rather than cure the illness. Nonetheless, the bottom line is that no one needs to endure the full brunt of the distresses and burdens of mental illness. Treatment is available, and treatment will help.

Unfortunately, there is further bad news.

Most people experiencing a mental illness do not get appropriate treatment. Of the millions of people in any year who will experience a mental illness, less than half will seek any sort of professional help. They do not seek or obtain appropriate treatment because they aren't sure that the problem is serious enough to warrant it, they don't know where to obtain treatment, they don't know what treatment would involve, or they are ashamed to admit they need it. Even then, fewer than half of those who seek help will get treatment from a mental health professional, that is, someone who is specially trained to treat mental illness. Instead, most will get care from a medical doctor with no particular expertise or adequate understanding of mental illness.

The church has a duty to understand and help persons with mental health problems and mental illness. This book is written to help church workers better understand mental illness so that they can identify it and refer people to appropriate professional resources.

Chapter 5

The Burdens of Mental Illness

"Come to me, all you who are weary and burdened,
and I will give you rest. Take my yoke upon you
and learn from me,
for I am gentle and humble in heart,
and you will find rest for your souls."
(Matthew 11:28,29)

Jesus speaks of weariness and burden, of the need for rest. Sharing our humanity, he knows our sorrows, trials, and needs. The burdens of which Christ speaks are amplified with mental illness.

In chapter 3, we saw that mental illness is diagnosed when distress, impairment, or both accompany behavioral or psychological symptoms. In this chapter, I present the burden of mental illness in those terms. I review the severity of distress and the immensity of impairment to both the individual and families.

The Personal Distress Caused by Mental Illness

The distress caused by mental illness can be categorized as emotional, physical, and cognitive. Beyond that, when someone develops a mental illness, he or she usually experiences shame and embarrassment. We discuss all of these versions of distress in turn.

Emotional Distress

It may seem odd to refer to emotional distress, as this seems part and parcel of all mental illnesses. However, not all mental illnesses are alike in terms of the severity of distress. Consider Becky and Betty, who have both been stricken with depression.

Becky is distressed by sad feelings that wax and wane throughout each day. But she makes herself smile and go to work, meet friends for coffee, and take care of her children. She generally enjoys these activities. It is when she is alone or not doing something useful that her melancholy comes calling. Becky meets criteria for depression, but her distress is not overwhelming.

Betty, in contrast, gets so depressed that she has trouble getting out of bed in the morning. Her husband must cajole and plead to get her going in the morning. The prospect of going to work fills her with dread. Her children get themselves ready for school. They make their own breakfasts and pack their own lunches, because they don't want to add to her burden. She knows this and it fills her with even greater shame and self-hatred. Both Becky and Betty meet the criteria for major depression (discussed in chapter 6), but Betty's distress is much greater.

Physical/Somatic Distress

Physical distress is not usually thought of when contemplating mental illness, but it is commonly experienced.

Probably everyone has experienced a headache at the end of a long, trying day (due to unconsciously clenching the teeth and tightening the muscles around the neck and shoulders). The muscle tension that continuously accompanies the anxiety disorders leads to similar bodily pain and fatigue. Fear and worry also cause gastrointestinal and digestive problems, including upset stomach, chronic diarrhea, and ulcers. Both anxiety and depression are associated with difficulty sleeping, and insomnia also leads to unpleasant physical distress. Of course, chronic alcohol and drug use do terrible things to the body.

Cognitive Distress

Cognitive distress refers to unremitting distressing thoughts, memories, and perceptions, and it is a common feature of many of the mental illnesses.

Depression and anxiety essentially rob a person of the capacity to make decisions. Depression causes cognitive confusion and fatigue, making the person feel incapable of decision making. A person with an anxiety will feel, obviously, quite anxious about making decisions, and he will either put them off or not make them at all.

Paul the Sales Guy

Paul described to me problems at work he was having because of his depression. "I cannot seem to concentrate or to remember anything. It feels like I have a blanket over my brain. I have trouble concentrating, which makes it difficult to have confidence in what I'm trying to think about, so I end up delaying or avoiding decisions." Being the sales manager of a team of ten salespeople, this caused serious problems for Paul. He was responsible for distributing sales assignments to the team. Before the depression set in, Paul made these decisions based on numerous factors, including previous sales assignments (the need to be fair), the match between the salesperson and the potential customer, and other things. Paul used to make these decisions easily and was able to defend them both to his team members and to his bosses. Since the depression, however, he had been second-guessing himself. Team members started to rebel when he repeatedly re-assigned sales calls or, worse, assigned two sales team members to the same call. Eventually he was asked to step down, temporarily, from the sales manager position.

Paul's boss knew that Paul was a valuable employee. They had known each other for almost nine years. She liked Paul and was genuinely concerned for him. She told him as much when they met to discuss his deteriorating work performance. When he described his difficulties, she told him that it sounded much like what her brother had gone through. She gently suggested that he see his doctor to determine what was going on. Paul was very grateful to her for the care and concern. Indeed, he had tears in his eyes when he described their conversation.

Shame and Embarrassment

Paul the sales guy was able to talk to his boss. In turn, she talked to him about seeking help for a mental illness that was interfering with his work performance, as most mental illnesses do. After several months of working with me to understand his depression and to develop strategies for decreasing it, Paul returned to his position as lead salesman.

There are two things unremarkable and two things remarkable about Paul's situation. The first *unremarkable* thing is that Paul developed a depression. Ten to fifteen million Americans will do so this year. The second *unremarkable* thing is that treatment was successful. Over the past five decades, mental health professionals have developed highly successful treatments for most mental illnesses.

The first *remarkable* thing is that Paul talked to someone about his depression. Most persons with mental illness do not talk to anyone. Most persons with mental illness are ashamed of being mentally ill. Despite this, Paul was able to open up to his boss about what was going on. He must have recognized, perhaps from prior interactions with her, that she might be able to understand. Unfortunately, this is not the common reaction to mental illness (see box below). Thus, the second *remarkable* thing was that Paul's boss did indeed respond with compassion. She did not make him feel defensive or embarrassed.

What did she do? She responded with kindness and with knowledge. She listened. She did not recoil in fear from his experiences and his distress. As important, she matter-of-factly stated that his situation was not unusual. She knew this from her brother's experiences. You now know this from previous chapters. She also informed him that treatment might help. As a result, Paul immediately felt better because he felt hope that, first, perhaps not everyone would see him as a freak, as he somewhat worried, and that, second, someone (his boss) was confident that treatment could help.

The reaction of Paul's boss exemplifies the reaction that Christians should have toward someone experiencing the depredations of mental illness. Christians realize that life can be burdensome and can make us weary. Knowing this makes them unafraid to embrace someone suffering. This is the first gift that communities of faithful Christians bestow on one another. We know that suffering is normal and inevitable, and we welcome and comfort the sufferer. (That is unless you embrace "prosperity preaching," in which case I request that you please refrain from saying anything to anyone who faces hardship in life. I address this more thoroughly in the later chapter entitled "A Proper Christian Understanding of Mental Illness.")

The second gift Christians can bestow on someone with mental illness, which I hope this book will help to develop, is the knowledge that mental illness is, unfortunately, quite common but also, fortunately, quite treatable.

Why Shame? Why Embarrassment?

My friend asked me, "How did you break your wrist?" I responded, "Yesterday I was drinking hot coffee, texting a friend on my cell phone, balancing my lecture notes, and trying to negotiate the concrete stairwell in the front of the building while wearing ice skates. I'm really not sure how it happened." My friend laughed and asked, "How long will you be in that cast?"

My friend asked me, "How are you doing?" I responded, "Not so well. I've been depressed for a while now." My friend looked uncomfortable and said, "Oh. That's . . . um . . . I'm sorry." She walked away as soon as she could.

Typical Reactions to Physical Hurt

Reactions to physical hurt are fairly predictable. If we tell someone we are physically hurt, we are not usually ashamed, and they do not make us feel embarrassed. When they ask what happened, I happily tell everyone how foolish I was behaving when I broke my wrist. They typically react fairly well. They express sympathy and they ask about treatment (who is doing the treatment, how long will it take to get better, etc.). People who have cancer, heart problems, cuts, scrapes, and breaks get similar reactions. Others ask what happened, where treatment is happening, and how treatment is going.

Typical Reactions to Emotional Hurt

Reactions to emotional hurt are also fairly predictable. They are not as nice. If we tell someone we are emotionally hurt (with depression, anxiety, substance use) or that someone we love is emotionally hurt, others typically don't know what to say. They act as if something shameful has just been disclosed. They look away, clear their throat, act uncomfortable, and try to extract themselves from the conversation (or change the topic). Somehow emotional hurt is something shameful, something we should not discuss with others out of embarrassment, and something they therefore react with discomfort.

Don't do that.

Time for a Change

When someone tells you about their emotional hurt, act the same way you would about physical hurt. Express sympathy and understanding: "Oh too bad. That's sounds difficult. A lot of people go through that." Ask about treatment: "Where are you getting treatment? How is it going? How long before you will get better?" Try this new way of reacting and you might just change the person's life for the better. (To help even more, see the following box on empathy.)

Distress to the Family Caused by Mental Illness

The family of a person with a mental illness suffers the distress of watching a loved one in pain and confusion. There is the potential of greater pain associated with the loved one not getting sufficient treatment.

I interviewed a mother about her son who had developed schizophrenia. "It was like learning to love a stranger. He looked like my son, and in many ways acted like my son, but he was no longer my son. He had become someone else, someone I did not know. So I went through grief when he became sick. Then when he died, even though in many ways he was gone long before, I had to go through grief all over again." Her son bled to death after attempting to cut off one of his own toes. He had developed the delusional belief that it was the reason their neighbor had suffered a heart attack. (I am not ashamed to say that I hope never to experience the distress she went through.)

Empathy to Reduce Shame and Embarrassment

Empathy is perhaps the single most valuable therapeutic attitude and behavior that a mental health professional can communicate to his or her patient. There have been whole books written on the topic and research conferences devoted to its study. Every how-to psychotherapy book devotes large sections to it. Fortunately, empathy is fairly easy to understand and to demonstrate.

Empathy means understanding and accepting how a person thinks and feels without evaluating those thoughts and feelings. To understand the way another person thinks or feels does not mean understanding *why* he or she thinks or feels that way, nor does it mean agreeing with her thoughts or feelings. It means successfully identifying those thoughts and feelings, accepting that they exist, and then communicating both of these things to the other person.

Empathic statements help in many ways. First, they show the person that his or her emotions or thoughts, while they might be uncommon, are nonetheless understandable by another person. Second, empathic statements help because they communicate that you are trying to understand.

As in this chapter, by reading this volume the reader will hopefully better understand the thinking, feelings, and behaviors that characterize the various mental illnesses, as well as the distress they cause and the devastation they wreak on lives. By understanding, readers will hopefully be better able to empathize and help.

Distress Related to Variable Severity

While some can be cured never to return, many mental illnesses last for years, decades, or even an entire lifetime. In the past, such mental illnesses have been called chronic mental illness, whereas the preferred term these days is serious and persistent mental illness, or SPMI. They include bipolar disorder, schizophrenia, and severe depression.

One of the most distressing things experienced by individuals and families who must deal with an SPMI is the variability and sometimes unpredictability of the illness. Severity waxes and wanes, meaning that there are periods of time when the symptoms and problems are relatively mild, but there are other times when they are relatively severe. There are several causes of the variability.

One cause is simply the nature of illness. Many medical afflictions wax and wane in severity. Someone experiencing pain will have good days and bad days. Someone dealing with diabetes will have good weeks and bad weeks. Mental illness, likewise, fluctuates in severity. Indeed, one of the SPMIs, bipolar disorder, is *defined* by mood fluctuating between extremes of depression and euphoria. There are causes for fluctuating severity, for both medical and mental illness, but they may be unknown or difficult to control.

A knowable cause of the fluctuations in illness severity is stressful events. For example, researchers on Long Island in New York found that the likelihood of a relapse for patients with bipolar disorder increased dramatically after the hurricane of 1985. Exacerbation of symptoms in persons with schizophrenia has long been associated with family stress, including a family's tendency to express anger openly. Many in the northern climes know that their depressive symptoms worsen over winter, when sunlight is less available (and at times nonexistent!). For this reason, it can be extremely important for someone coping with an SPMI to have a regular, predictable schedule. Such a schedule minimizes stress.

Another known cause of instability is the person's compliance with treatment. As with medical illness, many persons with mental illness may have difficulty or express resistance to complying with treatment. For example, when a person with mental illness begins treatment (e.g., a person with schizophrenia starts to take medication), he may fairly quickly feel better. As a result, he may decide he no longer needs medication.

Even with good compliance, however, illnesses can vary in severity from week to week. In sum, there can be unsettling and distressing unpredictability for family members of someone with a mental illness.

Distress Due to the Need for Constant Vigilance

Fear of recurrence or relapse might create in the family a sense of the need for constant vigilance. Family members might be on the lookout for early warning signs in the person with mental illness, or they may often ask the person, "How are you feeling?" or "Did you take your medication this morning?" This need for vigilance is entirely understandable. It is entirely understandable, but constant vigilance can be a serious source of contention between the person with mental illness and his family.

Imagine that you were diagnosed with bipolar disorder but have been in fairly good control for the past few months. Prior to the diagnosis, you spent a great deal of money during a "manic phase," although you and your spouse were able to get much of it back (by returning unopened merchandise). One Saturday you mention to your spouse that you would like to purchase a new flat-screen television. All across our great country, every Saturday, several thousand spouses say this, and it is probably said more often than not by a husband to a wife. For most couples, this does not cause a problem. A typical response will be "Sounds great" or "Let's wait" or "Get real" or some variation of these three.

For you, who have bipolar disorder, your spouse's reaction may be a bit different. Your spouse may respond by asking, "Did you take your medication this morning?" This may upset you, since you have been doing fairly well lately and, besides, wanting a new TV is not an indication of something abnormal. Except in your case it might mean the beginnings of another manic phase. The cyclical nature of mental illness, which is sometimes severe and sometimes mild, can cause a great deal of concern and distress to family members.

Distress Related to Shame and Embarrassment

The stigma of mental illness causes other burdens for families. One in five people in any given year will experience a mental illness, meaning that few people are unrelated to someone with a mental illness. Nonetheless, stigmatizing attitudes against mental illness thrive. Many in our society are ignorant about and afraid of mental illness. They react by rejecting those who have one.

These attitudes extend to the family of the person with mental illness. Surely, the attitude maintains, the parents must have done something wrong to have a child like that. Surely, these people reassure themselves, we are better than that and would never tolerate someone in our family having a problem like that.

Stigmatizing attitudes may be subtle or overt, but the results are predictable. First, the family might develop a sense of stigma towards itself. Mothers and fathers will ask themselves what they did wrong. They may look across the supper table and wonder what the other did wrong. Second, they will feel shame and embarrassment when admitting that one of their own has developed a mental illness. Even if they do not hold attitudes of stigma, they have seen stigmatizing attitudes often enough to assume that most other persons hold them. Finally, to the extent possible, they may try to hide the information. As I said in the previous chapter, if you don't know who in your church is experiencing a mental illness, it is not because they don't exist but rather because they have not come forward and told you.

Hopefully, this book will strengthen your resolve to find and comfort—with human empathic understanding and with the divine Word of God—those families in need.

Daniel Preus writes about both the distress of having a child with a serious mental illness as well as the comfort of the cross in *What Father Loves His Daughter Less?* The poem is reprinted, with his permission, at the end of this chapter (see p. 58).

Costs of Impairment

Earlier we organized impairment or dysfunction into three general areas: occupational impairment, which entails work and school; relationship impairment; and self-care impairment. All three types of impairment burden both individuals and families. Impairment will vary in severity, depending on the severity of the mental illness.

Occupational Impairment of the Individual

Having a mental illness makes it much more likely that you are not going to find a job. One study found that depressed persons were seven times more likely to be unemployed than non-depressed persons. In another study, children were followed for four decades to examine the long-term effects of having a childhood mental illness, such as attention deficit hyperactivity disorder (ADHD). Compared to their peers, adults who had a mental illness in childhood had less educational accomplishment, were much less likely to be employed, and had significantly lower incomes when employed.

Other research has shown that the symptoms and problems inherent in mental illness make it difficult for the individual to attain his or her potential either in school or within the workplace. Much of this research has been done with major depressive disorder and with the alcohol use disorders. This is due in part because these disorders are very frequent, making them easier to study than more rare illnesses such as bipolar disorder and schizophrenia. It is also because persons with these disorders are typically not completely impaired, meaning that they are often able to obtain and maintain employment at least to some extent. In other words, it is easier to study the effect of the illnesses on occupational functioning if the person has, or had at one time, a job.

These studies have found that persons with mental illness lose almost a day of work per week when their illness is in the acute (severe) phase. This comes in the form of absenteeism and sick days but also in lower productivity when they do work because of difficulty concentrating, being organized, and being efficient. Later chapters describe the symptoms that are associated with the various mental illnesses, and readers will easily imagine how these symptoms interfere with work. One study calculated the economic cost of mental illness to the United States as a whole to be $78.6 billion for the year 1990. This figure was related to lost workdays and lessened productivity but did not include the cost of treatment.

Occupational Impairment Within the Family

If we add the cost related to having to care for one's spouse, sibling, or child with a mental illness, the cost associated with occupational impairment soars. Expenses for the treatment of mental illness can be substantial. They are often assumed by the family, because insurance is unavailable or insufficient, or perhaps because mental illness is not covered by insurance at all. However, when tallying the burden of mental illness in economic terms, lost opportunities should also be taken into account. Family members must make adjustments and compromises that can prevent them from achieving their full potential in work. The ill child, sibling, or parent may need care on a frequent but unpredictable basis.

As a result, family members may need to take jobs that allow them flexibility to occasionally come in late, leave early, or not come in at all on some days. None of these behaviors benefit the employer, and even the kindest and most understanding boss may hesitate to praise and promote an employee who is not fully productive.

In summary, occupational impediments are rarely noted when tallying the cost of mental illness to a family, but they are very large indeed.

Relationship Impairment of the Individual

The emotional, cognitive, and behavioral symptoms of mental illnesses can be extremely injurious to relationships. A review of some of the most common symptoms of mental illness, meaning symptoms that are an aspect of many different illnesses, hints at the manner in which relationships might suffer.

Low self-esteem, shame, and feelings of worthlessness will make it nearly impossible for a wife to feel that her husband genuinely does love her and desire her. Since this simply cannot be possible, she may then worry that he desires to leave her or has already developed extramarital relationships.

Constant worry and anxiety about the future may make a husband and father work longer hours to make more money, since the family's destruction is barely being kept at bay. Since work does not include spending time with one's wife and children, those relationships may be damaged as a result. Even more damaging is the husband and father's angry outbursts towards wife and children, which are driven by his fear that they are being insufficiently vigilant about their safety and health.

Angry and abusive behavior is not required to diagnose someone with a substance use disorder, but it is a tragically commonplace effect. The alcoholic or addict may be irrationally angry while intoxicated or may become that way while drying out.

Someone whose symptoms include delusions, such as those seen with schizophrenia, severe depression, or the manic phase of depression, will believe things about others that are not only untrue but also hard to understand. If I borrow but return my son's cell phone and he later cannot find it, it's understandable why he may ask me if I still have it. On the other hand, if he accuses me of stealing his phone so that I could insert terrible thoughts into his mind, that would be difficult to understand.

Relationship Impairment Within the Family

Families must sometimes deal with the extremely disturbed and disruptive behavior that may be part and parcel of a mental illness. Household routines may need to be abandoned or adjusted drastically. Many families end up severely restricting their social activities. Invitations must be declined because one's spouse is too depressed to go or too anxious to interact with others. Going out at all may be avoided out of concern that something embarrassing—or worse—may happen. A daughter with autism or mental retardation may be incapable of normal communication, but she may nonetheless become frustrated when her needs are unmet, leading to a tantrum. Perhaps those dinner party plans at the house should be reconsidered.

In other words, not only might the relationships between the person with mental illness and his or her family be disrupted, so might the relationships between a family and other persons outside the family.

Even more commonly, relations with other family members can be severely tested. Mothers and fathers might disagree regarding what to do with a child with autism, or siblings might argue about what to do with Mom or Dad who is developing Alzheimer's disease.

I once interviewed a sister of a man with schizophrenia. He was living with her and her husband after their mother had passed away. The alternative to living with them was to have the brother live in a group home, which was extremely costly, or in a state hospital, which she had promised her mother she would never do. She and her husband were trying to adjust to his needs, which derived from his delusions. They could not buy chocolate ice cream, since he believed that communists made cocoa. Neither could they watch television when he was home because he believed that it was stealing and then broadcasting his thoughts. The worst was when he would come into their bedroom in the middle of the night and simply stand there watching them sleep (which they discovered when her husband woke up to use the bathroom one night, leading to a chaotic, loud, and almost perilous scene). As you may have guessed, she was in therapy with me because the stress of the situation was causing her and her husband to experience some serious marital conflict.

Self-Care Impairment of the Individual

Self-care behavior means engaging in behaviors that maintain or improve one's physical and mental health. Self-care behaviors include reading for pleasure, watching television and movies for entertainment, getting together with friends to enjoy their company, getting regular exercise, eating properly, getting enough sleep, taking time off from work, and seeking health care when needed (including taking medications that have been prescribed to recover or maintain health). One of the hallmark problems of mental illness is impaired ability for self-care. The severity of the impairment is an indication of the severity of the illness.

For example, individuals with severe mental retardation or autism are essentially incapable of keeping themselves safe or taking care of their own basic needs, such as shopping and preparing food. Many such individuals, when they reach adulthood, may move into assisted living or group homes, where they are either assisted with such basic tasks or where these tasks are taken care of entirely by other people.

In the case of mental retardation, inability to care for oneself is one of the criteria by which the disorder is diagnosed. Anorexia nervosa is similar, as a woman can be diagnosed if and only if her weight loss is so severe that it starts to compromise her health. As noted previously, some women with the disorder are so impaired that they endanger their own lives and may starve themselves to death (or be hospitalized and forcibly fed). Likewise, if a person drinks to the point of liver damage (cirrhosis), then he automatically meets one of the symptoms of alcohol dependence.

With most mental illnesses, the symptoms cause impairment. A person with schizophrenia may suffer delusions that lead him or her to neglect self-care, such as eating properly, taking care of personal hygiene, and finding a stable domicile. A problem for the United States is the fact that persons with schizophrenia are often too healthy to be kept against their will in a care facility. In a care facility, they can be convinced into taking medications that alleviate their symptoms. They get healthy and leave the facility, but unless they are in that facility, they stop taking medications. They then return to the acute phase of the illness, with attendant delusions and hallucinations, and end up incapable of self-care. The ultimate result of this "revolving door" is homelessness, which is as much an issue of mental illness as of poverty.

Depression entails another example of how symptoms of a mental illness causes impairment. Persons with severe depression can become so debilitated that they cannot function at the most basic level, such as getting out of bed. Or they can become so despondent that they attempt to kill themselves.

Self-Care Impairment Within the Family

A mentally ill person can compromise the self-care behaviors of families and couples. Family members often are forced to modify their social behavior or even abandon social interactions altogether. Days off work might need to be spent assisting the ill family member. Alternatively, people experience feelings of guilt for taking time off from such assistance to see a movie, visit with a friend, play a round of golf, or otherwise do something for themselves. Mental health professionals have begun to recognize the huge need of "caring for caretakers" (e.g., children responsible for caring for elderly parents or parents who must care for a child with severe disability). This amounts to encouraging caretakers to take care of themselves without feelings of guilt. If they don't, they may start to resent the ill person or even become incapable of providing adequate care (see box).

Caring for Caretakers

It is extremely important to encourage persons who are caretakers of others (whether they be elderly parents, a child, or a sibling with mental illness) not to neglect caring for themselves.

When working with clients who are caretakers, I often use the analogy of flying in an airplane, which most people have done. When I met with Camilia, she was exhausted from caring for her two boys with autism. Her husband had left years earlier. I asked Camilia if she had ever flown. She had, but not in years. I said the following to Camilia:

> When the plane starts to taxi away from the terminal and towards the runway for takeoff, one of the flight attendants will get on the speaker and instruct passengers about various things, such as where the flotation devices are. They also instruct passengers about what to do in case the plane loses air pressure. They explain to passengers that oxygen masks will drop from the consoles above their heads and that passengers should put them on. Then the flight attendant will say, "If you are traveling with a child, you should . . ." Camilia, how do you complete the instructions?

Camilia responded as I hoped she would. She said, "You should put it on your child first!" I said, "But Camilia, what happens if your child fights putting on the mask and then you both pass out?"

In fact, Camilia said exactly the opposite of the instruction. Flight attendants say, "If you are traveling with a child, place the mask on your own face first before assisting the other." In other words, if we do not take care of ourselves, we won't be able to take care of others.

Exacerbation of Medical Problems

Mental illness can have a major negative impact on medical treatment and thus on medical health. Numerous studies have found that people with mental illness are much less likely to follow medical advice and medical regimens. This is because of the symptoms that are part and parcel of mental illness, including confusion, difficulty following instructions, low energy, worry, and depression. It is not uncommon for someone with a mental illness to experience a loss of hope, wherein she may wonder "Why bother?" when instructed to follow medical advice.

In addition, mental illnesses cause serious disruption in relationships. As a result, supportive people who may otherwise encourage compliance with a special diet, exercise, or a medication regimen may not be available to do so.

Finally, persons with mental illness may frustrate and even annoy their medical providers because they no-show regularly or do not follow advice. This too makes it likely that they will not get adequate health care for medical problems.

Suicide

Suicide is a worldwide concern. In any given year about 15 out of every 100,000 persons will kill themselves. This is the general population rate, but different groups have higher rates. For example, males commit suicide at about four times the rate of females.

We review suicide in much more detail in a later chapter. For now, note that suicide attempts and completions are much more likely in persons with mental illness.

Faith and Mental Illness

Spiritual Solace

For all of the reasons discussed previously, belonging to a religious community is usually a source of immense comfort and solace to people dealing with mental illness. Research shows that persons with a mental illness often find comfort in religious beliefs and practices. Probably for similar reasons, research also shows that persons with relatively strong religious allegiance and faith are less likely to develop a mental illness in the first place. It turns out that knowledge of God's love and the comfort of the gospel are good for one's mental health. What a surprise!

Spiritual Problems

As with any trauma, the experience of mental illness, either directly as the individual afflicted or indirectly as family and loved ones, can cause spiritual problems. In brief, the misery that mental illness causes can negatively impact one's faith in a loving, caring God.

Readers must be prepared to reconcile suffering with the idea that God loves and cares. Those afflicted by mental illness, whether the individual or the family, might conclude, "God exists, but . . . " Joyce is a former client of mine, described in the following box, and she went through such a crisis of faith. If a person with mental illness retains belief that God exists, she may be brought back to a proper understanding of the life of the Christian and the theology of the cross.

It may thus be necessary to convince those suffering mental illness that suffering does not mean God has forsaken them. Some persons with mental illness (or perhaps their family) will question or doubt the loving essence of God. The person may think as Joyce did and conclude, "God hates me." A related thought the person might have is that God, despite what some say, does not care for everyone and that she is one of the unlucky ones who falls outside of his loving compassion. The person may respond, as did Joyce, by declaring that she hates God. The person may think, "God has rejected me, so I reject him!"

Alternatively, the person may experience intense confusion and hurt. In the same way that a child does not understand why some experience pain while others do not, the person will struggle to understand why God allows him such hurt or why God does not care. Perhaps they previously felt God's love, but now they don't. Or perhaps they see God's love for other people, how other people are happy and healthy, and are confused and hurt that God does not provide them with the same.

When God Forsakes His Children

Towards the end of our first session, Joyce said, "I hate God. It's quite obvious that he hates me, so why shouldn't I hate him back?" Joyce was adamant that she had no need for God. She believed God existed, but she insisted that God had abandoned her to a life of torment.

Joyce was the oldest of four children. Her parents were loving and kind. She recalled that they went to church every week. On warm, sunny, summer days, she would go lay quietly in the backyard grass and feel God's presence like a warm pressure on her chest. She knew God existed and that he loved her.

When Joyce was 13, her mother was killed by a drunk driver. Her world fell apart quickly and terribly. Devastated by the loss and feeling unable to cope, her father sent his children away. The youngest three went to stay with the father's brother and his wife across town. They did not feel they could fit all four kids, so Joyce was sent to her father's divorced older sister in a neighboring state. Joyce was the eldest and it would be least hard on her. It was supposed to be for only a while, until her father got things back together. But he never did. He began to drink too much, and then he lost his job. The temporary situation ended up being permanent.

Joyce's aunt's son Jack was two years older than Joyce. He had a mean streak. He would regularly beat up his younger sister and younger brother. Within two weeks of her arrival, Joyce was initiated into the family when Jack punched her in the stomach and blackened her eye. When her aunt saw the bruise on her face, she asked, "Jack did that?" She then walked away. She never again asked about bruises or scrapes or anything else.

When Joyce went through puberty, Jack added sexual assault to the physical abuse. This happened at least once a week, until Joyce moved out of the household at age 17. She was heavily into drugs and alcohol by the time she got her own apartment with an older friend. Joyce had her first child at age 19 and her second a year later. Both children were put in foster care after Joyce was arrested for the third time for prostitution and sentenced to six months in prison. She entered prison on her 21st birthday.

Incarceration included mandatory mental health treatment for anyone who tested positive for drugs at the time of arrest. She was diagnosed with post-traumatic stress disorder, or PTSD. Treatment helped her overcome PTSD. When I began seeing Joyce, she was married and had a young child. She was struggling with depression. It was during our first session that she mentioned that she hated God. Years later, I still vividly recall the stark contrast Joyce drew between her childhood, when she literally felt God's loving embrace, and her adolescence, when she descended into a life of unremitting wretchedness.

At one point, Joyce asked me if I wanted to hear the one Bible verse, from Psalm 22, that she still knew: "My God, my God, why have you forsaken me?"

Some patients with mental illness believe their mental illness is punishment from God. I worked many years with a woman with serious depression. She believed that her depression was a punishment from God. I pressed her on this, asking what she had done to deserve punishment. She declared that she was a bad mother to her two children and that God was punishing her by causing her to be depressed. I pointed out that her depression predated her marriage and children by at least 10 years (her depression started at about age 15, whereas her first child was born when she was 26). She rejoined that God is all-knowing and can predict the future, so she was being punished because God knew she was going to be a bad mother.

Abandonment of Faith

The most tragic reaction to mental illness is to conclude that God does not exist. This might be a more common conclusion for family members than for the one with the mental illness. Parents who must watch a child suffer with a severe mental illness or who must endure a child's suicide may become very angry with God. The paradox of a loving God who would allow such pain leads some to resolve the paradox in the only way they see possible, by rejecting the idea of a loving God.

Comfort in the Cross

It is hoped that persons experiencing the effects of mental illness will realize that God loves them even though he allows them to suffer. This is the critical and singular task that must be accomplished, and it is best done by preaching the theology of the cross. Obviously, it is not a task that mental health professionals are equipped to handle. They should refer to you for issues of theology, sin, and forgiveness, as you should refer to them for issues of biology and psychology. In other words, you should be involved in the mental health care of your church members.

I address all of these issues more fully in Part 3, entitled "The Proper Way for a Christian to Understand and Address Mental Illness." For now, let it be sufficient to say that Christians must embrace the theology of the cross. We take up our cross and follow him. We categorically reject the idea that suffering, including the suffering experienced by those affected by mental illness, is a form of God's punishment.

What Father Loves His Daughter Less?

What father loves his daughter less,
When overwhelmed by great distress
She cries in anguish and dismay
And sees her hopes all fly away?

What mother will not softly cry
Whose daughter's dreams are passing by
As mental illness captures her
And renders future joys unsure?

Shall father, mother, daughter fall
And brothers, sister stumble, all,
In hopeless desperation live,
Believing life acts as a sieve?

To filter out all joy and hope
And set her on a slipp'ry slope
Descending surely to despair
As though her joys were never there?

Shall life give way to endless shame
Engaging then in constant blame?
Shall caring and all love dissolve;
Shall trust into distrust evolve?

Is this the sure, relentless fate
That every person must await
When mental illness rears its head?
Must all its victims live in dread?

NO

No, hopes once dimmed shall be
restored,
And quiet joys once more be poured
Upon the spirits of the sad
And those who cried will then be glad.

No, weeping lasts but for a night
And morning comes and puts to flight
The sighs and fears of those distressed
And troubled spirits then will rest.

For fear may not extend its reign
In never-ceasing waves of pain;
The Savior stands upon the sea
And hears the sinking sinner's plea.

He reaches out his mighty hand;
He brings the drowning safe to land;
His Word speaks comfort to the soul
And heals and makes the broken whole.

Shall all afflictions, then, and tears
Be banished like the fleeting years
That mark our fragile hold on life?
Not yet, not yet the end of strife.

For this life offers happiness
And carefree days devoid of stress
And quiet nights of peaceful sleep—
All promises it cannot keep.

Are prayers then only helpless sighs,
Like mists dissolving in the skies?
No, he who hears and answers prayer
Has seen the heavy cross you bear.

And he has promised, "Come to me;
From trouble I will set you free.
Come unto me all you who live
With burdens great and I will give

The tranquil sleep for which you pray.
I'll ease your burdens every day.
Come unto me all you who yearn
For rest from toil and you shall learn

That rest and peace to all I give
Who trust in me and they shall live
With hope when tribulations rise
For I am strong and hear their cries."

Take heart, then, you who live in fear.
The Savior of the world is here.
His Shepherd's hand shall never fail
To guide you through this world's
dark veil.

YES

And look, another day is near.
Yes, Christ, the Lord shall soon appear
With all his angels in the sky
And on that last day—Death shall die,

All tears of woe evaporate
And Jesus shall new life create
Without the sorrow and the pain.
In joy and glory you shall reign

With him for all eternity.
Your song will one of gladness be
As then you see him face to face,
The one who saved you by his grace.

Yes, then shall come the brightest morn
Christ will himself the day adorn;
With all his glory he shall be
Your light for all eternity.

By Daniel Preus—January 29, 2008

Soli Deo Gloria

TWO

PART 2

DESCRIPTIONS OF SPECIFIC MENTAL ILLNESSES

Preview of Part 2

To review the first part of this book, it is extremely important to identify mental illness so that persons who experience it can be helped. The basic components of human experience (thoughts, feelings, behaviors, roles, and relationships) were discussed, and the formal definition of mental illness was provided (i.e., mental illness is a syndrome of behavioral, emotional, and/or psychological problems that is associated with serious and persistent *distress* and/or serious *impairment* in one's ability to fulfill obligations to others or to one's self). The burdens associated with mental illness, to both the individual and the family, were presented, and the important role that the church plays in aiding persons with mental illness was briefly discussed (to be elaborated on in a later chapter).

In this part of this book, the specific mental illnesses are presented. Each chapter will presents all or some of the following aspects of its disorders:

• *Specific Symptoms of Disorders.* As noted above and in chapter 3, a mental illness is diagnosed only if symptoms are associated with distress and/or impairment. Thus, which particular mental illness a person will be diagnosed with depends on what specific behavioral, emotional, or psychological *symptoms* a person is experiencing. These descriptions of the required criteria (i.e., the list of symptoms that must be present to diagnose someone) are derived from the *Diagnostic and Statistical Manual of Mental Disorders* (DSM), which was described in chapter 3.

• *Typical Presentation (The Face of the Illness).* While it is good to be knowledgeable about the symptoms of each mental illness, symptoms are usually only uncovered when asked about. For example, one of the hallmark symptoms of depression is insomnia, but you won't know if someone has insomnia unless you ask. So each chapter will also discuss the typical "presentation" of someone with a particular disorder. That is, each chapter will describe what the person will look like as you interact with him or her. These sections will be labeled "The Face of (Illness)."

- *Other Noteworthy Aspects of the Disorder(s).* Other aspects of the disorder that are worth knowing, such as risk factors for the disorder or the typical course of the disorder, will be presented in each chapter.
- *Distress and Impairment.* Each chapter will also describe the distress and impairment typically associated with the particular mental illness. Some relevant facts and figures about specific disorders are reviewed, as are important treatment issues and recommendations.
- *Treatment Exigencies and Encouraging Treatment Seeking.* Any unusual aspects about treatment of the disorder, as well as suggestions for encouraging a person with the disorder to seek treatment, will be presented.

The Depression and Anxiety Disorders

Chapters 6 and 7 review the most common mental illnesses: depression and the anxiety disorders. These are the two most common mental illnesses, and these are consequently the two longest chapters. Thus, whether you know it or not, you interact with people who have depression or anxiety every single day. Since the symptoms of depression and anxiety are internal, persons with these disorders can successfully hide their distress from others. They can pretend to be happy and force themselves to smile. But when you get to know them a bit, you realize they are chronically sad or overwhelmed with anxiety, and they cannot figure out how to feel better.

The Psychotic Disorders and Bipolar Disorder

Chapter 8 covers the psychotic disorders (most notably schizophrenia), and chapter 9 reviews bipolar disorder. In contrast to depression and anxiety, you would likely notice that you were interacting with someone who is experiencing severe symptoms of one of these disorders. The psychotic disorders and bipolar disorder are not as common, but they are usually much more devastating. Another difference in comparing depression and anxiety to schizophrenia and bipolar disorder is their duration. Depression and the anxiety disorders can endure for a long time, even if the person gets appropriate treatment. Indeed, some persons with these disorders remain in treatment (e.g., take meds) their whole lives. However, depression and the anxiety disorders can be cured if appropriate treatment is received. In contrast, psychosis and bipolar disorder are likely to last a lifetime. Treatment entails getting the individual to a relatively functional, perhaps even symptom-free state, then maintaining him there through ongoing medication management. For this reason, the psychotic disorders and bipolar disorder are sometimes referred to as "severe and persistent mental illnesses," or SPMIs.

Stress-Induced, Substance Use, Eating, Impulse Control Disorders, and Others

Chapter 10 covers the stress-induced disorders, including post-traumatic stress disorder. In chapter 11, we consider the substance use, eating, and impulse control disorders. These disorders have the commonality of being problems of behavior (using substances, eating, or controlling impulses). Chapter 12 reviews the dissociative, sleep, sexual, and somatization disorders. Chapter 13 covers the personality disorders.

Disorders That Emerge in Childhood and in Old Age

Chapter 14 reviews the mental illnesses that emerge in childhood (such as autism and ADHD), whereas chapter 15 covers the important topic of child abuse and neglect. Chapter 16 reviews the illnesses that do not usually emerge until old age, such as Alzheimer's disease, as well as the abuse and neglect of vulnerable adults.

Other Issues Relevant to Mental Health

In chapter 17, we review domestic abuse, whereas chapter 18 is dedicated to the topic of suicide.

A Paradox and a Plea

Before we begin our discussion of specific mental illnesses, I first present a paradox and a plea.

The Paradox of the Recognizability of Mental Illness

As reviewed previously, all mental illnesses have two aspects: distress and impairment. The graphical representation on page 67 shows these two aspects on a Cartesian system. We can place all mental illness in this system. For example, some mental illnesses are characterized by both high distress and high impairment, whereas others may be characterized by a low level of one and a high level of the other. (Different persons experience different levels of impairment and distress, and this between-person variability is shown by the arrows.) By definition, no mental illness has low levels of both distress and impairment. This figure illustrates the variability of the mental illnesses.

The profound paradox of mental illness is that the most serious mental illnesses are most easily recognized and remembered because the symptoms associated with them are the most disruptive, severe, and overt. That is, the symptoms cause a great deal of impairment. Examples of these mental illnesses are shown at the top of the figure. For example, schizophrenia might include symptoms such as hallucinations and delusions, which might lead the person to behave strangely. Bipolar disorder might include manic phase symptoms of aggressiveness, rapid speech, and irritability, and these will cause various psychosocial impairment. Some disorders are essentially defined by the profound impairment the person exhibits, such as dementia, the drug and alcohol use disorders, anorexia nervosa, and some disorders most commonly diagnosed in childhood (ADHD, conduct disorder).

Likewise, the mental illnesses that cause the most profound impairment are the type most likely to make the news. They are likewise the type most often presented in movies. Most know that John Hinckley tried to assassinate President Ronald Reagan and that he did so because he had delusions regarding the actress Jodie Foster. (He apparently was seeking to impress her.) It is likewise easy to recall Russell Crowe's portrayal of John Nash, the Nobel Prize winning mathematician, in the movie *A Beautiful Mind.* These individuals were characterized by extreme problematic behaviors that are memorable, and memorable examples tend to be remembered. As a result, when asked to describe a mental illness, most people describe problems and behaviors that would be characteristic of severe mental illness, such as the problems and behaviors being exhibited by a person in the midst of either a psychotic episode or a manic episode.

Paradoxically, these mental illnesses are the least common. In other words, the least common types of mental illness get most of the attention and are therefore most memorable.

In contrast, the more common type of mental illness is often overlooked and ignored. The second type is harder to recognize because the symptoms are more subtle with regard to impairment. With some effort on the part of the person experiencing them, they can be hidden from others. This type includes the depressive disorders and the anxiety disorders. People experiencing these disorders can put up a good front and, despite being in great distress, might be able to behave as if

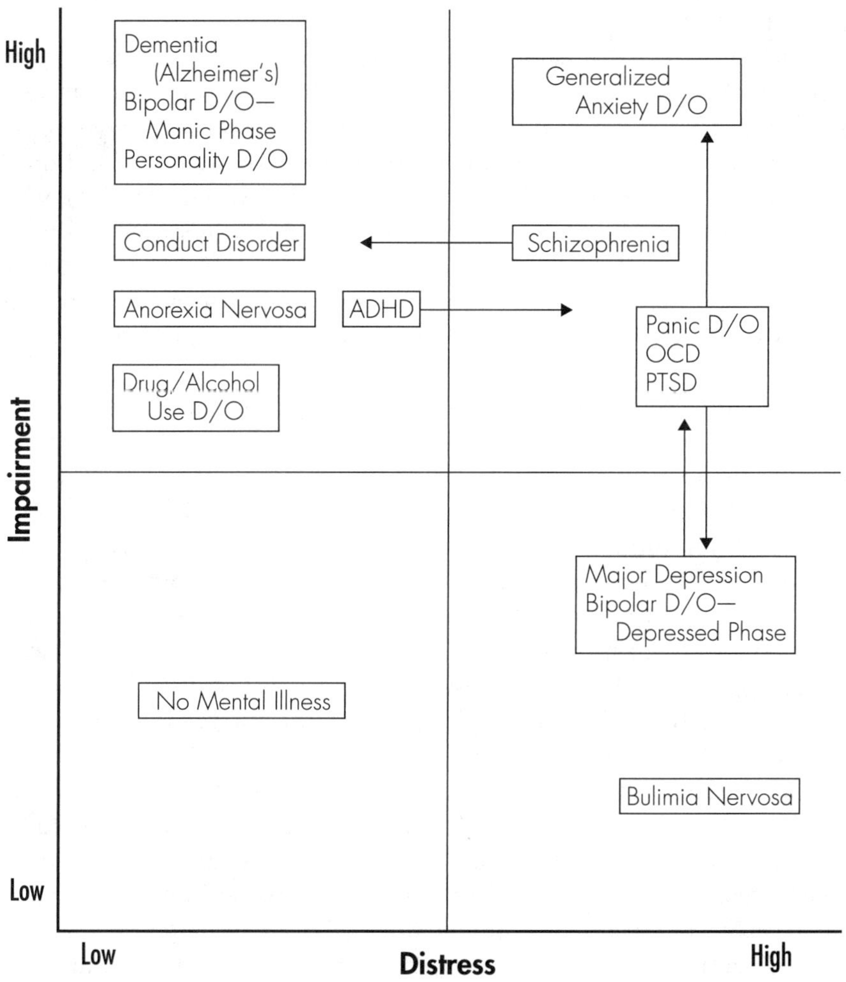

Distress Versus Impairment in Some of the Mental Illnesses

there is nothing wrong. (Note the arrows, however. These indicate that some persons with these disorders experience severe impairment.) Consider the following examples of persons with these mental illnesses who were able to exhibit little impairment.

John Madden, the great Oakland Raiders football coach who gained even greater fame as a football analyst, openly acknowledges that he has a phobia of flying. Years ago, he experienced severe anxiety while on a turbulent flight, and he has not flown since. Fortunately for him, he doesn't have to. Madden gets from city to city by Greyhound Bus, which outfitted a special ride for him (for the publicity it generated for their company). It may take John Madden longer to reach his destination than if he took a plane, but he can and does avoid planes. As a result, his phobia is never "activated," and if he never spoke about it, few would know about it.

Sir Winston Churchill (1874–1965) is widely known as the leader of the United Kingdom during World War II. His exhortation to his country that "we shall never surrender" is the high point of one of the most famous speeches of all time. It sounds like the attitude of a confident and hopeful man, and Churchill's activity during the blitz of London convinced many observers that he had boundless enthusiasm, optimism, and energy. Less well known is that Churchill suffered from profound depressions. A less famous quote from him reads as follows: "I don't like standing near the edge of a platform when an express train is passing through. I like to stand right back and if possible get a pillar between me and the train. I don't like to stand by the side of a ship and look down into the water. A second's action would end everything. A few drops of desperation." Churchill likewise made frequent references to his "black dog," what he labeled his depressive periods, which tended to be both intense and prolonged.

The great statesman Churchill did not exhibit odd behavior and was able to do his job despite his mental illness. The same can be said for Ashley Judd (actress); Owen Wilson (actor); Buzz Aldrin (astronaut); J. K. Rowling (author); Mike Wallace (newsman); Kurt Cobain, Billy Joel, and Sheryl Crow (musicians); Drew Carey and Jim Carrey (comedians); and many other persons both famous and not-so-famous. Recall from part 1 that approximately one in five persons will have a mental illness in any given year. People with mental illness, if they can, will hide it from others. Sometimes this is easier than others. John Madden managed to eliminate his anxiety by avoiding planes. Many readers have had the experience of talking with a friend who admits that she has been experiencing a serious depression lately, which she was able to hide from others, including you and her other friends. Some mental illnesses are practically defined by the fact that sufferers go to great attempts to hide them. An alcoholic will hide his drinking from others. A young woman with bulimia nervosa (the "binge purge" eating disorder) will go to extreme measures to hide her behavior from others.

The Consequence of the Paradox

The most serious mental illnesses are at the same time the least common and the most easily recognized and imagined. This leads to several negative consequences. First, if people assume that mental illness means psychosis, then other mental illnesses may go unrecognized or dismissed as minor or irrelevant. If they are "not so bad," then other mental illnesses will not be treated adequately. As will be shown in chapter 6, the "less serious" mental illnesses can cause intense distress and profound disability. Second, the idea that mental illness is the same as psychosis leads people to assume that all persons with mental illness can (or perhaps should) be forced into treatment or even locked up against their will. A related idea is that someone with a mental illness is unpredictable, unstable, and potentially dangerous.

Both of these notions make it very difficult for many people to accept that they have a mental illness or that someone they love has a mental illness. In the case of SPMI, the evidence becomes overwhelming and impossible to deny. If someone is attacking his refrigerator for acting threatening or emptying the bank account to buy property to start a supermodel school, then family members might be compelled to take action and force that person into treatment. The more serious, less-common mental illnesses, in other words, are the most likely to get treatment.

The much more common mental illnesses are not as disruptive, noticeable, and memorable. Persons with these illnesses (and their families) can ignore them for years on end. This is not a good thing. The purpose of this book is to help you convince persons with any type of mental illness that the illness exists, that effective treatment is available, and that they do not need to continue to suffer.

A Plea Regarding Terminology

I have a very strong opinion with regard to the terminology used to describe persons with a mental illness. Hopefully, readers will see that I follow my own rule consistently in what follows.

I have a very strong objection to describing persons with mental illness as their mental illness. I think it demeaning, stigmatizing, cruel, and hurtful to refer to a person as "schizophrenic," "depressive," "agoraphobic," or "anorexic." You will hear reference to a "schizophrenic's brain" or a "depressive's symptoms," and in my field you hear the lament "she's a borderline, what do you expect?" These terms imply that the person is the illness or that the illness is the primary and most important description of the person. To refer to the person by these terms disparages his or her individuality. The terms ignore the person as a mother or father; a brother or sister; a husband or wife; a worker or boss; a Christian, Jew, or Muslim; and all of the other ways we think of ourselves.

This is an unfortunately common practice among mental health professionals, who should but often don't know better. It is especially likely to happen when the mental health professional is frustrated with the patient for challenging the magnificence and munificence of the care the professional is providing by, of all the ridiculous things, not getting better! Thus, you may hear a mental health professional refer to his patient as an addict or a schizophrenic or a borderline (three examples of disorders that are challenging to treat). This is a universal signal that the therapist is either an ignoramus or frustrated by a patient or both.

In what follows I will refer to "a person with such-and-such disorder." For example, I will refer to the person with schizophrenia, the person diagnosed with depression, and so forth. This places the person in the primary position, suggests that the illness is an aspect (but not the only or most important aspect) of the person, and especially indicates that the person can recover from the illness. I strongly encourage the reader to adopt this practice in everyday language and especially when talking about or to someone with a mental illness.

Chapter 6

The Depressive Disorders

"Blessed are you who weep now, for you will laugh."
(Luke 6:21)

This chapter will help the reader better understand and empathize with persons who suffer depression. This will enable you to encourage them not to feel ashamed of being depressed but rather to recognize that effective help is available. The chapter begins with a review of major depressive disorder, which is the most common form of depression. It then briefly covers the less common depressive disorders: dysthymia, post-partum depression, seasonal affective disorder, and psychotic depression.

As will all subsequent chapters covering the specific mental illnesses, the chapter then attempts to give a sense of how a person with depression will actually look, or to use the terms of mental health professionals, the "typical presentation." The chapter also reviews some of the noteworthy aspects of depression, such as its different presentation in men versus women. The distress and impairment associated with depression are then discussed. The chapter ends with some advice on how to encourage someone with depression to seek professional help including a brief review of the most common treatment approaches.

Depression Is a Mood Disorder

To understand depression, it is important to understand the two terms that mental health professionals use to describe feelings: *mood* and *affect.*

It is also important to understand the two extremes of mood. Much of this information is repeated from chapter 2.

Mood and Affect

Mood is an extended period of feeling. Mood often reflects life circumstances. As a result, most of us experience various moods throughout the course of a day or week. On Monday, I was in an irritable mood, because I hate Mondays. On Tuesday, my mood was good, because my team won the football game the night before. Wednesday, which is my hectic day, I was in a tense mood. And so it goes.

However, what we feel will change, at least somewhat, according to what is going on around us. Such temporary, situation-determined feelings are called *affect.* Affect is temporary. Even when in a bad mood on Monday, I was cheered up (my affect changed) when chatting with a friend. Many of us have experienced having a good mood "ruined" temporarily by bad news. Our enduring feeling (mood) temporarily improves or deteriorates (affect) according to the situation.

Mood Disorder

Mood has two extremes. One extreme, or "pole," of mood is *mania,* which means the person is abnormally upbeat and cheerful. Behavioral signs usually accompany mania as well, including talking rapidly, being in constant motion, and doing foolish things. The other extreme of mood is *depression.*

Instead of having life influence his or her mood, someone with a mood disorder feels the same way all the time. Hence their mood is disturbed or "disordered." There are two types of mood disorders. Depression is referred to as "unipolar depression" because the person's mood stays at the extreme (pole) of sad mood. Someone with bipolar disorder, which used to be called manic depression, will fluctuate between depression and mania, the two poles of mood.

Sheryl is diagnosed with a mood disorder because she experiences unrelenting depression. She stays sad even when family, friends, and life in general give her reason to rejoice. She does not cheer up when her children come home from school, when a friend calls to say hello, or when she receives a compliment at work for a job well done. Her mood does not change to reflect the situation, but rather stays depressed.

Will has been diagnosed with a mood disorder because he remains abnormally upbeat and cheerful despite negative consequences of his behavior, bad news, and the admonitions of others. The situation does not warrant an ongoing good mood, but his mood does not change. (We would expect Will to later crash into depression, as a manic mood rarely occurs outside of bipolar disorder.)

The Other Mood Disorder: Bipolar Disorder

Bipolar disorder is a special type of depression. Persons with bipolar disorder will experience depression for some periods of time and mania during others. A person experiencing mania will be full of energy and have less need for sleep. She will be overconfident, talkative, and full of ideas (some unusual). As a result, she may take risks (e.g., go gambling, drive too fast) or do things that she normally would not (e.g., shopping extravagantly, sexual indiscretions). Bipolar depression is less common than depression and requires medical treatments (i.e., medication). Bipolar disorder is discussed in chapter 9.

Major Depressive Disorder

The DSM lists nine symptoms that must be present in some combination (at least five of the nine must be experienced) for *at least two weeks* for someone to be diagnosed with a major depressive episode. Some of the symptoms are obvious. The most obvious is feeling *persistently sad* most of the time. For some, this sadness is experienced as *anhedonia,* which is a sense of emptiness, boredom, or an inability to glean pleasure from life (including things they used to enjoy in the past). Of course, the person could experience both sad mood and anhedonia.

The person with depression will admit, when asked, to feeling *worthless and guilty.* Even when she is continuing to work and take care of her family, she feels like she is not doing well enough and that she is letting other people down.

Other symptoms of depression are not as obvious. (You will notice an either-or pattern in these next symptoms.) The person with depression may feel very *lethargic,* like her battery is depleted. Alternatively (or even at the same time), the person may feel an unpleasant, *restless energy,* such as you may feel when you are very tired but cannot sleep. Some persons react to the mental exhaustion of terrible, abiding sadness by overeating, with consequent *weight gain.* Others find they have no interest in food whatsoever and may *lose weight.* Depression will probably affect sleep. The person is most likely to experience *insomnia,* but some are so exhausted that they sleep too much (called *hypersomnia*).

Mark

Mark has experienced depression on and off since age 13. Mark is now 33 and has been married for four years. He has two children, ages 5 and 2. He and his wife began seeing me for marital counseling because his depression was interfering with their relationship. He said to me during our first meeting, "It is difficult to describe the despair that will overwhelm me. I feel like no one wants to associate with me, let alone love me. It's impossible for me to think Jill loves me, since I cannot be loved. At the same time, I start to get irrational about how things are going. I think I am going to lose my job and that we will go bankrupt, which is another reason Jill cannot possibly love me. I feel like I don't deserve to have a job (Mark is a well-paid executive in charge of strategy for a large computer company) and I don't deserve the money I am paid." Mark described how it was difficult to get out of bed in the morning and that he has to force himself to eat, since food has no enjoyment for him. Mostly, he was worried about whether he could possibly be loved by anyone, including his wife and two children. The whole time he was describing his mood disorder, his wife sat beside him, holding his hand and looking at him with loving concern.

Depression impairs one's ability to *think* quickly and effectively. As a result, the simplest of tasks (going to the store, making a phone call) and decisions (whether to go to lunch with a coworker, what to wear) seem overwhelming. None of this is helped by *difficulty concentrating.*

Mental exhaustion and a lack of ability to see beyond despair causes the person with depression to become convinced that the future is bleak. In particularly severe cases, he may feel not just *hopeless* but also helpless to improve things. As a result, the person with depression may have recurrent *thoughts about death,* such as that both she and others would be better off if she were dead. For some, these thoughts manifest as *suicidal ideation.* The person may consider taking her own life or may make an attempt at *suicide.*

The Varieties of Major Depression

Note that there are many possible combinations of any five (or more) of the nine symptoms and that some of the symptoms are either this or that. As a result, there are hundreds of varieties of depression (meaning different combinations of symptoms). All persons with major depression will experience either negative mood or anhedonia, but some may have appetite and sleep problems, where others don't. Some may have thoughts of suicide, but others won't. Some may feel enervated and run-down, whereas others will be agitated and angry.

Dysthymic Disorder

To be diagnosed with dysthymia, a person can have only two of the symptoms listed for a major depressive episode (including either sad mood, anhedonia, or both), but the symptoms must endure for at least *two years.* Dysthymia is thus *less severe* than major depression, but it lasts a very long time.

Double Depression

Major depressive disorder and dysthymia can occur together. Most typically, a person with dysthymia will develop the more severe disorder. Such "double depression" is extremely distressing and disabling. Persons with double depression are at particular risk of suicide.

Disruptive Mood Dysregulation Disorder (DMDD)

Children and adolescents can be diagnosed with major depressive episode or dysthymia. One noteworthy difference in diagnosing children and adolescents is that they often express sadness as irritability or anger. The thought is that children and adolescents do not understand their feelings well enough to express them genuinely (they substitute anger, an emotion that they are more familiar with, for sadness). A related explanation is that anger is more likely to attract attention from adults than will sadness, so children and adolescents are more likely to express it.

With the publication in 2013 of the new DSM, a mood disorder specific to children and adolescents was introduced. Disruptive mood dysregulation disorder was included in the DSM-5 to diagnose anyone under age 18 who exhibits persistent irritability and frequent episodes of behavior outbursts.

DMDD Criteria

DMDD might be diagnosed if a child or adolescent has repeated (several times per week) temper outbursts that are grossly out of proportion, in either intensity or duration, to the situation. The outbursts might be manifested verbally, in the form of screaming rages, or physically, in the form of aggression towards property or other people (such as other children, parents, teachers), or both. In addition, the outbursts will be inappropriate for the child's age (such as seeing an outburst reminiscent of the terrible twos in an 8-year-old). Finally, in between outbursts, the child's mood is observed to be persistently irritable or angry.

Ariel

Ariel is 12. She is not popular among her teachers, and her parents admit that they are somewhat afraid of her. Her emotions fluctuate wildly between giddiness and fury. Since infancy, she flies into a rage at the slightest provocation, such as being told "no." During one playdate at age 6, she angrily pushed another child off a short wall, requiring that child a visit to the hospital for stitches (and requiring Mom to find another friend for both herself and Ariel). She has drawn blood from family and friends more than a few other times.

DMDD or Bipolar Disorder?

The diagnosis of DMDD is controversial. One part of the controversy is related to diagnosis and the other to treatment.

Beginning in the late 1990s, more and more psychiatrists were diagnosing children with bipolar disorder (see chapter 9), which previously most researchers and clinicians agreed really could *not* be properly diagnosed until adulthood. Indeed, there were no established criteria for even diagnosing bipolar disorder in children. Those researchers and clinicians who argued that bipolar disorder, in fact, often *started* in childhood argued that the requisite manic episode was expressed as irritability and anger. As noted above, irritability is an alternative symptom to sad mood when diagnosing major depression in children.

Note that controversy and debate are part and parcel of any healthy science endeavor. It is necessary for scientists to disagree and to criticize one another's work in order to advance any scientific field. This is how research progresses. In this instance, the scientific debate revolved around the proper identification of a childhood mental illness.

However, this particular controversy was not always about science. Many believe that some had ulterior motives to diagnosing children with bipolar disorder. In particular, pharmaceutical companies began encouraging pediatricians and pediatric psychiatrists to use medications that were developed for use in the treatment of adulthood bipolar disorder (and schizophrenia) in children so diagnosed. This was "off label" prescribing, which means that the drug was being used in a different way than described in the FDA-approved drug label (which was based on many years of intensive, FDA-sanctioned scientific research). The end result was that the diagnosis of bipolar disorder in children and adolescents and its treatment, using drugs approved for different purposes, increased by a factor of 40! Many saw this as a problem.

Even more of a problem, longitudinal research examining children who had been diagnosed with bipolar disorder (which, being longitudinal, took about a decade to accumulate) was suggesting that many of these children were more likely to develop major depression or an anxiety disorder as adults, instead of continuing to meet criteria for bipolar disorder. This too was a problem. As we shall see in chapter 9, bipolar disorder usually persists throughout one's lifetime.

At the writing of this chapter, DMDD was a new diagnosis introduced in the DSM 5 (which came out in May 2013). By the time you read this, there may be more known about its validity and utility. As indicated earlier, research into the mental illnesses is neither quick nor easy. But mental health researchers do tend, eventually, to get it right.

Other Types of Depression

There are other types of depression.

Psychotic depression occurs when a person has such extreme depression that he also experiences some form of psychosis. These may include depressing delusions, which are false beliefs. A person with psychotic depression may believe he is responsible for the war in another country or for the recent death of a neighbor. Some persons with psychotic depression will experience hallucinations, meaning they may hear or see things that don't exist. Persons with this version of depression are usually treated with a combination of medications to address both the depression and the psychosis.

Two other types of depression are induced by specific circumstances. Research suggests that *post-partum depression* will be experienced by 10-15% of all women after giving birth. Post-partum depression may occur soon after delivery, within the first three months of delivery, or it may not show for up to a year later. Hormonal changes related to childbearing account for some of the depression. But there are numerous nonhormonal causes as well, including the overwhelming responsibility of caring for a newborn, changes in relationships, and a lack of sleep.

Finally, *seasonal affective disorder* (SAD) is a predictable visitor for some people. Sometimes called wintertime depression, this mood disorder arrives in the winter but generally abates by spring or summer. Even though it comes and goes, the severity should not be underappreciated. SAD is simply a subtype of major depressive disorder with a known cause. SAD is caused by the loss of sunlight. About half of persons with it can be effectively treated by exposure to bright, artificial light, whereas others are helped by antidepressant medication. For all who experience it, SAD is miserable. It is not uncommon for someone vulnerable to this disorder (which is diagnosed only while the depression is active) to be compelled to move to a warmer, sunnier climate.

Alyson

Alyson does not like winter. She lives in Bismarck, North Dakota, where winter comes early and hard. She has a very well-paying job in the oil industry; otherwise, she would move "in a heartbeat." Alyson is 52 and is well aware of the seasonal nature of her depression. She knows that by late November, soon after Thanksgiving, she will start to slide into a depression. She will lose energy, start to lose sleep, and begin to gain an indifference to things she usually enjoys, including gourmet cooking and reading long historical novels. She also knows that by April or May, she will start to come out of the depression if she forces herself to get outdoors, regardless of the cold, into whatever sunlight might be available. She and her medical doctor have developed a somewhat effective strategy for coping with her seasonal affective disorder. In late October, Alyson will start taking a small dose of antidepressant (fluvoxamine) and will increase the dose over the month. She also has purchased an artificial light that she uses for 30 minutes before work every morning, starting in November. These strategies help a great deal.

The Face of Depression

Others do not easily observe many of the symptoms of depression. (This is actually true for many of the mental illnesses.) For example, you will not know, unless you ask, whether someone is experiencing anhedonia, low energy, difficulty sleeping, and so forth.

On the other hand, it would be good to have a sense of how persons with depression may look or behave so that you can approach them, if you are concerned, and ask them that all-important and revealing question: "Have you been depressed lately?" (And then you can follow up with a referral to treatment.)

The face of depression is variable, but there are some typical aspects of the observable behavior of a person with depression. They can be divided into body language, interpersonal behavior, and commentary. The following are generalizations and are not true of everyone with depression. But if you observe these, it is a pretty good bet that the person is in psychological distress.

Body Language

Body language can be defined as nonverbal communication through facial expressions, gestures, and movements. Mental health professionals examine the body language of patients with keenness, as it reveals a great deal about their psychological state.

Not to make you regret reading this book by stating the obvious, but the depressed person *looks* sad and depressed. The person may look on the verge of tears, but more likely, to steal a phrase from *Man of La Mancha,* she will have a "woeful countenance." She doesn't smile easily. She won't react to life's simple pleasures, such as the smile of a friend, the smell of good food, or the laughter of a child. Her gaze will be somewhat vacant and nonreactive. She may also sigh frequently and wring her hands, giving off an aura of despair.

Someone with depression may display slowed gestures and movement. If asked, she may describe this as feeling as if her battery were low or as if she were walking through a fog. One strategy I have learned over the years is to walk behind a client when heading to the consulting room for the first meeting. If he or she is slower than normal, I will be alert to possible depression, especially if the person also displays depressed posture, such as slumped shoulders and inclined head. In short, the person with depression will look exhausted (which he or she is).

Interpersonal Behavior

The interpersonal behavior of someone with depression will tend towards avoidance. The shy person who is part of a group conversing won't likely say much but will still be in the group and will still react to the conversation. The person with depression, however, will not join the group. She will avoid social contact, even if the others honestly wish she would join in. Her logic is to "spare them" of her company, which she reasons is aversive to them.

Even when engaging in a conversation, it will seem that the person with depression is trying to avoid you. (He is not, but it will seem that way.) The person with depression will display a lack of eye contact, and speech may be slow and monotonous. You may notice an unusually long delay between utterances, either between their own statements or when responding to you. As a result, attempts at conversing with a depressed person can be trying, as it feels as if you are doing all of the conversational "work."

Commentary

The content of what the depressed person says is often brief and doleful. Their "commentary" on or interpretation of life will tend to be pervasively negative. What is said may have themes of hopelessness and helplessness. The person will express negative assessments of herself ("I'm a failure;" "It's all my fault;" "Nothing good ever happens to me;" "I'm worthless;" "No one loves me"). Others will be seen as untrustworthy and disappointing ("She invited me but didn't really want me to come to the party"), and the world will be characterized as hostile, cruel, and unforgiving ("People are mean like that;" "There is nothing good out there"). Perhaps, as a result, the person will see the future as bleak and frightening ("Life is not worth living;" "Things will always be bad"). Hopeless language in particular should alert you that the person may be contemplating suicide (see chapter 18).

Intense Shame

Perhaps the most noteworthy, seemingly universal aspect of depression is a sense of shame. I have been doing psychotherapy for 25 years and I have met with hundreds of people with depression. I have *never* met someone with the disorder who did not feel *ashamed* of having the disorder.

Sara, a mother of three beautiful and happy children, said to me, "It doesn't make sense that I would be so depressed. I have a friend who has cancer and she is incredibly upbeat and positive. I have another friend whose husband left her a year ago, and she is starting her own business. I feel like a loser. I hate myself for feeling this way!" Persons with depression are confused about why they feel this way, which leads to feelings of wrongness and shame. Somehow they feel that they are responsible or at fault for becoming depressed. As a result, they are reluctant to share with others that they feel depressed.

I find it useful to confront this directly with my clients. I confront it with admonitory humor. I state emphatically, "I don't understand why you feel ashamed of being depressed. It is not as if you want to be depressed. There would be something wrong with you if you wanted to be depressed. You're depressed, but there's nothing wrong with you. Stop blaming yourself for this, and let's try to get you out of this terrible place."

The Face of Depression in Adolescence

It is estimated that 1 in 20 teenagers will experience an episode of depression. Prior to puberty, males and females report similar rates of the disorder, but females show higher rates during adolescence and thereafter. Depression in adolescence is associated with a host of negative consequences, including higher risk of substance abuse, sexual activity and pregnancy, and school problems. Suicide is another possible outcome of depression. Although suicide is less common for youth than for elderly persons, it is the third leading cause of death in 15- to 24-year-olds. (In contrast to the elderly, who experience many things that cause death, young people tend to be healthy. Hence, although the rate is less than the elderly, suicide is a leading cause of death among youth.)

Depression in teens can look very different from depression in adults. If asked how he is feeling, a depressed adult will probably reply, "I've been somewhat depressed lately." If asked how he is feeling, a depressed teen *may* admit to being depressed. As likely, however, the depressed teenager will be grumpy, hostile, easily frustrated, and prone to angry outbursts. Some adults and parents believe that the normal adolescent is moody, unpleasant, and irritable. Probably all adolescents are this way *at times,* but a *chronically* irritable and unpleasant adolescent is likely suffering from depression. Thus, when asked how he feels, the depressed teen may snarl sarcastically, "I'm just great! Thanks for asking. I know you care so much!" The desire to say something rude in return, or to just simply turn and walk away, will be practically irresistible. Hard as it may be, try to resist the urge to do either.

It is not clear why depressed teenagers express their distress in such a disagreeable fashion, but understanding that teenagers are not much removed from childhood can help. It is likely related to low self-awareness and an immature understanding of normal and abnormal emotions. Related to this, depressed teens will frequently have vague physical complaints, such as headaches or stomachaches, which are "somatic substitutions" of emotional problems. It is also likely related to the heightened sense of vulnerability and the consequent need to appear tough that all adolescents experience. Finally, it may be related to the simple fact that an adolescent who has been anxious or depressed much of her existence does not know that to feel differently is an option.

Depressed teenagers are particularly susceptible to feeling worthless. All normal teenagers worry about their capacity to be successful adults. Indeed, we adults *want* teenagers to worry about what it takes to be successful, as this will motivate them to get a good education, learn to be nice to others, follow rules, and so forth. However, teenagers often have a mistaken and daunting view of what is required to be a successful adult (you can never be late, you can never make a mistake, and so forth). This is why parents must so often reassure their teenage sons and daughters that making mistakes is okay. "It's going to be okay. Everyone is late sometimes. Everyone forgets an assignment sometimes. Everyone messes up sometimes."

To reiterate, *normal* teenagers will worry about their future and some will do so to an unnecessary degree. The depressed teen, on the other hand, will be *extremely* anxious about her future. She will project her sense of worthlessness into her future and will be forced to conclude that no one will ever want to be her friend, no one will think her smart enough to hire, and no one will ever want to marry her. This has three effects. First, she will be extremely vulnerable to criticism, rejection, and failure, as these will "confirm" her worst fears. Second, she will react very badly to loss, such as a friend moving away, since she perceives herself as incapable of replacing anything she values. Finally, a sense of worthlessness will cause the depressed teenager to withdraw from people, including parents and friends. An alternative to this behavior is to start hanging out with a different, more "accepting" crowd of friends. Unfortunately, the gang that is most likely to accept someone regardless of her negative attitude may be made up of the kids who are most prone to unhealthy behavior, such as using drugs and alcohol or skipping school.

In summary, depression in children and adolescents may be suspected (and should be evaluated) if the child or adolescent (1) expresses unusual levels of irritability and acting out, especially if these are new behaviors; (2) starts doing more poorly at school; (3) appears to be socially isolated; (4) expresses a lot of somatic complaints; (5) seems excessively negative and worried about his future; or (6) develops unhealthy friendships.

Other Noteworthy Things to Know About Depression

Risk Factors for Depression

Risk factors are things about people that make them more likely to develop a disorder. Risk factors for major depressive episodes have been widely researched.

Depression affects all ethnic, racial, and socioeconomic groups. However, members of racial and ethnic minorities—especially African-Americans, Hispanics, and American-Indians—are significantly less likely to obtain any treatment or, if they do obtain it, adequate treatment for depression.

Stressful life events, especially chronically stressful things, put someone at greater risk of depression. These include employment problems, marital problems or dissolution, and financial problems.

Persons with a chronic medical illness, such as heart disease, diabetes, and cancer, are at higher risk for developing depression. Again, the never-ending stress of the disease and its treatment can lead to a sense of hopelessness and despair, which can develop into depression. Medical doctors are increasingly aware that proper treatment of these diseases means looking out for and treating depression, since someone with depression is much less likely to follow accurately and persistently the prescribed medical regimen.

Although depression can occur at any age, including childhood, elderly persons are at particularly high risk of developing depression because of the stress related to greater levels of physical health problems and social loss.

Episodes of major depression typically last from six months to a year. Moreover, depression is a recurrent disease: more than half who experience a first episode of depression will have at least one other episode in their lives. In other words, a primary risk factor for developing an episode of depression is a previous episode of depression.

Well-Known Persons With Depression

Numerous famous persons have suffered from depression. All of the following have openly acknowledged suffering depression:

Winston Churchill • Edvard Munch • Abe Lincoln • Walt Whitman
Buzz Aldrin • Stephen Hawking • Peter Gabriel • Sylvia Plath
Art Buchwald • Barbara Bush • Ray Charles • Eric Clapton
Dick Clark • Ernest Hemingway • Leonard Cohen • Sheryl Crow
Michael Crichton • Mike Douglas • Anthony Hopkins • Bonnie Raitt
Sarah McLachlan • James Taylor • Francis Ford Coppola

Depression in Men Versus Women

Women experience depression at twice the rate of men. Research has uncovered several reasons for this. Biological reasons include a greater genetic predisposition to inheriting depression (leading some researchers to wonder if depression vulnerability is passed through the X chromosome) and fluctuating hormone levels, especially during pregnancies and at menopause (both of which are associated with increased depression). Psychological explanations include the discovery that women spend more time than men thinking about problems. While helpful if the problems are solvable, ruminating on unsolvable problems can lead to depression. Also, women tend to focus on relationships more than men and to react more negatively when there are relationship problems or terminations. Finally, in contrast to previous generations, women today are as likely as men to work outside the home. Given that women focus more on relationships, however, they are more likely to do most of the housework and childcare. In short, women are more likely to experience the stresses of present-day living and are less likely than men to say that they have time to pursue pleasurable activities and to take care of their own needs.

Depression also presents differently in men and women. Women are more likely to respond to depression by acknowledging, to themselves and others, that they are depressed. Men, on the other hand, tend not to acknowledge depression, either to themselves or to others. Instead, men will tend to self-medicate their depression with alcohol and drugs. Thus, men have lower rates of depression but higher rates of substance abuse and dependence (i.e., alcohol or drug problems). In addition, men tend to blame others for their negative affect. They will thereby express depression with irritability, hostility, and perhaps aggressiveness.

In other words, women tend to feel depression honestly, whereas men tend to express it in other forms. The end result is that men who are depressed are less likely to obtain appropriate help.

Depression and Suicide

Recent longitudinal research has followed people with depression over long periods of time. The research shows that about 2% of those ever treated for depression at an outpatient clinic or office and 4% of those who at some point were hospitalized for depression will die by suicide.

The research also uncovered dramatic gender differences in risk of suicide in persons with depression. About 7% of men with a lifetime history of depression will die by suicide, compared to about 1% of women. While the latter rate is lower than the rate for men, keep in mind that the base rate of suicide in the population is .01%. In other words, women with depression are 100 times as likely and men with depression are 700 times as likely to die by suicide than persons without depression.

Depression and the Age of the Internet

The Internet is a wonderful thing, except when it is not. The Internet permits the free flow of information, which helps anyone wanting to know almost anything to obtain that information. Many readers probably use text messaging and social networking sites, such as Facebook. Many use these every day to keep in contact with colleagues, friends, and family. This is usually a good thing, but not always.

Both text messaging and social networking sites are relatively new, and research about their effects on people is just starting to be reported. Here are some of the things we are learning.

First, social media is seemingly inescapable. One in three persons who uses a smartphone (which will receive text messages but also connect to the Internet) admits to checking the phone before getting out of bed in the morning. On average, persons who text message receive over 400 messages in a typical month. Teenagers will receive an average of over 120 text messages every day! Teenagers in particular may feel compelled, rather than inspired, to maintain their social image on Facebook.

Second, the understanding that being connected 24/7 (i.e., 24 hours a day, 7 days a week) is voluntary and not mandatory seems to be lost on many people. Many teenagers and young adults especially will openly complain about the burden of being permanently and unceasingly connected to others. They dislike it, but they fear what will happen if they forgo it. Others may notice and talk about them or stop liking them. This seems like a trite concern, but to the young person it is not. Perhaps you can remember how anxious you were as an adolescent to fit in. You probably continue to have some of these same concerns about fitting in, which is why you comb your hair, brush your teeth, and put on clean clothes. This is voluntary behavior, but not really. It is necessary for your sense of fitting in.

Third, a growing concern among mental health professionals is that social media creates an unrealistically upbeat impression of what life is supposed to be like. Social psychologists speak of social comparison. This is the tendency for people, and especially adolescents, to appraise themselves by comparing themselves to others. Social media has made this absurdly easy to do, but the comparisons may be unrealistic. Try this experiment: Find a picture on Facebook of someone who is depressed. How about two pictures of people who are unhappy?

In summary, although social media is largely a positive phenomenon that allows people to get and stay connected, the connectedness can become overwhelming and cause stress, and the comparing of one's self to others may be especially painful for people who are experiencing depression.

Distress and Impairment

Depression is by its very nature highly distressing. For some, the distress is moderate (such as with dysthymia), but for others it is so profound that they feel it necessary to seek a way to end their own life. If the disorder endures long enough, the person may even forget what it feels like to be happy or content.

Depression's effects on self-esteem, motivation, and energy level often cause severe problems in family relationships and friendships. Adults who suffer from depression are less likely to get married and more likely to divorce. Social relationships are difficult to start and maintain if a person thinks she is worthless and a burden to others.

Depression impairs accomplishments. Persons with a history of depression have lower educational attainment and subsequent lower incomes. People with depression are seven times more likely to be unemployed. When working, the depression continues to impair. People with depression are twice as likely to take sick days. As might be guessed from a review of the symptoms (e.g., low energy, difficulty concentrating), depression causes decreased productivity at work or school. One study in the late 1990s found that the depressive disorders cause over $40 billion dollars in lost productivity each year. Another study suggests that depression is the leading cause of disability (i.e., being completely unable to work), both in the United States and worldwide.

Depression makes a person more likely to develop another disorder. Persons with depression are five times more likely than others to abuse drugs or alcohol. They are much more likely to either have or to develop a comorbid anxiety disorder (see next chapter).

Encouraging Treatment-Seeking

Without treatment, a depressive episode can last for weeks, months, or years. Treatment can help most people who suffer from depression, yet most people with depression do not seek treatment. This is especially true of dysthymic disorder, since the severity of the symptoms and impairment is not as great as with major depression. Part of the challenge of encouraging a person with depression to seek treatment is to get him or her to *hope* that treatment will help. Part of depression is a lack of hope, so the depression itself prevents someone from hoping to get better. Depression is thus self-perpetuating and can be extremely challenging to treat.

Depression: A Self-Perpetuating Illness

Despite how common it is, depression can be bewildering to observe. It can be difficult to understand how someone as likeable as Mary can act so self-loathing and depressed.

The person with depression is usually just as confused about why he feels the way he does. He knows he *should* not feel this way. He knows he is blessed; he knows that God loves him and has bestowed on him all kinds of underserved gifts, such as his wife, family, friends, employment, and health. He feels confused about how he feels, but he also feels ashamed about how he feels. (See previous section on p. 78 "The Face of Depression.")

In other words, the symptoms of depression, including the shame about being depressed, make it difficult for the person to fight the depression. The symptoms include difficulty thinking clearly, fatigue (partly related to sleep problems), a sense of hopelessness about the future, and an intense sense of worthlessness.

How to Encourage Treatment-Seeking

The confusion experienced by the person with depression provides a good opening for encouraging the person to get help. When you encounter someone with depression, you should share two things that you now know about depression. By sharing these, you implicitly encourage the person with depression to seek treatment. Then when you *explicitly* instruct them to do so, it will be easier.

First, inform them that depression is extremely common. It has been called the "common cold of mental illness." At any one moment, 15 million adult Americans (about 7%) will experience depression. (Another 6 million will report some depression symptoms, but not meet full criteria.) Thus, the first thing you should say to someone with depression is some version of the following: "Oh, that's too bad. Depression is really common. A lot of people experience depression. A lot of other people here (in the church or wherever) are also going through that."

In this way, encourage the person to realize that depression is not a sign of weakness or badness. It is not a sign that God has abandoned them, nor is it a result of them not having "strong enough faith." It might be helpful to point out the many persons in the Bible who suffered depression and doubts, including almost every main character in the Bible, including those who spoke directly with God.

The second fact to share is that their depression needs to be treated. Without treatment, the depression will likely last a long time. Moreover, without treatment the depression might alleviate spontaneously, but the person is likely to experience a recurrence.

Depression needs to be treated, and treatments are effective. Between 80% and 90% of individuals who suffer from depression obtain relief from their distress and are able to recover their relationships and work functioning. Treatment can include medications or psychotherapy. Ideally, it will include both.

With regard to medications, there are dozens of antidepressants now available, and they are successful in 60-80% of patients. No antidepressant has been shown to be more effective than others (although the newer ones have fewer negative side effects), but it will often be necessary to try different medications before settling on one that works well. Unfortunately, antidepressants will typically take several weeks before they start working. The typical treatment episode using antidepressant medications will last at least six months. (The rule of thumb is that treatment should last at least as long as the depressive episode.)

There are also a wide variety of psychotherapies that can be sought. However, some are specifically designed to treat depression and have been shown to be quite effective. These should be sought out (i.e., asked for by name!). Cognitive therapy (CT) and cognitive-behavioral therapy (CBT) focus on changing the negative thinking (e.g., hopelessness, low self-esteem) and the depressing behavioral patterns (e.g., social isolation) that cause and maintain depression. (Recall the association between affect-behavior-cognitions from chapter 2.) Interpersonal therapy (IPT) also focuses on thoughts and behaviors, but the explicit focus is on relationships. IPT teaches the person with depression relationship skills to help make relationships more fulfilling and enjoyable, which greatly helps to alleviate depression.

Thus, the second thing you should say to someone with depression (after telling them how sorry you are that they have such a dreadful but dreadfully common disorder) might be: "Where are you receiving treatment? Whom are you seeing? How is it going?" That is, you could take the approach of assuming that they are getting treatment, since they would be suffering needlessly if they were not.

Chapter 7

The Anxiety Disorders

"I have told you these things, so that in me you may have peace.
In this world you will have trouble.
But take heart! I have overcome the world."
(John 16:33)

The anxiety disorders are the most prevalent of all the mental illnesses. In any given year, one in five adults will experience one, and this prevalence rate is similar around the world. This suggests that the anxiety disorders are an exacerbation of something normal, necessary, and universal. In fact, this is exactly what they are.

This chapter begins with a review of the difference between normal, healthy anxiety and abnormal anxiety. The anxiety disorders are the phobias, panic disorder, agoraphobia, obsessive-compulsive disorder, and generalized anxiety disorder, and they are each reviewed. (Separation anxiety is another anxiety disorder, but it is only diagnosed in children, so it is presented in chapter 14.) For each of the anxiety disorders, the associated distress and impairment are discussed, as are other noteworthy things to know about them and treatment approaches that have proven useful.

The chapter then tries to give a sense of what someone with an anxiety disorder will look like in day-to-day situations. It ends with advice on how to encourage someone with an anxiety disorder to seek treatment.

Healthy Versus Disordered Anxiety

The anxiety disorders are the most common mental illnesses because anxiety plays such an important role in the lives of human beings. In order to survive, we *need* to be able to become anxious.

Healthy Anxiety

If we did not experience anxiety, we would not bother to avoid dangerous and potentially deadly actions. It is good that we (or at least most of us!) get anxious about picking up snakes. Anxiety prevents us from walking into busy streets and dark alleyways.

Healthy anxiety is both natural and necessary. It is also situation-specific, reflecting accurate discernment between truly dangerous situations and merely unpleasant situations. Healthy anxiety is time-limited. When the situation resolves, the anxiety goes away.

Both healthy and abnormal anxieties are anticipatory. That is, everyone experiences anxiety when something stressful (such as a public speech or exam) is about to happen. However, healthy anxiety motivates people to prepare (e.g., practice the public speech, study for the exam).

Abnormal Anxiety

Unlike the relatively mild, time-limited, and situation-specific anxiety caused by a scary object or a stressful event, the fear and dread of the anxiety disorders are excessive and inappropriate. They are chronic, progressive, and pervasive. As a result, they are incredibly disabling.

Normal Versus Abnormal Anxiety	
Normal Anxiety	**Abnormal Anxiety**
• Beneficial in that it keeps us away from danger and motivates us to prepare • Occurs only occasionally and is situational (and appropriate) • Limited in duration; usually of manageable intensity • Does not interfere with daily functioning (work/school, relationships, self-care); motivates people to do well	• No observable benefit (it is irrational or excessive) • Occurs frequently and pervasively • Lasts a long time or never goes away • Intensely distressing and disabling; feels unmanageable and intolerable • Interferes with daily functioning (work/school, relationships, self-care)

Excessive and Inappropriate

A person with an anxiety disorder will respond with excessive or entirely inappropriate fear to objects or situations. We do not diagnose a soldier about to enter combat with an anxiety disorder, but we would diagnose that soldier if he continues to exhibit fear and dread long after combat ceased. We won't diagnose a child who exhibits extreme fear of dogs as having an anxiety disorder unless the feared object (dogs) is actually harmless and the child is old enough to realize this.

It is not always easy to decide whether anxiety is healthy or abnormal. For example, fearing spiders and thunderstorms may not be problematic, since avoiding spider bites and going inside during thunderstorms is generally good for your health. As a result, mental health professionals must make a judgment that the fear is out of proportion to the actual danger in the situation. We look for indications that the anxiety is excessive, lasts longer or is more pervasive than what might be expected, and, most important, causes functional impairment.

Chronic, Progressive, and Pervasive

Healthy anxiety is time-limited. Anxiety arises when a scary object or situation is confronted, but when the object or situation goes away, so does the anxiety. Likewise, most of us outgrow childhood fears, even if they were fairly severe.

Abnormal anxiety, on the other hand, lasts long past the end of the anxiety-provoking situation (chronic). Likewise, abnormal anxiety is not typically outgrown. Instead, it tends to get worse over time (progressive). Finally, abnormal anxiety is pervasive because the fearfulness of the feared events and situations is entirely generated by the person's mind. Since our minds are with us all the time, the anxiety of the anxiety disorders, in contrast to normal anxiety, is pervasive. For example, a typical presentation of a person with generalized anxiety disorder is fear and distress that something terrible is going to happen, and not being able to identify what that terrible thing will be makes the anxiety even worse.

Operant Conditioning and Reinforcement

As will be seen in this chapter, many of the anxiety disorders include behaviors that are repeated again and again. These behaviors are easier to understand if you understand the concept of "reinforcement," which was developed by B. F. Skinner (1904–1990) as part of his theory of operant conditioning.

A behavior is strengthened, or "reinforced," if it leads to a desirable outcome. When Skinner's pigeons pecked the red dot on the wall, they got a food pellet. The behavior (pecking) led to a desirable outcome (food) and was thereby reinforced (the pigeon kept on pecking).

If telling a joke (behavior) leads to others laughing (desirable outcome), then telling a joke is reinforced and is likely to be repeated. If strapping on a seat belt (behavior) leads to cessation of the aversive beeping (desirable outcome), then strapping on a seat belt is reinforced and is likely to be repeated.

Applying the concept of reinforcement to feelings of anxiety is fairly easy. All people experiencing anxiety will try to do something to reduce that anxiety. For example, if you have to retrieve something from your trash can, afterwards you may feel anxious that your hands are dirty. You can relieve that anxiety by washing them. If leaving your house unlocked makes you anxious about getting robbed, then you are likely to lock the door before leaving for work. If thinking about an upcoming presentation makes you feel anxious, you can prepare for it and reduce that anxiety.

The anxiety experienced by persons with an anxiety disorder is extreme and sometimes long-lasting. Any behavior that leads to a reduction of that anxiety will be reinforced and is likely to be repeated. As will be seen, this concept applies to the behavior exhibited by persons with specific social phobias, agoraphobia, and obsessive-compulsive disorder in particular.

Disabling

For anxiety to be labeled abnormal (i.e., a disorder), it must cause problems. The anxiety of the anxiety disorders is so severe that the person will go to extraordinary effort to avoid and manage the anxiety. As a result, the anxiety disorders do indeed cause severe impairment.

The person with panic disorder might refuse to leave her home. The person with anxiety-provoking obsessions will engage in compulsions to reduce the anxiety, and the compulsions can take so long that she never gets to work on time. I knew a veteran of the Vietnam War who bedded down in the woods in order to avoid the loud noises of the cars and trucks traveling the street in front of his house. This helped neither his marriage nor his relationship with his kids.

As noted, healthy anxiety motivates people to prepare for stressful situations. In contrast, abnormal anticipatory anxiety will actual interfere with preparation. As a result, the person with abnormal anxiety may attempt to avoid the stressful situation. The person with severe social anxiety will delay making the sales call or find an excuse for avoiding the meeting. As a result, his job performance will suffer. The person with a phobia of flying may have to quit his job in order to avoid planes.

In summary, anxiety is a necessary part of human nature. It helps us to avoid danger and prepare for stressful situations. However, this natural and healthy anxiety can sometimes turn unhealthy. Anxiety is disordered if it is excessive, long lasting, pervasive, and disabling. All of the following anxiety disorders meet these criteria.

The Anxiety Disorders

The anxiety disorders include specific and social phobias, panic disorder (with or without agoraphobia), obsessive-compulsive disorder (OCD), and generalized anxiety disorder (GAD). Readers may notice that the anxiety disorders are the only mental illnesses to have widely known acronyms. I don't have a satisfactory explanation of this, but it may have to do with how common they are.

The common factor in all of these disorders is overwhelming fear and dread. What distinguishes one anxiety disorder from another is the stimulus, or cause, of the fear or dread. In the phobias, for example, the cause of anxiety is an object or situation (dogs, spiders, deep water, the dark). In OCD, the dreaded stimulus comes from one's own mind, such as the thought that one's hands are contaminated with germs.

The Fight-or-Flight Response

When extremely frightened or anxious, the body will have an automatic physiological reaction, often referred to as the fight-or-flight response, because the body prepares to either fight the danger or to run away from it.

To simplify an astonishingly complex process, the *amygdala* signals the *hypothalamus,* which activates the *pituitary gland* to release a hormone that stimulates the *adrenal glands* to release *adrenaline* (epinephrine) and other brain parts to release *cortisol.* Adrenalin and cortisol cause an increase in blood pressure, a release of sugar from the liver stores into the blood, and the release of fatty acids (also to be used as energy).

The physiological response is:

- Increased heart rate and blood pressure
- Increased respiration (i.e., panting) and perspiration
- Nausea (as the stomach shuts down to shunt energy to the muscles)
- Pupil dilation (to bring in more light)
- Shaking (and dizziness), chest pain
- Loss of hearing (to shut out distracting noises) and peripheral vision (to concentrate focus on their danger)

Specific Phobias

The specific phobias are intense and disabling fears of objects and situations that pose little or no actual danger. The person with a phobia may or may not recognize that the fear is irrational, but others will view it as so. I conducted an initial interview with a young woman who had an intense fear of public speaking, and I gently reminded her that the fear might be unreasonable given the lack of actual danger. She proceeded to relate a story of an actress who fainted (due to illness) and fell off the stage at a play and was killed. She was not going to let me get away with claiming that public speaking was not actually dangerous! (Likewise, persons with a phobia of flying can usually relate the most recent plane tragedy.)

The most common types of phobias are threefold: animals (dogs, snakes, spiders); the natural environment (such as heights, elevators, enclosed spaces, thunderstorms); and blood, injections, or injury.

Erik Sprints to School

Erik is 11 years old. He loves soccer and being outdoors. His grandfather has a wonderful backyard, but Erik doesn't ever go out there unless he knows Toby, his grandfather's Cairn terrier, is inside and locked in the basement. To his mortification, Erik needs his mother to walk him to school, which is four streets down, because he needs her to protect him if he should come across a dog. Earlier that semester, his teacher had called his mother to report that, for the last week, Erik had arrived at school each day panting and frightened. It seems that Erik had decided it was necessary to sprint to school in order to avoid seeing (although he could not avoid hearing) the houses where he knew there were dogs. Fortunately, Erik was open to the idea of seeing a psychologist that specialized in the treatment of phobias. Through gradual exposure to a variety of friendly dogs, combined with teaching Erik simple calming techniques (e.g., controlled breathing), Erik was able to overcome his phobia. He now walks to school by himself and loves to play with Toby. He recently asked his mother if he could get a dog for his birthday.

Distress and Impairment

To diagnose a person with a phobia, the fear must be both intense (and therefore distressing) and disabling. The intensity of the fear cannot be exaggerated. When encountering the feared stimulus (or anticipating it), the person's body will go into the so-called fight-or-flight response. This happens when the stimulus is encountered, obviously, but it also happens in anticipation of it. The person who has a phobia of needles, for example, will become intensely distressed when an appointment is made with a medical office, in *anticipation* of an encounter with a needle or two.

In order to avoid this distress, a person with a phobia will avoid the feared stimulus. To do this, people will limit their lives unnecessarily and regrettably. A child with a dog phobia, for example, may avoid going to a friend's house or his grandmother's house, as he knows they have dogs. He may also avoid attending birthday parties if he is uncertain whether the family has a dog or not. Likewise, the person with a needle phobia will avoid going to the doctor.

The impairment caused by phobias will correspond to the fear. The more pervasive the feared stimulus is, the more disabling the anxiety. In some cases, the feared stimulus is very limited. A severe phobia of snakes is probably not a problem for someone living in a high rise in New York City, since he can successfully avoid the feared object without excessive impact on his life. Indeed, if the feared stimulus is relatively infrequent or is easily avoided, then the person may not necessarily qualify for a phobia. In these instances, the person does not experience either distress or disability.

In other instances, however, the feared stimulus is unavoidable, pervasive, or unremitting. In these cases, the impairment will be intense. The person may then base important career or personal decisions on the need to avoid the stimulus. The more a person arranges his or her life around avoiding the phobic object, the more likely the person will experience both occupational and relationship impairment. For example, the person with a phobia of flying may turn down a job that will require frequent plane travel. The person with a phobia of enclosed places or crowds will likely seek to avoid going to restaurants, theaters, and baseball games, and doing other enjoyable activities with his family. The person with a blood or injection phobia may avoid going to the doctor, which could be health impairing.

Other Noteworthy Things about Phobias

Adults and adolescents with specific phobias will often recognize that their fears are unreasonable, whereas children will probably not.

The phobias are somewhat underappreciated with regard to empathy with the suffering of those experiencing them. Indeed, a sort of game has developed related to naming feared objects. The website phobialist.com lists 530 phobias, such as anuptaphobia (the fear of staying single), epistaxiophobia (the fear of nosebleeds), and verbophobia (the fear of words). The moderator of the site presents the list in a very serious manner, dubiously asserting that all of the phobias have been validated as real by cross-reference to medical articles or books. It is a fun list, but it cannot be taken particularly seriously. More problematic, since it is a fun list, it promotes the idea that phobias are fun and harmless and not particularly important. The reality is quite different. Having a phobia is not fun. Having a phobia can be quite harmful to one's life. Phobias are very important.

It was long believed that phobias were directly learned. For example, the child who gets knocked down and terrified by a dog develops a dog phobia. The person who almost drowns develops a phobia of water. While this argument seems logical, it did not survive empirical examination. Research has not supported this idea. Most persons with phobias report no negative experiences with the feared stimulus whatsoever, meaning no history of dog attacks, no experience of almost drowning, and no instances of treatment with incredibly painful needles. The phobias do not tend to come from actual experiences.

So where do phobias come from? Most phobias are learned via modeling. Children will watch an adult, probably a parent, react with intense fear or discomfort to something. The child observes this, reacts himself with intense fear (in sympathy with the parent's fear), and thereby learns that the object or situation is dangerous. Behaviorists refer to this as vicarious classical conditioning. An object or situation is paired with intense fear, which is transmitted not directly by the object or situation but vicariously through another person. The pairing results in associating the negative feeling and the object/situation (i.e., classical conditioning).

The phobia is maintained by something entirely different. When the person with a phobia confronts (or considers confronting) a feared stimulus, he experiences intense distress. The person will then escape from the feared object (or will avoid the confrontation). This behavior of escape (or avoidance) is powerfully *reinforced* by elimination of the fear. (See "Erik Sprints to School".) Treatment follows directly from this idea.

Treatment

Fortunately, the phobias are relatively easy to treat. Treatment of phobias entails two goals: the first is to teach the person active relaxation skills (such as slow, measured breaths and calming thoughts) and the second is to have the person, who now knows how to relax, endure progressively worse anxiety-provoking situations.

In other words, *exposure treatment* entails disallowing the escape or avoidance. The person with a phobia is made to confront (i.e., not allowed to avoid) the feared stimulus, and the person is then not allowed to escape. The body reacts with the fight-or-flight response, which is highly unpleasant. The body, however, cannot maintain this reaction. Eventually, the body returns to a relaxed state even though the feared stimulus is still present, and the person learns that the feared stimulus is actually not all that fearful. The treatment can be very unpleasant (confronting one's intense fears is never easy), but it is highly effective. The key, then, is getting the person to seek treatment. If sought through a competent professional, a cure is attainable.

If this procedure sounds familiar, it might be because many parents and other adults commonly use an informal version of it to help children overcome childhood fears. Imagine you have a niece who is terribly fearful of your very nice yellow Labrador. You will probably help her manage the fear by leashing the dog and then encouraging her to watch you pet the dog and have him do tricks. If she stays near the animal, her fear will subside. Eventually, she will likely approach the dog.

This is a gross simplification of treatment of phobias, but these are the general principles. If the person will consent to treatment, then a phobia will usually be cured within five sessions or so.

Social Anxiety Disorder (Social Phobia)

Social anxiety disorder, sometimes called *social phobia,* is an overwhelming and disabling fear of being scrutinized or negatively evaluated by other people. Sometimes these situations involve "performance," such as giving a speech. Even more often, however, the situations are as simple as a conversation, ordering off a menu, eating in public, or writing a check. Almost regardless of what they are doing, persons with social anxiety disorder have intense fears of being observed and evaluated.

Distress and Impairment

Social anxiety disorder is much more than just shyness. It is painfully distressing and extremely debilitating.

The fear experienced by someone with social phobia when anticipating or experiencing a social situation can be intense. The fight-or-flight response will kick in, with attendant nausea, sweating, heart racing, dizziness, and so forth.

The disorder leads the person to the avoidance of many potentially pleasurable and meaningful activities with other people. Many a choir has been deprived of wonderful voices whose owners had social phobia. Persons with social phobia have a hard time making and keeping friends. This is not because they do not want friends. The subsequent social isolation makes them lonely and sad, and it increases their risk of a comorbid depressive disorder or an alcohol or drug use problem.

School and work are also impaired. A high school student may be so overwhelmed by the fear of standing up to give a report that he can't complete assignments and fails classes. For many workers, social anxiety disorder impairs career advancement. They will have jobs well below their abilities because they are afraid to accept a promotion or are afraid of asking for that promotion, and they are likewise fearful of interviewing at another company for a better job. As a result, almost half the persons with social anxiety disorder fail to complete high school and most have fairly serious socioeconomic problems.

Michelle's Favorite Restaurant

Michelle had developed a reputation of being a good manager. She experienced intense anxiety whenever she had to talk to any group larger than two, such as at sales meetings. So she developed the "work around" of meeting individually with each salesperson. As a result, she developed a reputation of being a hands-on, involved, and caring manager.

Unfortunately for her, her reputation leads to being invited for after-work gatherings fairly often. Despite her anxiety, she has gone on several occasions. She always parks in a distant spot in the lot of the nearby Ace Hardware. She always parks there because then she knows she can always find her car, even if nearly blind from anxiety. While at the restaurant with her coworkers, she orders water, which she doesn't dare to touch, lest she knock over the glass. She sits quietly while, unbeknownst to her coworkers, her insides are churning and her brain is screaming at her to run away. She finally does make an excuse and leaves. (She sits in her car shaking for about 10 minutes, which is another reason to park so far away, until her vision returns to normal and she feels safe to drive home to her apartment.)

In our second meeting, Michelle referred to the usual gathering place as her "favorite restaurant." She has been there often enough now that the anxiety is manageable, at least for a while. It is the only restaurant she has ever voluntarily entered. (She once entered a restaurant at the mall by mistake. Mortified, she left quickly and drove home without completing her shopping errand.) She also has a "safe" parking place at the restaurant.

Other Noteworthy Things About Social Anxiety Disorder

Not surprisingly, research shows that people with social phobia are overly sensitive to criticism. They misperceive other people's reactions, seeing annoyance, criticism, disgust, and rejection where they are not. They have difficulty asserting themselves and usually suffer from low self-esteem.

The fear caused by social anxiety disorder may be compounded by a lack of social skills or by general inexperience in social situations. Readers may recall how nervous they were on their first date. You had no prior experience dating, and not knowing what to expect or what to do likely caused anxiety. Imagine, then, the anxiety someone might experience daily if she has never had any friends because of poor social skills.

Persons with social anxiety disorder imagine things quite often and quite actively. To be specific, they imagine the future, where they will likely have to interact with others, and they experience dread. To be more precise, they suffer anticipatory anxiety, which is a feeling of dread and fear about an upcoming situation. For weeks they will worry about doing something stupid at the upcoming wedding reception or office party. They will lose sleep because they are running out of food in the house and will soon have to go to the store where others will see them, watch them, and think critical thoughts about them.

Treatment

For a variety of reasons, social anxiety disorder is fairly difficult to treat, especially in comparison to the specific phobias. First, foremost and obviously, the specific phobias are specific. The feared stimulus is contained. A person with a dog phobia can probably go to work confident that no coworker has brought a dog to work, even if many have a dog living with them at home. In comparison, to even seek treatment, someone with social anxiety disorder has to encounter all sorts of fearful stimuli: she has to call for an appointment, which entails talking on the phone to a stranger; she has to arrive at the office, which includes walking across a waiting room full of strangers, talking to the receptionist, and (probably) completing paperwork; and then she must explain to a stranger (i.e., the therapist) what is wrong.

Treatment for social anxiety disorder entails a similar procedure as that used with specific phobias, but a little imagination will demonstrate that this too is much more complicated. Social anxiety disorder involves intense discomfort at being observed by others. There are many, many situations where this will occur.

Therefore, treatment usually involves helping the person to become non-phobic (if not exactly comfortable) in one or two social situations, and then encouraging the new skill to generalize to all social situations. For example, a patient may be trained to manage anxiety while at a coffee shop and while talking with friends, with the idea that the new skill will generalize to other restaurants and to talking with coworkers.

As with specific phobias, if a person with social anxiety disorder seeks treatment, a cure—or at least a large reduction in distress and disability—can be obtained.

Panic Disorder and Agoraphobia

Panic disorder entails the repeated occurrence of an intensely dreadful event and an intense fear of its recurrence. The dreadful event is a *panic attack*. Panic attacks are so awful that a person who experiences them might develop *intense fear* of having another. If the person has more than one panic attack and develops the fear of more, then she will meet criteria for panic disorder.

What makes a panic attack so bad? Panic attacks are 10-20 minute episodes of overwhelming fear that are accompanied by physical symptoms (such as heart palpitations and dizziness). The brain in panic mode directs the adrenal glands to excrete adrenaline, which causes the so-called fight-or-flight response (see box on p. 95). Most people have experienced this at least once. Most likely, it was during an actual panicky event, such as seeing your toddler standing in the street, realizing your bicycle brakes don't work, or having your car spin out of control on an icy street.

In a genuine panic attack there is no event causing the panic. The symptoms seemingly come from nowhere. The person thus experiences a sense of unreality and a fear of losing control. She may have difficulty breathing and become convinced she is going to die. If several panic attacks occur, the person may develop intense anxiety that more will happen in the future. At this point, the diagnosis of panic disorder would be appropriate.

Some persons (between 20% and 25%) with panic disorder will experience overwhelming anxiety in public situations, such as on airplanes, buses, and subways; in parking lots, stores, and theaters; or standing in a line with other people or being in a crowd. The anxiety is that if they have a panic attack, it would be difficult for others to help or for them to escape to somewhere safe. To deal with these situations, the person will need to be accompanied by a friend (like Logan, below) or suffer through the situation. In these cases, the person has developed comorbid agoraphobia. (The agora in Greek cities was the marketplace, the gathering place, or the place of assembly. It was outside—no covered malls in ancient Greece—and was the place where many people could be found.)

Logan's Panic

Logan reported the following to me in my office about three months ago: "It happened without any warning, a sudden wave of terror. My heart was pounding like mad, I couldn't catch my breath, and the ground underfoot seemed unstable. I was sure I was having a heart attack. It was the worst experience of my life." Logan had his girlfriend drive him to the emergency room. By the time they arrived, however, his attack had abated. She insisted that he go in, and he was evaluated for heart problems and other possible health causes. None of the tests showed anything abnormal, and he was sent home. A week later, he had another panic attack. Since then, he estimated that he'd had 10 or 12 more. It was getting to the point that he wanted his girlfriend to accompany him to the store and while doing other errands, in case he had another and would need assistance.

Distress and Impairment

Not to be glaringly obvious, but panic attacks are awful to endure. Most persons who have panic attacks report that while in the middle of one they feel as if they are going to die. Convinced of this, many people having a panic attack seek help at a hospital emergency room. These sensations start abruptly and build to a rapid peak, usually within ten minutes, so that a visit to the emergency room becomes an exercise in futility. (But see "Other Noteworthy Things" on the next page.) By the time they arrive, the panic attack and its attendant symptoms of racing heart, panting, and dizziness have abated.

The severity of impairment associated with panic disorder will largely depend on whether the person develops comorbid agoraphobia. This depends, in turn, on whether the person has identified panic attack triggers.

Some with panic disorder identify "high risk" situations that are relatively circumscribed. The intense fear of having another panic attack leads the person with panic disorder to try to avoid these situations. For example, they may avoid places that are crowded, standing in line, entering shopping malls, or riding in cars or on public transportation, which lead to only moderate impairment. However, for some, the panic attacks seem to come out of the blue, taking the person completely by surprise. In that case, avoidance seems impossible. How can one avoid something that comes out of nowhere? Avoiding everything may become the only solution, and agoraphobia and profound impairment will result.

People with agoraphobia will restrict themselves to their "zone of safety," which may be their home or apartment or, at best, the immediate neighborhood. Some are unable to work, and they may need to rely on family members to do the shopping and household errands, or at least to accompany them when they travel outside their safety zone. Some persons with agoraphobia become housebound for years or even decades. This has obvious impact on social relationships. In other words, the person with panic disorder and attendant agoraphobia typically leads a life of extreme discomfort, dependency, and disability.

Other Noteworthy Things About Panic Disorder and Agoraphobia

Panic disorder is not a panic attack. One in four persons will have a panic attack at some time in their life. Panic disorder is repeated panic attacks and the dread of future panic attacks.

If someone has a panic attack in the presence of some specific object or situation, he will likely develop a phobia instead of panic disorder. For example, someone who has had a panic attack while driving may develop a phobia of driving. John Madden, the highly successful football coach turned announcer, developed a phobia of flying because he experienced a panic attack during a particularly turbulent and frightening flight.

Stress makes someone more vulnerable to experiencing a panic attack. Attacks often occur during or within six months of marital problems, the death of a loved one, moving to a new home or city, the birth of a child, or a recent illness or surgery. They can also be triggered by large doses of caffeine or over-the-counter cold medicines, as well as ingesting cocaine or marijuana. On the other hand, most persons with panic disorder report that they have had a panic attack during sleep.

Going to the emergency room during an initial panic attack is actually not a bad idea. In fact, it could save someone's life. Conditions such as hyperthyroidism, myocardial infarction, cardiac arrhythmias, and certain types of epilepsy can cause panic attack symptoms.

Studies suggest that people who develop panic disorder overreact to their body's normal physiological activities. For example, feeling full after a large meal causes alarm for some people. I treated an individual with panic disorder whose first panic attack occurred when he got up after dozing on the floor. His brain and heart reacted to the change in body position by accelerating in order to drive blood into his brain so that he didn't pass out. He grew quite alarmed at this natural and necessary process. He did not understand what was happening, and the alarm grew into a full-blown panic attack. This misinterpretation of the body's activities is an essential aspect of the most effective treatment for panic disorder.

Persons with panic disorder are at particularly high risk of suicide, suggesting that the misery endured during a panic attack as well as the dread of having another one are intense and unbearable. According to one study, 20% of those diagnosed with panic disorder had attempted suicide.

Treatment

Panic disorder is extremely distressing and debilitating. Fortunately, psychologists have developed extremely effective treatments for it.

One key to treatment is teaching the person with panic disorder that the panic attack, in fact, does *not* come out of nowhere. Panic attacks occur because the person overreacts (misinterprets as catastrophic and life-endangering) to the body's fight-or-flight response. Education about the fight-or-flight response and about "healthy anxiety" is essential.

Another key is to conceptualize panic disorder as a type of phobia, where the feared stimulus is having another panic attack. As with phobias, the most effective treatment is a version of exposure treatment. The person undergoing treatment for panic disorder is taught that the panic, although highly aversive, is actually harmless. A common procedure as part of treatment is to expose the person to a panic attack. That is, the therapist will induce a panic attack in the person—during the treatment session in front of the therapist—so that the therapist can then aid the patient in confronting and enduring the panic. The goal is to teach the patient that panic attacks, while highly unpleasant, are ultimately harmless.

As with the phobias and panic disorder, agoraphobia responds well to exposure treatment. The person is taught relaxation skills and is encouraged to confront the outside world, first in the company of another person and then alone. Exposure to feared stimuli starts slowly, such as a walk into the front yard and then around the block. It then works up in intensity, such as a solo trip to the shopping mall.

If the reader was successful at imagining the horror of a panic attack, the reader might also be able to imagine how difficult it can be to talk someone with panic disorder into seeking treatment. The prospect of confronting one's intense fears is daunting. When the feared stimulus is a panic attack, which seems to arise from within (rather than something in the environment that can be avoided), the prospect is much more formidable. Encouraging treatment seeking in persons with the anxiety disorders is the last topic of this chapter.

Obsessive-Compulsive Disorder (OCD)

The person with OCD is ensnared in a pattern of repetitive thoughts and behaviors that he recognizes as senseless and that are enormously distressing, but the pattern is extremely difficult to overcome. As the name indicates, obsessive-compulsive disorder involves obsessions and compulsions.

Obsessions are repeated, intrusive, and unwanted ideas or impulses. The most common obsessions involve fears of contamination (e.g., germs are contaminating everything), making mistakes (e.g., an important action such as locking the door or turning off the stove was missed), and overwhelming impulses (e.g., being unable to stop oneself from groping, assaulting, or screaming at a stranger). Obsessions cause intense anxiety, which is highly aversive and which the person is compelled to reduce.

Thus, the obsessions cause compulsions. Compulsions are a behavior or set of behaviors that works to reduce anxiety. Compulsions are therefore strongly reinforced. This makes it likely that the person will engage in that behavior again in the future when experiencing the same anxiety. If the behavior again works to reduce anxiety, it becomes stronger still. Soon, the behavior has become a compulsion, because it is effective at reducing the anxiety.

The relief tends to be temporary, however. Someone with a phobia can obtain complete, enduring relief from anxiety by avoiding the feared situation. In OCD, however, the anxiety-inducing obsessions are difficult to avoid because they are internal (i.e., thoughts). The anxiety-provoking obsessions are relieved by the compulsions, but they do not go away for long. They assail the person again and again. As a result, the anxiety-reducing behaviors become compulsive, since the person feels "compelled" to do the behavior again and again.

Common compulsions include cleaning and hand washing, repeated checking (oven turned off, door locked, etc.), counting and arranging (related to obsessions with order and symmetry), hoarding (related to the obsession that something bad will happen if something is thrown out), and intensive rumination to make sure one doesn't make a mistake or commit a sin. Many persons with OCD develop "rituals" surrounding their compulsions to ensure that the compulsion is conducted correctly. (If it is not, it has to be redone or repeated.)

Distress and Impairment

OCD is profoundly distressing and extremely disabling. The person with OCD understands that the fears are unrealistic. He "knows" that he locked the door, but he nonetheless cannot avoid anxiety related to the idea that he somehow, some way, actually did not lock the door. The anxiety provoked by the thoughts seems unbearable.

The impairment or disability associated with OCD is probably self-evident. One of the biggest issues is the amount of time spent on the compulsive behavior. It can be very difficult to get to work on time if one has to return home repeatedly to make sure that the door is locked and the coffee maker is turned off. It can be equally difficult to complete tasks at work if one is obsessed with not making a mistake.

Relationships will also be seriously compromised. Because of the time spent on rituals, persons with OCD will be unable to do things with people who are important to them. Going to your son's soccer game or taking your wife to dinner becomes an ordeal when you have to spend hours making sure the house is safe. Several years ago, I started couples therapy with a couple, except that she did not show to the first meeting. She could not leave the house because she was still cleaning the bathroom, a process that usually took either exactly 60 or exactly 90 minutes, depending on how well the ritual went. Her husband, to say the least, was somewhat frustrated with the state of their marriage.

Other Noteworthy Things about OCD

OCD affects several million adults (2-3% of the population) in the United States. It strikes men and women in roughly equal numbers.

Most persons suffering from OCD have numerous obsessions, but the obsessions tend to cluster around certain themes, such as cleanliness or safety. For example, a person with OCD may be obsessed with germs on himself and dirt on the floor. Another may be obsessed that she will commit an act of violence against her child, but also obsessed with groping a stranger at the grocery store.

Persons with OCD do *not* get pleasure when performing the compulsions. Typically, they will spend at least one hour a day engaged in their rituals, but it can be much more than that.

One-third of adults diagnosed with OCD report that their symptoms developed during childhood. The typical age for the first diagnosis is 19.

Symptoms of OCD may improve or worsen at different times. Symptoms will worsen during times of stress.

Persons with OCD know they have OCD. They know that the obsessions are irrational and that the compulsions are unnecessary. They realize that others do or would believe that their thoughts and behaviors are strange, and they feel intense shame. One study found that the average time for a person with OCD to seek treatment is seven years. The same study found that these treatment seekers needed *another seven years* before they admitted to a therapist that they had obsessions and compulsions.

Jim's Obsessions

Jim has safety obsessions. He leaves for work after his wife on most mornings, but even when he leaves first it doesn't help. He must set aside an extra 30 minutes to leave for work so that he can have time to complete his checking compulsions. He will walk around their home checking that every door and window is locked, then check to see that the stove, toaster, microwave, and coffee maker are off. He does this routine five times. If he doesn't do it in the correct order, he must start the whole routine over again.

On mornings when his wife leaves after him, to avoid the embarrassment of conducting it in front of her ("I know the ritual doesn't make sense, and I am deeply ashamed of it"), he will do the routine only once. More and more frequently, however, he will arrive at work and be bothered by thoughts that he missed something, and he will need to return home. He has had to cancel several meetings in order to do this.

Treatment of OCD

Treatment of OCD, as with all of the anxiety disorders, is both effective and efficient. The most effective and common treatment is called exposure and response prevention. The person is exposed to the obsession (for example, a person with a "dirty hands" fear will be asked to rub her hands along the floor) and then disallowed to engage in the compulsion (for example, the person is not allowed to go wash her hands). As with all of the exposure techniques, eventually the person's intense anxiety will abate. The body simply cannot maintain the fight-or-flight response for an extended period of time. The liver metabolizes adrenalin and cortisol, and the anxious response dissolves. Using this procedure, the person will gradually learn that the obsessive, anxiety-provoking thoughts, while unpleasant, do not actually cause harm.

A person with OCD usually understands that others would see his obsessions and compulsions as odd, so he will go to great efforts to hide them. At the same time, the anxiety associated with the obsessions (such as anxiety about germ contamination) makes the prospect of confronting the anxiety-inducing stimulus during treatment an exceedingly daunting task. As a result, many persons with OCD never receive treatment.

Generalized Anxiety Disorder (GAD)

Everyone worries about the health, safety, and future of their family, but most are able to either reassure themselves or stop thinking about such things for a while. Someone with generalized anxiety disorder (GAD) worries about these things and many other things, even when there is little or no reason to worry. Someone with GAD is worried about the past (something went wrong and is about to announce itself), the present (something is wrong and it will soon be found out), and the future (something will go wrong). GAD has been called basic anxiety, because it really has no cause. Anxiety seems to just be there.

For the person with GAD, simple things that most people enjoy can become overwhelming sources of anxiety. Life would be better if things would just stop, but, instead, dinner must be made (what to make?), parties must be attended (what to wear?), and holidays and birthdays keep approaching (what to get the person?).

Distress and Impairment

People with GAD experience intense physical tension. The tension can lead to difficulty sleeping, poor eating, chronic fatigue, muscle aches, headaches, and nausea. They are apprehensive and hyper-vigilant. They almost always anticipate the worst, even though there is no real reason to expect it. Being convinced that something bad is inevitable, they are constantly on the lookout for danger. This excessive vigilance often causes "autonomic reactivity," which most people refer to as jumpiness. That is, people with GAD tend to startle easily.

GAD will interfere with social relationships, school, and work. Persons who suffer from GAD worry excessively and nearly constantly about seemingly minor things. The free-floating nature of the anxiety encourages the person to try to pinpoint (in order to eliminate) the source of the anxiety, so she will constantly question friends, fellow students, teachers, coworkers, and bosses "Did I do something wrong?" and "Are you upset with me?" Concern about doing something wrong will interfere with school and work efficiency, causing problems in these areas.

Moreover, it is often unpleasant to be in the company of people suffering from constant anxiety. Persons with GAD may be accused of "looking for things to be anxious about" or of being happy "only when worried." Such comments are somewhat understandable, as the person with GAD cannot specify what it is she fears. Such comments are nonetheless unhelpful and unkind. GAD is not a happy disorder.

Mary Fears Nothing and Everything

Mary reported the following problem to her therapist in the first session: "I wish I could tell you exactly what's the matter, but there really is no one thing. It's sort of everything. There's this constant fear that something awful is about to happen or has happened without me knowing it. Sometimes I feel like something terrible has just happened. I'll call the school where my kids are or call my mom, but it is always the case that nothing has happened at all. Most of the time I can't point my finger at something specific, but if there is anything at all, even something little, I will focus on that. Last week, I thought a supermarket clerk had overcharged me for an item. She showed me that I was wrong and I left the store, but that didn't end it. I worried the rest of the day. I kept going over the incident in my mind, feeling terribly embarrassed at having raised the possibility that the clerk had made an error. I called the store and asked to speak to her to apologize, but I didn't know her name. Then, I got embarrassed about that, as the manager was clearly exasperated with me and kept putting me on hold to deal with other things. The tension was so great, I wasn't able to go to work in the afternoon."

Other Noteworthy Things About GAD

About 3.1% of the US population meets criteria for GAD in any given year. Women are twice as likely to be affected. It is relatively more common among persons of lower socioeconomic status, which is related to the greater likelihood of such individuals living in genuinely dangerous situations, such as an unsafe neighborhood.

In addition to basic anxiety, GAD has sometimes been referred to as free-floating anxiety because there is no specific object (as in specific phobia), situation (as in social phobia), experience (as in PTSD), or cognitive activity (such as the obsessions of OCD) that causes the anxiety.

Insomnia and somatic complaints are common for persons with GAD. The thought of tomorrow and everything that it will bring produces anxiety that interferes with sleep. Anxiety causes gastrointestinal problems, headaches, muscle aches, and fatigue. Consequently, someone with GAD may seek medical care repeatedly for headaches and trouble falling asleep. Unfortunately, medical doctors are often times poor at recognizing mental illness.

If not treated, GAD tends to become progressively worse. Treatment is necessary to halt the disorder.

Treatment for GAD

Both psychological and medicinal treatments have been used to address GAD. Research suggests that both are effective.

The most common psychological approach for GAD (and all of the anxiety disorders) is cognitive-behavior therapy (CBT). In this therapy, the person with GAD is taught new cognitive and behavioral skills. Regarding cognitions, the person is taught to recognize and change negative, worry-based, anxiety-provoking thinking. Behavioral skills that are useful include relaxation and stress management.

Biological treatments are most commonly used to treat GAD. Simply put, the medications reduce the feelings of tension and anxiety. For reasons that are not entirely clear, the SRI antidepressant medications (such as fluoxetine or Prozac) have proven especially effective.

The Face of Anxiety

The face of anxiety is variable, and the following are generalizations and are not true of everyone with anxiety. Nonetheless, there are some typical aspects to the observable behavior of a person with an anxiety disorder. They will have a prototypical body language, interpersonal behavior, and commentary. Because they are anxious about what others think of them, people with anxiety will work hard at hiding their distress.

Body Language

If you are face-to-face with someone who has an anxiety disorder and is in the middle of a highly anxious moment, you may find yourself looking around the room to try to find where the danger is located. The alarm on her face will be evident. Her bodily sensations, including racing heart, upset stomach, sweating, trembling, dry mouth, shortness of breath, lightheadedness, and blurred vision, will not be evident to you. The person who experiences these will attempt to cover them up. This often entails avoiding or precipitously leaving.

The person with an anxiety disorder will also look intensely unhappy when not in the midst of acute anxiety. The unhappiness is largely because the person with an anxiety disorder feels lousy. As noted, all of the anxiety disorders entail extremely unpleasant physical symptoms, which are ultimately exhausting.

Interpersonal Behavior

Persons with an anxiety disorder can sometimes come across as antisocial. They will tend to focus their attention on themselves during social situations. This is not a self-centered, grandiose focus but rather a focus on their performance and whether they are "leaking" signs of how anxious they feel. As a result of not concentrating adequately on the actual content, their conversations may be superficial and can come across as indifferent. Hence, the person can appear to be lacking social skills.

Furthering this impression, persons with an anxiety disorder tend to organize their lives around avoidance and safety. This means avoiding (e.g., not going to the party) or escaping (e.g., leaving the party early) social situations. During social situations, they will do things to protect themselves from embarrassment or negative evaluation (e.g., staying quiet, avoiding eye contact). This might severely limit their social behaviors and, indeed, might leave others with a negative impression of them.

Commentary

The internal commentary of someone with an anxiety disorder is rife with negativity. Typical thoughts will include: "That was a stupid thing for me to say;" "She doesn't like me;" "They think I'm weird;" "I offended her;" and "No one will talk to me."

Occasionally, the internal commentary will make its way into the person's speech. The person with an anxiety disorder will occasionally make incredibly negative and harsh comments about himself.

Encouraging Treatment-Seeking

There is both good news and bad news about treatment of the anxiety disorders. On the one hand, some of the most effective treatments of mental illness have been developed for these disorders. On the other hand, the very essense of the anxiety disorders impedes treatment-seeking.

Treatment Efficacy

The anxiety disorders respond well to both biological (medications) and psychological (psychotherapy) treatment.

Regarding medications, there are two types of agents commonly used. Anti-anxiety (or anxiolytic) medications relieve anxiety very quickly and very effectively. As a result, the anxiolytics are experienced as highly reinforcing. Unfortunately, these medications can promote psychological and sometimes physical dependency. The best example of this is Valium, which was widely prescribed and widely abused in the 1960s and 1970s. The anxiolytics are therefore best used as "rescue" drugs, to be taken only when the anxiety has become overwhelming.

Antidepressant medications that target the neurotransmitter serotonin are called serotonin reuptake inhibitors, or SRIs. For unclear reasons, they also relieve anxiety symptoms. The huge advantage of the antidepressants is that they do not tempt abuse (there is nothing immediately reinforcing about taking them) nor do they promote dependency. However, the antidepressant drugs take longer to work (needing anywhere from four to eight weeks before effects are seen). Quite unfortunately, in the early phase of SRI treatment, many persons, whether being treated for depression or anxiety, experience *increased* anxiety.

A common treatment approach for the anxiety disorders is to prescribe antidepressant medication concurrent with a short-term prescription of anxiolytic to suppress the anxiety-provoking initial phase.

Several different methods of psychotherapy have proven very effective for the anxiety disorders, such as panic control therapy for panic disorder, exposure response therapy for OCD, and systematic desensitization for the phobias. Therapy helps the person with an anxiety disorder anticipate and prepare for situations that cause anxiety. Illogical thinking patterns (e.g., this situation is dangerous) and misinterpretation of bodily sensations (e.g., I am having a heart attack) are common targets of psychotherapy for the anxiety disorders. In this way, therapy can help a person become less sensitive to the frightening bodily sensations that accompany most anxiety disorders. In addition, the person may be taught breathing exercises to help promote relaxation and to prevent hyperventilation that often occurs during a panic attack.

The best and most long-lasting treatment effects for the anxiety disorders come from a combination of medications and psychotherapy.

Treatment Reluctance

Paradoxically, mental health professionals have developed extremely effective treatments for the anxiety disorders, but the anxiety disorders are some of the least frequently treated. Whereas almost 70% of persons with a mood disorder will seek treatment, only about 33% of persons with an anxiety disorder will do so. This is due to several factors.

First, persons with the anxiety disorders can create strategies to avoid the things about which they are anxious or to reduce their anxiety. It is not particularly problematic to have a snake phobia if you live in a city, and people who have extreme fears of dogs can avoid them with some effort. If one does get anxious, alcohol, which is both legal and widely available, can reduce it fairly effectively. A very common way for someone with panic disorder to reduce the fear associated with having another panic attack is to not go anywhere without a companion. So, people with the anxiety disorders can address them, so to speak, without professional help.

In addition, the anxiety disorders are easier to hide from others than are other disorders. Someone with depression will look depressed. The behavior of a person with a psychotic disorder is obvious. A substance use disorder (i.e., alcohol or drug problems) might be successfully concealed for a while, but it is usually eventually found out. In contrast, people can fairly successfully hide feelings of extreme anxiety, so much so that others will learn about the problem only if the person admits to it. However, they tend not to admit it due to shame.

Indeed, the anxiety disorders seem to generate more shame than the other disorders (with the exception of the substance use disorders), which makes it unlikely that a person will admit to having one. Over the course of growing up, children are regularly informed that fears and anxieties are silly and unnecessary. Adults encourage children with such expressions as "It's safe," "There's nothing to be afraid of," and the occasional "Look, your little sister is not afraid." It is not bad to say such things to encourage children to overcome groundless fears (e.g., of dogs, going to school, spending the night at a friend's house). In the long run, however, fears and anxieties tend to develop a quality of needlessness. We learn the rule: "There is no need to ever be afraid."

Encouraging Treatment Seeking

You can help a person with an anxiety disorder using some of what you have learned. That is, inform her that the anxiety disorders are extremely common but that they are also highly treatable. This is the same approach as suggested for depression (see the end of chapter 6). With the anxiety disorders in particular, it is helpful to address the reluctance to seek treatment directly by addressing both the person's shame and confusion. Even if the person with the anxiety disorder does not admit to either, you can probably assume that they are there.

Remind the person with an anxiety disorder that many people in the Bible had irrational fears, and yet they are looked upon as examples of people with great faith. Having faith does not prevent anxiety. Abraham had direct assurances from God that all would be okay, but he felt it necessary to lie about being married. Peter walked side-by-side with Christ, but he lied about being a disciple out of fear. Although she may feel ashamed of her anxiety, assure her that God is not upset with her for being anxious and that no one, including you, will condemn her for it.

Acknowledge the person's confusion and perhaps admit that you share it. It is confusing to you that Bill is anxious about something that is so unlikely to happen. Of course, it is more confusing and upsetting to him. It seems unhealthy and strange that Mary worries so much about something terrible happening to her children in the future, even though she lives in a nice neighborhood and sends her kids to a good school. She knows it doesn't make sense, but she cannot help herself. Accept their confusion and admit to them that such tremendous anxiety indeed does *not make sense.* (Review the beginning of this chapter, where it was noted that the fear of the anxiety disorders is usually recognized by those with one as excessive and irrational.) Remind them that the anxiety disorders, like illness, natural disasters, and other terrible things, don't have to make sense in order to exist.

Address the lack of sympathy of so many other people. Observers, including spouses and friends, will sometimes accuse a person with an anxiety disorder of overreacting or of being "hysterical." The person is repeatedly reassured that everything is fine but cannot believe it, and the individuals doing the reassuring sometimes become impatient and upset.

Mostly, encourage the person with an anxiety disorder to realize that he or she does not have to have it. Treatment is available and effective, and they need to seek it.

Strawberries With Sugar: Mass Hysteria Is Actually Collective Anxiety

In May 2006, an outbreak of a contagious virus was reported in Portuguese schools. Over 300 students at a dozen schools reported symptoms that were similar to those experienced by characters in a recent episode of a TV show that was especially popular with teenage girls called "Morangos com Açúcar" (or "Strawberries With Sugar"). Symptoms included rashes, dizziness, and difficulty breathing. Some schools temporarily closed. Portugal's Institute for Medical Emergency eventually dismissed the outbreak as caused by mass hysteria.

One of the most notorious cases of mass hysteria occurred in Salem, Massachusetts, in the late 1600s. The witch trials began when a 9-year-old girl and her 11-year-old cousin began to have fits. They screamed and made strange sounds, threw things, and contorted themselves into peculiar positions. Other young women in the village began to exhibit similar behaviors. Following accusations of witchcraft, 19 people were hanged, one man was pressed to death, and as many as 20 died in prison.

As interesting as cases of mass hysteria are, their cause is fairly mundane. Mass hysteria is spread by causing others to think that there is something terribly wrong. No one can identify the something, and no one can stop it either. Thus do episodes of mass hysteria usually begin with one or two individuals who are affected by strange and unexplainable symptoms. The symptoms cause consternation and anxiety, and the anxiety causes the symptoms to spread to others.

Documented episodes of mass hysteria have usually been limited to women, but not always. The condition *Koro* is the belief that one's genitals are gradually disappearing into one's body, which will eventuate in death. In 1967, hospitals in Singapore needed to reassure hundreds of men seeking care for Koro. Some men had tied pieces of string around their genitalia, just in case.

Modern communication methods, including instant news reporting, the Internet, Facebook, and Twitter, allow incredibly fast transmission of false or incomplete information. In other words, we can expect that contagious anxiety (and mass hysteria) will be more common in the future.

Chapter 8

Schizophrenia and Other Psychotic Disorders

"My comfort in my suffering is this: Your promise preserves my life."
(Psalm 119:50)

The well-functioning brain takes in sensory information, including sights, sounds, touches, smells, and tastes. It then processes those sensations in order to create perceptions, such as faces we recognize, sounds we understand, the feel of a breeze, the smell of a fire, and the taste of wine. In other words, the well-functioning brain enables us to perceive the world as it actually is.

The well-functioning brain usually thinks in ways that are accurate reflections of the world. We understand which people like us and which people don't. We recognize when we have done something well and when we have done something poorly. We remember what happened earlier today, yesterday, and last week. We sometimes make mistakes, such as forgetting someone's name or recalling that we had a conversation with Jack when it was really with Jill. In general, however, the healthy brain both thinks about things and remembers events with fairly good, if imperfect, accuracy.

For a person with a psychotic disorder, these very basic brain processes have gone terribly wrong.

The term *psychosis* is used to indicate that a person is experiencing a *disturbance of perception and thought* that is so severe that he or she has lost contact with reality. The person within a psychotic episode experiences a world that is animated by products of his or her mind or psyche. Because of the disconnection to reality (i.e., the world as others experience it), someone with a psychotic disorder may experience profound impairment. He or she may have difficulty relating to or communicating with others who do not understand or appreciate what he or she is experiencing.

Psychosis is not a diagnosis but rather a very important symptom. Someone exhibiting this symptom may be diagnosed with any of a variety of disorders, which are reviewed in this chapter. There are several different disorders, but the most common by far is schizophrenia. After reviewing schizophrenia and the other, less-common psychotic disorders, the chapter reviews other noteworthy aspects of and the typical presentation of the psychotic disorders. The distress and impairment associated with the psychotic disorders are discussed, as are special considerations related to treatment. The chapter includes a discussion regarding how to encourage someone with schizophrenia to seek and, more important, *continue* treatment. The chapter ends with a discussion of the effects of deinstitutionalization.

The Genius

John earned his doctorate from Princeton University at age 22 and began teaching at MIT at age 23. One mentor's letter of recommendation consisted of a single sentence: "This man is a genius." The new professor did very well. He solved a supposedly unsolvable problem posed by a 19th-century mathematician. To this day, normally staid mathematicians describe the solution as "astonishing." Many joke that the math professor is most famous these days for his trivial work in economics, for which he earned the Nobel Prize.

When he turned 30 or so, however, things began to go bad. He began to express odd beliefs, claiming there was a communist conspiracy fomenting against him, organized by men who favored red ties. His lectures became increasingly nonsensical, and at one point he abandoned his classes altogether and fled to avoid those intent on harming him. He wrote letters to government officials, warning them of the conspiracy of the men in red ties. In everyday conversation, he became unintelligible. One colleague said, "There was no way to talk to him or even follow what he was saying."

His new wife had him hospitalized at McLean Hospital, and he was diagnosed with schizophrenia. Some believed that he had died. He had not died, but his life became hellish. Upon his release from the hospital, the professor resigned, cashed out his pension, and fled to Europe. Officials in Switzerland recognized his impaired mental state and refused to allow him to give up his US citizenship. His wife followed him to Europe, and she convinced the officials to deport him back to the United States. After treatment, they returned to Princeton, where the professor had done his graduate work. He spent his time hanging around campus, talking about himself in the third person, writing bizarre postcards, and making phone calls to former colleagues to discuss numerology and world political affairs.

In 1994, at the age of 66, Dr. John Nash received the Nobel Prize in Economics for his work on game theory. By then, he had learned to distinguish his delusions from reality, and his problematic behavior became less severe. He has since been given an office at Princeton, where he continues to explore mathematics, the world in which he first succeeded. Many readers have probably seen the movie about his life called *A Beautiful Mind.*

Schizophrenia

Schizophrenia is a devastating brain disorder. It causes intense distress, and the profound impairment to which it leads compromises all areas of functioning. It interferes with a person's ability to think clearly and make decisions, to manage emotions, to behave in socially appropriate ways, and to relate to others. Schizophrenia literally translates as "split mind," which makes some think that schizophrenia means the person has multiple personalities. The term *schizophrenia* was, in fact, coined by a Swiss psychiatrist who wanted to emphasize his theory of its cause, which he believed was a disconnect between the emotional and rational functions of the mind.

Symptoms of Schizophrenia

The symptoms of schizophrenia can be divided into three categories: disorganized thoughts, positive symptoms, and negative symptoms.

Disorganized Thinking

The hallmark symptom of schizophrenia is confused thinking. Most basically, it is the inability to follow one thought with a related thought. Confused thinking causes confused speech, resulting in severe problems in communication with other people. For example, someone with schizophrenia may have trouble communicating in coherent sentences or carrying on conversations with others. Recall that Dr. Nash's colleague noted, "There was no way to follow . . . what he was saying."

Disorganized thinking may affect emotions as well. A person with schizophrenia may express emotions that do not seem to fit with the situation. He may act very angrily for no apparent reason or because of a delusion that others are speaking ill of him. He may laugh when told bad news. Disorganized thinking will impact relationships. Speaking nonsensically and repeatedly expressing emotions that do not fit the situation can be quite disconcerting to others.

A person with schizophrenia may exhibit disorganized behaviors. She may engage in actions that do not make sense to an observer. She may move more slowly than others or repeat certain gestures or movements, such as walking in circles or pacing.

Positive Symptoms

Positive symptoms are an excess of something normal. The most prominent positive symptoms are hallucinations and delusions. Hallucinations are perceptions of sight, sound, smell, and smell or taste that have no basis in reality. A person with schizophrenia may see people or hear voices that are not there, such as choirs singing or voices criticizing everything the person does. Hallucinations may be distortions of real images, such as seeing someone grow bigger and then smaller.

Someone in a psychotic episode may have delusions, which are beliefs that have no basis in fact. Some common delusions are the conviction that people are reading their thoughts or plotting against them or that they can control other people's minds. Paranoid delusions are false beliefs that others are trying to harm you or are plotting against you. Delusions of grandeur are false beliefs that you are more important, powerful, or famous than you actually are. John Nash had both paranoid and grandiose delusions. He fled to Europe partly out of concern that the US government was not taking seriously the threats that the men in red ties posed to him. He was convinced that others were secretly monitoring and threatening him.

Negative Symptoms

Negative symptoms entail an absence or decline of emotional, cognitive, or behavioral functioning. For example, persons with schizophrenia may exhibit emotional flatness or lack of expression, appearing bored with or disinterested in their environment and its inhabitants. They may react to sad, irritating, or exciting events or information with little emotional response. Negative symptoms may be exhibited as apathy, including an inability to start and follow through with tasks. Again, this may be most obvious in social situations. For example, they may exhibit speech that is overly brief (e.g., responding to queries about well-being with one-word answers) and lacking in meaningful content (e.g., When asked what she thought of a certain book, one of my patients responded, "There were a lot of words," which was probably true but was also uninformative). Unfortunately, someone with schizophrenia may not just appear to be disinterested to others, she may actually experience a lack of pleasure or interest in life. One person with schizophrenia wrote her father, "I wish I could feel really bad; it would be better than feeling nothing."

Other Psychotic Disorders

There are several other psychotic disorders. The commonality to all is the experience of a psychotic episode, which is characterized by delusions, hallucinations, and/or impaired thinking. These disorders are not as commonplace as schizophrenia, so they are less well-studied and less well-understood. As a result, our approach to treating these disorders tends to rely on what we know about treating schizophrenia.

The first two of the following disorders are identical in appearance to schizophrenia, except that they appear and disappear rather rapidly (within 6 months), whereas the next two are distinguished from schizophrenia because they are caused by a biological insult to the brain. Schizoaffective disorder is diagnosed when psychosis co-occurs with depression. The final disorders presented next are noteworthy because they involve delusions only.

Short-Term Psychotic Episodes

Persons with brief psychotic disorder or schizophreniform disorder exhibit all the symptoms of schizophrenia, but their symptoms appear and abate quickly. *Schizophrenia* is the appropriate diagnosis if a psychosis endures more than six months. However, *brief reactive psychosis* is the appropriate diagnosis if the psychosis endures less than one month, whereas *schizophreniform disorder* endures between one month and six months.

Someone with brief psychotic disorder will exhibit psychosis for a few weeks only and then return to normal functioning. The disorder is called brief *reactive* psychosis, because it typically develops in response to an extremely stressful event. Most commonly, brief reactive psychosis is seen in wartime.

The person with schizophreniform disorder exhibits the symptoms of schizophrenia, but the symptoms last less than six months. The disorder develops more quickly than is typical for schizophrenia. That is, the person diagnosed with schizophrenia usually exhibits a long "prodromal" (prior to illness) phase of gradual deterioration in functioning. In schizophreniform disorder, in contrast, symptoms of psychosis tend to develop quite suddenly and will, by definition, resolve within six months.

Because these disorders resolve so rapidly, impairment does not intensify to the same degree as with schizophrenia. Persons who recover from schizophrenia that, by definition, lasts a long time often have residual symptoms, such as mildly delusional thinking and an odd social presentation. Persons diagnosed with these brief disorders are likely to have a full recovery with no residual problems.

Ryan the Marine

Ryan developed hallucinations and delusions soon after a traumatic experience in Sadr City during Operation Iraqi Freedom. His two best friends, while walking beside him, were killed by roadside bombs. He later helped retrieve their body parts that had been scattered. That night, he started hallucinating that one of his two dead friends was searching for the other and he tried to leave camp in order to help find him. He also developed a somewhat convoluted set of beliefs that his commanding officer—a blonde-haired, decorated combat veteran from Nebraska—was actually an Iraqi infiltrator. Ryan was sent to a military hospital in Iraq, where the hallucinations and delusions fairly quickly stopped. He was discharged from the Marines not much later, however, and was still being seen for post-traumatic stress disorder five years later.

Psychosis Due to Substance Use or Due to a Medical Condition

Extensive or intensive use of drugs or alcohol can cause a psychotic episode. The psychotic episode may be an exacerbation of the normal effect of the drug. For example, someone who takes a hallucinogenic drug (such as LSD) may experience hallucinations that continue after the drug use has ended. Or a psychotic episode may be a side effect of extended use of drugs that normally don't cause hallucinations. For example, extensive use of cocaine can cause hallucinations and paranoid delusions. Stopping an extended period of drug use may cause a psychotic episode. Suddenly stopping using heroin or alcohol after a binge can cause the person to experience hallucinations due to withdrawal.

Some medical conditions can cause a psychotic episode, such as severe fever, head injury, or a brain tumor. For example, confusion is a common symptom of early-stage Alzheimer's disease, which is a disease caused by a degenerative process in the brain. Some persons with the disorder get very upset by the confusion, but others might exhibit delusional thinking. For example, the person may not remember where she put her purse and accuse others of stealing it. In more advanced cases of the disease, the person may have delusions about being poisoned or spied upon. As recognition capacity starts to fail, the person may express belief that he is being held captive in someone else's house. Someone with Alzheimer's disease may accuse his wife, daughter, or son of being an imposter.

As with Jacob (see box), treatment of these disorders means discovering and treating (if possible) the underlying cause. When the cause is eliminated, the disorder usually disappears.

Jacob's Headaches

Jacob is a 27-year-old Latino male. His family finally coerced him into a psychiatric ward because his auditory hallucinations and delusions of grandeur were worsening. They had begun about nine months previously. Jacob was inconsistent in taking prescribed anti-psychotic medication, but even when he did take them, they had no effect. Jacob was not resistant to taking them. Instead, the hospital staff observed that he was genuinely very forgetful. Moreover, he frequently complained of severe headaches. Jacob was transferred to a medical floor where they did scans of his brain and discovered a tumor. Within two weeks of surgery to remove it, his symptoms disappeared and have never returned.

Schizoaffective Disorder

Someone with schizoaffective disorder experiences symptoms of both schizophrenia and a mood disorder. The symptoms of schizophrenia, such as hallucinations and delusions, occur simultaneously with the symptoms of either an episode of major depression or alternating cycles of depression and mania (i.e., bipolar disorder).

As illustrated by the story of Melanie (see box p. 124), persons with schizoaffective disorder seem to suffer more than most. The combination of psychotic and depressive symptoms is more miserable than either are alone. In cases of depression alone, the distress leads the person to seek treatment. In cases of schizophrenia, delusions and hallucinations often bother a person a great deal, so that he is also willing to seek treatment. In cases of schizoaffective disorder, the person may have the false belief that the depression is deserved, which interferes with help-seeking behavior. Melanie reasoned, "Why would I feel so depressed if God did not hate me?"

Schizoaffective disorder is not as common as schizophrenia, which itself is far less common than the anxiety, depression, and substance use disorders. As a result, schizoaffective disorder has not been as often studied and is therefore not as well understood. Moreover, when doctors search for a treatment regimen, they tend to rely on what is known about schizophrenia and depression. Typically, then, a person with schizoaffective disorder will be prescribed some mix of antipsychotic and antidepressant medications.

Melanie's Depression and Psychosis

Melanie was a mother of two with a husband who loved her dearly. Since she was a teenager, she had long experienced fairly severe episodes of depression, but things seemed to have turned a corner after college. She married and obtained a job as a call center supervisor for a wireless phone company. Soon after the birth of her second child, her phone company merged with another company. All call centers were sent overseas, and she was offered the opportunity to move to India with her family to supervise several such centers. Instead, she went to India for six months to oversee their establishment and then came back to the United States without a job. By that time, her increasing despondency about her career had developed into severe depression. After she got home, things began to get alarming. Her husband could not convince her to return to the psychiatrist they had consulted upon her return. The psychiatrist's nurse was "rude and probably an illegal alien." When Melanie refused her doctor's suggestion to go to the hospital, he gave her some pills he "pulled out of his drawer" that were "actually poison." She only pretended that she would fill the prescription, and she certainly was not going back. Besides which, God was clearly punishing her for being a bad mom, a bad wife, and a bad worker. She deserved to suffer. Melanie met criteria for both major depression and for a psychotic disorder, and she was therefore diagnosed with schizoaffective disorder.

Disorders Characterized by Delusions Only

The most severe manifestation of a psychotic disorder will include hallucinations, which means that the person sees, hears, and perhaps feels and smells things that are not there. The last two psychotic disorders to be discussed may be considered less severe since persons with them do not experience hallucinations but rather delusions only.

Someone may be diagnosed with *delusional disorder* if she has persistent beliefs that have no factual basis in reality. Common delusions are that one has some dreadful disease, is being followed, or is being conspired against by family, friends, coworkers, and strangers.

The major difficulty in diagnosing this disorder is establishing that the beliefs are in fact untrue. One may actually have a disease that doctors keep missing or for which there is no test. Note, for example, that persons with relatively rare diseases, such as Lyme disease (which causes diffuse pain and headaches and can actually be quite serious), are sometimes diagnosed with a psychiatric disorder, because medical professionals erroneously believe that the lack of evidence of a biological disease indicates that it is all in the patient's head.

Wanda and Wally

Wanda was in a long-term relationship with Wally, who had schizophrenia that was relatively mild. Once when younger, Wally had a severe but brief psychotic episode that necessitated him leaving college after he had barricaded himself in his dorm room for a week. Wally, who was one-quarter French, seemed to make a full recovery after a brief hospitalization. Medications immediately alleviated his delusions about the resurgence of the Triple Alliance (late 19th-century European powers allying against France), as well as the command auditory hallucinations (in which voices alternated between French and German accents) that insisted that he needed to warn the French consulate. It soon became evident to his friends and family, however, that Wally never recovered his easygoing and rational nature. He seemed tense and irritable, and he increasingly withdrew from relationships. With Wanda, however, things were different.

Ten years after leaving college, Wally met Wanda at the library, where he liked to read European newspapers and magazines. After he and Wanda moved in together, he shared with her some of his "secret knowledge." Over the years, Wally had developed fairly elaborate delusions about the cause of his problems at college. The department of foreign languages had several professors who resented him quite a bit, mostly because he understood European history and the current unions, alliances, and antagonisms between the various European countries better than they did. His explanations to Wanda, both about the professors and about Europe, were rife with factual details and exceptional in complexity. Moreover, Wally was transformed into a dynamic, invigorated, and passionate advocate for Europe's working classes when discussing these things. Wanda was swept up by his fury and his zeal, and she soon bought wholeheartedly into his delusional system.

Shared psychotic disorder is a disorder that develops as a result of an extended, intimate relationship with a person who has delusions. Shared psychotic disorder is diagnosed in the person who comes to share the delusional belief.

Note that Wanda and Wally were both able to function despite their delusions. Sometimes shared delusions turn deadly, however. David Koresh was a self-appointed messiah who convinced several dozen other adults of his importance and greatness. He, 54 other adults, and 28 children were killed in a raid on their Branch Davidian compound outside of Waco, Texas, in April 1993.

Other Noteworthy Things About Schizophrenia

Age of Onset

Schizophrenia typically begins in early adulthood, between the ages of 18 and 25. A new diagnosis of schizophrenia is quite rare for people over age 40. On average, men develop schizophrenia at a younger age than women. The average age of onset is 18 in men and 25 in women. Moreover, the disease tends to be more severe in younger males, with a much higher rate of required hospitalization (due to dangerousness or severe impairment). As with all mental illnesses, the earlier schizophrenia is diagnosed and treated, the better the outcome for the person and the more likely a sustained recovery.

Prevalence

Approximately 1.1% of the world's population over the age of 18 (about 51 million people) currently meets criteria for schizophrenia. Schizophrenia occurs in all societies regardless of class, race, ethnicity, religion, or culture. Some persons are more at risk for the illness than others, however.

Risk Factors

The exact causes of schizophrenia are not known. As will be discussed more thoroughly in the second volume of this work, the diathesis-stress model is probably the best way to understand the disease. The model holds that people get a disease because they are born with a predisposition (diathesis) that is expressed only under certain environmental conditions (i.e., stresses). This model explains why identical twins (who are identical in their genetic makeup) don't have perfect concordance with the disease. That is, if one identical twin has schizophrenia, the likelihood that her twin will also have it is about 50%. Both twins have the biological predisposition, but only one twin develops the disease, presumably because of differences in environmental experiences.

The risk factors for schizophrenia are consistent with this model. They include a family history of schizophrenia; exposure to viruses, toxins, or malnutrition in utero; stressful life circumstances; and using psychoactive drugs, such as marijuana, during adolescence and young adulthood.

The Course of Schizophrenia

Receiving a diagnosis of schizophrenia does not necessarily mean that a person will always have it. Some persons are diagnosed following an episode of psychosis and then seem to recover completely. Up to one in three persons diagnosed with schizophrenia will recover either entirely or mostly. Most have to cope with the disease for all of their life, however. Fortunately, the disorder can be managed quite successfully, and impairment can be kept to a minimum. In general, success depends on appropriate and ongoing management via regular contact with psychiatrists and adherence to medication prescriptions.

In other words, schizophrenia is a highly treatable and manageable illness, if the person understands and acquiesces to the need for treatment. Unfortunately, the disease itself can present problems in this regard.

The Face of Schizophrenia

Schizophrenia is probably one of the easier mental illnesses for others to recognize. This is particularly true if the person is actively psychotic. This will be the case if the person has not yet been diagnosed or if the person has stopped treatment (i.e., stopped taking medications).

The symptoms of the disorder are difficult to conceal by the person, and they will profoundly impact the person's ability to interact with others. The person experiencing a psychotic episode may be delusional, in which case he or she may mention unusual beliefs. Someone with paranoid delusions may act suspiciously or report concerns (or convictions) that others are attempting to monitor his behavior or to hurt him. Someone experiencing delusions of grandeur may report that God has a special love (or hatred) of him and that God accordingly planned to elevate him over all other creation (or to destroy him). Delusions of reference may more accurately be labeled delusions of communication. The person with these will report that others (e.g., aliens, the CIA) are sending messages to her through unusual means (e.g., TV broadcasts, street lights) or are stealing her thoughts.

The person experiencing hallucinations will be hearing, seeing, feeling, or smelling things that other people, including you, are not. The person will, accordingly, be quite distracted. While interacting with you, she will be hearing sounds that will, at least temporarily, demand her attention. As a result, someone who is hallucinating will exhibit slowed reactions, meaning longer than normal delays in conversations.

The person may not share or admit the hallucinatory experiences without prompting. Previous experience doing so (and getting shocked stares, odd looks, or outraged denunciations in response) will have taught her to keep hallucinations to herself. On the other hand, if you ask the person about hallucinations (e.g., "Are you hearing anything or seeing anything that maybe others are not hearing or seeing?"), she will not likely deny them. In fact, she may be relieved to talk about them.

It is actually somewhat more difficult to discern pathology in a person experiencing delusions only versus someone experiencing hallucinations (which probably are coexisting with delusions). The person with delusions only is not impaired by hallucinations, and the delusions may not be immediately evident because they don't cause obvious impairment.

What is the best way to respond to a person with delusions or hallucinations? I believe it is best to acknowledge the two realities of the situation. One reality is that you and others do not share the delusions and are not experiencing the hallucinations. The other reality is that the person is experiencing them, that they are quite real to the person, and that they may be quite bothersome.

Distress and Impairment

As is the case with any illness, whether cancer or the common cold, there are variations in severity of schizophrenia.

Distress

The disorder can cause profound distress to the person. Imagine believing that you are a source of evil and that you should be and eventually will be punished by God himself. Evidence of profound distress is that one in ten persons with schizophrenia will attempt suicide, which is a higher rate than that seen in depression.

Other persons with schizophrenia may not experience such profound distress. This may be because the symptoms are not that severe or are being well-managed with medications. Or it might be because the person experiences anosognosia, which is the lack of awareness that she has an illness. As will be discussed in more detail later in this chapter, anosognosia interferes with treatment seeking. (Why seek treatment for a nonexistent illness?)

Impairment Related to Symptom Severity

The severity of impairment will be related to the severity of symptoms. The severity of symptoms, in turn, will largely hinge on the success of psychiatric treatment.

At one extreme, the individual with schizophrenia may manage the disorder very well. She will seek and continue treatment as needed. She will marry, have children, have a successful career, and lead a positive and fulfilling life.

On the other hand, despite being in treatment, a good proportion of persons with schizophrenia will experience residual symptoms. As a result, they may experience some degree of relationship and role impairment. If no one else hears the voices he hears or understands the beliefs he believes, it will be difficult for others to understand what someone with schizophrenia is going through. As a result, the person with schizophrenia whose treatment is only partly successful may have difficulty forming and maintaining relationships, perhaps related to difficulties in trusting others, as well as difficulty finding and keeping work. The disorder may thus render the person incapable of holding a job. Work performance may become essentially impossible, partly due to impaired relationships but also because the person has difficulty formulating organized thoughts and actions.

Unfortunately, the 40% of persons with schizophrenia who receive no treatment at all will likely exhibit serious impairment and face considerable dangers. Estimates are that untreated schizophrenia accounts for about one-third of the homeless population. The homeless are regular targets of criminals. One study found that one in four homeless persons admitted occasionally eating from garbage cans, and one in ten reported that garbage cans were their primary source of sustenance.

Other research indicates that persons with untreated schizophrenia comprise one-sixth of the total jail and prison population. Moreover, on average, they will be kept in prison twice as long as those without schizophrenia. Some admit that they purposely break rules, leading to longer or extended sentences, in order to remain incarcerated where they feel safer and are better fed. Others break rules because of the symptoms (delusions and hallucinations) of their illness.

Poorly managed schizophrenia is very costly to both families and society (see also chapter 5). Families have to endure the horror of watching a loved one suffer, and they often struggle to get the person adequate treatment. Estimates of the cost in the United States alone in 2002 were $62.7 billion, of which about one-third was associated with health care and the rest to lost productivity on the part of both the individuals with the disorder and the individuals' families.

The SPMIs and Violence

A common misconception about persons with schizophrenia is that they are much more prone to violence than persons without schizophrenia. However, it is equally wrong to believe that having schizophrenia (or bipolar disorder) does *not* confer any risk of violence. Research indicates that a diagnosis of schizophrenia confers greater risk of violence, but that the risk is nonetheless quite small.

Schizophrenia and bipolar disorder (chapter 9) are referred to as serious and persistent mental illness (SPMI). Of the estimated 16,000 total homicides in the United States each year, it is estimated that 10% are committed by persons with untreated schizophrenia or bipolar disorder.

Persons with untreated serious mental illness are much more likely to "self-medicate," meaning they use alcohol and drugs in order to reduce the severity of their symptoms and the intensity of their distress. Some research suggests that much if not all of the increased likelihood of violence entirely disappears if persons with SPMIs who have comorbid substance use disorders are excluded. In other words, an individual with schizophrenia or bipolar disorder who is not using substances and is obtaining adequate treatment is not more likely to be violent than someone from the general population. Moreover, if a person with an SPMI becomes violent, the violence is usually directed at family members and tends to take place at home. Finally, it should be noted that people who are not mentally ill at all still commit the vast majority of violence.

Special Considerations in the Treatment of the Psychotic Disorders

The good news is that treatments for schizophrenia are generally successful and are improving every year. There are over a dozen medications currently in development for the treatment of schizophrenia. Psychological treatments, such as cognitive therapy (e.g., teaching the person to distinguish rational and irrational thoughts), are proving successful.

That said, schizophrenia is categorized as a serious and persistent mental illness (SPMI). This is the term used by mental health professionals to describe mental illnesses with *complex symptoms* that require *ongoing* treatment and management. The most common SPMIs are schizophrenia and bipolar disorder, which is covered in the next chapter. The SPMIs have unique treatment exigencies.

Symptom Management

Persons with schizophrenia and bipolar disorder will typically not experience symptoms at a consistent or steady level. Rather, symptoms will fluctuate in severity over time. Because of the variable symptoms, someone with an SPMI may be able to function independently for periods of time, but at other times will need intensive support to maintain health, housing, school or work, and social relationships.

It is important to note that symptoms will worsen most predictably when the person with either schizophrenia or bipolar disorder is experiencing stress. Consistency, predictability, and support for stress management are important for all diseases, but are essential in managing these particular diseases.

Crisis Care

Persons with SPMIs are more likely than those with other mental illness to require hospitalization, because symptoms can be especially severe. A person with bipolar disorder in the throes of a manic episode may require hospitalization for his own safety and the safety of others (e.g., the person continually drives too fast). Someone with severe depression may require hospitalization to prevent suicide. A person with acute symptoms of schizophrenia may need to be hospitalized to forestall acting on homicidal thoughts that are related to delusions of paranoia or because the person is unable to care for himself (e.g., walks around outside in winter wearing only a T-shirt).

Scientology's War on the Treatment of Mental Illness, Part 1

Almost immediately after drug treatment for schizophrenia was developed, some began to attribute the symptoms of the illness to the drugs. This is because the first generation of antipsychotic medications tended to have tranquilizing effects. These early medications were related to the recently discovered antihistamines, such as Benadryl, and most people know the sleepiness and lethargy they cause. The logic was simple. If someone without schizophrenia took an antipsychotic drug, he would become sleepy and lethargic. Similarly, a person with schizophrenia will often respond slowly, have trouble making conversation, and appear to be in a fog. Therefore, the medications must be causing the symptoms!

Simply wrong, however. Antipsychotic medications did not and do not cause the mental fog associated with schizophrenia. Physicians, including Hippocrates, have observed these symptoms in persons with schizophrenia for centuries. Contrary to causing them, antipsychotic medications help symptoms significantly. The first-generation medications helped particularly with the positive symptoms of hallucinations and delusions, whereas more present-day medications for the treatment of schizophrenia are also effective in the treatment of the disorganized and negative symptoms (i.e., communication difficulties).

The idea that the medications cause the symptoms has been promoted vigorously by Scientology, which claims that persons with schizophrenia are being mistreated if given medication. Scientologists have exerted tremendous effort and spent much money to denigrate and disparage the mental health treatment system in general and medication treatments in particular. Scientologists claim that mental illness does not exist. They openly assert that doctors and pharmaceutical companies, due to avarice and despite a lack of empirical evidence, purposefully mislabel as mental illness what are actually spiritual problems. Not to impugn their motives, but I note that scientologists promote Scientology as the only legitimate recourse for obtaining mental health. The depredations Scientology has inflicted on persons with mental illness, especially children and their parents, is discussed in more detail in subsequent chapters.

The Necessity of Medications

Persons with an SPMI almost always *require* medication to prevent symptom reemergence (referred to as "relapse") and to maintain functioning. The primary medications for schizophrenia are called *antipsychotics,* and the primary medications for bipolar disorder are called *mood stabilizers.* As with drug treatments for physical illnesses, many persons with severe mental illnesses may need to try several different medications before they find the medication or, more likely, the combination of medications that works best.

Symptoms Can Interfere With Treatment Adherence

One report summarized five different high-quality surveys and found that, on average, 50% of persons being treated for schizophrenia were noncompliant with medications. The single biggest reason why individuals with schizophrenia (and bipolar disorder) do not take their medications is anosognosia, which is a lack of insight or awareness of the illness.

Anosognosia is the result of disease-related damage to the brain, and it affects half of those with schizophrenia (and just slightly fewer of those with bipolar disorder). Ironically, for some, awareness of the illness improves as a result of medications. Other factors associated with noncompliance are a negative attitude toward medications, a poor relationship with one's treatment provider, and a comorbid substance use disorder.

In other words, many persons with schizophrenia may be disinclined to take medications because of the very symptoms of the illness itself. In addition to anosognosia, individuals with schizophrenia may have delusions of paranoia and believe that the medications are actually an attempt to poison them.

Alternatively, someone with schizophrenia may start taking medication but then stop because she believes the medication is not helping, is no longer working, or is making things worse. In truth, there may be some legitimacy to these complaints. According to one study, even among persons with schizophrenia who were compliant and receiving "optimal" treatment, about two-thirds persistently experienced symptoms.

Paradoxically, the medications may work so well that the person becomes convinced that they are no longer necessary. Others stop taking prescribed medications because of unpleasant side effects.

As a result of these barriers to effective self-management, the treatment of schizophrenia and bipolar disorder often involves family members encouraging or coercing those with these disorders to seek and to comply with treatment (e.g., take medications as prescribed, go to the doctor's office when scheduled). The stress of this can be dreadful. What should be a loving relationship may transform into a paradoxical contest of wills. For example, a mother finds herself quarreling with her son in order to do what is best for him. Organizations such as the National Alliance for Mental Illness (NAMI) have been founded to help families deal with the stress of having a family member with an SPMI.

Families and the Course of Schizophrenia

The emotional environment within one's family plays a role in the progress of schizophrenia (but not in its genesis). After observing that many patients with schizophrenia who went back home to stay with parents (after a period of hospitalization) relapsed more frequently than patients who went to other environments, psychiatrists conducted some studies. Most such studies have used the concept of "expressed emotions" by family members towards the individual with schizophrenia. In particular, studies have focused on highly negative expressions of emotion, including critical comments and hostility. Subsequently, studies from all over the world have demonstrated that expressed emotionality predicts relapse (i.e., the reemergence of symptoms). There is related evidence that improving the emotional environment within families helps to prevent relapse.

Encouraging Treatment-Seeking and Treatment Commitment

Schizophrenia and the other psychotic disorders are extremely serious, causing extreme distress and profound impairment. Fortunately, treatments for them have improved dramatically.

Compare these two findings. According to the National Institute of Mental Health (NIMH), in 2010 it was estimated that approximately 40% of individuals with schizophrenia were untreated. However, because of the intervention of others, most persons with schizophrenia obtain treatment at some point in their lifetime. If most persons with a psychotic disorder have had treatment at some point but only just over half within the last year, that means that many started but then stopped treatment. With these disorders in particular, then, continuing treatment is a major focus.

Encouraging treatment seeking and compliance for persons with schizophrenia and the other psychotic disorders entails working with both the individuals and their families.

Talking With the Individual

It can be difficult to know how to respond to someone with schizophrenia who makes strange or clearly false statements. Remember that these beliefs or hallucinations seem very real to the person. It is not helpful to say they are wrong or imaginary. But going along with the delusions is not helpful either. Instead, calmly say that you see things differently. Tell them that you acknowledge that everyone has the right to see things his or her own way. In addition, it is important to understand that schizophrenia is a biological illness. Being respectful, supportive, and kind without tolerating dangerous or inappropriate behavior is the best way to approach a person with this disorder.

If the person is not in treatment, emphasize its necessity. If the person is in treatment, congratulate the person and be prepared to encourage the person to see that treatment will need to be ongoing. With either case, it can be helpful to contrast the difference between how things go when taking medications and how they go when medications are abandoned.

Be specific with examples, such as, "I can't help but notice that you seem to do so much better when you are taking medications than when you are not. When you take your meds, you come to church, you are friendly and warm, and you seem happy" (and so forth). The more specific you can be, the more encouraging and caring will your words be received.

Helping the Family

Someone with schizophrenia will hopefully be receiving help from health care professionals, including psychiatrists, social workers, psychologists, case managers, and other caregivers. However, family members are likely the person's primary caregivers.

Hopefully, the family will encourage the person with a psychotic disorder to take medications and keep doctors' appointments. Family members will hopefully be supportive of rational thinking and healthy self-care behaviors, such as eating and sleeping well. Research clearly shows that persons with a psychotic disorder do much better if their families are appropriately supportive and encouraging. However, this can be exhausting to families, especially if the symptoms are severe or the disorder proves particularly resistant to treatment.

Some families struggling with a severe form of this disorder may need to occasionally force issues. To be specific, they may occasionally need to force the person into the hospital. If they cannot do so themselves because of agitation, threatened or real violence, or other problems, they may have to have the police take the person to the hospital. This is at best extremely stressful and at worst a devastating experience.

At the very least, the families of persons with schizophrenia and the other psychotic disorders need your prayers, encouragement, support, and understanding. Encourage them in the loving work that they are doing. Openly admire their efforts, while being empathic with their struggles with this dreadful disorder.

Chapter 9

Bipolar Disorder

"For I am convinced that neither death nor life, neither angels nor demons, neither the present nor the future, nor any powers, neither height nor depth, nor anything else in all creation, will be able to separate us from the love of God that is in Christ Jesus our Lord."
(Romans 8:38,39)

Bipolar disorder can be one of the most difficult and devastating mental illnesses. This chapter will help the reader better understand and empathize with persons struggling with bipolar disorder and with the families of those with the disorder.

Bipolar disorder is a mood disorder. As noted previously, mood is an extended period of feeling. For most people, mood reflects circumstances. All of us experience good moods and bad moods. We get in a good mood after a good day and in a bad mood after a bad day. Someone whose mood stays the same way all the time, regardless of the situation or circumstances, may be diagnosed with a mood disorder. As was seen in chapter 6, someone with major depression is in a negative, sad, and depressed mood nearly all of the time. Nothing that happens will change the person's depressed mood. Hence, he or she has a mood disorder.

In major depression the person will experience only one of the two extremes of mood. Some psychiatrists will thus refer to major depression as "unipolar depression." In contrast, someone with bipolar disorder experiences both extremes of mood. She will fluctuate between depression and mania, the two poles of mood.

This chapter starts with a review of the symptoms of the disorder, followed by an effort to give a sense of how a person with bipolar disorder may seem in person. This chapter reviews some of the noteworthy aspects of bipolar disorder, as well as the distress and impairment associated with it, not just for the individual afflicted but also for the individual's family. The chapter ends with a brief review of treatment exigencies associated with bipolar disorder in particular.

Manic Episodes Within Bipolar Disorder

The symptoms experienced by the person diagnosed with bipolar disorder who is in the midst of a depressive phase will be identical to the symptoms already described in the person with a depressive disorder. (Some persons with bipolar disorder will assert that their depression is worse because of the contrast to the manic phase.) The symptoms of mania, being at the other end of the mood continuum, are entirely different. As with the diagnosis of depression, not all of these symptoms need to be present for a person to meet criteria for a manic episode disorder.

Mania is characterized by affective, behavioral, and cognitive symptoms.

Affective Symptoms

Concerning the feelings experienced by the person with bipolar disorder in a manic episode, they feel great. Patients in a state of mania are cheerful to the point of euphoria. They won't recall having ever felt badly, nor do they expect that anything will happen in the future that may make them feel less joyful than they feel at the moment. The person in the throes of a manic episode may occasionally feel irritable. Other people and the world in general seem to move too slowly to the person in a manic phase, which might lead to intense feelings of impatience. Irritability may be especially pronounced as the episode of mania is "winding down" and exhaustion (and eventually depression) starts to emerge.

Behavioral Symptoms

The behavior of a person in a manic episode can be generally characterized as "excessive."

When talking to others, speech will be excessively fast, garrulous, loud, and enthusiastic. Speech content may rapidly flit from one subject to another, sometimes called a flight of ideas. Thus might the person's talking give the impression of being under a lot of pressure, as if his mouth cannot keep up with the thoughts running through his mind (pressured speech).

Others will see the person's energy level as excessive as well. She will have trouble sitting (or will move or fidget a lot if required to sit) and will move quickly. Both large and small actions will be impulsive. If in your house, she will pick up things on your tables, flip through magazines and books, and seem intensely restless. Regarding large actions, the person may experience intense sexual arousal, which might be expressed through inappropriate sexual activity. Overall, there is increased activity and involvement in pleasurable activities without thought for consequences. Individuals in a manic episode may go on spending sprees. The overactivity can cause the person, eventually, to collapse from exhaustion. At that point, the piper needs to be paid, so to speak. Obviously, sexual indiscretions and financial recklessness can cause intense damage to relationships.

The excess energy might be seen as a decreased need for sleep. Indeed, the person can go for days without sleep without feeling tired. Some sleep may be obtained, but the person will arise after one, two, or three hours feeling refreshed and ready to conquer the world.

Cognitive Symptoms

The "pressured speech" described above provides evidence of the cognitive state of the person in a manic episode. Most persons describe their thinking during manic episodes as overly fast and overly full. The term used is *racing thoughts,* which is a nice description of the sense that one's mind is going faster than one's mouth can keep up. Hence, the cognitive state produces pressured speech.

The person in a manic episode may exhibit grandiosity (the delusion that he is important, special, or lucky). Related to grandiosity may be unrealistic beliefs in abilities and powers. The person is happy, confident, and enthusiastic, believing that nothing can possibly go wrong. This attitude might combine with excessive behavior, such as driving too fast, spending too much money, and getting extremely impatient with how negative other people are about such great ideas and plans. These beliefs may contribute to inappropriate social behavior, such as spending sprees (using money that he doesn't have or "will be getting soon!") and inappropriate sexual activity.

Unfortunately, many manic episodes are much less pleasant than buying too many clocks or starting painting projects in the middle of the night (see box below). Persons in manic episodes can become enraged at others for thwarting their plans (for example, by cutting off their credit cards), may put their family's reputation and savings at risk, and may endanger others with their behavior, such as driving too fast. Excessive and unrealistic confidence in grand schemes may lead to disastrous business deals and reckless behavior.

Finally, a manic episode may worsen to a psychotic state. For some, thoughts become delusional. They may hold onto false beliefs—such as the idea that they have extraordinary skills and powers—and cannot be convinced otherwise. For some, hallucinations (especially of voices) can occur.

Mania or Hypomania?

Clinicians refer to the varying presentations of bipolar disorder as the "bipolar spectrum." The fact that the disorder is more severe in some than in others has become incontrovertible. Indeed, there are now two subtypes of bipolar disorder. In a near-complete failure of imagination, the committee that named the two subtypes called them bipolar I disorder and bipolar II disorder. The distinction between the two is whether the person experiences a "full blown" manic episode or merely a "hypomanic" episode. Hypomania is much less severe.

Marjorie and Trent

Marjorie is a 34-year-old mother of two who recently purchased several hundred cuckoo clocks. Most are in the basement, but several dozen are in her minivan. She has been quite busy going from one apartment to another in the high-rise where she and her family live. She is convinced that she can sell them so that they will become rich and be able to move into a beautiful home with a huge garage (for the cars they will be able to afford) and a swimming pool. She has difficulty understanding her husband's concerns about how much money she has been spending. He works the evening shift at the factory and drives a snowplow during winter months, but he does not make much money, and she doesn't understand why he doesn't see this as an opportunity to change their lives. When pressed, she admits that she stayed up much of the night surfing the Internet for more great deals that could also be turned for tremendous profit. Even more concerning, which ultimately led to her being hospitalized, was that she had left the children (ages 3 and 7) in the minivan to follow and continue arguing with the local grocery store manager, who objected to her trying to sell the clocks in the store parking lot. The police were called, and Marjorie was located. She became quite irate and verbally abusive. The police called her husband and she avoided arrest only by agreeing to a referral to see a psychiatrist, who then admitted her to the hospital. Marjorie was diagnosed with bipolar I disorder.

Trent's most recent manic episode began, as they do for many people with bipolar disorder, with a night of sleeplessness. He finally got up to go to the bathroom, where he noticed that the bathroom needed painting, which he began to do. During a break to get some water from the kitchen, he noticed that the kitchen also needed painting, which he also began to do. You can guess what happened later that morning when he went to the living room to turn on the radio. His wife and he joked (I think it was a joke) that they waited to consult with his psychiatrist until after he had finished the various painting projects. Given that Trent's mania was not particularly pathological—and indeed his wife said he was very pleasant during these times—Trent was diagnosed with bipolar II disorder.

The full-blown manic episode is alarming to others. The person in a manic episode will be irrationally optimistic, overly talkative, fast moving and energetic, and have no need for sleep. He will have difficulty completing tasks because of a shortened attention span, and at the same time he will complain about others being overly slow, boring, and unimaginative ("How can you fail to see how great this idea is?"). Someone in a manic episode might endanger themselves or others (through reckless driving, inappropriate sexual activity, etc.) and damage vital parts of their lives (through excessive spending, inappropriate behavior towards bosses and coworkers, etc.). He might have to be hospitalized, against his will, to prevent such danger and damage.

In contrast, the person experiencing hypomania will usually not alarm other people (although they will notice the change in mood and be somewhat concerned). Someone in hypomania may actually be more productive and creative than usual, related to increased energy, but the person won't have difficulty completing tasks. She may display some talkativeness and decreased need for sleep but will recognize that these are happening. She will usually remain cheerful but can be serious when appropriate. She will have only occasional poor judgment and impatience but will know enough to apologize. She may be more sexually active, but it will be with her husband, not with strangers. Since the behavior is not as severe, someone in a hypomanic episode will likely not have to be hospitalized. She may damage her social reputation to some extent but will not likely endanger herself or others.

Be aware that hypomania is a spectrum and some episodes can lead to serious consequences, especially if the person is experiencing *excessive* self-confidence and optimism (which are likely) that border on conviction. In other words, hypomania can impair judgment, but since the hypomanic episode is subtler than a full-blown manic episode, others may miss the impaired judgment. As a result, they will not intervene. Being convinced that I will catch a fish tomorrow morning may lead me to waste a few hours on our lake. Being convinced in spending my retirement savings on a can't-miss/no-risk financial opportunity may lead to a much more serious problem.

Anosognosia

As suggested, an important difference between the two bipolar disorders is anosognosia. The person in a manic episode is much more likely than the person in a hypomanic episode to fail to recognize what is going on, that the behaviors and feelings are related to a mental illness. He is likely to get irritated with others who suggest something is wrong.

The person with bipolar II disorder who experiences a hypomanic episode may experience anosognosia for a while. After all, who is going to think that feeling great is a problem, much less go to a doctor and complain about it?

In both disorders, the manic and hypomanic episodes are usually followed by depression. The post-depression manic episode in bipolar I disorder will likely be accompanied by anosognosia, as the intense rush of good feelings and energy overwhelm the memory of the misery of depression. The subsequent hypomanic episode of bipolar II disorder, in contrast, is not as seductive, and the person is more likely to accept that the episode, though pleasurable, is a product of a disorder.

Diagnosis bipolar I disorder or bipolar II disorder

If someone exhibits any episode of mania, he or she will be diagnosed with bipolar I disorder. If the person only exhibits hypomania, then the diagnosis will be bipolar II disorder. However, the distinction between mania and hypomania can be subtle, making the decision of which to diagnose difficult for mental health professionals to make. The distinction is made based on impairment severity.

A psychiatrist I know summarized the difference as follows: "Someone in a hypomanic episode will buy 5 purses, whereas someone in a manic episode will call the factory in France and order 500, then get mad that they can't be delivered the next day." But what if the person orders 5 purses yesterday, 25 today, and 100 tomorrow? Compounding the difficulty of distinguishing mania and hypomania is that mania usually builds in severity over time. In other words, hypomania will precede mania.

For this reason, many psychiatrists give a preliminary diagnosis of bipolar II disorder with the notation that it will be changed to bipolar I disorder if the hypomanic episode devolves into a manic episode, that is, if things worsen considerably.

The Face of Bipolar Disorder

The face of someone in a bipolar depressive episode will be identical to that of someone with major depression. If you know the person, however, the difference in mood between the previous times you saw him will likely be striking. Someone in a major depressive episode will be depressed for months or even years. Someone in a bipolar depressive episode, however, will likely have seemed exceedingly cheerful not too long ago.

The severe stage of a manic episode is fairly difficult to miss. The person will be obnoxiously loud, talk fast without pause, not allowing others to say something, and respond with irritation, if not anger (and possibly aggressiveness), if concern is expressed about whether his mood and behavior may be abnormal. In other words, the person in a manic episode will laugh and yell, sometimes within moments of each other; will be difficult to interrupt; and will not entertain any reason to see that something may be wrong.

Someone experiencing hypomania might not worsen into full-blown mania (i.e., he has bipolar II disorder) or might indeed proceed to a manic episode (i.e., he has bipolar I disorder). The person in a hypomanic episode may appear charming and disarming. It is likely that others who are close to the person have begun to see some concerning signs, such as decreased sleep, increased energy, or irritability. However, if confronted about concerns by family, a health professional, or perhaps you, the person will be able to pull it together, smile politely, and shrug off the concerns.

Others in a hypomanic episode may be uncharacteristically impulsive, irresponsible, and careless. He may start missing or arriving late to meetings when he is usually prompt, because other things were distracting him. Or she may blurt out comments or questions during the meeting when she is usually reserved.

Other Noteworthy Things to Know About Bipolar Disorder

In previous decades, bipolar disorder was known as manic-depression. *Bipolar disorder* is the preferred term as it reflects the fact that persons with the disorder fluctuate between the two "poles" of mood. The disorder is characterized by cycling between severe highs (mania) and lows (depression).

The annual prevalence of bipolar disorder has been estimated at 1.1%, with about 60% having bipolar I disorder. Except for a family history of the illness, there are no identifiable risk factors. It affects men and women of all races and ages about equally (although the older one gets, the less severe the manic or hypomanic episodes manifest).

Worldwide epidemiological surveys suggest that the United States has a higher rate of bipolar disorder than other countries. Speculation as to why this is includes that there is less stigma attached to the disorder in the United States, meaning that survey respondents were more willing to respond affirmatively to questions about symptoms. Others have speculated that the United States has historically attracted immigrants who are somewhat overly optimistic, energetic, impulsive, and creative, which are some of the signs of hypomania.

In bipolar disorder, mood changes can be dramatic and rapid, but they are gradual more often than not. If the person experiences four or more episodes of mania and depression in any given year, the qualifier "rapid cycling" will be added to the diagnosis.

Mania then depression is the usual order of things. The manic or hypomanic episode will almost always precede the depressive episode. It is as if the mind and body respond to the elevated mood and excess energy by a punishing depression.

For most people with bipolar disorder, sleep problems are the most common signal that a period of mania is about to emerge. Sleep problems may be due to an increase in stress. Both sleep problems and stress are known triggers of relapse.

Major depressive disorder, which is characterized by low mood only or only one pole of the mood continuum, is therefore often referred to as "unipolar depression." However, there is no "unipolar mania" disorder. There is no experience of mania without subsequent depression.

Distress and Impairment

Whether the person with bipolar disorder will experience distress or not depends on whether she is in a depressive or manic episode. Impairment is inevitable, however.

Distress or Not

The distress in the depressive episode of bipolar disorder will be identical to that of a person with a depressive disorder. Distress will be moderate to profound. If the episode endures long enough, the person may forget what it feels like to be happy or content. As one may guess from a review of the symptoms (e.g., low energy, difficulty concentrating), depression causes decreased productivity at work or school. Depression's effects on self-esteem, motivation, and energy level often cause severe impairment in family relationships and friendships (see below).

In contrast, manic episodes are not typically accompanied by distress but can be associated with destructive impairment. The impairment within a manic episode tends to be related to diminished judgment, which affects social behavior in ways that can cause serious problems (such as financial difficulties) and embarrassment. The severity of impairment will be related, of course, to the severity of the manic episode, which in turn leads to categorization into a diagnosis of either bipolar I or bipolar II.

There is also cumulative distress associated with the enduring nature of the disorder (and with schizophrenia as well). Simply put, it is wearisome to cycle through mania and depression without any relief in sight. According to the National Institute of Mental Health, 10-20% of patients with bipolar disorder commit suicide. These are not all persons in a depressive episode. Instead, some have recently emerged from a depressive episode that followed a manic episode, and they are looking around at the damage they have inflicted on their lives. Indeed, the depressive episode is potentially safer than the recovery period, as the latter is often accompanied by increased energy levels, which makes acting on suicide impulses more easy (and thus more likely).

Impairment

Whereas distress is variable, depending on which pole of the mood disorder is being experienced, impairment in relationships and occupational functioning is probably inevitable in bipolar disorder.

Marital and family relationships can be severely damaged by bipolar disorder. Impulsive and risky behavior during manic episodes, such as spending large sums of money or staying away from home all night or for days at a time, will endanger trust and can devastate financial stability. At the other end of the mood spectrum, it can be quite difficult to know how to deal with someone who is profoundly depressed and perhaps talking about suicide. During both manic and depressive episodes, communication can become extremely difficult. During a manic or hypomanic episode, the person with bipolar disorder will interrupt and talk incessantly. The content of words will likely come across as unreasonable and self-centered. There is also a substantial risk of irritability and anger. Both mania and depression interfere with one's capacity to pay attention to what others are saying both aloud but also through body language and emotional expression.

Moreover, the transition from hypomania to mania to depression can be overwhelmingly stressful. Hypomania can imbue a relationship with laughter and love, whereas mania may infuse a relationship with annoyance, obnoxiousness, both potential and real aggression, recklessness, and danger. Then depression sets in, with attendant low energy, low self-esteem, and a desire for isolation.

Add to that the possible repeated hospitalizations, dealing with the legal system (related to arrests, appeals for rescinding foolish purchases, declarations of bankruptcy, and so forth), and explaining to friends why some irrational behavior (middle of the night phone calls, attempts at seduction) happened. It may not be surprising, then, to learn that some studies show that marriages will fail for nine in ten persons with bipolar disorder.

Marriages and families will also suffer because of work-related impairment. One study estimated that persons with poorly controlled bipolar disorder (whether due to nontreatment or poor response to treatment) lose over $600,000 in wages over their lifetime. This includes days lost from work, getting terminated from employment, and difficulty regaining employment.

Families are also severely and negatively impacted by having to care for a person with bipolar disorder. As with schizophrenia, family outings and leisure activities may prove unmanageable to organize and implement. Crises and health care visits can take a giant toll on the capacity of family members to be productive at work.

Finally, both families and work functioning may be impacted by comorbid substance use problems. One study found that about half of persons with bipolar disorder had a substance use disorder.

Special Considerations in the Treatment of Bipolar Disorder

Bipolar disorder and schizophrenia are considered serious and persistent mental illnesses (SPMIs), which by their very nature present unique challenges. To reiterate from the similar section in the previous chapter, there are special considerations in the treatment of bipolar disorder, including the potential need for crisis care, the advantage of combining medications with counseling, and resistance to treatment related to the illness itself.

Crisis Care

Persons with bipolar disorder will typically not experience symptoms at a consistent or steady level. Symptoms will fluctuate in severity over time. In other words, a person with bipolar disorder may require hospitalization when symptoms become severe. Someone in a manic episode may behave recklessly with finances (e.g., emptying bank accounts, running up huge amounts of debt) or endanger his own safety and perhaps the safety of others. After the manic episode ends, severe depression usually follows. (Note that the two mood extremes tend to run in parallel, meaning a mild manic episode will be followed by a mild depression and a severe manic episode by severe depression.) Someone in a severe depression may require hospitalization to prevent suicide.

Symptoms Can Interfere With Treatment Adherence

As with schizophrenia, the symptoms of bipolar disorder may deter medication compliance. Someone in the midst of a manic episode will feel great (or highly irritable) and be convinced that there is actually nothing wrong (or that the problem is those other irritating people). No one goes to the doctor complaining of being in a great mood, and the same goes for someone in the manic phase of bipolar disorder. As a result, the family members of the person in this state usually have to initiate treatment, usually over the person's objections (which will be strenuous in the case of full-blown mania and at least spirited in the case of hypomania).

Finally, it is estimated that about 40% of persons with bipolar disorder experience some level of anosognosia, which is the lack of awareness that symptoms are present, that they are problematic, or that they are caused by an illness (or all of the above). Anosognosia will obviously prevent someone from seeking or maintaining treatment.

Medications and Psychotherapy

Persons with bipolar disorder benefit most from a combination of medications and psychotherapy.

Medications. Different medications serve different purposes. Someone in the manic phase of bipolar disorder will be given medications to attempt to rein it in, such as an antipsychotic or an anxiolytic (antianxiety drug). Someone with bipolar disorder in a severe depressive episode might be given an antidepressant.

The typical goal of medications, however, is to prevent the reemergence of the illness or a relapse. Typically, manic episodes precede depressive episodes. Treatment thus entails medications called *mood stabilizers* that are intended to prevent manic episodes.

This makes treatment a challenge, however. In contrast to treatment of depression, where treatment causes the person to feel better, treatment of bipolar disorder is not intrinsically rewarding. Treatment is intended to prevent a manic episode (and a subsequent depressive episode). In other words, the medications are intended to maintain a stable mood.

As with other medical illnesses, such as high blood pressure, if medications are successful in managing the disorder, the person with the disorder may begin to think that medications are no longer needed. As a result, she may stop taking them, leading to a relapse.

Finally, many persons with bipolar disorder experience unpleasant medication side effects (including weight gain, drowsiness and fatigue, chronic thirst, and gastrointestinal problems), which also act as a disincentive to compliance with the treatment regimen.

Related to this, ongoing medication compliance is something that spouses and families, who have experienced the worst of manic and depressive episodes, strongly desire. Ongoing medication compliance might manifest as one's spouse or family members encouraging or coercing. This can cause a great deal of hurt feelings, resentment, and frustration.

Psychotherapy. To repeat the story from chapter 5, imagine that you have bipolar disorder but have been medication compliant. One day you mention to your spouse that you would like to purchase a new flat-screen television. Even if this is a great idea (because your current TV only covers half of the living room wall) or a completely ridiculous idea (because you just got a new TV last month), a typical spouse will respond with "Let's talk about it" or "Don't be ridiculous." But for you, who have bipolar disorder, your spouse responds, "Did you take your medication this morning?" This type of conversation happens frequently when a couple or family is dealing with bipolar disorder.

For this and other reasons, psychotherapy can be very beneficial to persons with bipolar disorder. A good therapist can help the couple or family develop the *extraordinary* skills (i.e., skills not ordinarily needed by most couples and families) to manage this type of situation (i.e., the constant need for vigilance against the mental illness and the desire to be treated like everyone else).

Psychotherapy can also prove very beneficial in encouraging proper self-management. Regular meeting with a therapist can focus on the importance of ongoing medication compliance. A therapist can work with a patient to help him understand that the pros (no more doing irrational things, no more awful depression) outweigh the cons (unpleasant side effects) of continuing to take medications.

Finally, psychotherapy can help the person with bipolar disorder learn stress management skills. Symptoms will worsen most predictably when the person with bipolar disorder is experiencing stress. Learning stress management skills and keeping one's life as consistent and predictable as possible are essential in managing this disease, making counseling or psychotherapy indispensable.

Encouraging Treatment-Seeking and Treatment Commitment

As with schizophrenia, encouraging someone with bipolar disorder to seek and then stick with treatment entails working with the person and the family. The key to working with the individual, for both you and the family, is to do so during the "normal" phase, when the person's reason and judgment are not impaired by mania or depression. This can be tricky.

Talking With the Individual

Given the distress and impairment issues, it should not come as a surprise to learn that patients with bipolar disorder voluntarily seek treatment when they are experiencing a depressive episode but don't see a need for treatment during a manic episode. The manic or hypomanic stage can be highly pleasurable. Beyond that, anything less than the manic or hypomanic stage can feel insufficient. People with bipolar disorder may be afraid to seek treatment because they are afraid that they will feel flat, less capable, or less creative.

Empathizing with this will help. Acknowledge the advantages of not taking medications, but emphasize that these fears must be weighed against the benefits of getting and staying well. (See chapter 11 box on motivational interviewing p. 178.) Do not hesitate to emphasize the necessity of treatment. A person may feel good while manic but may make choices that could seriously damage relationships, finances, health, home life, or job prospects. Someone with bipolar disorder experiences extreme highs but also devastating lows. Emphasizing the latter can help, especially if the prophylactic effects of ongoing medication compliance are likewise emphasized.

If the person is not in treatment, ask why. If treatment was recently ceased, be aware that this is a hallmark sign of early hypomania or mania.

If the person is in treatment, congratulate the person and be prepared to encourage the person to see that treatment will need to be ongoing.

Helping the Family

The family members of someone with bipolar disorder will benefit from encouragement and support, even if they do not ask for it. They might not reach out because mental illness in general is considered shameful and is stigmatized by much of society. But bipolar disorder, in particular, may lead the affected families to remain silent because of the impulsive and irrational behavior of the family member with the disorder during the manic phase. Knowing what you now know about the disorder, you can empathize with the family and help them to place the blame for the behavior where it belongs, that is, not with the person or with the family but with the disorder. The behavior is part of the disorder. It is unfortunate, and it must be dealt with (via apologies, explanations, court appearances); however, it is not voluntary nor is it shameful.

With all mental illnesses, it is important to assign blame correctly for certain behaviors and problems to the illness, rather than to the person. The person with depression does not want to be withdrawn and sad, but he cannot help it. These are signs that further treatment is needed. The person with schizophrenia does not want to deny having the disorder (anosognosia), but because of the disorder, half of those with schizophrenia will struggle to admit they have it (and resist treatment, say they don't need medications, and so forth). The person with bipolar disorder does love his family, but he cannot help but do impulsive and foolish things that damage the family while in the manic phase.

Hopefully, the family will understand this, and you should encourage them to do so. It may take a while for the reality of this to sink in. If the diagnosis of bipolar disorder is fairly recent and the spouse or family members are thus somewhat unfamiliar with the disorder, it will be natural for them to blame the person. After several years, it will become evident that the person truly cannot help herself when in the throes of mania. Encourage them to recognize that the behavior is due to the disorder.

Research clearly shows that persons with bipolar disorder do much better if their lives are predictable rather than hectic. Regular sleeping and eating habits are essential. (For example, a person with bipolar disorder should *never* take a job involving shift work, where some weeks she works one schedule and other weeks she works an entirely different schedule.)

In general, keeping stress to a minimum is highly important. Since life doesn't stop throwing stressful things at us, stress management skills (such as effective communications, problem solving skills, etc.) are essential. Psychologists and other mental health professionals specialize in training people in these skills, so encouraging them to seek couples or family therapy will be very helpful.

In other words, persons with bipolar disorder do much better (meaning they experience fewer relapses) if their families are supportive and encouraging. It must be acknowledged, however, that this is asking a great deal of the families. If the symptoms are severe or the disorder proves resistant to treatment, then the turmoil endured by and the damage inflicted upon the family can be tremendous.

Families coping with bipolar disorder may need occasionally to strongly encourage or perhaps even force the person into treatment. This will at least involve a call to the person's psychiatrist and may even involve calling the police. In the case of schizophrenia, the person in crisis is likely irrational and potentially dangerous, and getting the person hospitalized is somewhat straightforward (but not easy). In contrast, forcing someone with bipolar disorder into the hospital during a manic phase can be quite difficult. The person is not likely endangering his own or others' safety. The things being endangered are his and their livelihood, legal standing, marriage, reputation, or financial well-being. Endangering these, however, does not allow a medical doctor to hospitalize someone against his will. Forcing the issue is extremely stressful and is sometimes impossible. Incredible as it may sound, psychiatrists and families are often left in the position of waiting for things to deteriorate to the point of life endangerment before they can act.

To repeat from the previous chapter, at the very least, the families of individuals with bipolar disorder need your prayers, encouragement, support, and understanding. Encourage them in the loving work that they are doing. Openly admire their efforts, while being empathic with their struggles with this dreadful disorder.

Chapter 10

The Stress-Induced Disorders

"So do not fear, for I am with you;
do not be dismayed, for I am your God.
I will strengthen you and help you;
I will uphold you with my righteous right hand."
(Isaiah 41:10)

This chapter reviews post-traumatic stress disorder (PTSD) in detail. After reviewing the criteria for diagnosing PTSD, the chapter tries to give a sense of what someone with PTSD will look like. It then presents other noteworthy things about the disorder, followed by a review of treatment approaches and how to encourage persons with PTSD to seek treatment. The chapter ends with an overview of the adjustment disorders, which are mental health problems caused by difficulty adjusting to a challenging situation.

Post-Traumatic Stress Disorder (PTSD)

PTSD is the mental illness with the most descriptively accurate name. All that one needs to know about the disorder is right in the name. PTSD is a stress (or anxiety) disorder that develops after (post) a traumatic event. The trauma *causes* the disorder to develop. For the trauma to cause the disorder, the person must be exposed to it. There are varieties of both trauma and exposure.

Defining Trauma *and* Exposure

To qualify as traumatic enough for PTSD, the traumatic event must be death, serious injury, or sexual violation. The trauma may be actual experience or it may be a serious threat of such an experience. Sadly, trauma comes in many forms. For females, the most common traumatic events are sexual assault and domestic abuse. Trauma may be a person-to-person assault, such as a mugging or car jacking, or a random, impersonal, public event, such as a shooting at a school or place of work. It may be due to human behavior, such as motor vehicle accidents, industrial accidents, home fires, or plane crashes; or it may be due to natural disasters, such as floods, tornadoes, and earthquakes.

Exposure may be direct or indirect. It may be actual experience (i.e., being the victim of the traumatic event). On the other hand, it may involve witnessing the traumatic event happen to another person. For example, most of us did not know someone in the World Trade Center towers, but thousands of people did. The collapse of the towers was broadcast real-time and worldwide, and many witnesses who watched the demise of a loved one developed trauma-related mental illness. The trauma may be learning about a traumatic event that happened to a close family member or friend, or firsthand repeated or extreme exposure to aversive details of the traumatic event. Thus, the disorder may develop in the parents of murdered children, in spouses of rape victims, in emergency medical service workers, police, firefighters, search and rescue workers, and mental health professionals helping those with PTSD (who hear their stories over and over again).

The exposure may be brief, and the trauma may be a onetime event. Violent assault and motor vehicle accidents, for example, are usually sudden, brief events, but the trauma is so extreme that PTSD might develop. Alternatively, the exposure may last for months, and the trauma may be relatively modest in severity. Many military personnel hold noncombat support roles, such as maintaining helicopters, trucks, and tanks, but they are in a war zone. Repeated exposure to potential danger or to the damages of warfare can have a cumulative effect, and many of these individuals also develop PTSD.

The most certain cause of PTSD, however, is prolonged exposure to repeated, horrifying events. Military personnel who have combat roles, civilian emergency personnel such as firefighters and police officers, and others who experience or witness repeated trauma are at particular risk for the development of PTSD. As well, children who are neglected or sexually, physically, or verbally abused, which are traumatic experiences that tend to be both prolonged and terrible, are at high risk of developing PTSD.

Brett

I interviewed Brett, a veteran who had experienced intensive combat during his tours of duty. He voluntarily lived in a tent in the woods near his house—deep in the woods, that is. He did this because the cars and trucks driving by his home, where he lived with his wife, reminded him of the sounds of his trauma. In particular, when cars and trucks would screech their tires or, worst of all, when the trucks would explode with a backfire of the combustion in the engine's cylinders, "I instantly find myself back in combat." This would happen at almost any time, including at night. More than once he awakened his wife by trying to pull her under the bed while screaming at her to keep her head down. These flashbacks were obviously quite distressing to both him and his wife, and one weekend he moved to the deep woods where at least the sounds would not cause them.

The Symptoms of PTSD

PTSD comprises four types of symptoms. *Persistent reexperiencing* of the trauma may include recurrent nightmares and intensely distressing, intrusive, and sudden recollections (flashbacks). Sometimes flashbacks are triggered by external events, such as loud noises.

The person with PTSD may engage in *avoidance behavior,* wherein he attempts to limit his exposure to external reminders. For example, someone who has been in a severe car accident may avoid riding in cars, or at least avoid taking the highway on which the accident occurred. He will likely try to avoid thinking about or remembering the event whatsoever, and he may be so successful at this that he can legitimately state that he cannot remember key aspects of the event. Also, persons who have been through trauma understand that others probably do not want to hear about the trauma, such as the combat they experienced, the rape they endured, or the death they witnessed. As a result, persons with PTSD can come across as cold, distant, and withdrawn. Likewise, not thinking or talking about something terrible can be exhausting.

The third type of symptom is *negative cognitions and mood.* The person with PTSD is likely to be irritable and depressed. Previously enjoyed activities, such as bowling, hunting, going to parties, or watching sports on television, may be viewed with indifference or even scorn. This may lead to a distancing from others, including spouses and children, and a markedly diminished participation in activities.

Finally, some persons with PTSD exhibit increased arousal, which is related to extreme vigilance to cues that the trauma might occur again. (You can easily imagine how such "hypervigilance" would be a good thing during combat.) They will also experience guilt and depression, often related to not acting "perfectly" during the traumatic event. "If only I had seen the enemy sooner, things would have turned out differently" or "If I hadn't taken that route home, this would not have happened to me." Persons with PTSD may have difficulty falling or staying asleep. It is difficult to relax and fall asleep when nightmares await you on the other side. Arousal may be marked by more externally focused behavior, such as aggression towards others and reckless or potentially self-destructive behavior.

OIF/OEF and PTSD (Part 1: The Numbers)

At the time of this writing (August 2015), more than two million American military personnel had been deployed to Operation Enduring Freedom (OEF, the war in Afghanistan) and Operation Iraqi Freedom (OIF, which has been called Operation New Dawn since September 2010). Almost 6,000 coalition service members have been killed in these conflicts, and almost 42,000 Americans have returned from combat with physical injuries, many of them resulting in permanent disability.

Studies suggest that as many as one in six (over 300,000) of the US troops report symptoms that are consistent with PTSD, and as many as one in three will have either PTSD, depression, or a substance use disorder. In other words, the rate of psychological injury in OEF/OIF veterans is as high as the *lifetime* rate of all mental illnesses in the general public. Service members from OEF generally report less combat experience, and OEF veterans therefore seem to have a lower rate of PTSD than OIF veterans.

It should be noted that these are problems the troops acknowledge. The chances are very high that many troops are either minimizing or denying problems (see p. 159), which means that the real rate is probably even higher.

Distress and Impairment

PTSD is usually accompanied by extreme distress, as review of the symptoms would suggest. The distress of PTSD is intense and ongoing. This is because of the near-constant psychological presence of the traumatic event. It is always there, in the background, dominating the person's emotional functioning. Either the person cannot stop thinking about it or the person is putting forth great effort to avoid thinking about it. In both cases, it is the dominant force in the person's life, and the distress is usually palpable. It may be classic distress, including depression and anxiety, which come with the sense of hopelessness that the event will always be with the person, year to year, day to day, moment to moment. Or the distress may be irritability at the constant presence of the event, which the person does not want to think about anymore. Or the distress may be buried, observed as a change in the person who used to be active and outgoing but is now distant and disinterested, lest something or someone remind him of the event.

Moreover, PTSD leads to other mental illnesses, such as depression, anxiety, or substance use disorders. These comorbid disorders make treatment of PTSD more difficult, and they make impairment more severe.

The disorder can cause severe impairment. The person may have trouble returning to work or socializing with friends and loved ones. As noted above, one of the symptoms of PTSD is acting cold, distant, and withdrawn. This is not good for marriages, parent-child relations, and other close relationships, such as with friends and coworkers. A common observation of those close to the men and women who have served in combat is that they seem distant and withdrawn. Unfortunately, distancing oneself from others, suppressing the memory of traumatic events, and stifling negative emotions cause all sorts of problems.

Over the last decade, since the advent of the wars in Iraq and Afghanistan, the Department of Defense (DOD) and the Veterans Administration have expended great effort developing treatments for PTSD. As a result, we have numerous effective treatments.

OIF/OEF and PTSD (Part 2: Changing Military and Greater Stress)

The military trains men and women to be tough. Troops are trained to high levels of physical and psychological strength and stamina so that they can perform the duties expected of them. This has always been the case and probably does not surprise most readers. What may surprise readers are the demographic changes of the military in the last 25 years. These changes, as well as changes in their experiences in both noncombat and combat arena service, have exacerbated the likelihood of extraordinary strain and stress.

Currently, the US military is made up of 89% men and 11% women. Most service members (68%) are in their 20s (although almost half of all officers are in their 30s). Two-thirds are white; 16% are black; 10% are Latino; 4% are Asian; and 4% are listed as "other."

Unlike previous military operations, both OIF and OEF have relied heavily on members in one of the Reserves or the National Guard. These members are not full time, and are very likely to have regular jobs, and spouses and children. Half of service members are married, and half of the married have children (the majority younger than age 14). OIF and OEF have been characterized by both more frequent and longer-lasting deployments than past conflicts. Almost 40% of current services members have been deployed at least twice. As a result, employment problems, financial hardship, and family conflict are more likely to exacerbate the "routine" stress of serving in an occupation where one is expected to put one's life at risk.

The type of conflict has also changed. It is more random and unpredictable. In all the wars up to and including World War II, the great battles were named because they took place at a location for a confined period of time. For example, in the American Civil War, the Union and Confederate armies both marched on Gettysburg and clashed for three days in July 1863. During WWII, Patton's Third Army chased the German army until it got close enough to force it to turn and fight. In between battles, the armies ate, marched, sang, and slept knowing that they would probably have at least some forewarning ("The enemy army is near!") before the next battle.

OIF and OEF (and Vietnam to a large extent) have been quite different. They have been characterized by the guerilla tactics characteristic of insurgency warfare. Violence and death are not constrained to battle. Indeed, there are few battles at all, since there is no enemy army to seek out and destroy. Instead, one may be attacked anywhere at any time. Three in four of all injuries in these theaters of operation have resulted from explosions from roadside bombs, car bombs, suicide bombers, and other versions of the improvised explosive device (or IED, a term that did not exist prior to OIF).

Acute Stress Disorder

If someone experiences a traumatic event and develops symptoms of PTSD *immediately* or within a month, then the appropriate diagnosis is acute stress disorder. If the symptoms subsequently endure more than a month, or if they do not appear for at least a month (sometimes PTSD takes several months to manifest), then the diagnosis changes to PTSD.

The Face of PTSD

The several ways that PTSD may present depend on the traumatic event and on the person's subsequent environment.

The publicity of the event will influence how the person may appear. One face of PTSD is easily seen if you look. Some events, such as fires and accidents, are better publicized than others. Prayers may be offered for the person. Everyone talks about the event for a while, and the person who was traumatized is well known.

Another face of PTSD is more difficult to see because other traumas are more secret. The various types of abuse that men perpetrate on wives (domestic abuse) and that parents inflict upon children (physical, emotional, and sexual abuse) are not publicized and are not typically the focus of prayers.

The distress of those with the disorder is universal, however. Thus, the universal face of persons with PTSD is that they seem to be carrying a psychological burden. Moreover, they understand very well that no one wants to hear about it. This is partly true. Even those who are willing to hear about it at first eventually grow weary of hearing about it, which is a fact they don't want to communicate but which ultimately gets communicated anyway. On the other hand, however, it is partly not true. They may believe others don't want to hear about the event any longer, partly because they are tired themselves of thinking about it and of having it affect their lives so deeply.

Other Noteworthy Things to Know About PTSD

Perhaps one in ten persons will experience an episode of PTSD at some time in their life. PTSD can occur at any age, including children. Females seem to be at higher risk for PTSD. The most common cause of PTSD in females is sexual assault.

Male and female veterans are at equal risk of developing PTSD. Unfortunately, female service members may develop PTSD not due to combat experience but due to sexual assault or victimization within their own unit.

In general, the symptoms seem to be worse if the event that triggered them was deliberately initiated by a person, such as a rape or kidnapping, or involved loss of life of another person, as is commonplace in war.

OIF/OEF and PTSD
(Part 3: Underrecognition Leads to Undertreatment)

Since the elimination of compulsory service, men and women have joined the military for various reasons. Some have a desire to serve their country, while others see service as a good occupation or as a source of useful training. Although

PTSD is common and treatable, many military personnel are very reluctant to admit having a mental health problem. The reluctance is due to realistic if unfortunate concerns about how others will perceive them. Of particular concern is that other unit members and their superior officers will perceive them as weak or as incapable.

Unfortunately, the concern is realistic, as others often see persons with mental illness as weak. Most persons who are not in the service may be able to overcome fear of that reaction by telling themselves that people who matter, such as loved ones and close colleagues, will not perceive them that way.

In the military, however, the fear of being perceived as weak cannot be as easily mitigated. No employer, including the military, can guarantee that it will not terminate someone for mental health reasons. This is perhaps especially so for the military. In actuality, the functioning and fitness of military personnel who have a mental illness may indeed be seriously and perhaps permanently impaired. If someone cannot perform his job, he cannot remain in the job. The military routinely sends its personnel on arduous missions, armed with lethal weapons, to potentially dangerous places. Physical and mental toughness and durability are job requirements. Weakness is either overcome or purged during training, for the simple reason that weakness during combat can lead to calamity.

In short, admitting a mental health problem could be detrimental to the career aspirations of someone in the military. As a result, many military personnel experiencing mental health problems do not admit them and do not get them treated.

Encouraging Treatment-Seeking in PTSD

Some individuals with PTSD who do not receive care gradually recover over a period of years. However, treatment maximizes both the rate and likelihood of recovery. PTSD in persons who are receiving treatment has an average duration of approximately three years, compared to more than five years for those not receiving treatment. Whether treated or not, more than one-third of persons with PTSD never fully recover. Recovery is more likely if treatment begins fairly soon after the traumatic event, if the person has a supportive network of family and friends, and if there is not a comorbid mental illness, such as a substance use disorder.

Spouses and children are affected both by the traumatic event and by the subsequent illness. They may experience intense and enduring fear for the person, whether the trauma was short-lived (e.g., an accident) or ongoing (e.g., service overseas in a war zone). Family members will bear the brunt of the person's alienation towards others, which may cause them to feel anger toward the person with PTSD. It may be difficult to communicate with the person with PTSD, especially if she does not want to talk about the event (which most do not). The arousal that accompanies PTSD may lead to unusual, unforeseen angry outbursts or assaultive behavior. The person with PTSD may develop a substance use disorder.

Families should engage in counseling if anger, addiction, or problems in school or work become issues. Stress and anger management and couples therapy are possibilities. In any event, families should try to maintain their outside relationships and should continue to be involved in pleasurable activities. Readers should encourage treatment by informing the individuals and the families affected by trauma that treatments are particularly extremely effective for these disorders. Express empathy and understanding that treatment, which will require confronting the traumatic event, will be difficult. But encourage them to get treatment so that they can be happier and more content.

The Adjustment Disorders

A diagnosis of adjustment disorder is appropriate if someone develops emotional or behavioral symptoms in response to a stressful event or situation. (Note that PTSD is caused by a severely traumatic event.) The symptoms must be more severe than what would be expected for the type of event that occurred, and they likewise must be severe enough to affect the person's work or social functioning (i.e., to cause impairment).

Adjustment disorders begin within three months of the event or situation, and they end within six months after the stressor stops or is eliminated. If the adjustment problems continue after the event resolves, then another diagnosis (such as PTSD) is appropriate. Subtypes of adjustment disorder are specified according to the primary symptoms. Mental health professionals will thus diagnose "adjustment disorder with," and then specify the primary problem, such as "depressed mood," "anxiety," or "a mixture of behavioral and emotional problems."

OIF/OEF and PTSD (Part 4: Our Nation's Response, Your Response)

Veterans of OIF and OEF have unusually high rates of suicide. Recent research suggests that suicide is not directly related to service in OIF or OEF. Instead, suicide is related to mental illnesses caused by service in OIF or OEF, including PTSD, alcohol-related problems, depression, schizophrenia, and bipolar disorder.

The foremost issue is that current and former soldiers are disinclined to admit that they have a mental health problem and are reluctant, even if they admit it, to seek help. The dramatic and alarming increase in suicides among active and retired OIF and OEF military personnel is almost certainly related to reluctance to seek help. The Department of Defense, the Veterans Administration, and researchers and clinicians around the country are doing their best to understand and address this issue. But the issue is extremely complex.

The military needs its soldiers to be strong. It does not, however, want them to mistake strength for resignation to a life of psychological pain. The military wants soldiers to admit if they have a mental health problem, but the military may be forced to discharge someone from the military if the mental health problem is too severe.

Certain military leaders, both active and retired, believe the word *disorder* makes many soldiers who are experiencing PTSD symptoms reluctant to ask for help. They have urged renaming the disorder "post-traumatic stress injury," a description that they say is more in line with the language of troops and would reduce stigma. In the newest version of the DSM, the American Psychiatric Association recognized this but retained the word *disorder* anyway.

Your response should be empathic and realistic. The need to be strong in the military is realistic, but the perception of what strong means can be exaggerated. Tough and strong people feel stress, get scared, feel lonely, desire the companionship of others, miss their families, and sometimes cry. Tough and strong people, moreover, can learn to cope with stress, sadness, fears, and loneliness by talking with professionals with specific training in those issues. Mild to moderate problems can be alleviated before they become major problems. Also, the realistic but sometimes exaggerated sense of needing to be tough endures past service termination, or it endures because service never quite terminates. Recall that members of the Reserves or Guard, who finish a tour and go back to their families and lives, may be called up for another deployment. Being tough and strong with other soldiers is necessary. Being tough and strong (and distant, cold, angry, and imperious) with one's spouse, children, friends, and colleagues is not usually necessary and can cause serious marital, family, social, and occupational problems.

Events That Cause Adjustment Problems

Usually, but not always, the stressful event causing an adjustment disorder is an ongoing situation, such as financial problems, problems with a son or daughter's behavior, severe marital discord, or a severe setback, such as job loss. The event may be a one-time thing, however. For example, adolescents may develop an adjustment disorder after their parents' divorce, which is obviously an ongoing situation, or after a severe disappointment, such as not getting into their favored college, which is a onetime event. Many events are sudden and time-limited but have long-lasting repercussions. These may include natural disasters, such as an earthquake or tornado; events or crises, such as a car accident or being diagnosed with a major illness; or the death of a loved one.

It is not clear why the same stressful event causes some people to develop an adjustment disorder, whereas others seem to deal with it without difficulty. Predisposing factors that may put someone at risk for developing an adjustment disorder include intelligence, a family history (meaning genetic vulnerability) of anxiety and depression, and whether or not the person has adequate coping strategies. Therapy for an adjustment disorder tends to be fairly short-term, and it should focus on developing better coping strategies, such as reaching out to friends for support and finding available resources, such as temporary governmental assistance.

The Importance of Coping

For some individuals, problems overwhelm their capacity to cope. Either the problems are really big or their coping skills are insufficient, either in general or for that particular problem.

Consider the experience of millions of parents whose young child is diagnosed with type 1 diabetes. For this particular problem, they probably do not, at that time, have the capacity to cope. Medical caregivers treating the child know this, and they have many training sessions in which they will teach the parents (and child) how to manage the disease. The parents and child need to be taught new coping skills that they previously did not need (and which most children and parents will never need). Learning coping skills in these unusual situations is usually fairly straightforward, and quick.

Problem-Focused and Emotion-Focused Coping

Suppose you, like millions of other people each year, lose your job. You will probably then engage in both *problem-focused* coping and *emotion-focused* coping.

Problem-focused coping means trying to resolve the source of the stress. In this example, that means finding another job. You will update your resume, make phone calls, ask friends about possible positions at their places of work, and prepare for interviews. These are things you will do to resolve the problem.

Emotion-focused coping is also important. Losing a job will make you upset and angry. You may also feel anxious about finding another one. Many people have developed emotion-focused coping strategies for dealing with such tension (i.e., emotional stress). A long bike ride or a hard workout at the gym can release tension and anger. Talking with a sympathetic friend helps improve mood. Going for a walk, listening to music, working on a hobby, or taking a day off work are all good strategies for coping with stress.

In other words, if you lost your job, you could probably cope with it. You probably have the resources to find another job (resolve the problem), and you hopefully have the wherewithal to get through the emotional turmoil.

Such problems happen to many people, and they vary in their severity. Losing a job but then getting another is a stressful problem. Losing a job and not being able to find another is extremely stressful and may overwhelm someone's capacity to cope. Having a child diagnosed with diabetes is a stressful problem. Having a child diagnosed with severe autism is extremely stressful, as the child will likely not learn to care for himself.

Some individuals simply do not have the capacity to cope effectively with any stressful situation. Many faced with stress engage in unhealthy emotion-focused coping strategies, such as using drugs and alcohol or otherwise trying to suppress the emotion. Although most people are fortunate enough to have supportive friends and family to help them get through tough situations, others don't. Their friends have their own problems to deal with, and their family members simply don't know what to say or do that could help.

In any of these situations, the person might seek professional help to learn new coping strategies. They may ultimately be diagnosed with an adjustment disorder by the treating mental health professional.

Is the Diagnosis Legitimate? Is Treatment Necessary?

The reader might observe that the criteria for this disorder are broad enough to capture many people. For this reason, mental health professionals often use this diagnosis when a person does not have enough of the other symptoms for another diagnosis. (A formal diagnosis is necessary in order for treatment to be paid by insurance.) However, that is not the same as saying that the diagnosis is not justified.

First, it is likely the case that many people experience an adjustment disorder and that most do not ever seek professional treatment. It is likely that they adjusted to the situation on their own or with informal help, for example, by following the advice of a friend who went through something similar.

Also, since an adjustment disorder interferes with functioning, seeking treatment is justifiable. If someone cannot adjust to the situation, then a more severe mental illness may develop. Moreover, mental health professionals have many tools and strategies to help persons deal with situations that are overwhelming them.

Finally, when the mental health professional diagnoses an adjustment disorder, she is declaring that the disorder is relatively mild and will be short-lived but that it is nonetheless causing impairment and therefore qualifies for treatment.

Chapter 11

The Substance Use Disorders, the Eating Disorders, and the Impulse Control Disorders

"Who has woe? Who has sorrow? Who has strife?
Who has complaints? Who has needless bruises?
Who has bloodshot eyes? Those who linger over wine,
who go to sample bowls of mixed wine.
Do not gaze at wine when it is red, when it sparkles in the cup,
when it goes down smoothly! In the end it bites like a snake
and poisons like a viper. Your eyes will see strange sights,
and your mind will imagine confusing things.
You will be like one sleeping on the high seas,
lying on top of the rigging.
'They hit me,' you will say, 'but I'm not hurt!
They beat me, but I don't feel it!
When will I wake up so I can find another drink?'"
(Proverbs 23:29-35)

I admit that at times the Bible is not entirely clear to me. There are some passages that I have difficulty understanding. Like the eunuch encountered by Philip, I need to have them explained to me. Chapter 23 of the book of Proverbs is not one of those passages. In all the psychological and psychiatric explanations that I have heard or read, I have not come across a finer explanation of the problems associated with the misuse of alcohol.

Hopefully this chapter will help you to understand better the disorders related to impulsive behavior (i.e., the substance use, eating, and impulse control disorders). By better understanding them, you can help more effectively. Each disorder is reviewed, followed by a description of the distress and impairment typically caused by each. The various presentations (faces) of the disorders are presented, as are some treatment-related issues. The chapter begins with an overview of the similarities between these disorders, which led to them being grouped into the same chapter.

Overview of the Disorders

These three types of mental illness have some common core issues that make treatment particularly challenging, including the following:

Behavioral Problems

These disorders are due to problematic *behavior.* The substance use disorders (SUDs) are problems in the misuse of substances, the eating disorders are problems associated with eating, and the impulse control disorders are problems with self-control.

Minimalizing and Externalizing

Most persons with these disorders will likely express resistance to the idea that there is anything wrong. Earlier, *anosognosia* was described as the lack of awareness of being ill that some persons with bipolar disorder and schizophrenia have. For persons with the substance use disorders, eating disorders, and impulse control disorders, there is not pure ignorance that anything is wrong. Rather, they recognize that others are upset by their behaviors, which they fully realize are out of the ordinary. Rather, they minimalize and externalize. They don't accept that the problem is all that bad (instead, it's that his wife exaggerates the problems caused by drinking) or that it resides within them (parents and doctors overstate the dangers of losing weight; others cause him to lose his temper). If the woes, sorrow, and strife are not their fault, they should not be held responsible for making things better.

Lack of Distress Reduces Motivation for Treatment

Persons with these disorders tend not to experience distress, except when others get upset with them. As a result, they often lack motivation to seek treatment. It is estimated, for example, that 90% of persons with a substance use disorder (SUD) do not seek or obtain any treatment. When asked why not, the vast majority states that they did not recognize they needed it.

Most frequently, they seek treatment when their disorder causes severe enough problems in either relationships or roles that others feel compelled to force the issue. For example, an alcoholic may seek treatment when his spouse threatens to leave, when his boss threatens to fire, or when the judge threatens to imprison. Even then, they may not acknowledge that they have a problem. They may seek treatment only to satisfy another person. They are not at all convinced that they have a problem, but if the "old lady" or the "awful parents" or that "jerk of a boss" insists, they have no choice.

The Challenge to Care

These issues underscore another common factor among these disorders: persons with these disorders can challenge our capacity for compassion. It can be difficult to understand why they do what they do and why they don't stop. They tend to minimize the problems and to blame others, and persons with these disorders will likewise lie about how they are doing and about what happened.

To be blunt, it can be difficult to like them. The challenge to remain caring is true for friends, colleagues, and families, but it is also true for health care professionals.

Specialty Caregivers

For these reasons, to treat these disorders requires special training. Essentially all mental health professionals are qualified to treat anxiety and depression, but there is special training required to treat the substance use, eating, and impulse control disorders. (You may keep this in mind when referring someone with one of these disorders for treatment. On the other hand, you don't have to keep this in mind, since the first nonspecialist professional the person sees will refer him or her to a specialist.) These specially trained clinicians learn to take special care to remain objective, empathic, and invested in the person's well-being. They learn that these individuals act this way because of the disorder, not because they are actually unlikable. Many of these clinicians have themselves been diagnosed with and treated for the disorder in the past. For example, it is very common for a substance abuse counselor to be in recovery from an SUD himself.

The Substance Use Disorders (SUDs)

The Bible informs us that wine was given to people for good. Noah planted a vineyard after the flood. The first miracle of Jesus was changing water into wine. Jesus used wine when he established the new covenant. Wine was given to people for good, but the Bible has numerous examples of its improper use, including Lot and King Saul. As noted in Proverbs, those who consume excessively ("linger over wine") will likely encounter many problems.

Substance use disorder (SUD) is the umbrella term for alcohol and drug use disorders. Substances are psychoactive, which means they affect thinking, feelings, and behaviors.

Diagnosing Someone With a Substance Use Disorder

The SUDs are unique in that they are diagnosed regardless of the subjective report of the person. Mental health professionals evaluating someone for an SUD do not ask about feelings or thoughts. Instead, they will focus almost exclusively on the effects of the use of the substance. Someone can be diagnosed with an SUD if and only if using the substance causes *problems.* The problems caused by use may be physical (problems with health), social (problems with colleagues, friends, and family), or occupational (problems fulfilling work or school responsibilities).

Distress (or Not), but Definitely Impairment

People who are experiencing an SUD may experience distress about their situation, including feelings of guilt, shame, and low self-esteem. However, it is probably more common for someone with an SUD to feel no distress about the drug or alcohol use itself but rather about the effects of that use. Paradoxically, such feelings may encourage the person to use even more, in order to numb the negative feelings or to forget the problems. Hopefully, instead, distress will encourage treatment-seeking. Ultimately, however, some persons with SUDs experience no distress whatsoever.

SUDs cause varying levels of impairment. Mental health professionals must make note of the severity when making the diagnosis and treatment recommendations. The SUDs are all categorized as either "mild," "moderate," or "severe." Severity ratings increase as the person increases the intensity and frequency of use and as problems caused by that use escalate.

Biological Changes

As use gets more severe and prolonged, the individual's body goes through dramatic changes. Extensive substance use causes alterations to the brain, which has three consequences. First, the person will experience symptoms of withdrawal when he stops using. Withdrawal can be extremely unpleasant. As stated in Proverbs, in the case of withdrawal from intense and prolonged alcohol use, delirium tremens (DTs) cause auditory and visual hallucinations: "Your eyes will see strange sights, and your mind will imagine confusing things." DTs also lead to intense anxiety, disorientation, and muscle tremors: "You will be like one sleeping on the high seas, lying on top of the rigging." An individual with a severe SUD will experience intense cravings for the substance, sometimes related to a desire to eliminate symptoms of withdrawal: "When will I wake up so I can find another drink?"

Second, the person will exhibit tolerance, which refers to the biologically based need for increasing amounts of a substance to get the desired effect. Hence the not uncommon observation that a large dose of alcohol that would make most of us dangerously intoxicated has no seeming effect on the heavy drinker.

Finally, the person with a severe SUD may experience unintended excessive use in terms of either amount of substance or time spent using (i.e., binge episodes). Research suggests that binges are caused by a brain change in which the person is no longer able to perceive the amount being consumed or the amount of time passing.

Psychosocial Impairment

The more severe the SUD, the more the person rearranges his life around using. Someone with a severe SUD will spend a great deal of time doing things associated with using the substance. These activitities include spending a lot of effort trying to obtain the substance, especially if the substance is illegal, such as cocaine, marijuana, and heroin. They include extensive periods of using (going on a "binge") and needing extensive time to recover from use. In direct reference to this, the psychosocial problems caused by spending so much time either seeking to become intoxicated, being intoxicated, or recovering from intoxication include impaired relationships, problems at work or school, and problems with the legal system.

Relationship impairment includes problems with one's family, due to arguments, abusive language and behavior, passing out on the floor, missing important events, and so forth. Missing one of your child's basketball games because you are intoxicated might be an indication of a "moderate" alcohol problem. If your child doesn't bother to tell you about upcoming games anymore, knowing that you won't bother showing up, this may indicate a more serious problem.

Occupational impairment at work or at school includes arriving late, decreased productivity, and absenteeism.

A diagnosis of SUD is always appropriate if the person runs into *legal problems* related to use. Anyone arrested for drunk driving essentially automatically meets criteria.

Finally, a diagnosis of SUD is appropriate if the person exhibits *self-care impairment.* This includes use that causes danger to one's self, such as being intoxicated while walking along a busy street or while using a chain saw. Picking fights with people while drunk ("They hit me and I've got the bruises to show for it, but I didn't feel anything!") counts as meeting this criterion. Bodily damage, such as liver or brain damage, also counts as meeting this criterion.

Mild, Moderate, or Severe Impairment?

The distinction between mild, moderate, and severe SUDs can be a difficult distinction. The distinction is made according to impairment.

Being late to your child's soccer game because you are hungover may be a "mild" alcohol use problem. Missing one of your kid's soccer games because you are intoxicated may be an indication of a "moderate" alcohol problem. If your kid doesn't bother to tell you about his upcoming games any more, knowing that you won't be there, this might indicate a "severe" problem.

Getting drunk and then sick on a regular basis at college may indicate a "mild" problem. Occasionally missing assignments or classes at college or at work may be a "moderate" problem. Dropping out of college or getting fired indicates a "severe" problem.

The Face of Substance Use Disorders

The SUDs have many different faces among the three distinct phases of the disorder. The disorder starts with the phase of denial, when the person is using to the extent that problems are appearing but the person denies that the problems are there. (Again, an SUD is diagnosed if the substance use causes problems.) The next phase is the acknowledgement phase, which may or may not involve attempts to quit or moderate the substance use, and a subsequent phase may then include (or not) treatment attempts. The final phase is typically referred to as "recovery," when the person is no longer using the substance but remains at risk for relapse into using.

The Faces of Denial

Probably every person with an SUD goes through a phase of denial. The person who drinks too much or who uses drugs in an unhealthy fashion will not realize this right away. Instead, he will rely on family or friends to tell him that they are concerned about the bad things the use seems to be causing. It is quite normal and natural, and therefore should be expected, that the person will deny that things are bad.

In other words, the first face of the first phase of SUD is a mix of surprise, agitation, irritation, and denial. Hopefully, the face of consternation and self-reflection follows that face. The manner in which the person is approached at this point is very important (see p. 178).

An alternative face at this phase is more classical denial, wherein the person has experienced many problems associated with her substance use and probably has been confronted about these problems already. But the person will nonetheless insist on minimizing the problems or outright denying the problems are due to substance use. This person is more likely to react to your concern with feigned surprise or pretend amusement, after which she is likely to avoid you (which she will justify by telling others that you are unkind) lest you confront her again.

The Faces of Acknowledgement

Acknowledgement of a problem with substance use is a good thing. It is the first step towards attempting to make things better, with resultant (although probably not immediate) improvement or recovery. But acknowledgment does not always lead to an attempt to change.

I vividly recall my experience 25 years ago with one of these faces. A gentleman had been brought by ambulance to the emergency room because he had been found unconscious on the street. I was younger then, and I may have looked somewhat innocent and naïve (although I did dry behind my ears every morning before reporting to work). Upon awakening in the ambulance, the gentleman insisted they let him go, but they were obligated to bring him to the hospital. When I entered his room, he was happy to chat and happier to inform me that he regularly used "speedballs" (heroin and cocaine mixed) and had no intention of stopping. As I tried to talk him into accepting a referral for treatment, he repeatedly smiled broadly while suggesting that I do anatomically impossible things to myself. Simply put, like many persons with SUDs, he knew exactly what he was doing and the damage it was causing him, but he was not experiencing any distress whatsoever. He was not interested whatsoever in treatment intended to get him to stop using.

Ironically, this type of person who acknowledges an SUD is easier to deal with than the more common type. The more common type wakes up after a night (or week) of intoxication and expresses immense remorse and regret. She swears she has learned her lesson, and she promises things will be different in the future. Then she does it again. That is, for many of us, the honesty of the "hardcore" and impenitent person with an SUD is preferable to the one who is apologetic, minimizing, and ultimately dishonest. It is difficult to maintain patience with a person who repeatedly promises to quit using but then uses again and again.

You are likely to have negative reactions to persons with SUDs. They can be a challenge for the best of us, but we are obligated to rise to that challenge. One of the most unlikeable persons in the Bible was a man named Saul, who hunted down and killed the followers of Christ. This chief of sinners knew firsthand about the grace of forgiveness and underserved love that others bestowed upon him. We reach out to these persons and try to help them because they are no different than we, "for all have sinned and fall short of the glory of God" (Romans 3:23).

I recommend three attitudes simultaneously. Acknowledge that you are repulsed and perhaps angered by the behavior, recognizing that the anger is because you care about the other person. (We don't get angry with people we don't care about.) Do not express your anger and disgust, as that will not help. Be honest that you are upset if the person asks. At the same time, attribute the behavior to the disorder.

The Faces of Treatment

There are many faces of treatment. There is the hopeful face, where the person is fearfully hoping that treatment will help. There is the hidden ambivalent face, where the person enters treatment with a seemingly positive attitude, smiling and so happy to be there and getting the help he really needs, but secretly harbors resentment that others dare think he needs it. There is the veteran face, which has been in treatment many times previously and knows the drill well enough to direct it. (Many recovered persons in fact do become SUD specialists.)

There are many faces of treatment, but when talking to someone in treatment, *you* should display only one. Any effort to eliminate an SUD through formal treatment (i.e., seeing a mental health professional) should be enthusiastically embraced by others, even as we acknowledge that treatment is ultimately more likely to fail than succeed (see following paragraphs below). That is because the faces of treatment are impossible to distinguish from one another and from the face of the committed person who is intent on putting the SUD behind him. Assume that is the face you are encountering, and try to be positive and encouraging.

The Faces of Recovery

Persons who have recovered from an SUD are likely to need treatment for a comorbid mental illness that was being "self-medicated" by the substance use. This might be depression, an anxiety disorder, bipolar disorder, or a psychotic disorder. Without treatment for the newly discovered mental illness, the person will be at serious risk of relapse.

The ideal face of recovery is the person who has moved beyond shame and into acceptance. This person will accept the reality of the SUD and all the damage that it caused in relationships. The person will speak openly of ongoing recovery efforts, such as attending meetings. In actuality, openly speaking of ongoing recovery efforts is an aspect of ongoing recovery.

Self-Help Groups

Many mental health professionals who provide treatment for SUDs often encourage or insist that the person attend informal treatment, commonly known as self-help groups. For the SUDs, AA (Alcoholics Anonymous) and NA (Narcotics Anonymous) are the most well known. These are sometimes called 12-step programs because they organize around 12 steps to recovery.

Attendance at self-help groups during formal treatment is a common request, and attendance after formal treatment is almost always expected. This is related to three facts about SUDs. First, persons with SUDs feel intense shame about their pathological behavior, and attending a group with other persons who have recovered from SUDs reduces the sense of isolation and shame. It also enhances a sense of hope that one can recover, as these others have. Second, the person trying to recover from an SUD has many friends whom he can no longer see, because they are continuing to use. Attending a self-help group provides a new community.

Finally, someone with an SUD will need the encouragement and skills provided by treatment for longer than the usual treatment lasts. Self-help groups can provide ongoing encouragement and reinforce the skills needed for recovery.

Some Christians are uneasy with groups that follow the 12-steps, because the steps explicitly reference "God as we understand him" and a "Power greater than ourselves." In my opinion, a Christian can derive benefit from AA or NA. Although the groups are filled with persons with different religious beliefs or with no religious beliefs at all, members are not to question or challenge the beliefs of others. Indeed, what 12-step programs profess has some similarities to what Christians confess. Twelve-step programs profess that persons with SUDs are captive to the substance (as Christians by nature are captive to sin); that they are powerless, in and of themselves, to stop using; and that the using is destroying their lives.

Other Noteworthy Things to Know About the Substance Use Disorders

A substance use problem is diagnosed if substance use causes problems. It is really as simple as that. However, the problems that substances cause, especially alcohol, are far from simple.

According to the National Institute of Drug Abuse (NIDA), drug abuse (counting illegal drugs, tobacco, and alcohol) costs the US economy approximately $600 billion each year ($193 billion for drugs, $235 billion for alcohol, and $193 billion for tobacco) due to increased health care costs, crime, incarceration and enforcement, and lost productivity.

For tobacco, the costs are about evenly divided between health care costs for tobacco-related diseases and lost productivity because of those diseases. For drugs, the main costs are lost productivity and interdiction efforts (the "war on drugs"). Health care costs related to illegal drugs are about 5% of the total cost.

Alcohol is much more commonly available (being legal) than drugs, and as a consequence is much more costly. Health care is about 13% of the total cost. Since alcohol is not illegal, there is relatively little money spent on interdiction. To what then are the costs attributed? Alcohol is a factor in one-third to one-half of all suicides, homicides, physical assaults, rapes, and accidental deaths (fatal motor vehicle accidents, falls, fires, and drowning). It is also a factor in most cases of domestic violence.

A Simple Preliminary Assessment of SUDs: CAGE

CAGE is an acronym of four questions that can be asked to evaluate whether the person may have an SUD. An affirmative response to any of these questions should lead to a referral for a more thorough evaluation.

1. Have you ever felt you ought to **CUT DOWN** on drinking or drug use?
2. Have you ever felt **ANNOYED** at someone who questioned or criticized your drinking or drug use?
3. Have you felt **GUILTY** about your drinking or drug use?
4. Have you ever had a drink or used drugs as an **EYE OPENER** (i.e., first thing in the morning) in order to steady your nerves or to get rid of a hangover?

Treatment Considerations

The first thing to note about treatment is that it is not always necessary. Many persons with SUDs are able to quit without treatment. This was observed on a large scale in the Vietnam War. Many of the soldiers who served in Vietnam extensively used drugs. Researchers and clinicians expected that when the soldiers returned to the United States, there would be an epidemic of problems related to ongoing addictions. To their surprise, the vast majority of soldiers were able to quit without any help whatsoever. Subsequently, researchers have discovered that this self-quitting phenomenon is fairly common.

Most persons with SUDs will require some treatment, however. The typical treatment episode entails monitoring by a medical doctor, as well as some version of counseling in conjunction with ongoing involvement in a self-help group, especially a 12-step program. These programs are useful because they allow persons with SUDs to interact closely with others who have had similar problems, which helps reduce the shame associated with the problem. They also allow them to see that others also struggle to maintain sobriety (with varying degrees of success). Twelve-step programs are somewhat controversial. My professional opinion is that they are inherently neither good nor bad but that some specific programs are good and some specific programs are bad. Thus, it is advisable to check the reputation of any specific program before recommending it to a parishioner looking for one to join.

Formal treatment is more likely to be necessary as the SUD becomes more severe. Success rates in the treatment of mild to moderate SUDs are fairly good. Persons who enter treatment at these stages can fairly readily learn to quit entirely (i.e., attain abstinence) or to use the substance without engendering problems (i.e., learn to control their use).

Treatment of severe SUDs, in contrast, is much less likely to be successful. It is estimated that perhaps 10% of persons with severe alcohol use problems enter treatment in any given year. Over 50% of patients who enter treatment drop out before it is completed, whereas about 30% of those who begin treatment remain abstinent for a year after treatment. On the other hand, the best predictor of successful resolution of an SUD is prior treatment. It seems that each time someone enters treatment, he or she learns something until, eventually, treatment succeeds for that person. Thus, the best advice to offer someone with an SUD who has tried treatment in the past is "Go back. Hang in there. Keep trying."

Even if a person with a severe SUD successfully quits, he or she will be in danger of relapse. For this reason, the SUDs are never said to be "cured." Rather, a person who has successfully halted use of a substance will probably continue to refer to himself as an alcoholic or addict, or more likely as "in recovery." This emphasizes the need for constantly engaging in behaviors that promote the maintenance of sobriety.

An Effective Way to Approach Someone Who May Have an SUD: Motivational Interviewing

Bill Miller is a psychologist who developed an effective way to approach someone who is exhibiting signs of an SUD. The approach is intended to minimize the risk of upsetting the person (making him defensive) while maximizing the likelihood that he will consider the need to do something about the problem. The approach is called motivational interviewing. It emphasizes a loving, affirmative attitude, wherein the person is treated with respect and concern, but also emphasizes an honest, unflinching, and open discussion of concerns.

Collaborate, don't confront. Approach the person in a spirit of collaboration, and avoid any confrontation (even if the other person seeks to turn the conversation in that direction, which might happen in an effort to derail what you are trying to do). You are not to be an "expert" in what the other person is doing wrong, but, rather, you are one of the two of you who have a relationship. Emphasize the importance of the relationship (i.e., the other person) to you.

Be empathic. This is the most important and essential thing one person can do for another. (It is the *sine qua non* by which psychotherapy works or fails.) Empathy means seeing the world through the way the other person sees the world. It means understanding and accepting how the other person is feeling (but not necessarily feeling the same way). The other person feels picked on and misunderstood. You don't necessarily agree that such feelings are "correct" but you don't have to agree. You do have to understand and accept that he feels that way, however. Empathy will enable the other person to feel like he has been heard and understood, which strengthens your relationship. This, in turn, makes it more likely he will be honest in expressing other things, as well as more likely he will listen to you as you express concerns.

Frame concerns as discrepancies. Tell the person about your concerns in a "this way, but that way" fashion. Frame concerns as a mismatch between "where you are right now with your health, your relationships, and your work" and "where you want to be." The person is a good guy. He wants to be a good dad, a good husband, a good friend, and a good worker. In a collaborative, empathic fashion, conduct an examination of the discrepancies between (a) his current behaviors and situations and (b) what he wishes to be doing, what he values, and what he hopes for the future. Encourage him to recognize that if things continue as they are, then things will continue as they are.

Expect resistance, but don't fight it. The person won't like the conversation, regardless of how collaborative and empathic you are. He will resist. Don't argue and don't confront. Instead of fighting the resistance, roll with it. Empathize with the resistance using statements such as "I realize this is hard to hear" and "I know you don't really see it like this." Perhaps most important, emphasize that the choice is his. Emphasize the person's autonomy, which is indisputable in any case. (If he doesn't choose to change, he won't change.) However, don't forget to emphasize that the bad situation will continue if things don't change, and encourage the person to realize his capacity to change if he chooses.

The Eating Disorders

The eating disorders involve extreme emotions, attitudes, and behaviors involving weight and food. Anorexia nervosa, bulimia nervosa, and binge eating disorder are the three eating disorders to be discussed. They share some qualities, but they are distinct. As we will see, a person can be diagnosed with only one of the three eating disorders.

Each year, millions of people in the United States are affected by a serious and sometimes life-threatening eating disorder. The vast majority are women who are either in their adolescence or young adulthood. The two most common eating disorders are anorexia nervosa and bulimia nervosa.

Anorexia Nervosa and Bulimia Nervosa

Persons with anorexia nervosa and bulimia nervosa are extremely concerned with body shape and weight. They evaluate their self-worth on their shape and weight, and especially the latter. Persons with these disorders will start their days well or poorly—they will leave home in a good mood or a bad mood—depending on the number displayed by their scale. Moreover, they will openly admit this preoccupation.

Because of the preoccupation, persons with anorexia nervosa and bulimia nervosa engage in a long-standing pattern of unhealthy behaviors involving food. To be specific, they attempt to control their weight and shape by engaging in strict dieting. As a result of the dieting, they experience intense hunger.

Anorexia Nervosa

Persons with anorexia nervosa ignore their intense hunger and continue to diet to the point of extreme weight loss. They nonetheless will exhibit a distorted body image (an unrealistic perception of body shape). Indeed, one of the most frightening aspects of the disorder is that people with anorexia continue to claim that they look fat and need to lose more weight, even when bone-thin. A lack of body fat will cause another prominent symptom, which is that prepubescent girls will not develop a normal menstrual cycle and girls already menstruating will cease doing so.

Kathryn the Runner

Kathryn lost a lot of weight over a nine-month period, beginning when she was 14. Like most American girls, when she entered adolescence, she became obsessed with her body's appearance. She had little self-confidence and life was becoming more stressful. An only child, her parents had recently separated, and her mother told her they were likely to have to move. Kathryn looked at the shiny, happy, thin people in magazines, on TV, and online, and she wondered if getting into better condition and losing weight might help her feel better about her life. She first cut out fats, then carbs, and soon after would only eat cottage cheese and probiotic yogurt from the dairy group. Her main diet consisted of rice cakes, apples, and carrots. She began to lose weight and life started looking better. Her desire to look and feel better soon gave way to a desire to achieve perfection. Her growth spurt stopped at 5'4". Her weight dropped from a healthy 120 pounds to 87 pounds. She started running and worked up to between 5 miles (on a "lazy day") and 12 miles (on an "okay day"), but she always wished she could run farther.

Her hair began to fall out, her skin cracked and sometimes bled, and her monthly periods stopped. Twice she fainted in the shower after a long run.

Yet, she still didn't believe she was thin enough. The girl she saw in the mirror every morning was fat and unattractive. The girl was lazy and needed to become more perfect.

When her mother took her to the doctor for a checkup prior to fall track season at school, the doctor took one look at Kathryn and sent her to the emergency room for a psychiatric evaluation. She was hospitalized immediately, first on a medical floor to stabilize her heart (which had become arrhythmic) and then on the psychiatric floor, where she spent two months regaining weight and obtaining therapy for anorexia nervosa.

Bulimia Nervosa

In contrast to anorexia nervosa, persons with bulimia nervosa "succumb" to hunger caused by intense dieting and engage in binge eating, which is defined as the consumption of an unusually large amount of food within a short period of time. The food is often sweet, high in calories, and easy to eat quickly. People with bulimia nervosa usually report feeling a lack of control during eating binges. During the binge, the food is eaten secretly and rapidly, with little chewing.

Combining the extreme weight and shape concern with such an intense violation of their diet (i.e., binge eating) leads individuals with bulimia nervosa to feel extreme guilt and shame. The binge-eating episode is thus usually followed, fairly immediately, by compensatory behaviors to counteract the caloric content of the ingested food. The guilt caused by the binge-eating episode will later lead the person with bulimia nervosa to engage even more assiduously in dieting behavior, setting off the diet-binge-compensate cycle once again.

The most commonplace compensatory behavior is self-induced vomiting, in which the person attempts to "purge" her body of the consumed food. Another type of purging behavior is to take drugs to stimulate bowel movements and urination. Some persons with bulimia nervosa engage in nonpurging compensatory behaviors, such as fasting and dieting, taking drugs that supposedly speed up metabolism, and exercising frantically. It has been observed that persons with bulimia nervosa have an unusually high rate of cigarette smoking, which is likely because nicotine suppresses appetite. In the DSM, persons with bulimia nervosa are categorized as either the purging or nonpurging subtype.

Amanda's Eating Habits

At age 25, Amanda is entering her seventh treatment episode (at seven different clinics) for bulimia nervosa. A cardiologist, to whom her gynecologist sent her after detecting heartbeat irregularity, prompted this particular referral. The cardiologist told her that her heart is being damaged by her behavior.

Since age 18, her first year of college, Amanda has revolved her life around binge eating and vomiting. She estimated that the worst it ever got was 10-15 times daily.

Presently, she binges and purges 3-4 times each day after work, but more frequently on the weekends. She stops by a grocery store on the way home (a different store each day of the week so that no one notices her buying so muchfood). She puts the food in the kitchen, takes some to her bedroom to eat it, and then returns to the kitchen for more. When she feels overly full, she forces herself to vomit, then returns to the kitchen. This pattern is repeated until she consumes the entire purchase. The amount of food she purchases varies according to how much tension she feels from work. After the episode, she feels intense shame.

Binge-Eating Disorder

Binge-eating disorder is the most common eating disorder. A person will be diagnosed with binge-eating disorder if he or she engages in binge eating, as defined here, without subsequent compensatory behavior. As with bulimia nervosa, binge eating is defined as eating an unusually large amount of food in a defined period. The episode is usually associated with intense emotional distress, most especially shame, and a sense of loss of control.

Which Disorder?

As shown in the box on the next page, there is a great deal of overlap between the eating disorders. In both anorexia nervosa and bulimia nervosa, the person is preoccupied with weight and shape and engages in unhealthy behaviors to try to control them. In both bulimia nervosa and binge-eating disorder, the person engages in binge eating.

However, a person can be diagnosed with only one eating disorder at a time. That is, no two diagnoses are given simultaneously. For example, in recognition of the greater severity of anorexia nervosa, if a person loses weight to the point of endangering her health, then she will be diagnosed with anorexia nervosa regardless of whether she also binges and purges (i.e., meets criteria for bulimia nervosa).

As a result, many individuals will be diagnosed with different eating disorders over time. In fact, most persons in treatment for bulimia nervosa report that they have had anorexia nervosa in their past. The development of anorexia nervosa in individuals who initially present with bulimia nervosa has also been reported, but it is less common. Persons with binge-eating disorder will be diagnosed with bulimia nervosa if they start to purge the binged food, whereas persons with bulimia nervosa will have their diagnosis changed to binge-eating disorder if they *stop* purging but continue to engage in binge-eating episodes.

Similarities and Differences Between the Eating Disorders		
Anorexia Nervosa	**Bulimia Nervosa**	**Binge-Eating Disorder**
Primary Criteria • Severe preoccupation with weight or shape • Strict dieting • Severe weight loss • Lack or loss of menstrual cycle	*Primary Criteria* • Severe preoccupation with weight or shape • Binge-eating episodes • Compensatory behaviors • Moderate to severe distress	*Primary Criteria* • Binge-eating episodes • Moderate to severe distress
Associated Issues • May engage in compensatory behaviors • Minimal distress • Life-endangering due to starvation	*Associated Issues* • Strict dieting • Normal or slightly above-average weight • At greater risk for heart events and other health problems	*Associated Issues* • Usually obese • Obesity linked to many health-related problems

Other Noteworthy Things to Know About the Eating Disorders

Prevalence and Onset

The lifetime prevalence rate of the three eating disorders in the United States is around 10%. The most common disorder is binge-eating disorder, with a lifetime prevalence rate of about 5%. Binge-eating disorder is more common in adults and is equally common in men and women, whereas anorexia nervosa and bulimia nervosa are more common in relatively young females. The lifetime rate of the latter is estimated at about 3.5%, whereas the lifetime rate of the former is estimated at about 2%. Anorexia nervosa and bulimia nervosa usually develop during adolescence or early adulthood. The most common ages of developing these are the start of high school and the start of college. Not coincidentally, these are the times when probably everyone feels social stress (i.e., to be accepted) most acutely. (The prevalence rates for all three eating disorders are *extremely* hard to estimate. Most persons with these disorders will knowingly, out of shame, or unknowingly, out of denial, refuse to acknowledge symptoms of the eating disorders. As a result, most epidemiological surveys of mental illness do not even attempt to include them.)

Certain sports and activities convey greater risk for the eating disorders. Male wrestlers and body builders who feel compelled to gain and lose weight rapidly are at risk for bulimia nervosa. Female runners, ice skaters, and gymnasts, where a slim body shape is considered important, are at particular risk for anorexia nervosa . Both men and women who act, model, or dance are at higher risk.

Other Features of the Disorders

Although the term *anorexia* literally means "absence of appetite," this isn't true. People who have anorexia nervosa are, in fact, usually very hungry. They refuse to eat, which gives them a sense of satisfaction and a sense of control. Someone with anorexia nervosa will repeatedly check her weight, perhaps dozens of times per day, and her mood will fluctuate depending on whether the scale reports good news (weight loss) or bad news (weight gain).

Instead of eating to satisfy hunger, which is eating's most basic attribute and purpose, persons with anorexia nervosa often fixate on the food preparation and consumption process. They might prepare elaborate meals for others that they themselves don't eat. They might collect recipes and pictures of food. They may develop strange eating habits, such as carefully weighing and portioning food, cutting food into tiny pieces, and hiding (but never actually consuming) food. Many engage in other behaviors to reduce weight, such as intense exercise, self-induced vomiting, or the use of laxatives, enemas, and diuretics.

Depending on the severity of malnutrition, nails and hair may become brittle and skin may become dry and yellow. Someone with anorexia may complain of feeling cold (hypothermia) because her body temperature has dropped, which is due to the body's attempt to conserve calories or the fuel necessary to keep the body at a normal temperature.

Persons with bulimia nervosa and binge-eating disorder are more likely to smoke than others. Nicotine suppresses appetite, which is seen as an advantage. Unfortunately, an increase in appetite is a common side effect of quitting smoking, making it especially difficult for persons with these disorders who do smoke to quit.

The severe dieting, binging, and purging behavior of the person with bulimia nervosa can usually be successfully hidden, especially since persons with bulimia nervosa are usually normal weight. Persons with anorexia nervosa are, by criteria, severely underweight, and most persons with binge-eating disorder are overweight or obese.

Defining Healthy Weight

Over the last few decades, debate about properly defining "healthy weight" has been lively. Most of us remember the weight charts at the doctor's office, which showed the "ideal" weight (or a range of weight) for persons of a certain height. "Remember" is the operative word, because they don't exist at many doc-tor's offices any longer. They have been abandoned as inaccurate and insufficient. Currently, there is still debate about how to evaluate weight as healthy or unhealthy, but most researchers and clinicians agree that the Body Mass Index, or BMI, is a good if imperfect indicator.

The BMI is a ratio of weight and height. To be specific,

BMI = pounds * 703/inches squared

A BMI between 20-25 is optimal for health and long life, whereas 18-20 is somewhat underweight and 25-27 is considered somewhat overweight. Obesity is over 30, whereas the usual cutoff for anorexia nervosa is 17.5 or less.

Sophisticated modeling of healthy weight also takes into account body frame, allowing those with larger frames to have higher BMIs and those with smaller frames to have lesser BMIs and still be considered healthy.

Distress and Impairment

The three eating disorders vary in terms of the distress they cause to the person, which of course has implications for help-seeking behavior. The primary impairment for all three is health-related, which is perhaps not surprising given that disturbance of the basic biological need of eating is their hallmark.

Distress

Persons with anorexia nervosa tend to not experience much distress regarding their self-destructive behavior. Instead, they may appear proud or self-satisfied that they are able to control the universal and usually overpowering urge to eat. Almost without exception, then, others coerce persons with anorexia nervosa into treatment. The person with anorexia nervosa may be distressed that parents and medical doctors are upset, but she is unlikely to agree that the concern is legitimate. As a result, few persons with anorexia nervosa will seek treatment voluntarily but rather must be forced into treatment by others.

In contrast, persons with bulimia nervosa and binge-eating disorder tend to be extremely distressed by their situation. They recognize that what they are doing to themselves is pathological, but they feel both trapped and out of control. Out of a desire to look differently or lose weight, individuals with bulimia nervosa get trapped in a vicious cycle of diet-binge-purge. They will starve themselves until the desire to eat becomes overwhelming and they feel compelled to binge eat, which makes them feel guilty and engage in purging behavior. As with persons with binge-eating disorder, they feel out of control when they engage in binge eating. The difference between the binges of someone with bulimia nervosa versus someone with binge-eating disorder is that the former is usually compelled by intense hunger caused by dieting efforts.

Psychosocial Impairment

Persons with anorexia nervosa usually fare pretty well in regard to school and work functioning. Indeed, perfectionism is a common trait among persons with anorexia nervosa, and this attitude leads them to be good students, good workers, and generally compliant citizens. Instead, for persons with anorexia nervosa, the impairment tends to be in relationships. Relationships tend to suffer, as self-starvation becomes the focal and primary activity of their lives. Parents, family members, and friends who become concerned about the dangerous behavior will meet anger and derision. Relationships will become conflicted as, for example, parents attempt to exert their authority and get their daughter to eat, whereas she responds by increasing her efforts to be in control, not just over her weight but also over her life. Anorexia nervosa is a frightening and frustrating disorder.

Persons with bulimia nervosa and binge-eating disorder tend to have less extreme self-control than those with anorexia nervosa. They also are less in denial about the pathological nature of their behavior, so arguing about whether or not there is a problem is less likely. Thus, relationships tend not to be as impaired. On the other hand, persons with these disorders tend to hide their binging and purging behaviors, with the result that their relationships come to be characterized by dishonesty and secretiveness.

Persons with bulimia nervosa and binge-eating disorder are also more likely to be anxious or depressed, as well as more likely to have a comorbid substance use problem.

Health Complications

Persons who suffer from the eating disorders will experience a wide range of health complications, leading to relatively high rates of mortality. The starvation experienced by persons with anorexia nervosa can cause damage to vital organs such as the heart and brain. One in ten cases of anorexia nervosa leads to death from starvation, cardiac arrest, or other medical complications. If comorbid problems, most particularly suicide, are taken into account, one in five will die earlier than her peers.

Bulimia nervosa can also cause serious medical problems. Persons with the disorder can severely damage their bodies by frequent binging and purging. Electrolyte imbalance and dehydration can occur and may cause cardiac complications and, occasionally, sudden death. In rare instances, binging can cause the stomach to rupture. Also, persons with bulimia nervosa may experience the erosion of dental enamel (due to the acid in vomit) and scarring on the backs of the hands (due to repeatedly pushing fingers down the throat to induce vomiting).

Finally, persons with binge-eating disorder tend to be overweight or obese, and the health complications of those conditions are well known, including heart disease, high blood pressure, cancer, type II diabetes, and breathing problems, as well as sleep apnea and asthma.

The Faces of the Eating Disorders

There are two faces of the eating disorders.

Persons with anorexia nervosa are not distressed by their disorder because they do not believe there is a disorder. The face they see when they look in the mirror is quite different from the face that everyone else sees. When a person with anorexia nervosa looks at herself in the mirror, she sees someone who is fat and who needs to lose more weight. The face of anorexia nervosa, in other words, is the classic face of denial of the reality that others see. When parents, doctors, mental health professionals, and anyone else see her, they see someone who looks like she is starving to death—which in fact she is.

So the person with anorexia nervosa denies that there is anything wrong, rebuffs the notion that she is desperately unhealthy and in need of help, and is appalled by the idea that others will insist, perhaps forcibly, that she gain weight.

To be blunt, the face of anorexia nervosa is bewildering. As noted, it is not that these (usually) young women don't feel hunger. It is mystifying to others that they won't eat despite the fact that their bodies are screaming at them to eat, just as our bodies would if they were in that condition. It is even more disorienting to observers that the person with anorexia nervosa denies the blatant, flagrant, seemingly undeniable reality of the numbers on the scale. Others will confront them with this truth, saying, "No one your height should weigh as little as you do. It is unhealthy, and if you keep this up, you will die." But she will deny this with serenity and with conviction, as if she knows something that others do not.

To my students and colleagues, I have compared the bizarre mentation of persons with anorexia nervosa to that of persons in a psychotic state. The lack of association with reality is almost delusional. It is not voluntary, however. Persons with anorexia nervosa have lost the ability to be rational when contemplating their circumstance, making decisions, and maintaining their health. This is partly due to brain damage secondary to the state of semi-starvation. The brain atrophies (grows smaller), while the ventricular areas of the brain (the fluid-filled sac separating the various lobes) grow larger.

In contrast, the faces of persons with bulimia nervosa and binge-eating disorder are the faces of shame. Persons with these disorders go to great lengths to hide their illness from others. Since persons with bulimia nervosa tend to be normal weight (in contrast to the extremely low weight of persons with anorexia nervosa), they are usually successful at doing so. Thus, when you learn from someone that she is in treatment for bulimia nervosa, you will likely be quite surprised. You will not have had any notion that anything was wrong. Similarly, persons with binge-eating disorder are also intensely ashamed of their situation. However, like persons with anorexia nervosa who are easy to see because of their low weight, persons with binge-eating disorder are also usually easy to see because of obesity caused by the disorder. As a consequence, if that person admits that he is considering treatment, has just started treatment, or is currently in ongoing treatment, you might not be particularly surprised.

In the case of bulimia nervosa, I recommend that you do your best to hide your surprise, which might aggravate the sense of shame. In contrast, in the case of binge-eating disorder, I recommend that you not act as if you were expecting such news, which might also aggravate a sense of shame. Instead, act somewhat surprised. In both instances, empathize with the person about the difficulty of the situation, congratulate them on doing the right thing (i.e., getting help), and ask them to let you know if there is anything you can do to help.

Treatment Considerations

Anorexia nervosa, bulimia nervosa, and binge-eating disorder strike young women, and the earlier treatment can be initiated the better the outcome. All three disorders have immense physical health consequences, and the longer they last the more likely the damage will be either long-term or permanent.

Outpatient Versus Inpatient Treatment

While some persons with anorexia nervosa can be treated as outpatients, others will need to be hospitalized in order to force them to regain the weight (and avoid death by malnutrition or starvation). Fortunately, many of the problems experienced by persons with anorexia nervosa are reversed when they gain weight.

In contrast, most people with bulimia nervosa can be treated as outpatients because they aren't in danger of starving themselves as persons with anorexia are. However, if the bulimia is out of control, a stay in an eating disorders treatment program may help them let go of their behaviors so they can concentrate on treatment. Group therapy can be effective for college-aged and young adult women because of the understanding of the group members who have had similar experiences.

Blaming the Parents?

Quite dissimilar to other disorders, there is a special indignation that families are likely to encounter in the treatment of the eating disorders. Freud's notion was that parents, and especially mothers, were to blame for psychological problems that people have as adults. Freud was comprehensive and included all of the mental illnesses in this formulation. Even though numerous subsequent psychiatrists and psychoanalysts further developed this idea (blaming parents for, among other things, schizophrenia and autism), research finally caught up with the idea. It has been roundly criticized and rejected as both unscientific and cruel. At least, it has been rejected by most.

The single category of mental illness where blaming mothers still holds credence, among *some* mental health professionals, is the eating disorders. The idea that the eating disorders are merely the "expression" of serious dysfunction and pathology in a family has a long history that, unlike other areas, is still accepted by many. Books such as *The Golden Cage,* which emphasizes that girls with anorexia nervosa are merely attempting to live up to their parents' need for them to be perfect creatures who could be shown off to others, were huge sellers among professionals who treat these disorders. Likewise, family therapy proved to be one of the only successful approaches in the treatment of anorexia nervosa and bulimia nervosa. When they see the age of the victims of the disorders and that family therapy is recommended, some mental health professionals come to believe that the disorders are *caused* by dysfunctional family factors.

In fact, the eating disorders are related to family issues in two ways. First, eating (i.e., meals) is typically a family-centered event. Second, most persons who develop anorexia nervosa and bulimia nervosa are younger females who live with their parents. Hence, family therapy remains an essential component of treatment. However, it is simply untrue that the disorders are *caused* by dysfunctional family factors.

Why bring this up? Because readers should keep in mind that when a family seeks treatment for such a disorder, it will likely be confronted and insulted (and probably made to feel both confused and guilty!) by this outmoded way of thinking. Either directly or subtly, parents (and especially mothers) who seek treatment for their child with an eating disorder are often made to feel that they are being blamed for creating the illness.

This is not to say that parents and families are *never* to blame for the development of an eating disorder. Everyone learns eating and health habits from his or her family. As well, every family in the United States is heavily influenced by sociocultural norms, including what foods are good to eat, what foods should be avoided, and how much should be eaten. It can be hard to distinguish the causes of the disorder. If the mental health professional determines that the cause is at least partly the family's influence, then the family's unhealthy attitudes and behavior may become a focus of treatment.

Western Beauty Ideals and the Eating Disorders

As noted, the majority of persons with both anorexia nervosa and bulimia nervosa are female. Women are particularly vulnerable to the eating disorders because of Western society's intense focus on beauty as an indicator of worth. The pressure to meet a certain beauty ideal is associated with a pressure to be thin, which causes women to diet in order to achieve such an "ideal" figure.

An important aspect of treatment of the eating disorders, then, is to confront this idea that beauty and worth are interdependent. If young women can accept that this notion is ubiquitous but extremely unfair, then they may be able to be convinced to stop dieting. Eating regularly alleviates the central issues in both anorexia nervosa and bulimia nervosa. The person with anorexia nervosa will gain weight, and the person with bulimia nervosa will no longer be prone to binge eating, which is the consequence of feeling starved.

The Impulse Control Disorders

These disorders involve problematic behaviors that the person either cannot control or has difficulty controlling.

Tourette's Disorder and Trichotillomania

Tourette's disorder and trichotillomania are motor (body) behaviors of, respectively, tics and hair pulling. For both disorders, the problem behaviors are impulses that the person either cannot control or has great difficulty resisting.

Tourette's Disorder

Tourette's disorder (TD) is characterized by motor and vocal tics. These are repetitive involuntary movements or utterances. The tics are rapid and sudden, and they must persist for more than a year to meet diagnostic criteria.

TD affects about 1 in 500 people, and males are affected three to four times as often as females. The disorder almost always emerges in childhood, with symptoms appearing between the ages of 4 and 8. The first symptom that appears is usually a tic on a small area of the face, usually around the eyes or mouth. It is estimated that 20-25% of the general population have tics at some point during their lives, especially during times of stress, but they usually disappear after a short time. With TD, the tic remains and worsens to involve other muscles of the face, neck, arms, and legs.

Coprolalia is the term for vocal tics that are bad words or phrases. It is the most well-known vocal tic, but only about 10% of persons with TD actually exhibit it. More common tics are eye blinking, shoulder shrugging, and throat clearing. The types of tics may change, and their frequency and severity may increase or decrease over time. For some, the tics become so severe that they negatively impact both relationships and achievements. Persons with tics often get teased. Even worse, they may be blamed, derided, and scolded by family and peers. The distraction of tics can lead to difficulties at school and at the workplace.

The tics are entirely involuntary. They are due to a combination of neurological problems and environmental stress. Persons with TD report that they become aware of an urge to do the tic, similar to the urge to scratch an itch or to sneeze. Engaging in the tic relieves the increasing tension. Suppressing the urge (e.g., in social situations) causes increased tension and mental exhaustion, which actually increases the likelihood that a tic will be expressed. In most persons with this disorder, symptoms increase with anxiety, stress, and fatigue.

Trichotillomania

Like Tourette's disorder, trichotillomania (TTM) is a disorder of impulse control. TTM is compulsive hair pulling that causes substantial and noticeable hair loss. The hair pulling is usually to the scalp, but it can also occur at the eyebrows, eyelashes, or anywhere else hair grows on the body. Hair pulling is usually done one hair at a time, and hair-pulling episodes may last for hours.

TTM is usually associated with great shame, and as a result it is not clear how common it is. The limited research that has been conducted suggests that as many as 1 in 20 people may have TTM. Adults are as likely as children and adolescents to have the disorder, and women are four times more likely than men to be diagnosed.

TTM is classified either as "automatic," wherein the hair pulling occurs without conscious effort and perhaps without awareness (e.g., during sleep), or as "focused," wherein the hair pulling is done consciously and perhaps ritualistically after a period of increasing tension.

Treatment Considerations

Several treatments for both TD and TTM have been developed in the last decade. Medications have proven somewhat effective in reducing the tics of TD, but the disorder is most common in children and adolescents and there is (or at least should be) understandable hesitation to use them. Medications have not proven successful in the treatment of TTM.

Psychological treatments for both disorders involve recognizing and addressing internal tension and external stressors. Treatment includes teaching persons to recognize stressful situations, as well as teaching stress management and other calming techniques to reduce the internal tension that cues the tics and hair pulling. It will also likely include the advice to leave a stressful situation, permanently if possible, but at least temporarily.

Training someone to recognize stressful situations is an aspect of psychoeducation, which is extremely important in these disorders. Both TD and TTM are fraught with misunderstanding and misinformation. For the person with TTM, knowing that stress exacerbates the urge can be both revealing and incredibly helpful. With regard to TD, psychoeducation entails teaching the child, parents and siblings, and school that the tics are involuntary. Anger and blame can be replaced with understanding, support, and compassion. Knowing that the tics will be made worse by stress (e.g., by getting in trouble at school when they happen) is essential for their management. This is equally important for the person with the disorder to understand. Many with TD can suppress tics for brief time periods, and they may experience confusion and shame that they cannot do so all of the time.

"Habit reversal training" has proven quite effective for many persons with these disorders. This therapy was first developed to treat what were then called nervous habits, such as nail biting and smoking. The person with TD or TTM is taught to recognize the urges or feelings that precede the tics or hair pulling. They then are taught to perform a behavior that will reduce the urge or be incompatible with the tic or hair pulling behavior. For example, someone with a throat-clearing tic may be trained to focus on slow, rhythmic breathing to reduce the urge to clear his throat. The person with the urge to pull her hair may be taught to comb or brush her hair calmly for ten minutes, which is both incompatible with pulling and may also reduce the urge.

Anger Management Problems (Intermittent Explosive Disorder)

Anger is a completely normal emotion. In and of itself, anger is neither a problem nor a sin. After all, Jesus got angry with the Pharisees and with the moneychangers. Anger is an emotion people feel when something is bothering them a great deal.

For some people, however, anger expression becomes inappropriate and problematic. Inappropriate expressions of anger include screaming, name calling, swearing, threats of violence, destroying property (e.g., throwing things, breaking objects, punching walls), and violence towards others.

Someone who has repeated episodes of impulsive, aggressive, and violent behavior towards others or property or repeated episodes of angry verbal outbursts (or both) may be diagnosed with intermittent explosive disorder. The diagnosis may be appropriate if the person reacts "grossly out of proportion" to the situation, meaning in a manner in which most people would not behave. Road rage or other temper tantrums may be signs of intermittent explosive disorder.

Impairment Leads to Distress

Inappropriate expressions of anger cause fear in other persons and reduce the likelihood that an aggravating situation will be resolved effectively. Out-of-control anger will cause problems in one's relationships at work, with friends, and especially at home. As a result of damage done to relationships after an outburst, the person may feel intense distress in the form of remorse, regret, and embarrassment.

The Cycle of Violence

This regret will lead to excuses and promises to change ("I just get so angry I cannot control myself;" "This won't happen again;" "Next time I'll aim my fist at the wall"). Then the person will try to be good.

However, since the person has no good strategy for coping with stress and tension, these promises actually have a detrimental effect. The promises to do better lead to "excessive" niceness and the ignoring of stressful situations, which therefore won't be resolved.

The stress and internal tension will build until finally another explosion of anger occurs, followed by remorse and promises to do better, and so it goes. This "cycle of violence" in domestic abuse is further elaborated in chapter 17.

Encouraging Treatment-Seeking

Intermittent explosive disorder will cause extreme damage to marital relationships. Thus, if someone has repeated episodes of explosive, inappropriate anger, then treatment is absolutely necessary. Simply put, the person is stuck in a bad habit from which he will not be able to extricate himself. Unfortunately, the shame and embarrassment will likely cause the person to resist a referral. Judicious use of motivational interviewing, described in one of the boxes in the SUD section earlier in this chapter, is recommended in these situations. Emphasize to the person that he wants to do better and to be a better father and husband, which is a wonderful thing. But also emphasize that the problematic behavior keeps occurring and will continue to occur in the future, unless he learns new habits through psychotherapy.

As with TD and TTM, treatment usually involves becoming aware of the increase in tension (i.e., the urge) and developing strategies for resolving or releasing the tension in an appropriate manner. For anger management problems, a combination of education and psychotherapy, often with a group of other persons who have in the past struggled with anger management, is most effective. Help him to see that he needs to learn to express his anger constructively rather than destructively. Finally, be ready with a referral source, and be ready to make the phone call with him ("I'm glad you agree. I know someone good. Let's call right now and get you an appointment").

Chapter 12

The Dissociative, Sexual, Sleep, and Somatic Symptom Disorders

"The righteous person may have many troubles,
but the LORD delivers him from them all."
(Psalm 34:19)

This chapter briefly reviews some less common mental illnesses. The dissociative disorders are caused by severely stressful events. The sexual disorders are likely in couples having relationship difficulties (as either cause or effect). The sleep disorders are very common and can be profoundly distressing. Finally, the somatic symptom disorders are characterized by the redirection or sublimation of emotional distress into physical complaints.

The names of these particular disorders are alliterative, and the chapter title is therefore quite fun to say out loud. However, that is the only commonality among them (and not the reason for grouping them together).

The Dissociative Disorders

There are four categories of dissociative disorders, and they are reviewed below. Overwhelming stress, which may be the result of traumatic events, accidents, or disasters that may be experienced or witnessed by the individual, usually causes the disorders. The common issue for all of the dissociative disorders, which seems to be the result of the stress, is profound cognitive disturbance. This may include changes in the person's memory, consciousness, or identity, as well as diminished awareness of themselves and their surroundings.

The dissociative disorders are some of the most dramatic and extraordinary, and thus they have been portrayed many times in TV shows and movies. As a result, there is an incredible amount of misinformation. There is also quite a bit of controversy related to questions about their validity.

Dissociative Amnesia

Dissociative amnesia is caused by a single, severe, traumatic event. Dissociative amnesia is a fairly common occurrence in traumatic situations, and the validity of the diagnosis is incontrovertible. Given the frequency of traumatic events, the disorder is fairly common. Usually, it resolves fairly quickly, but there have been documented cases that have lasted years. Duration usually depends on the severity of the traumatic event.

Military and police personnel are at risk for the disorder given the dangers of their profession. Causal events may be a firefight in Iraq or a shoot-out in downtown Los Angeles. Female rape victims may develop dissociative amnesia. Children who are traumatized may also develop it.

Corporal Patten Wanders Away

Lance Corporal Patten was near the end of his second tour with his Marine Corps unit when he was found wandering in the Iraqi desert about a quarter-mile from base camp. He was not wearing his helmet and did not have his weapon. When he was brought to the medical tent, he could not tell anyone how he got into the desert, where he was supposed to be, where the rest of his squad was, or even who he was. He was wearing identification, so these mysteries were quickly resolved, as was his condition. It turned out that his fellow marines had been anxiously looking for him for the last few hours. Corporal Patten had been part of a patrol when three improvised explosive devices (IEDs) exploded in quick succession, followed by an extended attack. The first IED exploded in front of the patrol, and the second and third exploded on either side of the line of marines. The second IED killed one of his closest friends, and when he turned to look for cover he witnessed another friend killed by the third. According to the other marines who were part of the patrol, Corporal Patten was effective in the subsequent firefight, including their hasty withdrawal to the cover of an abandoned house. When other marines rescued the other members of the patrol, they found Corporal Patten's helmet and weapon, but not Corporal Patten. They knew he was alive, and they feared that he had been captured.

The treatment of dissociative amnesia is fairly straightforward: the person must be forced to remember what happened. In most cases, dissociative amnesia resolves quickly. Once memory and identity are restored, dissociative amnesia is cured, but, unfortunately, the person may develop another disorder, such as PTSD.

Dissociative Identity Disorder (DID)

DID is much less common than dissociative amnesia, and it is much more controversial. A person with DID will display two or more distinct personalities or identities. These subpersonalities take turns being in charge, and each will have a distinctive pattern of thinking and relating to others. In most cases, some of the personalities are unaware of each other, although there is usually a primary personality that is aware of all others. Because one personality may be unaware of another, the individual with DID may be unable to recall experiences and information that is relegated to a personality about which he does not have awareness. The subpersonalities are often dramatically different.

In contrast to dissociative amnesia, which resolves as quickly as it arrives, DID lasts a long time. Also in contrast to the other disorder, the cause of DID tends to be prolonged. To be specific, DID appears to be caused by extreme and prolonged trauma in childhood, such as childhood physical or sexual abuse. The theory is that in order to deal with repeated traumatic experiences, a child will create alternative personalities so that the trauma can be compartmentalized. In this way, she deals with the ongoing trauma.

Chris Sizemore's Three Faces

The most famous case of DID is Chris Costner Sizemore, made famous in the classic book, *The Three Faces of Eve,* which then became a classic movie, starring Joanne Woodward. One of the three Eves was a sweet, conservatively dressed, conscientious worker and devoted mother, whereas another Eve was coarse, seductive, impulsive, and adventurous. The third personality was Jane, who was able to work with her psychiatrist to uncover the cause of her problems. Supposedly, the traumatic experiences leading to the splitting of Ms. Sizemore's personality at a very young age was witnessing an accidental death at a lumberyard, seeing her mother cut herself badly, and seeing a drowned body.

DID is a controversial diagnosis because many mental health professionals doubt that it exists at all. Some skeptics believe that many supposed cases of DID are actually iatrogenic in nature, meaning that the therapist somehow encouraged a susceptible client to adopt the symptoms. Alternatively, some believe that patients may pretend to have DID to get attention or to excuse their behavior, including criminal behavior or sexual acting out.

What should be concluded about DID? First, most experts agree that there are true cases. Second, they also agree that the disorder is probably extremely rare and that mental health professionals should be very careful before diagnosing someone with DID.

Dissociative Fugue

Dissociative fugue is a form of dissociative amnesia that involves unplanned travel or wandering. Case studies suggest that it too is precipitated by stressful events. Some are suspicious of the validity of some supposed cases of fugue, however. In some instances of fugue, the person in the fugue may go so far as to establish a new identity, which would seem a difficult task for someone in a state of cognitive confusion and distress. Moreover, some cases have been suspicious in that the person may have been motivated to disappear and then reappear elsewhere as someone else.

Agatha Mysteriously Disappears

A famous case of fugue involved the mystery writer Agatha Christie. She disappeared one evening in early December 1926, from her home in Berkshire, England. Although a successful author by then, she was depressed about her mother's recent death and by discovering that her husband was being unfaithful. The immediate speculation about her disappearance was that she had committed suicide or had been murdered. The police organized search parties and had her husband followed. Her picture appeared in newspapers across the country. Some residents at a spa in the town of Harrogate suggested to one of the guests, Mrs. Teresa Neele, how much she looked like Agatha Christie. Mrs. Neele laughed off suggestions that she was the missing author. Finally, the police took her husband there. He identified her and took her home. Neither Agatha Christie nor her husband ever spoke of the incident. To many observers, the most likely explanation is that she simply wanted to get away from a bad situation and embarrass her husband, who was doing little to disguise his extramarital dalliances.

Depersonalization/Derealization Disorder

Depersonalization/derealization disorder is a confined period of time wherein the person experiences a profound sense of surreal detachment from himself or his surroundings. He may experience a lack of control of himself or a sense of being outside of himself. Due to the sense of disconnection, the person will also experience significant difficulties or distress at work, in relationships, or in other important areas of life. Similar to amnesia, severe stress seems to be the most common precipitating event. In both instances, it appears that the mind "retreats" from reality, either entirely (in the case of amnesia) or at least partly (in the case of depersonalization).

Repressed (but Then Recovered) Memories Versus Dissociative Amnesia

Dissociative amnesia is a genuine disorder. People who experience a sudden and extremely traumatic event may temporarily lose track of where they are, what happened, or even who they are.

Unfortunately, the increased acceptance of dissociative amnesia as a legitimate disorder has led to exaggerated accounts of repressed memories. The recent past saw a veritable parade of adults (including many celebrities, such as Roseanne Barr) who did not remember until adulthood that they had been severely abused as a child. Supposedly when the trauma occurred, they immediately repressed its memory, but for some reason the memory came back. Most controversially and in contrast to an enormous amount of scientific research, these individuals have insisted that their formerly repressed (but now recovered) memories are entirely accurate. Indeed, there have been criminal prosecutions and convictions based on recovered memories.

Dr. Elizabeth Loftus is one of the world's leading experts on memory. She tells the story of a family reunion where her uncle told her that 30 years ago, when Elizabeth was 14, Elizabeth found her mother's dead body in the swimming pool. She did not remember that event, but her uncle insisted. Over the next few days she started to recall the image of her mother floating face down in the pool. She wondered if this explained why she was such a workaholic and perfectionist and why she still got upset when thinking about her mother, who died almost 30 years ago. When she later spoke to her brother about it, she was surprised to hear him say that their uncle was wrong. She had not found the body. The memories that Dr. Loftus had been recalling were, in fact, fabrications of her mind.

Dr. Loftus has conducted several decades of research into memory, and she and others have shown that memory is quite fallible. In laboratory work, she has shown that each time a person imagines that something happened, as she was imagining that she had found her mother's body, the person creates an image of it happening. If the person continues to think about the event, the image becomes more familiar. Details become more detailed, and the event becomes more believable and more real. It takes on the properties of a real memory, to the extent that people will come to consider it a factual aspect of their past (i.e., a memory of an authentic event). In one of her more famous experiments, she told research subjects, "Your mother told us that when you were a young child, you got lost at a shopping mall." This was a fib and none of the subjects remembered the event. Nonetheless, many of the subjects came back a week later with extensive details about the "event," such as being given gum by a nice lady and talking to the mall guard. They had "remembered" an event that never actually happened after being given the suggestion that it had happened. Could this be happening with recovered memories? It certainly could. Indeed, some seem to encourage false recollections.

A book about recovering from incest, called *The Courage to Heal,* informs readers that incest survivors often do not remember being abused because repression and denial are so common (which is not true). The book also provides a list of feelings experienced by incest survivors, such as shame about matters of sex, the occasional sense of unworthiness, and feelings of vulnerability. (Of course, such feelings are fairly common, if not outright universal.) The first edition of the book advises that readers ought not be fooled if they don't remember specific instances of abuse, since "If you are unable to remember any specific instances but still have a feeling that something happened to you, it probably did."

Finally, it should be remembered that most traumas are not forgotten. Indeed, this is the basis for many an unpleasant memory and for the diagnosis of PTSD. Most people who experience trauma would give anything to forget it, and some go to great lengths to do so (such as excessive drinking).

So we can answer some important questions.

- Does sexual abuse and incest happen? Absolutely yes.
- Do people sometimes forget things only to remember them accurately later? Almost certainly yes.
- Is dissociative amnesia real? Absolutely yes.
- Is memory perfect? Absolutely not.
- Can people remember things that did not happen? Absolutely yes.
- Do people misremember things? Obviously yes. (How many times have you argued with a sibling or spouse about whose memory is correct? By the way, research suggests that you are probably both wrong!)

We can answer these questions about memory in general, but we cannot answer any question about someone's particular memory. We simply cannot say whether someone who "recovers" a lost memory has genuinely done so, is convinced that she has done so even if the memory is not authentic, or is lying about doing so. All we can do for certain is listen, try to understand, and try to help.

The Sexual Disorders (Sexual Dysfunctions)

Sexual dysfunction can be defined as impaired ability or complete inability to enjoy sexual intercourse. The sexual disorders are fairly common. It is estimated that at least half of all persons will experience, probably temporarily, a sexual dysfunction at some point in their life. The disorders are sometimes, but not always, associated with a great deal of personal distress. They are likewise sometimes, but not always, a cause of marital distress, which is a type of impairment.

The disorders can be categorized according to which phase of the sexual response cycle is affected: desire, arousal, performance, and orgasm.

Desire Phase Disorders

The desire phase of the sexual response cycle is just what it sounds like, the emergence of a desire to have sex. *Hypoactive sexual desire* is diagnosed when a person has deficient or absent sexual desire.

Regarding distress and impairment, most persons with low levels of sexual desire don't see it as problem. Not desiring something does not tend to cause distress, whereas desiring but not obtaining something might. For this reason, a dissatisfied husband or wife may prompt treatment-seeking for inadequate desire problems in his or her spouse.

Arousal Phase Disorders

Regarding the arousal phase, both males and females may experience difficulty with the biological/physical aspects of sexual functioning.

Male erectile disorder (which is without doubt the most redundant term in medical history) used to be called impotence. The term was seen as pejorative and stigmatizing, however, so the more medical term is now preferred. It used to be believed that psychological issues were the primary cause of erectile disorder (ED). However, most cases of ED are resolved using drug treatments (perhaps you've seen a few million commercials), which has led to the conclusion that it is most often a biological issue. Whether biological or psychological (e.g., caused by marital distress or anxiety), there are effective treatments available for men.

In women, the equivalent of ED is called female sexual arousal disorder. It is the persistent inability to attain or maintain arousal. The 2013 version of the DSM, in fact, combines desire and arousal phase disorders into one category for women (female sexual interest/arousal disorder) to reflect the basic idea that a woman who does not desire to have sex is going to have difficulties with arousal.

Performance/Orgasm Phase Disorders

After normal arousal and the initiation of intercourse, dysfunction may still occur. For example, if a woman has arousal problems but attempts to have intercourse anyway, this may lead to the experience of pain. This performance phase disorder is called genito-pelvic pain. It is much more common in women than in men.

Orgasm phase problems, on the other hand, seem equally likely in men and women. Men only will experience premature ejaculation, but both sexes will experience delayed orgasm or the absence of orgasm.

Treatment of Sexual Disorders

These disorders are, in principle, fairly easy to treat. Treatment needs to be provided by either a medical or a mental health professional.

The first step in treatment is to determine that there are no medical or physical causes. A referral for a medical workup is absolutely required, especially if the person reports that her relationship is otherwise happy, healthy, and satisfying. Common medical causes of sexual dysfunction are age-related changes (i.e., changing levels of hormones), medications (e.g., antidepressant medications), and chronic medical conditions (such as diabetes or hypertension).

In the past two decades, researchers have recognized that whether or not medical issues are present, there will be psychological factors involved in any sexual dysfunction. Even if the cause is a medical condition, for example, the emergence of a sexual problem in a relationship is highly likely to cause shame and embarrassment, if not resentment and anger. Psychological issues need to be addressed. However, the psychological issues are, by definition for these specific disorders, interpersonal.

In this regard, then, the best treatment involves working with the couple. Most couples benefit from *education* about what is normal and appropriate in relationships. For example, most new couples can be fairly spontaneous regarding sexual relations, whereas more established couples with children may need to be less "romantic" and more purposeful about such pragmatic issues as privacy, timing, and availability.

Even more likely is the need for the couple to learn techniques to develop better *communication* skills. The communication may need to be sex-specific, which can be difficult for some people to be comfortable doing. It can be embarrassing and difficult, for example, to tell your spouse that you are unsatisfied. However, this is probably preferable to avoiding sex altogether, and with professional help most couples can overcome most of the problems listed above.

Even more likely still, however, will be the need to develop *conflict resolution* skills. It turns out that being chronically angry and upset with one's spouse will interfere with a satisfying sex life.

The Sleep Disorders

There are a variety of sleep disorders, as shown in the box. This section reviews the most dangerous to physical health (i.e., sleep apnea), as well as sleepwalking and night terrors. The next section reviews insomnia.

Sleep Disorders: An Incomplete List

There are a bewilderingly large number of sleep disorders. Here is an incomplete list.

- Adjustment sleep disorder (acute insomnia)
- Paradoxical insomnia (formerly sleep state misperception)
- Idiopathic insomnia
- Insomnia due to mental disorder
- Inadequate sleep hygiene
- Primary central sleep apnea
- Obstructive sleep apnea
- Sleep-related nonobstructive alveolar hypoventilation, idiopathic
- Narcolepsy
- Recurrent hypersomnia
- Kleine-Levin syndrome
- Behaviorally induced insufficient sleep syndrome
- Circadian rhythm sleep disorder
- Sleepwalking
- Sleeptalking
- Sleep terrors
- Recurrent isolated sleep paralysis
- Nightmare disorder
- Sleep-related groaning (catathrenia)
- Exploding head syndrome (hearing a loud bang within one's head)
- Sleep-related hallucinations
- Sleep-related eating disorder
- Restless legs syndrome (including sleep-related growing pains)

Sleep Apnea

Sleep apnea is not a psychological problem, except that insufficient sleep can cause exacerbation of other problems, such as ADHD, anxiety, and depression. I review it here because it is a substantial health problem that is easy to diagnose and, essentially, completely curable.

What is sleep apnea? Sleep apnea is diagnosed when a person's breathing is interrupted during sleep. Obstructive sleep apnea is caused when the soft tissue in the back of the throat collapses during sleep. This happens most often in men over the age of 40, especially if they are overweight. When the tissue collapses, it will either partially or completely block the airway. People with sleep apnea stop breathing repeatedly during their sleep, perhaps hundreds of times over the course of the night. Sometimes this is observable by others, whereas sometimes it is not. As a result, the brain does not get enough oxygen, and the brain awakens the person (although not to complete wakefulness) enough to get the body to gasp and force air past the obstruction. Significant snoring is thus a hallmark sign of someone with sleep apnea. Mild and occasional snoring is fairly common in both men and women. However, snoring that is associated with heavy, deep, and labored breathing is caused by air being forced through the obstructive tissue.

Because the brain is constantly partially awakening the person in order to get air and oxygen into the system, the person with sleep apnea cannot enter the deep sleep necessary for genuinely refreshing, restful sleep. This can be dangerous both in the short term and the long term. In the short term, sleep apnea causes the person to feel tired during the day. This causes poor performance at work, at school, and behind the wheel (leading to motor vehicle accidents). Over the long term, sleep apnea will cause substantial cardiovascular problems. Essentially, the heart has to work much harder than normal to deliver more blood to the brain and body because the blood is insufficiently oxygenated. Overworking your heart causes the heart to grow larger, leading to substantially increased risk of high blood pressure, strokes, and heart attacks. (Obesity causes cardiovascular problems via the same mechanism.)

Diagnosis and treatment of sleep apnea. Sleep apnea is diagnosed at sleep centers, where the person being evaluated can be "plugged into" various machines that watch the brain and body sleep, such as the EEG (to measure the brain's electrochemical activity) and EMG (to measure muscle activity). Over the course of several hours, it will be evident if the person's breathing is being interrupted and if the brain is not entering deep sleep. Treatment often involves the use of a CPAP machine (continuous positive airway pressure), which delivers a continuous flow of air into the nostrils to keep the airways open so that breathing is not impaired.

Sleepwalking and Night Terrors

Sleepwalking and night terrors both occur mostly in children, and both are usually outgrown. Sleepwalking, also known as somnambulism, occurs when the child arises while still asleep and walks around. Sleepwalkers will have no memory of the behavior, since they were not awake and conscious even though their eyes are open. Night terrors are episodes of extreme terror that do not seem to occur during the dream stage of sleep. The peak age for sleepwalking is between 4 and 8 years, whereas night terrors occur between 3 to 12. Treatment for either disorder is usually unnecessary (unless the child endangers himself or herself during sleepwalking episodes).

Insomnia

The average adult sleeps 7.5 to 8 hours per night. Children sleep more, and elderly people sleep less.

In a typical night, an adult will go through four or five 90-minute sleep cycles. During each, two brain states alternate. Slow wave sleep (SWS) is deep and restful, as the electrical activity of the brain slows down. In rapid eye movement (REM) sleep, the electrical activity of the brain looks similar to wakefulness. During REM sleep, the eyes make rapid, back-and-forth movements and the person is usually dreaming. REM sleep occupies about 25% of sleep time. It is less restful than SWS. The reason for REM sleep is unclear, but it appears to be essential to mental health.

After centuries of study, we still don't know why we sleep. We do know what happens when we don't get enough sleep, however. People who experience insomnia feel miserable, are at higher risk of serious mental illness, and are in danger of problems associated with being sleepy and tired during the day, including poor work and academic performance and motor vehicle accidents.

The most well-known form of insomnia is difficulty falling asleep. Less well-known but equally common is having trouble regaining sleep after awakening in the middle of the night or awakening in the early morning. In many cases, the person experiences insomnia because of medical (e.g., pain), emotional (e.g., anxiety), or environmental (e.g., too much light) causes. On the other hand, "primary insomnia" is sleeplessness that cannot be attributed to some cause.

Distress and Impairment

Insomnia causes intense distress. Over 25 years of clinical work, I have repeatedly seen that insomnia is one of the most aggravating symptoms that can be experienced. It is often the straw that causes the proverbial camel to break, meaning that it is often the difference between someone seeking and not seeking professional help. Insomnia can also lead to life-threatening impairment. Difficulty sleeping causes a person to be tired, with attendant problems concentrating, staying awake, making decisions, and reacting quickly. Not all jobs require quick decisions and lightning-fast reactions, but probably anyone's job performance will suffer if one has insomnia. One study estimated loss of work productivity due to insomnia at over $15 billion dollars annually. Most people drive cars, and insomnia-induced tiredness leads to accidents every year, including an estimated 1,500 fatal accidents.

Insomnia can be self-perpetuating. Consider that to attain sleep means to relax. If someone has difficulty sleeping and is bothered a great deal by such difficulty, relaxing in order to sleep will become more difficult.

Insomnia Treatments

There are two types of treatments for insomnia. One is highly popular but dangerous and questionably effective. The other is much less popular but of proven effectiveness and with no risk to health.

Drug treatments. The most popular method of treatment for insomnia is drugs. Some of these medications can be purchased over-the-counter, by anyone, whereas a physician must prescribe others.

Over-the-counter drugs, such as Excedrin PM and Tylenol PM, typically contain diphenhydramine. Diphenhydramine was developed to alleviate allergy symptoms. Similar to Benadryl, one of its primary side effects is drowsiness. Although unwanted in an allergy medication, drug makers saw the benefit of such an effect to help people with mild insomnia. Diphenhydramine is not particularly helpful to persons with chronic or persistent insomnia, however.

Prescription drugs to help people sleep act on the GABA (gamma-aminobutyric acid) neurotransmitter system in the brain. These include Ambien and Lunesta. These drugs purport to slow brainwave activity, which encourages people to relax, feel drowsy, and fall asleep. These drugs are useful for short periods of time. They induce sleep, and in my opinion occasional use to overcome a temporary problem is not objectionable.

However, some doctors allow patients to use these drugs on an essentially permanent basis, despite contraindications and potential dangers to health with long-term use. Long-term use is contraindicated by the fact that their effectiveness is reduced and dependence may develop. In other words, the drugs won't work as well after about two weeks, and the person taking the drugs may come to rely on them to sleep. Combining these two phenomena, the person may end up taking considerably more than is appropriate.

The dangers of these drugs are well documented. If someone stops taking the drugs, he may experience depression, anxiety, and anger. He may experience withdrawal symptoms such as lightheadedness, stomach and muscle cramps, nausea and vomiting, and profound tiredness. Even worse, there will likely be a rebound effect wherein the person will have difficulty falling asleep or staying asleep. Ironically, these problems associated with ceasing the drugs are actually mild in comparison to the problems that are associated with taking them. These drugs cause day-after drowsiness, and especially in elderly people they increase the risk of falling. There are documented cases of somnambulism in persons taking these drugs, including instances of driving a car, preparing and eating food, making phone calls, and having sex. Other possible changes that may be attributed to the use of sleep medications include memory problems, difficulty concentrating, confusion, increased aggressiveness, agitation, slowed speech or movements, anxiety, depression, and thoughts of suicide.

In summary, sleeping pills are acceptable as a short-term solution. For someone who occasionally has insomnia or for someone experiencing a short bout of insomnia, sleeping pills can be useful. However, long-term or chronic insomnia is almost always a psychological and/or behavioral issue. Long-term insomnia is self-perpetuating, as previously noted. Not sleeping causes intense distress and concern, which interferes with sleeping. Since it is a psychological and behavioral issue, long-term insomnia should be addressed accordingly. Moreover, psychological and behavioral treatments are highly effective and safe. The long-term use of prescription sleeping pills for chronic insomnia is not uncommon, but it is almost always medically improper (as the drug makers themselves will attest) because it is dangerous.

Psychological and behavioral treatments. Unlike drug treatments, the psychological and behavioral treatments of insomnia are not well-advertised and are not well-known. Research conclusively suggests, however, that psychological and behavioral treatments are far superior to medications in the treatment of insomnia. They are highly effective, and the effects endure because, unlike sleeping pills, these techniques help one overcome the underlying causes of sleep problems. Moreover, the treatments are absolutely safe. The treatments have two main themes: help the person change thoughts that are causing or worsening sleep problems, and help the person develop sleep strategies that will encourage relaxation and sleep.

With regard to thinking, psychological techniques involve identifying and changing thoughts that cause or worsen insomnia. Recall that the way we think influences how we feel. Negative thoughts can cause worry and tension, which is bad for sleep. Thoughts that may lead to sleep problems include unrealistic expectations (such as, "I should be able to sleep well every night, like everyone else does!"), exaggeration ("I can never sleep! This is going to kill me!"), and hopelessness (e.g., "I'm never going to sleep well again!"). None of these are rational or realistic, and all of them can be identified and changed.

As shown in the box below, improving sleep hygiene fosters better sleep for everyone. Also presented are techniques specifically developed by psychologists to help people who are experiencing insomnia.

Sleep Hygiene (Plus Some Advice for Overcoming Insomnia)

Psychologists refer to "sleep hygiene" to describe sleep-related habits. Some people have lousy sleep hygiene. Here are seven aspects of sleep hygiene that may help anyone sleep better. Also described are three steps that someone with insomnia might take (in addition to improving sleep hygiene). These latter steps are probably unnecessary for someone not experiencing insomnia, but they work well for people who are. The basic idea is that the bedtime routine, the bedroom, and the bed will become "cues" to your body to sleep.

Seven Aspects of Good Sleep Hygiene

Develop a bedtime ritual.

Follow the same routine every night before you go to bed. This signals your mind and body that it is time to relax. Most people have some version of a regular routine, such as washing up, brushing teeth, and putting on pajamas. If you engage in any other behaviors, such as reading or watching TV, be sure that they are not overly stimulating.

Be aware of when and what you eat.

The discomfort of being either too hungry or too full may keep you awake. If you eat before going to bed, don't eat anything that will make your stomach work extra hard, such as spicy or complex foods. Instead, eat something simple and comforting, such as cereal and milk.

Be aware of when and what you drink.

If you drink too much before bed, you will need to get up, perhaps more than once, to visit the bathroom. Caffeine takes hours to wear off and should be avoided in the afternoon. Finally, drinking alcohol before bedtime is terrible for sleep. Alcohol may make you feel sleepy at first, but a large awakening effect occurs as it leaves the brain.

Check the comfort status of your room.

Ideal sleeping conditions are cool, dark, and quiet. Therefore, consider getting darker window shades and using either earplugs or a white-noise noisemaker. Spending a bit of money on a quality mattress and pillow that you consider comfortable is probably worth the cost. Finally, if you have children or pets, don't let them sleep with you (especially if you want to have more children!).

Exercise

Regular exercise uses energy and makes us tired, which promotes sleep.

Learn to relax.

Some have an easy time relaxing, but many do not. Fortunately, the skill of getting your mind and body to relax can be learned. Strategies and techniques have been developed, and they are easy to find (e.g., free audio files on the Internet), learn, and master. These include autogenic relaxation, progressive muscle relaxation, and visualization.

Reign in your brain.

Have a pen and pad of paper by your bed. If you think of something important, write it down. This prevents worry about remembering it.

If you don't sleep, try not to worry about it. It does and will bother you, but try not to let distress devolve into worry. If you have a bad night of sleep, you will be tired the next day, but nothing more.

Three More Steps to Address Insomnia

Stick to a sleep schedule.

Go to bed and get up at the same time every day, even on weekends, holidays, and days off. That means that early in this regimen you will be getting up after not having slept well the previous night. That's fine. You will be that much more tired when you turn in that night.

Use the bed for sleep (and sex) only.

Do NOT watch TV, use the computer, or read in bed. Do not use the bed for worry. That is, if you don't fall asleep within 15 minutes or so, get up and do something relaxing. Return to bed when you feel ready to sleep. Repeat as necessary. The goal is to train your mind to associate getting into bed with sleeping.

Eliminate naps.

The single most difficult piece of advice for someone with insomnia to hear is the most essential: no more napping! Daytime naps interfere with nighttime sleep. If absolutely necessary, nap for no longer than 10 to 20 minutes. Again, this will mean you are tired by the end of the day, but that is a good thing.

Disorders Characterized by Bodily Complaints

Somatic Symptom Disorder

A person who is overly concerned with her health may be diagnosed with somatic symptom disorder (SSD). The person will have numerous, probably vague, somatic complaints ("aches and pains"), such as fainting spells, nausea, headaches, fatigue, and heart palpitations. The person may be convinced that there is some underlying, terrible disease accounting for the symptoms, or the person may focus on the symptoms themselves. In either event, these complaints may or may not be attributable to a diagnosable medical condition.

While the complaints are genuinely distressing and may cause significant impairment, the complaints and the person's reaction to the complaints are nonetheless exaggerated. That is not to say that the person is intentionally or voluntarily producing them. She is not intentionally deceiving others but, rather, is truly distressed. She will complain of and, by all appearances, actually be experiencing the physical symptoms of an illness. To meet criteria for this disorder, the person must be found to be giving a lot of thought on the seriousness of the somatic symptoms and to be exhibiting a high level of anxiety about the concerns. In addition, the concerns must dominate her behavior (such as seeking medical consultations, complaining to others, and seeking information online). The person may spend years or decades going from doctor to doctor seeking help.

Functional Neurological Symptoms Disorder

Some persons have physical complaints that suggest there is something wrong with them neurologically (i.e., with their nervous system), such as weakness or paralysis in their arms, legs, or entire body; impaired hearing or vision; tingling sensations in their fingers and toes; or impaired speech. If the person is thoroughly examined and found to have no actual neurological problems (such as multiple sclerosis), she may be diagnosed with functional neurological symptoms disorder.

In most instances, some psychological factor or cause can be identified, such as a traumatic event (e.g., a recent divorce, job loss, witnessing a traumatic death). Hence the disorder was previously called conversion disorder, in recognition of the psychoanalytic explanation that the neurological symptoms were "converted" from the hard-to-express psychological factors. (In one of Freud's most famous cases, which helped lay the foundation for the theory of psychoanalysis, Anna O. converted anger at her father, which she could not admit to herself because it caused too much guilt, into pain and paralysis.) Because the term *conversion* was definitively psychoanalytic, and because the symptoms are more accurately perceived as having a functional quality (i.e., a purpose), the term *functional neurological symptoms disorder* has been adopted.

The disorder is extremely complex and little understood. Hopefully, more research will shed light on it.

Treatment Issues

Persons with these disorders tend to be in a great deal of distress, which leads to treatment-seeking behavior. However, they believe their complaints are genuinely medical, so they seek treatment from medical professionals. Even after a medical doctor reassures them that there is no underlying biological cause, they remain unconvinced. Since they are highly unlikely to recognize that psychological factors are causing the somatic complaints, they are highly unlikely to seek psychological treatment. As a result, these disorders tend to be very difficult to treat.

Chapter 13

The Personality Disorders

"In their own eyes they flatter themselves too much to detect or hate their sin. The words of their mouths are wicked and deceitful; they fail to act wisely or do good. Even on their beds they plot evil; they commit themselves to a sinful course and do not reject what is wrong."
(Psalm 36:2-4)

This chapter covers the personality disorders, which are a special class or category of mental illness. They are problems in the way that a person customarily thinks about himself and others, leading to extremely dysfunctional interpersonal behavior and consequent extreme difficulties in relationships. Unlike the other mental illnesses, which can be time-limited because they go away (e.g., treatment leads to a cure of depression) or which can be mitigated in severity although they never quite go away (e.g., the use of medications reduces the severity of the hallucinations and delusions of schizophrenia), by definition the personality disorders persist over time and in severity.

Personality and the Environment

To understand what a personality disorder is, one must first have a clear understanding of personality and how it combines with environment to produce thoughts, feelings, and behaviors.

Personality Versus Environment

Personality is the habitual and usual way a person thinks, feels, and behaves across a variety of situations. Personality is what is meant when we say that someone behaves (and thus presumably thinks and feels) in a consistent and therefore predictable manner. Tyler is shy in almost all situations, so we expect him to be shy at the birthday party. Joan is careful and responsible in most areas of her life, so we are surprised when she is not prepared for the presentation. Francis is agreeable with nearly everyone, so it was a shock to see her get so upset at her coworker.

The *environment* is the other major influence on how we think, feel, and behave. We act, think, and feel one way at a worship service, another way at a baseball game, and still another way at the bank. People don't cheer at the pastor for delivering a great sermon the way they do at their favorite player, and most don't scream at the bank teller for doing a lousy job the way they yell at the umpire. You probably tend to think kind thoughts about the people in front of you in line to shake hands with the pastor, slightly less kind thoughts about those in front of you in line for a hot dog, and even less kind thoughts about those "holding up the line" at the bank. You feel relatively more relaxed and contemplative at worship but more excited and eager at the game. At the bank, you probably feel nothing in particular, which we refer to as bored.

Personality and Environment Combine

For most people, *personality* and the *environment* combine to cause thoughts, feelings, and behaviors. In environments where there is no expected behavior, personality differences in people can be seen fairly easily. On the playground, there are few expected behaviors (by definition, any play behavior is okay), and the differences in children are easy to see. Some are loud and rambunctious, whereas others prefer to spend the time with a single playmate. Some office workers are neat, prompt, and organized, whereas others don't seem bothered when they can't remember the location of their desk. At the same party, some people will dance, even if they don't know how, whereas others are mortified by the idea that others might see them near the dance floor.

At other times the environment is the main determinant of thoughts, feelings, and behaviors. That is, sometimes the environment demands certain behavior. Everyone at a church service acts the same during the sermon (i.e., sits quietly). It is hard to tell who the shy child is when the whole classroom is quietly taking a test. When looking at rows of soldiers lined up for inspection or rows of musicians lined up for marching band practice, it is difficult to tell one personality from another. The children's and soldiers' and musicians' behavior in these situations is explicitly prescribed.

An OCEAN of Personality Traits

Psychologists who study personality agree that there are five main traits across which everyone varies. They are referred to as "the Big Five," and the acronym for them is OCEAN. These are ways of describing people. Being either relatively high or relatively low on any of these traits is neither problematic nor advantageous (although being very high or very low on any trait may cause a person occasional problems).

- *Openness* to experience is an indication of a person's willingness to try new things. People high on this trait tend to be tolerant, flexible, creative, and perhaps impulsive. People low on this trait tend to be conservative and conventional, and perhaps rigid and narrow-minded.
- *Conscientiousness* is an indication of a person's tendency to take responsibilities seriously. Someone high on this trait will be seen as persistent, stable, consistent, and perhaps rule-bound and obedient. Someone low on this trait might be more free, easygoing, relaxed, and perhaps irresponsible.
- *Extroversion* is an indication of the degree to which one is outgoing versus relatively reserved with regard to interactions with other people. Someone high on this trait (i.e., an "extrovert") will be expressive, enthusiastic, friendly, sociable, or perhaps annoying. Someone low on this trait (i.e., an "introvert") will be relatively quiet, restrained, and inhibited, perhaps to a degree that others might misperceive him as cold and unfriendly.
- *Agreeableness* is an indication of cooperativeness and niceness towards others. Someone high on this trait will tend to be concerned, perhaps excessively, about others' feelings. Someone relatively low on this trait might have a tough, take-care-of-yourself attitude toward other people.
- *Neuroticism* is an indication of general psychological arousal, which means the tendency to be naturally somewhat nervous and high-strung versus relaxed and unreactive. If you are the "jumpy" type, then you may be high on this trait. If nothing tends to bother you, on the other hand, you may be low on this trait.

For most people, personality is flexible and "reacts" to the environment. The shy child can give an assigned speech when necessary. The disorganized worker cleans his apartment when company is expected.

The extrovert manages to sit quietly at a wedding. For most, personality and environment combine to determine how a person thinks, acts, and feels.

For example, imagine that a shy person (an introvert) attends a basketball game with an outgoing person (an extrovert). Introvert and extrovert are commonly known personality traits. The two friends witness a great play by their team's star player. The basketball game and the great play are both environmental factors. The play causes them both to think happy thoughts, to feel happy, and to express happiness. But the extrovert will probably feel happier, think a greater quantity of happy thoughts, and most assuredly will act in a much more happy and obnoxious way than will the introvert. (All of us have sat in front of the extrovert at a game!) As with most people, their personalities combine with the environment to generate their thoughts, feelings, and behaviors.

Personality Disorders

For some people, however, their personality is overwhelmingly and unpleasantly the major determinant of how they think, feel, and act. For them, personality traits are *rigid and unchanging.* They do not change the way they think, feel, and act regardless of the situation. This can lead to serious problems in work, social, and romantic relationships. When this happens, the person may be diagnosed as having a personality disorder.

Someone with a personality disorder will likely have difficulty accepting that there is anything wrong. The person's way of feeling, thinking, and behaving seems normal and natural to him. Likewise, it is common for someone with a personality disorder to *not feel distressed.* Instead, when confronted with dysfunctional relationships and situations, the person may blame others for the problems. The person is simply being himself and is not aware that "himself," that is, his never-changing way of thinking, feeling, and behaving, is responsible for his problems in roles and relationships. Persons with a personality disorder cannot fathom that others think they are doing something wrong.

As a result of this feeling of normality and the lack of distress, it is common for someone with a personality disorder not to seek treatment. Why seek treatment, which entails admitting that I must change, when I am doing nothing wrong? Distress and treatment-seeking might be initiated only after several years—or even decades—of problems in roles and relationships or at the insistence of others who are affected by the dysfunctional behavior. Even if the person with a personality disorder seeks treatment, however, doing so does not necessarily entail an admission of a need to change. As a result, the personality disorders tend to be *very difficult to treat.*

The DSM lists ten personality disorders, and they are briefly described in the box below. This chapter focuses on the three most frequently diagnosed, meaning that you are most likely to see one of these. Also, they are by far the most disruptive to society and to relationships.

The Personality Disorders

Antisocial: disregards and violates the rights of others

Avoidant: socially inhibited; intense feelings of inadequacy; hypersensitive to perceived criticism

Borderline: unstable relationships; unstable self-image; impulsive; emotionally labile

Dependent: excessive need to be taken care of; exhibits submissive and clinging behavior; intense fear of separation

Histrionic: constantly craves attention; excessively emotional

Narcissistic: grandiose fantasies; inappropriate self-aggrandizing behavior; intense need for admiration; lacks empathy for others' feelings or needs

Obsessive-Compulsive: preoccupied with orderliness and neatness; lack of openness; inflexible; despite adherence to rules, usually very inefficient

Paranoid: distrustful and suspicious of others; interprets others' motives as malevolent

Schizoid: detached from relationships; restricted range of emotion

Schizotypal: acute discomfort with close relationships; cognitive or perceptual distortions; eccentricities of behavior

Narcissistic Personality Disorder

Xavier was a 26-year-old seminary student who had been suffering from depression for several years. He came to see me for psychotherapy at the recommendation of one of his professors at the seminary he was attending. He was home for summer and was wondering whether to return the following year. Xavier described himself as an overachiever who always performed at the top of his class as an undergrad.

When asked, he admitted that he didn't always receive the top grade, but that was either because he found the class boring or because the instructors did not know what they were doing. Xavier knew when he came in that I was a professor at Marquette University (he admitted that he had looked me up on the Internet and had downloaded my curriculum vitae [CV]). It was easy to observe that he was carefully watching me while he criticized his professors. He did not seem worried about my reaction, but he was obviously interested in it, and a slight smirk occasionally flitted across his face as he described particularly foolish things his professors had done.

Xavier had read my CV, which he had downloaded from my Marquette website. He brought in a copy of his CV to our first session. He also brought in printouts of his autobiographical statement, which he had submitted to the seminary as part of the admission application. He presented both packets to me and insisted that I read them before the session began. "I know about you, since I looked you up. You should probably learn something about me before we start. It might help you to understand me better." He then questioned me about how long I had been at Marquette, how often I did psychotherapy, and what therapeutic orientation I followed. He knew from my CV where I had attended graduate school, and he declared in an attempt to be kind that "it is actually a pretty good school. I was accepted there, but I decided I really needed a bigger school with a better reputation in order to be challenged."

During subsequent sessions, Xavier went on at length about his disdain for his seminary professors and classmates. It seems that many of the professors were "not that bright" and had only "rudimentary understanding of basic theological concepts." He recounted several instances when he shut down a theological discussion by a declamation that no one, not even the professor, could counter. They tried, to be sure, and they sometimes acted like they had more theological understanding than he did. Their jealousy sometimes forced him to drop classes.

Xavier was openly proud of his physical appearance and his conditioning. At one point he marveled that other students at the seminary, who were less attractive and less athletic, were either in serious relationships or married, whereas he had a lot of difficulty finding a "suitable woman" (meaning someone of unimpeachable beauty who was willing to submit herself to him).

Narcissus

In the late 19th century, a British psychologist first used the term *narcissism* to describe pathological self-love. The term was adopted from the myth of Narcissus.

According to the Roman poet Ovid, the father of Narcissus was the god of rivers and his mother was a nymph. Narcissus was so good-looking that many fell in love with him. But Narcissus rejected them all, including a nymph named Echo, who was so devastated that she shriveled up until all that was left of her was her voice. Another spurned would-be lover begged the goddess Nemesis to punish Narcissus. She caused Narcissus to view his own reflection in a river. He was so enraptured by his own image that he stayed by the river until he died. A flower grew where he died. The narcissus still grows commonly on the shores of rivers and lakes.

Xavier became somewhat distraught when he described that he had no close friends. It was distressing because people could not match his high intellectual and physical standards. "I have trouble having conversations with people who don't have the intellectual background that I have. I find them boring. Also, I could never be a friend to someone who was fat. Fat people disgust me."

Xavier exhibited many of the DSM criteria for narcissistic personality disorder. He had an inflated sense of self-importance, exaggerating his achievements and talents and harboring the expectation that others, such as his fellow students and the professors, would recognize him as superior. He harbored the belief that he was special and unique, such that he could only be appreciated by a specially qualified therapist (hence his questioning my competence) and should only associate with other equally special people (nobody too stupid or fat, please). He had a need for admiration and a highly developed sense of entitlement.

One of the reasons that persons with this disorder have trouble in relationships is that they have great difficulty with empathy. They are either unable or unwilling to recognize that other people have feelings and needs. A single-minded pursuit of one's own needs gets in the way of considering others' needs. Moreover, when someone with such an intense need for admiration is not treated with all due deference, he can react with scorn or rage. The person with this disorder recognizes himself as a special person who deserves special consideration and to whom the rules of everyday life do not apply. Others may not understand his wonderful greatness, but that is their problem.

Antisocial Personality Disorder

The case of Gary Gilmore illustrates many of the characteristics of the antisocial personality disorder (ASPD). Gilmore began drinking at age 10 and displayed antisocial behaviors early. In spite of high intelligence, he did poorly at school and was often truant. Schoolmates regularly accused him of stealing. At age 14 he was sent to a detention center for stealing a car and was subsequently sent to jail several times for burglary. While in prison he gained a reputation for cruel and violent behavior. He never had a steady job or a long-term relationship. On one of his short forays into the world outside of prison, he killed two people while committing armed robbery. He instructed them to lie on the floor, and he shot them. Because of the seeming senselessness of the murders, the judge ordered that his sanity be evaluated. He was found to have an IQ of 129, which is very high, and there was no indication of an organic problem or of a psychotic process. He reported feeling fine: he slept soundly, had a good appetite, enjoyed reading, and was neither depressed nor worried. Gilmore was convicted and sentenced to death, but he had no sympathy for himself either. He refused to appeal his sentence (although others filed appeals on his behalf). Instead, he insisted that he be executed by the method of his choice, and he chose firing squad. In 1977, a Utah firing squad granted his wish. He was the first person to be put to death in the United States in 11 years.

Antisocial personality disorder has been researched most extensively because of the flagrancy of the disorder (i.e., they don't attempt to conceal their depravity). ASPD has a tremendous cost to society. The essential characteristic of the person with ASPD is chronic amoral behavior. They will regularly and without remorse take advantage of other people. These individuals seem to be incapable of taking into account how another might feel about or be affected by their behavior. If they seem to have positive feelings for another, close inspection will reveal that it is an act they play for their own selfish purposes. They can be superficially charming but will react with rage when caught in deception.

The primary emotions a person with ASPD will feel are irritability and hostility. Incredibly egocentric, the person with ASPD sees the victims of his crimes and actions as deserving because they were stupid, weak, and unsuspecting. People with ASPD are usually impulsive and have difficulty delaying gratification. In combination with their lack of empathy for others, they will get caught doing illegal things because they cannot resist doing them and because they are seemingly unaware that others might object. Similar to someone with narcissistic personality disorder, people with ASPD will have great difficulty dealing with authority figures. As a result, they tend to be quite unemployable.

Someone with ASPD obviously will feel little distress about his illness. Distress occurs when they are convicted of a crime and are put in jail. That is not to say that all persons with ASPD are con artists, thieves, murderers, and drug dealers. People with ASPD cut across all professional fields; they take jobs as business executives, DJs, professors, politicians, physicians, plumbers, and candlestick makers.

Nonetheless, many persons with this disorder end up in prison despite the fact that they are, on average, of higher intelligence. The lack of empathy for anyone, including themselves, somehow precludes them from learning from their mistakes, with the result that they get caught and sent to jail. Many prisoners are offered treatment or are mandated to treatment, including persons with ASPD. Unfortunately, there is little evidence that this disorder, in particular, can be successfully treated.

Borderline Personality Disorder

When Don was asked by friends how Sherri was, he would always respond, "Fine, she's doing great." This was not especially true, however. Everyone who knew her would agree with Don's assessment of his wife. She seemed to be doing great. Sherri was very pleasant towards her coworkers and towards the parents of her children's friends. But she was not particularly close to anyone, besides Don. What people on the outside saw was not what he, her children, and her parents experienced.

Sherri often complained to Don that no one knew the real her. He could not disagree. Sherri never felt happy or content inside. She had a terrible self-image, and she always felt very anxious that others would find out what she was really like and would reject her. She acted pleasantly towards colleagues and acquaintances, but she acted horribly towards those closest to her. She alternately adored Don for staying with her and despised him because he would eventually leave her. She was desperate that he not leave but was convinced he ultimately would. In the course of a single morning or afternoon, she would transition from extremely happy to uncontrollably angry. She would be loving one moment and aggressive the next. She might be generous in one sentence, but spiteful and vindictive in the next. Mostly, she felt depressed, empty, worthless, and confused.

Early in their marriage, Don went on a two-day business trip. Sherri could not be convinced that the trip was really for business and insisted that he was going to see someone else and would never return. Don did his best to convince her, at one point having his boss talk to her about the trip (he laughingly told his boss that she was the anxious type and needed to be assured that he would be safe). Rather than be reassured, however, Sherri grew more upset that Don's boss would lie to her to cover for his betrayal. She grew more despondent when he left. She called him that first night to tell him that she had taken her entire bottle of antidepressants. He was forced to call emergency services to take her to the hospital, subsequently cancelling his trip before the first meeting the following day. Don was forced to take another job, for less pay, that would not require business travel. Since that day, Sherri has fairly regularly threatened self-harm or suicide.

Borderline personality disorder (BPD) is characterized by extremes in self-identity and in relationships. The person with the disorder will have extremely poor self-esteem, such that she will have difficulty trusting another person to be genuinely friendly, loving, or committed. The fear of abandonment, even by one's parents, is pervasive. One patient with BPD once noted, "If parents could legally divorce their children, I'm sure mine would have filed the papers by now!" If asked what she is like or what she likes, the person with this disorder will typically answer, "I don't know." The disorder is characterized by a lack of sense of self or of identity. Thus, the person with the disorder will often feel empty, bored, and without purpose.

A person with BPD will likewise be extremely sensitive in relationships, perceiving things in extremes such that her views of others will change quickly. In intimate relationships, someone diagnosed with this disorder will tend to go back and forth between an attitude of idealization and an attitude of detestation. The person with whom they have a relationship will be alternately adored and despised. Someone with BPD will often react unreasonably to perceived slights, with verbal and occasionally physical expressions of anger that are wildly overblown and inappropriate. At the same time, the person with this disorder is desperately fearful of losing friendships and relationships, and she will later come back with extreme expressions of remorse and regret. Needless to say, maintaining a relationship with a person with this disorder can be very difficult.

Given the problems in relationships, it might not surprise readers to learn that this personality disorder, more than any other personality disorder, usually has comorbid mental illnesses. Someone with BPD is likely to have also either an anxiety disorder (such as PTSD), a mood disorder (especially major depression), or a substance use disorder (especially alcoholism). Indeed, it is more likely that she will have a comorbid problem than that she will not. What may surprise readers is to learn that persons with this disorder are also at higher risk for medical problems, such as hypertension; liver, stomach, and heart problems; arthritis; and sexually transmitted diseases.

Current research suggests that the primary cause of BPD is being overwhelmed by emotions. Persons with the disorder don't feel normal levels of emotions, rather they experience emotions to an extreme degree. They don't feel happy, rather they feel deliriously happy. They don't feel insulted, rather they feel unforgivably affronted and offended. This overwhelming nature of emotions appears to be partly biological and partly psychological. There is some evidence that the parts of the brain that are primarily responsible for emotions (i.e., the amygdala and hippocampus) do not function properly. Perhaps because of resultant extreme experiences of emotions, persons with the disorder often report that they feel that no one understands what they are going through. As children, they never get the sense that parents or others (e.g., teachers, coaches, friends) understand, which makes them feel that their perspective is both unappreciated and unimportant. This causes problems with identity development, not to mention an ongoing but unresolvable ache for connectedness to others.

BPD is also unique from the other personality disorders in its association with distress. Someone with BPD will feel miserable much of the time. It is a personality disorder, however, meaning that the sufferer will have difficulty understanding how the problems are her fault. Her thoughts, feelings, and behaviors feel entirely natural because they have in some form or another always been present in her life. Nonetheless, the serious damage that BPD does to relationships will likely lead the person to experience profound distress, which will hopefully lead to seeking treatment.

Finally, BPD is unique among the personality disorders in that the mental health profession has a fairly effective treatment for it. Called dialectical behavior therapy (DBT), the treatment takes a long time and must be administered by a specially trained therapist. But there is good evidence that DBT works, offering hope to both the person with BPD and her family.

Chapter 14

Mental Illness in Children and Adolescents

"If anyone causes one of these little ones—
those who believe in me—to stumble,
it would be better for them to have
a large millstone hung around their neck and
to be drowned in the depths of the sea."
(Matthew 18:6)

This chapter covers the mental illnesses that typically begin during childhood or adolescence: attention deficit hyperactivity disorder (ADHD), oppositional defiant disorder (and conduct disorder), the autism spectrum disorders, separation anxiety disorder, intellectual disability, and reactive attachment disorder.

The chapter provides an overview of the symptoms that are seen with these specific illnesses. It also attempts to give readers a sense of how a child or adolescent with mental illness, and also the child's family, will appear. Issues related to distress and impairment are presented, as are treatment exigencies related to children and adolescents.

Before discussing the disorders, special considerations related to youth and mental illness are considered. The chapter ends with a discussion on controversies associated with the diagnosis and treatment of mental illness in children.

For purposes of this chapter, childhood begins after about age 3, whereas adolescence is usually defined as the age between the onset of puberty and the beginning of adulthood. Also, the issue of disorders related to children and adolescents is lengthy and important. As a result, this is one of the longest chapters of the book.

Special Considerations Related to Children and Adolescents

This section starts by reviewing the manner in which children and adolescents are specifically vulnerable, which is related to the fact that they rely completely or partially on adults for their basic needs. Also considered is the influence of distress and impairment on help-seeking behavior, which is different in children and adolescents than in adults. The issue of mandated reporting (what it is and why it exists) is also discussed. The challenge of conducting research with this population is also reviewed. Finally, a brief review of "normal adolescence," which some think does not exist, is provided.

Specific Vulnerabilities of Children and Adolescents

It is exceptionally troubling to adults when children suffer. Childhood is not supposed to be an endless episode of carefree joy, but most adults probably recall their childhoods fondly. Most are especially distressed when they see a child being hurt by illness or bad circumstance, because they recognize that children are especially vulnerable.

Reliance on Adults

Children and adolescents are limited in their capacity to help themselves. They invariably rely on adults for their basic needs, including healthy food, clean water, and safe living conditions. They are vulnerable to the pathologies, whims, desires, and decisions of adults. Children are not able to seek medical or mental health care on their own but must be taken by a parent or legal guardian. If that person is purposefully abusive or unintentionally neglectful, perhaps due to severe poverty, strained circumstances, or their own mental illness, the child is unlikely to receive needed medical and psychological treatment. Untreated problems that emerge during childhood or adolescence have the potential to endure a long time. Emotional problems in childhood, especially if they go untreated, are likely to endure into adulthood.

Abnormal Can Become Normative

What people experience as children will become normal to them. If Bob was raised in a household that had pets, Bob thinks having a pet is normal. He is much more likely than Bill, who did not have pets growing up, to have a pet in the household he establishes as an adult. If the television was always on in Mary's childhood home whereas Molly's childhood home was full of books and readers, no one would be surprised that adult Mary's TV is always on whereas Molly is always reading.

Emotional problems experienced in childhood may likewise become normalized. Whereas an adult who develops anxiety or depression will probably recognize the feelings as unusual and indicative of a problem, the child with anxiety or depression may grow into adolescence and adulthood supposing that those negative feelings are normal. Children and adolescents lack a mature understanding of mental illness and are much less capable of dealing with it than most adults. Thus, the chapter on depression noted that the child or adolescent might express depression not as sad *affect* but rather as irritability or anger.

Likewise, if intimidation, fear, and abuse are a regular part of someone's childhood, then intimidation, fear, and abuse are likely to be a regular part of that person's adulthood. A child who endures enough maltreatment might come to experience it as appropriate. Most readers are familiar with stories about the sad plight of adults who were abused as children. Abused boys and girls may become abusive men and women. More pathetically still, abused girls might become women who seek out abusive partners, mistaking the abuse for an expression of love and belonging.

Lack of Discernment

A related concern is that children and adolescents do not entirely understand the difference between appropriate and inappropriate adult behavior. They are less likely to recognize that they are being mistreated and abused. Indeed, a favorite tactic of abusers is to convince the child that the abuse is actually normal (or that it is her fault).

The Vulnerability of Parents

Children and adolescents are obviously vulnerable. However, parents of children and adolescents who have a mental illness are also vulnerable. Parents who are desperately unhappy about a child's illness are vulnerable to exploitation. Parents want their children to be well, and there have been grotesque attempts to turn such concern into profit. Many people have succeeded in doing just that. Three egregious examples are covered in this chapter. The first is the story of a man who attempted to use the fear of autism to convince parents not to have their children immunized with the MMR vaccine to increase the use of a vaccine his company was selling (see following box). Another concerns the overselling of ADHD medications (see box on p. 247). The chapter ends with Scientology, which decries all mental health professionals so that persons with mental illness will use their expensive and bizarre technique of treatment.

Distress, Impairment, and Treatment-Seeking

Distress predicts treatment in adults. The more distressed an adult, the more likely an adult is to seek treatment voluntarily. On the other hand, if an adult is severely impaired but not particularly distressed, such as in the case of schizophrenia or severe alcoholism, others may force him or her into treatment. Being forced into treatment is much less likely (and less effective) than voluntary treatment.

However, children and adolescents rely on adults for health care. Except in medical emergencies, it is illegal for a health care provider to treat a child or adolescent without the consent of the parent or other legal guardian. (Some states make exceptions for older adolescents.) Whether distressed or impaired, the child or adolescent is "taken" to treatment by a parent or legal guardian.

Consequently, for children and adolescents, the association between distress, impairment, and treatment-seeking is reversed. Distress is not predictive of treatment-seeking, whereas the more impaired the child is, the more likely he is to be taken to treatment. As a result, children and adolescents are the least likely to receive treatment.

Understanding the difference between externalizing and internalizing disorders may help to explain this.

Profiting From the Childhood Disorders, Part 1: Andrew Wakefield Creates the MMR-Autism Controversy

In 1998, the British journal *Lancet,* one of the most well-respected and prestigious medical journals in the world, published an article whose lead author was Andrew Wakefield. In the article the authors stated, "We identified associated gastrointestinal disease and developmental regression in a group of previously normal children, which was generally associated in time with possible environmental triggers." That meant they found evidence that the vaccine against measles, mumps, and rubella (also known as German measles), the so-called MMR vaccine, seemed to be causing some children to develop pervasive developmental disorder or autism. Fairly quickly, vaccination rates declined, in large part because self-proclaimed "autism activists," such as Jenny McCarthy, spread the word that they were unsafe.

In 2011, the *British Medical Journal* published a remarkable statement written by its editor in chief, deputy editor, and associate editor. The article was entitled "Wakefield's Article Linking MMR Vaccine and Autism Was Fraudulent." The article credited the investigative journalism of Brian Deer, who published a series of articles investigating the original *Lancet* article's methods and findings. The journalist showed that Wakefield had misrepresented the methods used and had altered numerous facts about the medical histories of all 12 of the report's subjects to support his claim of a link between MMR and autism. The article asked rhetorically, "Is it possible that he was wrong, but not dishonest?" and answered definitively, "No. A great deal of thought and effort must have gone into drafting the paper to achieve the results he wanted." The original article was purposely fraudulent. According to reports, Andrew Wakefield was motivated by greed. He had financial interests in a company that was producing a vaccine that would be an alternative to the MMR vaccine.

Since its publication, a decade of epidemiological studies involving thousands upon thousands of children who have and have not received the vaccine has uncovered no evidence whatsoever of a link between the MMR vaccine and the autism spectrum disorders.

Did this stop Wakefield and McCarthy? It did not. One might excuse the latter as being a zealous, concerned, misinformed, and misguided parent, but the former simply wanted to make money from many parents' worst nightmare.

Has the story ended? No. The article's claim was widely publicized, and irresponsible and unbalanced media reporting fueled fears. As a direct result, many parents did and do choose to not vaccinate their children out of concern for the vaccine's safety. Hundreds of thousands of children in the United States and the United Kingdom (and elsewhere) are going unvaccinated. Measles, mumps, and rubella are all virus-based diseases, and all are contagious. The diseases usually do not kill, but some children who contract these infections have died because of the fabricated controversy.

Externalizing and Internalizing Disorders

Researchers and clinicians sometimes categorize childhood and adolescent disorders as either "externalizing" or "internalizing." (By the way, these categories could easily apply to the adult disorders.)

Externalizing disorders are those that tend to bother other people, such as parents and teachers, whereas the child does not experience much distress. Hence, the problems are external to the child. The externalizing disorders are essentially defined by impairment in task performance and in relationships.

The best example of an externalizing disorder is attention deficit hyperactivity disorder (ADHD), which is reviewed in detail later on in this chapter. A child with ADHD will have trouble sitting quietly, paying attention, and doing his schoolwork. He will not do well on schoolwork, and his behavior will bother the teacher and other students, causing damage (impairment) to his relationships with them. Affected children are often not distressed by the externalizing symptoms, but may become distressed at the impairment caused by the symptoms (such as constantly being in trouble at school, not having friends, etc.).

In contrast, the internalizing disorders are considered to be internal to the child. These disorders are characterized by negative feelings, such as anxiety and depression. By definition, these disorders cause children a lot of distress. However, the disorders are not usually disruptive to others. Indeed, the child with anxiety will do her best not to be noticed by others, including the teacher and her peers. Children with an internalizing disorder will not do well on schoolwork, as the anxiety or depression interferes with performance. But since the child is not bothering others, the failure will likely be attributed to lack of ability, not a mental illness.

Who Is Referred for Evaluation and Treatment?

Consider Max and Jessica, who are both in second grade at St. Paul's Lutheran Grade School. Max has ADHD and is his teacher's most challenging student. Max has difficulty staying in his seat, constantly interrupts, and has to be reminded several times what task he is supposed to be doing. Jessica has severe anxiety. She is very quiet, never leaves her seat, and never speaks to other children. She does occasionally weep quietly, but the teacher will sometimes ignore this knowing Jessica will eventually stop.

Which child is more likely to be identified by adults as having a problem that may require professional attention?

Children with externalizing disorders are more likely to receive treatment. Teachers will report to parents that the child is performing poorly and is disrupting the classroom, or teachers and the principal will tell the parents that an evaluation is being recommended. The parents want the child to do well, so they will bring him in for evaluation and possibly treatment to make him less irritating and so he does better at school. The problem will hopefully be properly addressed.

The child with an internalizing problem is sometimes not so lucky. Neither externalizing nor internalizing children are capable of recognizing what is going on, but it matters more for the latter. The externalizing child gets into treatment despite never making a complaint or expressing any distress whatsoever. The disruption gets attention. The internalizing child, on the other hand, is not disruptive, so she is not noticed and marked as needing intervention. She does not know, any more than the externalizing child, that what she is feeling and doing indicates that there is something wrong. She does not know, for example, that continuous sad or anxious feelings are an indication of a problem. She is unlikely to complain to her parents except in vague, nonspecific ways (e.g., that she doesn't want to go to school because her stomach hurts). She is thus unlikely to be identified as needing care.

This is a gross simplification. Many externalizing children do not get needed care, and many parents of internalizing children are acutely attentive to anxiety and depression and seek appropriate care. But, generally speaking, the association between distress, impairment, and treatment-seeking is different for children and adolescents than it is for adults.

Mandated Reporting

Because children and adolescents are more vulnerable to abuse and to receiving inadequate care, most states have "mandated reporting" laws. Teachers, nurses, doctors, and others who have regular contact with children and adolescents are mandated to make a report to their state's protective services agency when they discover that a child is being abused or neglected. They are legally obligated to make a report. The laws stipulate, essentially, that professionals are not allowed to rely on their own judgment about the extent, severity, or impact of the abuse or neglect. Mandated reporters either make a report or they break the law. When a report is made, usually to the state's children's protection agency (or some version thereof), the state makes an investigation and potentially becomes involved in securing the well-being of the minor (such as removing the child from the home and placing her in foster care).

Mandated reporting laws have been modified over the years in attempts to define more clearly what is meant by abuse or neglect. Despite this, there remain some controversies and concerns about whether and when a report should be made.

There are two things to understand about mandated reporting. First, as discussed in the next chapter, while most states also demand reporting of abuse or neglect of vulnerable adults, (defined as someone over the age of 18 who, because of either physical or emotional disability, relies on another person for care), but there is not mandated reporting for otherwise healthy adults. For example, if a husband abuses his wife, she might file assault charges with the police, but therapists are not obliged to make a report to state protective agencies. As discussed in chapter 17, some states require some providers, such as those working in emergency departments, to report any assault, but there are not consistent laws cross states as in child abuse.

Second, state agencies are almost always willing and prepared to consult confidentially with anyone, including teachers, physicians, nurses, and mental health professionals, about whether a report needs to be made. It is not necessary to reveal your name, the name of the child or family, or anything else, even if they advise that a report must be made.

Research With Children and Adolescents

Doing research with children and adolescents is much more complex than with adults. For one thing, to study any person under the age of 18 requires parental consent. Such consent is not impossible to get, especially when the researchers only want to ask questions, but it is much more difficult than obtaining consent from an adult. Another problem is that children and adolescents are not as cognizant about their feelings and behaviors as are adults, which calls into question the validity of their self-report of problems.

For these reasons, the childhood and adolescent disorders have been the least researched. Thus, this chapter's information should be understood as "works in progress." Fortunately, research is proceeding quickly and well, and in the last three decades there has been a proliferation of understanding of and effective treatments for these disorders.

Prevalence Rates of Mental Illness in Children and Adolescents

Research shows that children and adolescents experience a similar rate of mental illness as adults. In any given year, between 15% and 20% of children and adolescents will experience or exhibit a diagnosable mental illness. The types of illnesses change as people grow into adults, but the rate is remarkably similar. Also similar to adults, children and adolescents develop mental health problems that are not severe enough or long-lasting enough to be considered diagnosable illnesses but which, nonetheless, cause some level of distress and impairment.

Adolescence Is Not a Mental Illness

In 1992, a 15-year-old killed his mother, father, sister, and brother, and then fled to another state. The event made national news. As I drove to work the following morning, I was appalled to hear a local DJ say he was not surprised by the event. He said, "I'm surprised we don't hear about this kind of thing all of the time. Teenagers are so crazy! They've got hormones raging in their bodies. They don't care about the difference between right and wrong. They are totally whacked out. Not only am I not surprised, fact is I am surprised we don't read about this stuff everyday."

No one sharing the broadcasting studio with him that morning disagreed. This DJ had expressed one of the many popular but entirely mistaken "myths" about normal adolescent development, which is that the "normal teenager" is as likely to murder his family and flee to another state as to eat breakfast and go to school. My guess is that many radio listeners likewise agreed that "most teenagers are nuts." Yet good portions of those very listeners were at the time living with perfectly normal teenagers. That morning, they walked into their place of work and then called home to remind their teenager to let the dog out one more time before going to school. They ended with, "Oh, and good luck in your soccer game; I hope to get there before halftime."

The idea that normal adolescence is tumultuous is not new nor is it limited to the general populace. Anna Freud (Sigmund's daughter), who became famous in her own right as a child psychiatrist, wrote about the normal "Sturm und Drang" (storm and stress) of adolescence. Other mental health theorists have referred to the "normal psychosis" of adolescence.

In other words, there has long been the belief that the normal adolescent is impulsive, moody, unhappy, and rebellious. An exaggeration of this idea is "Oh, sure, he killed a few siblings and both parents, but he'll grow out of it. It's just a normal stage. Those crazy adolescents!"

Normal Adolescence

Research conducted over the last five decades, including ongoing research that is following children through adolescence and into middle-age adulthood, has established that most adolescents are happy, well adjusted, and emotionally healthy. Most adolescents report that they love their parents, want to do well in school, hope to get a good job, and hope to be able to contribute meaningfully to society. Contrary to the belief that teenage worries are irrelevant, surveys of adolescents consistently find that one of their primary worries is how their parents are doing. Another common worry, which doesn't seem that odd or awful, concerns whether they will be able to find gainful employment and a happy relationship as adults.

That is not to say that all adolescents are happy and healthy. As noted earlier, about one in five teens experiences significant depression or anxiety, drug or alcohol related problems, school or work problems, or interpersonal problems. This parallels the figure for adults.

Myths and Realities About Adolescence

Myths (based on popular notions)	Facts (based on research)
• Adolescents rebel against their parents' values • Adolescents hate hard work • Adolescents are emotionally unstable • Adolescence is painful and difficult for most • Peer pressure is always bad • Teen worries are minor and meaningless	• Adolescents tend to express values similar or identical to their parents • Adolescents value hard work and accomplishment • Most report enjoying the period of adolescence, although (like adults) about one in five will have a mental illness • Peers may pressure friends to study, join clubs, not smoke, and go to church • The most common adolescent worry is whether their parents are okay

Physical Development

The physical development that occurs during the adolescent years is called puberty. The body matures biologically and becomes capable of reproduction, a process that takes about two years. The body also grows larger, as anyone who has ever been responsible for keeping food supplied in a household containing a teenager or two can attest. Puberty begins and ends, on average, about two years earlier for girls than for boys. It probably comes as a complete shock to readers to learn that cognitive development (i.e., intelligence) and emotional maturity also begin sooner in girls than boys.

Cognitive Development

Mental ability expands dramatically during the adolescent years. One of the primary cognitive changes between childhood to adolescence—the change that most befuddles parents—is the greater ability to understand another's perspective. Consider what this new ability enables.

When the child asks if he can spend the night at a friend's house, he does not know if his friend's mom gave approval, is not sure where his friend lives, and has no idea how he would either get there tonight or get home tomorrow. This shows that children tend not to think ahead and to plan, but it also shows that most children don't anticipate what their parents will think or ask about.

In contrast, when the adolescent asks if she can spend the night at a friend's house, she has already thought through most of her parents' questions, concerns, and potential objections. Yes, her friend's parents are really nice and they will be home. No, they won't be allowed to stay up late, because they have to get up early the next day. Yes, they will be having pizza for supper, and so can she have some money? When in such conversations, parents can feel as if they are being overwhelmed with information or as if they are being tricked into a debate for which they had not prepared.

Compared to the child, the adolescent has the capacity to understand others' thoughts and perspectives. This new skill has both good and bad aspects. The good aspect is that adolescents are more capable of predicting what will happen in the future and of understanding how others are feeling. A bad aspect is that teenagers become terribly concerned about how others view them. Children don't realize that others think about them, which is why parents need to remind them to change their shirt, brush their hair, and take a bath. Adolescents presume everyone is always thinking only about them. This leads to newly developed apprehensions about hair, clothing, and other style issues. Thus they complain that they cannot find a decent shirt to wear and spend hours in the bathroom, first emptying the hot water heater and then fixing their hair.

Emotional and Social Development

Adolescence is a time of intense emotional and social development. In both areas, identity development plays a major influence. Indeed, identity formation is considered by many to be the primary "task" of adolescence.

Identity is an understanding of who you are. When asked identity questions, children and adolescents will respond differently. When asked who she is, the child will respond with concrete facts: she is 9 years old, is in fourth grade with Mrs. Baker, and is the daughter of Jack and Betty Walker. The child's identity tends to be framed in terms of identification with important others.

Because of newly developing cognitive powers, the adolescent will think more deeply and complexly about her identity. Whereas children report on what they see and experience, adolescents are capable of abstraction. The adolescent remains the daughter of Jack and Betty Walker, but the adolescent realizes that she *could* have been born the daughter of another couple. She *could* be attending a different school. She *could* have been born in a different country, within a different culture with different beliefs. The adolescent is able to picture different versions of herself and especially of her future. This is both exhilarating and frightening. Her identity is no longer fixed but rather is in flux. During this time, the adolescent might try different identities to see how they fit. One day she loves country music, the next day punk music. One morning he has a Mohawk, that afternoon a crew cut. Various looks, preferences, and even attitudes are tried.

During the process of identity development, the relationship between parent and adolescent can change dramatically. The adolescent will *pull away* from her family, ignoring or avoiding them and maybe acting like she'd rather be anywhere else than with them. At the same time, there will be a drastic increase in the importance of friends. Parents' opinions about clothing, hair, music, and interests determine how children look, what they listen to, and what they do. Adolescents seek out their friends' opinions in these matters.

This can be difficult and painful for parents, but it is also normal and necessary. For most adolescents, the safest place to try a new identity is at home. Despite protestations to the contrary, the adolescent cares very much what her parents think. She is confident that her parents will not reject her regardless of what she does. Parents may get upset, but they won't abandon her. Thus she can test her new identity within the safety and security of her family before she trots it out in front of her friends. Better to try a new hairstyle, new music, new avocations, and new attitudes with people who will love you no matter what you do. Being rude with your parents may get you in trouble, but it is almost always forgiven. In contrast, being rude with your friends may end those friendships. So adolescents will test-drive new behaviors and attitudes within their families, to see how things turn out, before using them with friends.

So the difficult adolescent striving for independence is not necessarily the poorly adjusted adolescent. In fact, I tell parents that when the adolescent pulls away, it's a good indication that they have done a good job raising him. The well-adjusted adolescent *must* establish a relatively independent identity. Hopefully, he will hang on to much of what his family has taught him (such as remaining in the faith), but he also must begin the process of becoming the unique person he will be as an adult. After all, he is going to need an identity when, in a few short years, he becomes an adult and either joins the workforce or attends college, where he will be independent and be held responsible for his behavior.

Distinguishing Normal Adolescence From Mental Illness

The period of adolescence can be "crazy making" for parents, as their predictable and dependent child transforms into an unpredictable teenager who seems to go out of her way to find things about which to disagree. However, this is not the same as mental illness, where the individual is emotionally distressed and psychosocially impaired. It's important to understand when an adolescent is developing normally versus when an adolescent is experiencing mental health problems.

The problem with the myth that all teenagers are crazy is that when a teenager does exhibit emotional problems, she may be overlooked or ignored rather than assisted and, if necessary, referred for formal help.

Disorders That First Emerge in Childhood and Adolescence

The five most prevalent mental illnesses of childhood and adolescence are reviewed in this section. Some illnesses are familiar but have slightly different presentations. Some illnesses are unique to childhood, meaning that they cannot be diagnosed in an adult if they were not apparent when the person was a child. For example, one cannot develop autism as an adult; by definition, autism begins in childhood. (Although sometimes a mental illness that was present in childhood is not recognized and diagnosed until adulthood.)

Attention Deficit Hyperactivity Disorder (ADHD)

One of the most common mental health disorders in children is attention deficit hyperactivity disorder (ADHD), an extremely serious illness that has potential long-term, negative consequences if it is not detected and treated appropriately. ADHD is usually classified as an externalizing disorder. ADHD is a problem of attention and hyperactivity.

Children and adolescents (and adults) with ADHD have difficulty staying focused. Research suggests that the part of their brains that sustains attention is underactive. As a result, children with ADHD often fail to finish tasks (such as homework assignments, projects, and chores). They make frequent, seemingly careless mistakes; have great trouble getting or staying organized; have difficulty following directions; and often lose things. These attention-related problems become most evident when the child begins school.

Signs of hyperactivity are also obvious in the classroom but are usually evident prior to that. At home, children exhibit hyperactivity by running excessively, climbing things that shouldn't be climbed, playing loudly, and talking excessively. At school, hyperactivity manifests itself as difficulty sitting still. Children with ADHD will fidget and leave their seats at inappropriate times. They will act without thinking, commonly called impulsivity. They will blurt out answers without being called upon, will have difficulty waiting their turn, and will interrupt both the teacher and other students.

Although the term ADHD suggests otherwise, to meet criteria for a diagnosis of ADHD does not require that the child exhibit *both* attention problems and hyperactivity. Symptoms of hyperactivity are not universal in the disorder. Likewise, most but not all children with ADHD have attention difficulties. As a result, mental health professionals will specify the disorder as "ADHD primarily inattentive," "ADHD primarily hyperactive," or "ADHD mixed presentation."

ADHD appears to be a biological problem that is exacerbated by environmental factors. The brains of children with ADHD appear to be either underdeveloped or underactive in the areas associated with attention. Inadequate attention capacity causes problems at home and at school, with which most parents and most teachers are unprepared to cope unless specially trained to implement specific behavioral strategies.

Distress and Impairment

There is minimal distress or impairment in preschool children with ADHD. Adults take care of everything for young children, so being inattentive is not a particular problem, and it will likely go unnoticed. Most young children tend to be somewhat impulsive, such that the impulsive child (with ADHD) may likewise not be noticed. However, the externalizing problems can cause serious internalizing problems characterized by self-hatred and significant distress as the child grows into a teenager and then an adult.

Bobby

By age 2, Bobby was terrifying his mother and father. He was an early crawler and walker, not bothered by falls and bumps into furniture. One cold and rainy day, when the doors and windows were all shut, they simply couldn't find him. After 20 frantic minutes of searching and calling, they heard him giggle from the top of the 6-foot tall bookcase in the family room. Other times they would find him on top of the refrigerator or stove (he loved playing with the dials) or walking along the edge of the kitchen counter.

Bobby was an extremely loving child who couldn't get enough hugs. His hugs tended toward the violent, however, as he would literally fling himself into his parents' arms, strangle them, poke around with his knees and elbows, and then escape. Father compared it to hugging the Tasmanian Devil of Bugs Bunny fame. After several drops and near-drops, they learned not to stand when hugging him.

If his mother did not watch him closely in the park, he would wander off. On one occasion, she became involved in discussion with another mother and later found Bobby on another street, staring into the window of a home, either unaware or uncaring that he had become lost.

Bobby is now in third grade. He sits in the front row on a special pad, designed for kids like him to enable constant but *quiet* squirming. Locating Bobby here enables his teacher to redirect him to the task at hand. Bobby asks endless questions, most of which are irrelevant to the material being studied. He hums and drums his pencils on the top of his desk or book or occasionally his own head. His desk is terribly disorganized, with notebooks, papers, and crayons falling onto the floor. He is still a very loving and loveable child.

Impairment becomes evident quickly when the child with ADHD starts school, although distress will remain minimal for a while. The most basic requirements of school are perfectly contradictory to the illness: sit still and pay attention. In other words, even though ADHD is unassociated with intelligence, children with ADHD are perfectly prepared to fail the requirements of school. Aside from family, school probably ranks as the most important influence on a child's emotional development. From a young age, much of our lives are spent at school, which almost always entails some sort of formal evaluation of capability and achievement. School is where the smart, capable, and likeable are discovered. Alternatively, school is where a child may realize that he is none of these things.

Thus, if left undiagnosed or untreated, the child with ADHD will develop substantial impairment at school. School problems have fairly comprehensive and far-reaching consequences, including school dropout and employment problems. Problems of attention and impulsivity also cause serious problems in relationships.

This impairment eventually leads to fairly severe distress. Being at a place of constant failure for six to eight hours per day, five days per week, is not good for a child's self-esteem. Quite understandably, the child with ADHD may learn to despise school and, more generally, authority figures. It can be hard to like and appreciate teachers, for example. Teachers constantly remind the child with ADHD to pay attention and try harder. Teachers regularly provide feedback to the child and to the child's parents that he is not doing as well as he could be. As ADHD is unrelated to intelligence, teachers are correct in observing this. The observation is correct, but it is entirely unhelpful.

The attention problems of ADHD will affect friendships. The child with ADHD, being less attentive, is less likely to pick up on important social cues, such as smiles or frowns. Attention to others' wants and needs is essential if one is to be a kind and considerate person. Since attention is a problem for the child with ADHD, he is less likely to be socially appropriate with peers, and he is less likely to be liked by others. The third grader at recess who cannot wait his turn or follow the rules of games will have trouble making and keeping friends. In some of the saddest research one can read, teachers, children, and parents consistently rate children with ADHD as less likeable.

Impulsivity also causes substantial problems in relationships. Impulsivity is expected in a two-year-old. Before any two-year-old enters the living room, her grandmother will quickly go around the room putting certain figurines and other valuable objects out of reach. Impulsivity in an eight-year-old is more surprising and aggravating. The eight-year-old who breaks one of his grandma's things might be forgiven; the eight-year-old who breaks one of his grandma's things every time he visits might develop a reputation. The eight-year-old who breaks a classmate's favorite toy airplane, which is being passed around during show-and-tell, might develop problems making and keeping friends.

Children with ADHD have these types of experiences fairly continuously. As a result, they are at higher risk for developing poor self-esteem and worse. Adult outcomes of children with ADHD include higher rates of depression, drug and alcohol use problems, and other emotional problems. There are long-term effects on the child's attitude toward school and work: those with ADHD are twelve times as likely to drop out of high school and one-fourth as likely to graduate college or to have a professional job as an adult.

For these reasons, one might say that ADHD starts as an externalizing disorder but develops into a combined externalizing and internalizing disorder.

Other Noteworthy Things to Know About ADHD

ADHD affects between 3% and 5% of children in the United States. It used to be believed that it was primarily a boys' diagnosis, but more extensive research has suggested that the rates are similar for the two sexes. It seems that boys are more likely to exhibit the behavioral problems (i.e., hyperactivity) and are thus more likely to be diagnosed and treated.

ADHD is highly comorbid with other conditions, including learning disabilities and oppositional defiant disorder.

In contrast to most mental illnesses where the subjective experience of the person is important, ADHD is diagnosed solely on the basis of adults' observation of symptoms. This is because children cannot reliably report that they have attention, hyperactivity, or impulsivity problems.

Over half of children with ADHD will continue to experience symptoms as adults.

Some children with ADHD are never diagnosed, and many enter adulthood with substantial educational, relationship, and occupational impairments. Some will seek treatment as an adult (such as after their child is referred for an evaluation and they recognize the similarities between their own and their child's behavior and problems). To be diagnosed with the condition for the first time as an adult, the person must have exhibited ADHD symptoms in childhood. Evaluation of adults for possible ADHD should entail examining the person's educational and work history, as well as interviewing parents (about the person's behavior as a child). A diagnosis of ADHD can bring great relief to an adult. The diagnosis explains the reason for the problems they had as a child and continue to have now, which may alleviate their shame and distress.

Diagnosis and Treatment

It is extremely important to diagnose and treat ADHD so that children with the disorder will not be impaired by the illness and perhaps suffer negative psychological consequences for the rest of their lives. The proper diagnosis of ADHD is reviewed later. The treatment options are now reviewed.

Medications. Medications are typically the first choice in treatment for this disorder. Usually the medication is some version of psychostimulant medication. As the name implies, psychostimulants stimulate the brain and help the child with ADHD focus. Caffeine is a mild psychostimulant, and many adults use some version of caffeine in the morning to rouse themselves and to improve their ability to concentrate. Psychostimulant medications are much more potent, and they have a similar effect.

The medications are variable. They may be a pill, liquid, or skin patch. Some are short acting and must be taken throughout the day, usually in collaboration with the school nurse. Others are extended release, allowing the child to take the medication once a day before school.

Hundreds of clinical trials have been conducted and have shown that these medications significantly reduce the attention and hyperactivity problems of children with ADHD. In these research studies, one group of children is given a medication whereas another group is given a placebo. The effects are noticed almost immediately, such that teachers and parents report that they know easily when a child has not taken his medication. Long-term studies have shown that children with ADHD who take medications, compared to children with ADHD who do not, are more likely to finish high school and attend college. As adults they earn more in their employment.

Children with ADHD seem to respond to medication because it addresses the underlying biological problem, which is underactivity in the part of the brain that is responsible for attention and focus. The medications do have common side effects, some of which can be quite unpleasant or even dangerous. These need to be monitored carefully (see section on controversies on the next page).

Psychological Treatment. To summarize, research has shown that medications can be beneficial to the child, adolescent, and adult with ADHD.

However, long-term follow-up of children and adolescents with ADHD who took medications suggest a somewhat complicated picture. It is found that compared to children and adolescents with ADHD who did not take medications, the children and adolescents with ADHD who took medications fare much better. However, they still fare much more poorly than their non-ADHD peers.

The anti-ADHD medications improve attention and reduce hyperactivity, which help improve school performance to some extent. However, the skills to do well at school, as well as the skills to do well in social settings, will not improve with medications alone. By the time the proper diagnosis is made and appropriate treatment is initiated, children and adolescents with ADHD are typically lagging far behind non-ADHD peers in essential skills. Regarding schoolwork, children with ADHD, even if taking medication, will continue to lag behind with regard to the essential school skills, such as breaking tasks into manageable parts, organization and preparation, and sustained effort. Social skills, such as waiting one's turn, engaging in cooperative play and conversation, and being a good friend, are also likely to continue to be deficient.

Research strongly suggests, then, that psychological treatment is a necessary adjunct, and perhaps a sufficient alternative, to medications. Psychotherapy for ADHD tends to focus on practical strategies for dealing with attention problems and impulsivity. For example, a therapist will teach a family to set up homework time to minimize distractions to the child (e.g., making sure that the television and radio are off, keeping other children and the parents quiet). Likewise, a child may be taught to think through tasks (i.e., organize work before beginning it) and to think before she speaks. In social skills training, the therapist teaches appropriate social behaviors so that the child can develop and maintain friendships.

So, medications or psychotherapy? The former is easier and will lead to immediately observable improvement in attention capacity and hyperactivity. Moreover, it may be the only viable option for some families. But medications will not address essential skill deficits. Psychotherapy takes longer and requires more effort on the part of both the child and parents, but it teaches necessary life skills that have not developed normally.

In summary, medications are necessary for some children, but other children do as well with psychotherapy alone. Also, medications are more effective in the short run, but psychotherapy is more effective over the long-term. Finally, the combination of medications and psychotherapy is the most effective treatment of all.

Important Controversies Regarding ADHD (Including Proper Diagnosis)

The diagnosis and treatment of ADHD has been controversial in the last few decades. To a great extent—and probably more than most readers are aware—this controversy has been created and promoted by Scientology. As discussed in the last section of this chapter (and more thoroughly reviewed in chapter 19), Scientology has a financial interest in getting people to reject the idea that ADHD or any other mental illness exists (so that they will instead join Scientology, which is the only legitimate way to address their "real" problems). Of course, this "controversy" started by Scientology is not a controversy at all: mental illness, including ADHD, is real, and ADHD in particular can cause profound psychosocial impairment in children, which puts them at risk for lifelong problems and therefore needs to be diagnosed and addressed.

The two authentic controversies regarding ADHD are concerns about the safety of medication treatment and concerns that more and more children are being diagnosed with and treated for the disorder than actually have it.

Concerns about the safety of ADHD medications. Because of the high likelihood of improvement, psychostimulant medication is the standard of care for ADHD. Potential side effects will be familiar to anyone who has ever taken an excessive dose of caffeine: decreased appetite, stomachaches or headaches, sleep difficulties, anxiety, and irritability. The appetite and sleep disturbances are particularly worrisome, as children need to eat and sleep well in order to maintain their normal trajectory in weight and height gains. Ingesting excessive amounts causes more extreme side effects of the drugs. They are very rare but also very dangerous, and they include heart problems or psychotic-like symptoms (probably because the drugs increase the activity of the neurotransmitter dopamine in the brain).

There are other concerns about ADHD medications in addition to side effects. Psychostimulant medications are popular drugs of abuse. It is estimated that 10-20% of all *prescribed* ADHD medications end up being abused.

A dramatic increase in ADHD diagnosis. Many more children and adolescents are diagnosed with ADHD than in years past. For example, the Centers for Disease Control and Prevention (CDC) published data showing that the rate of diagnosis of the disorder in children and adolescents between 4 and 17 years of age climbed about 5% every year from 2003 to 2011 and that a diagnosis of ADHD had been made in

15% of high school children. (By the way, adults are also being increasingly diagnosed with ADHD.)

There are two reasons that ADHD is diagnosed now more than previously. First, the increase in diagnosis and treatment reflects progress. ADHD has become more well-known and well-understood over the last several decades. So part of the increase in diagnosis is likely due to better recognition by schools, parents, and pediatricians.

The second reason, however, is that ADHD is being overdiagnosed. A diagnosis of ADHD is too frequently given to children and adolescents who do not actually have it. Several studies have confirmed this. For example, one study found that many children and adolescents who were prescribed medications for ADHD did not have it but more often had oppositional defiant disorder (ODD).

Mistakenly diagnosing a child or adolescent with ADHD when he does not have it is an extremely serious issue. The diagnosis is likely to lead to treatment with anti-ADHD medications, which can cause potentially serious side effects. For a child with ADHD, parents and physicians will make a careful decision as to whether the risk of untreated ADHD outweighs the risk of side effects. Likewise, concerned parents, pediatricians, and especially pediatric psychiatrists will mitigate those risks by carefully monitoring the side effects to decrease the potential for harm to the child.

But there are few legitimate excuses for giving these medications to a child who does not actually have ADHD. Mistakenly diagnosing a child with ADHD when the child does not have it reflects a failure on the part of teachers, pediatricians, and parents to ensure that the diagnosis is legitimate. Parents of children suspected of having ADHD should always consult with an appropriately trained mental health professional who specializes in pediatric populations (i.e., pediatric psychiatrists and psychologists), as only they are specifically trained to distinguish the various causes of problems at school, including possible ADHD.

Profiting From the Childhood Disorders, Part 2: Pharmaceutical Companies

The most common treatment for ADHD is medications. Pharmaceutical companies develop and market medications in the hope that the medications will sell, and no one (including the author, who has type 1 diabetes) who has ever relied on a medication to save his or her life will have a problem with drug companies making profits from medications.

On the other hand, drugs for ADHD have proven extremely profitable to pharmaceutical companies in large measure because of advertising efforts that ultimately encourage their overuse. Sales of these medications in 2002 were almost two billion dollars, whereas in 2012 they came close to nine billion dollars.

The advertisements for anti-ADHD meds are ubiquitous, appearing on television and in popular magazines. The advertisements tend to exaggerate the influence of ADHD (suggesting that it causes any and all problems with otherwise wonderful and brilliant children). Moreover, they tout the benefits of the drugs while underemphasizing their dangers (which are presented at fast speed or in very small font). They typically suggest that ordinary childhood behaviors, such as forgetfulness, disagreeableness, and commonplace school issues, such as not liking school and not wanting to do homework, are actually ADHD-induced problems that can be solved with medication. Some companies advertise directly to children, including producing comic books in which superheroes tell the reader, "Medicines may make it easier to pay attention and control your behavior!"

As a result, the Food and Drug Administration has repeatedly fined pharmaceutical makers of the major anti-ADHD drugs for false and misleading advertising.

The Importance of Competent Diagnosis and Treatment

Ironically, one of the reasons ADHD is overdiagnosed is that the disorder can be very successfully treated with medications. Such success has led to an overreliance on medication treatment and not enough utilization of psychological techniques (see above). It has also led to sloppiness on the part of health professionals, especially pediatricians, who prescribe anti-ADHD medications to children and adolescents without verifying that they actually have ADHD. As noted, evidence strongly suggests that anti-ADHD medications are often prescribed for problems other than ADHD.

Pharmaceutical companies that want to increase profits have driven the overdiagnosis of ADHD (see box above). The advertising has had the effect of convincing some teachers, doctors, and parents to simply and simplistically think, "We'll try these meds and see if they work," without fully acknowledging that the medications are not risk free and can, in fact, be dangerous. Common side effects are insomnia, appetite problems, and psychological dependence (the feeling that you cannot cope without them), but heart damage, psychosis, and suicidal thoughts are also possible.

Without careful evaluation of the entirety of the child's situation, a diagnosis of ADHD might be given when it should not. For this reason, parents should *never* allow a nonmental health professional to convince them that their child has ADHD. Parents, teachers, and nonpsychiatrist medical doctors can certainly help recognize that a child may be exhibiting symptoms of ADHD, such as problems at school. However, regardless of how many children they have had in their classrooms or they have seen at their offices, teachers and pediatricians are not experts in ADHD. Only experts should be allowed to diagnose a child as meeting the criteria for ADHD.

Differential diagnosis by a mental health professional. Despite what pharmaceutical companies would have you believe, sometimes difficulties paying attention and focusing are not due to ADHD. Some children arrive at school hungry, which makes paying attention difficult. Sometimes (believe it or not) a teacher is boring and children have trouble staying interested and paying attention. Sometimes a child has never been taught how to pay attention, to follow through on tasks, or to do as he is told. Sometimes a teacher simply dislikes a certain child, which the child will sense and which may cause the child to be less motivated to do well at school. Sometimes problems at home cause the child to have problems at school. In other words, problems at school are not just due to ADHD. Treating all such problems with medication is often done, but it is inappropriate.

ADHD does not cause problems just at school. The problems of attention and hyperactivity should show up everywhere, not just in certain situations or during certain tasks or with certain teachers. Therefore, assessment should involve evaluation of the child's attention capacity and behavior across a variety of situations. A proper, comprehensive evaluation will involve ratings by parents and teachers, as well as a clinical interview (of the child and parents) and testing of attention capacity, usually through some specially designed test. Only mental health professionals specializing in children can conduct such an evaluation.

Tom Doesn't Have ADHD

Consider Tom, who is eight years old and in Mrs. Johnson's third grade classroom. He has trouble paying attention, and as a result he talks to other kids and distracts them. He gets upset when scolded, and Mrs. Johnson gets the distinct impression that he is not intentionally being disruptive. He is also forgetful and disorganized, and he often claims that he completed the homework or assignment but cannot find it. For these reasons, Mrs. Johnson thinks Tom likely has ADHD. But Tom did okay for Mrs. Andersen last year. In addition, he doesn't show attention or behavioral problems either at home or at Sunday school.

Suppose that the teacher and principal recommend that Tom might have ADHD and the parents take Tom to a pediatrician instead of to a pediatric psychologist or psychiatrist. Although generally unqualified to determine whether Tom's problems are due to ADHD or to one of hundreds of other possible causes, the pediatrician nonetheless prescribes psychostimulant medication. Tom ends up taking the drug for no legitimate reason. Even worse, the medication actually helps Tom's behavior improve, which lends credence to the idea that he does actually have ADHD and increases the likelihood that Tom will be kept on the medication in years to come.

Now suppose that Tom is instead seen by a pediatric psychologist who conducts a full psychological evaluation, including an evaluation of Tom's attention capacity, intelligence, school achievement (including intensive evaluation of Tom's capacity in reading, mathematics, and writing), and family and social environments. The testing shows that Tom's family is relatively happy and healthy but that Tom's father had been diagnosed as having a learning disability as a child. The testing further reveals that Tom's attention capacity is normal, his vocabulary is normal, and he is a quick thinker. It also shows that Tom has specific difficulty processing letters. So he knows the typical number of words that any third grader knows, but his brain has difficulty processing letters, with the result that written words are sometimes jumbled for him. Tom doesn't know that this is going on inside his brain; all he knows is that he isn't understanding school stuff very well and the teacher keeps getting mad at him.

If properly diagnosed, Tom will not be given inappropriate medications. Instead, his reading problems will be addressed.

Proper treatment means monitoring and caution. Treatment of ADHD with medications is a very serious business. For this reason, a pediatric psychiatrist should monitor their use for ADHD. With proper monitoring, the risks of psychostimulant medications can be minimized or eliminated. Clinicians and researchers agree that the risk of stimulant treatment is overwhelmed by the risk of not treating ADHD, which would allow a child to proceed through life hating school, perceiving himself as defective and unlikable, and being unable to succeed at college or in a career.

Oppositional Defiant Disorder and Conduct Disorder

It is fairly normal for a child to go through a phase when he or she is defiant and difficult. "Terrible twos" is a popular expression that suggests the normalcy of a developmental period wherein the child is loud, demanding, and unpleasant. Most children outgrow this phase under the guidance and nurture of their parents, who set limits and refuse to cater to unreasonable demands. However, some children never outgrow it and other children seem to return to this "terrible" attitude and behavior after seemingly outgrowing it.

Oppositional defiant disorder and conduct disorder are two distinct disorders, but they are grouped together because they are similar in many ways. Bad behavior on the part of the child or adolescent is the hallmark of both disorders. Oppositional defiant disorder is less severe than conduct disorder. The former can develop into the latter if the behavior goes from bad to worse.

A child with oppositional defiant disorder (ODD) regularly acts negatively and hostile. He will exhibit defiant behavior (hence the name of the disorder), including frequent temper tantrums, defying rules, and arguing with adults when they confront him about his misbehavior. Children with ODD will deliberately antagonize and annoy other people. They are likely to blame those same other people for their behavior.

ODD is not a pleasant disorder to confront. Conduct disorder (CD) is downright unpleasant and frightening. CD encompasses all of the behaviors of ODD, but it is more severe in that it entails serious violations of other people's rights. A child or adolescent with this disorder will act aggressively towards others, for example, by bullying or forcing unwanted sexual contact. Someone with the disorder will casually and habitually lie, both in order to avoid punishment but also, seemingly, because he simply sees no benefit to ever telling the truth. Violations of the law are seen with this disorder also, such as the willful destruction of property and stealing. Other serious rule violations will include school truancy, staying out all night, or running away from home.

ODD is more common for boys before puberty, but it is equally common among boys and girls after puberty. In contrast, boys consistently outnumber girls with regard to being diagnosed with CD. Although some children seem to be born to be bad, the best current explanation for both disorders is family problems. Poor discipline practices (i.e., nonexistent or inconsistent responses on the part of parents to children's misbehavior) and general disregard and neglect (i.e., not attending to the child's needs, especially their social and emotional needs) are excellent predictors of the development of ODD and CD. A child whose parents do not discipline him does not have the chance to learn self-discipline, and he will not develop the capacity to act appropriately with other adults. Doing what he is told is simply a foreign concept. In contrast, a child who is essentially ignored by his parents will yearn for adult attention. He may learn quickly that he gets lots of attention by misbehaving. To adults, it will seem odd that a child would enjoy aversive and punishing attention. To the child, even this type of attention is better than no attention.

Distress and Impairment

As might be guessed, children and adolescents with ODD and conduct disorder tend to experience minimal distress. The obnoxious behavior, lying, defiance, rule violations, and mistreatment of others does not cause them remorse or discomfort. They may feel distress if they get in trouble, but not usually otherwise.

On the other hand, impairment is fairly serious in both disorders. Children and adolescents with ODD will be in regular trouble at school. Having the more severe disorder, children and adolescents diagnosed with CD may end up in the juvenile criminal justice system and may be referred to residential treatment programs.

Relationship impairment will be particularly serious. Children and adolescents with these disorders will be extremely unpopular with other kids, and they will be especially unpopular with, if not outright detested by, teachers and other adults. Both disorders are much more common in homes where antisocial behavior on the part of adults and other children is customary. Impairment in family relationships is therefore also commonplace, but the relationships were probably pathological prior to the development of the disorders rather than as a result of the disorders.

Claire Doesn't Need to Try

Claire was not Mrs. Matthews' favorite 4th-grade student. Not by a long shot. Claire was disagreeable on her best days, and she seemed to spend as much time in the principal's office as in the classroom (which suited Mrs. Matthews just fine). But the principal also had no luck with Claire. When told to do something, Claire demanded an explanation as to why she should do it. Whether she received an explanation or not, Claire would usually not do the assignment or activity but would instead pester other children. When scolded, Claire would talk back and occasionally throw a tantrum.

Claire's father was brought in for a chat with the principal and Mrs. Matthews. Despite being asked not to do so, he brought Claire along to the conference. There was no other place to send her, so the teacher and principal allowed her to stay. She insisted on climbing into her daddy's lap. As the conference proceeded, she pestered him to use his phone, to show him how to start the game on it, to show him how to play the game on it, and to watch while she played the game on it. To the increasing irritation of Mrs. Matthews and the principal, Daddy simply put up with it. He occasionally asked her to settle down and let the adults talk, but he was completely ineffective. The conference ended, one weeping fit and one tantrum later, with a promise from Claire to try harder. She didn't.

Claire is now in 8th grade. She smokes and has two different boyfriends. She has been suspended three times so far this year, once for cursing at teachers, once for threatening the assistant principal, and once for stealing.

As is the case for so many children (i.e., when there is no intervention for the earlier disorder), Claire is on her way to progressing from oppositional defiant disorder to conduct disorder.

The Different Faces of ADHD Versus ODD/CD

ADHD, ODD, and CD are all externalizing disorders and share some common symptoms, but they have very different appearances to others.

The child with ADHD is trying to do better, but is literally incapable (given the limitations of his attention span). Likewise, the parents of the child with ADHD are usually trying very hard to figure out what to do differently and how things could go better. They will likely be grateful for help. In brief, the child with ADHD might be difficult to like sometimes (see p. 242), but he and his parents are usually trying.

The children with ODD and CD, on the other hand, do not try to do better. They too exhibit problems at school and with relationships, but they are not interested in changing things. The parents may protest that they are doing their best, but their best is usually pathetically ineffective. Sometimes the parents are simply uninterested and barely involved. As a result, adults will find themselves not liking children and adolescents with ODD and CD. Being defied and cursed at causes adults, who usually think they deserve better, to become impatient and irritated.

Treatment Considerations

Given that distress on the part of the child is minimal and that problem parenting (either ineffective discipline or insufficient attention to the child) is a likely cause, formal help for these disorders is usually not voluntarily sought. Rather, children and adolescents with these disorders will find themselves taken to treatment by parents or legal guardians or mandated to treatment by schools (which may make treatment a contingency for return to school) or by the court system (which may make treatment a contingency for staying out of an institution).

As noted, ODD and CD are not brain-based disorders. Chaotic and unpredictable environments cause these disorders. The only legitimate treatment for these disorders is psychological, which must involve both the parents and the child. Treatment needs to focus on getting parents (and perhaps teachers) to react differently to the child so that he or she learns what behaviors will and will not be tolerated. In other words, adults in the child's environment are trained to manage the child's behavior. These techniques are thus referred to as "behavior management."

The vast majority of parents probably use behavioral management techniques (see box). But some parents need to be trained in behavioral management. For some, their child's behavioral problems are more extreme than most parents must confront (such as in ADHD), and so these parents need to learn special behavioral management skills that most parents don't need to learn. In the cases of ODD and CD, the parent or parents usually have little sense of what it means to train a child. They don't know how to do it and they have never done it, and the child develops ODD and CD as a result.

Behavior Management in Three (Sort of) Easy Steps

The essentials of behavioral management are threefold.

A good mental health professional can help parents develop effective behavior management strategies. First, desirable behaviors, such as complying with requests or saying please and thank you, are reinforced. Every time the behavior occurs, it is rewarded, such as with a treat or with praise. (Mental health professionals call praise and compliments social reinforcement. It would amaze readers to realize how infrequently some parents either praise or compliment their children.)

Second, certain undesirable behaviors that are simply annoying, such as arguing or whining, are ignored. If behaviors are ignored, they go away.

Third, unacceptable behaviors are punished. For example, if a child violates curfew or infringes on the rights of others, such as by stealing or bullying, then an appropriate punishment is implemented.

Effective punishment can be tricky. For example, parents should avoid punishing themselves when they punish their child. I have *never* understood the popular technique of grounding a child or adolescent who misbehaves. Spending the evening with a petulant, irritable, resentful, and disagreeable child punishes the parents as much or more than the child. Instead, I recommend giving the child a ten-minute odious task that needs doing but that no one likes,such as doing the dishes, cleaning the toilet, or picking up the dog's droppings from the yard. At the same time, remove a privilege that the child cherishes (e.g., TV, computer, cell phone) until the child completes the task. As soon as it is finished, the child gets the privilege back and all is forgotten.

Autism Spectrum Disorder

Autism spectrum disorder (ASD) can be among the most severe disorders to affect children. However, there is a range of severity of the disorder (hence the term *spectrum* right in the name). A child or adult with ASD may have mild or severe communication deficits, social difficulties, and behavioral idiosyncrasies.

Communication Problems

Language is fairly predictable in terms of development. By her first birthday, a typical toddler uses single words and turns her head when she hears her name. By age 2, most children begin to put together sentences like "See doggie" or "More juice" and can follow simple directions. Language ability explodes after that, so that the typical seven-year-old is able to form whole sentences, convey personally relevant information, and communicate meaningfully with other children and adults.

In contrast, children with the ASDs have communication problems. The problem may be relatively mild. In mild ASD, the child may have difficulty understanding another person's perspective. A typical problem for someone with a relatively mild manifestation of the disorder is picking up on subtle language clues, such as sarcasm and irony. Moving along the spectrum towards the more severe ASDs, a child's language development may be severely delayed. Normal infants are easily attracted to sounds, whereas an infant with ASD may appear deaf. Indeed, concerns about hearing ability are a common reason that parents bring their infant to the pediatrician, and they are stunned to later learn that their child has been diagnosed with ASD.

Even after rudimentary language skills develop, general language capacity may be severely limited, without ability to generate meaningful sentences or repeating the same phrase no matter the situation. Children without ASD go through a stage where they repeat what they hear, but they typically outgrow this by age 3. Some children with ASD exhibit "echolalia," wherein they parrot what they hear. What they repeat may be a question they were just asked, such as "What's your name?" It may be an advertisement from radio or television. In its most severe manifestation, someone with an ASD may never learn to communicate.

Juan

Juan is eight years old and has severe ASD. He is a sweet child, but only if he is left alone. He doesn't have much interest in other people. He never has. At an age when most infants enjoy being picked up and played with, Juan would squirm and push away. (Needless to say, this was very hard on his parents.) Juan started walking late, and by three years old he was still not talking.

Now, when others try to address him, he doesn't acknowledge them at all. (His therapist must take hold of his chin to make Juan look at her.) If someone tries to come close, he will start to hum, which gets louder and louder if the person does not move away.

Juan doesn't have much interest in people, but he is obsessed with order. He lines up his blocks (but never builds anything with them), keeps his books (which he cannot read) on the bookshelf in order of height, and straightens the kitchen chairs over and over for hours on end, unless his mother distracts him with something else. He doesn't like to be distracted when he is doing his straightening, however, and he throws a tantrum when someone moves anything he has straightened. He also doesn't like loud noises and has a special aversion to the sound of the dishwasher. As he has gotten older, his tantrums have become worse. He sometimes throws things and has three times smashed a window. Other times he will bite himself or hit his head on the floor.

Social Difficulties

Language development problems contribute to problems in social relationships, but such problems start earlier than language. Most infants are extremely social. They stare at people, turn toward voices, clutch fingers, and smile in response to engagement—the child with ASD does not. The child with a severe ASD may be essentially unaware of the comings and goings of others, including parents. Even when approached, she will appear indifferent. She does not respond to social interactions, such as smiles, hugs, and warm, loving attention. Whereas the normally developing infant will be practically enrapt by his mother's face, studying it while being held and delighting in her expressions, infants with an ASD may actively avoid eye contact and will seem disinterested in faces. Some will passively accept attention, including hugs and cuddling, but others will actively resist such attention and physical affection. A normally developing child will become upset when her parent leaves, but the child with ASD does not. Neither will she show pleasure when the parent returns. Considering what most parents are expecting from their infant and child, this is extremely painful for them.

Some observers believe that the ASDs are a problem in the part of the brain that processes and interprets social cues. As a result, children with ASD have difficulty understanding (and appropriately responding to) what others are thinking and feeling. Everyone tends to rely on subtle social and facial cues to distinguish the meanings of words and situations. For example, "What a great idea!" has potentially very different meanings: in one context, the person is being sincere; in another context, the person is being sarcastic and essentially stating that the idea could not be worse. The person with an ASD misses such subtle cues, and social problems ensue. The tone of voice and the smirk or the smile doesn't register.

Without the ability to interpret gestures and facial expressions, the social world will be intensely confusing. Exacerbating the situation, someone with an ASD will have difficulty understanding another person's perspective. He will not understand that all of us have different information, feelings, and desires. This inability leaves the person with ASD unable to predict or understand the actions and reactions of others. It also makes it difficult for them to express what they need. As a result, children with ASD may simply scream when upset or grab what they want. As noted, social difficulties may be related to a brain-based problem in interpreting other people's facial expressions.

Unusual, Stereotypical, or Repetitive Interests and Behaviors

A child with ASD may exhibit odd, repetitive motions, such as repeatedly flicking her fingers or rocking back and forth. Some will repeat certain actions for hours at a time, such as spinning a plate or dropping and picking up a ball. A person with ASD may become fixated with certain objects, such as clocks or watches. I knew a child who was fascinated by the imagery of a door closing. Whenever he was being walked down a hall or in a room, he would suddenly escape his adult escort and rush to the door to open and then swing it closed. These repetitive behaviors may be related to an unusual need for consistency. A person with ASD may insist on the same foods at the same time in the same order on the plate every day. A minor change in routine, such as the cancellation of a TV show or a snow day off from school, may be tremendously upsetting.

Why We Don't Let Jenny McCarthy Be Surgeon General

Jenny McCarthy's son has autism. Ms. McCarthy has insisted, in persistent and public fashion, that the disorder was caused by vaccinations. She has been on a mission to stop parents from vaccinating their children.

Research has resoundingly and repeatedly found no connection between vaccines and autism spectrum disorder. Several decades of research with thousands of children around the world has found no evidence whatsoever to support this assertion. Of course, no one should claim that vaccines are risk free. A small number of children each year will have severe and potentially fatal allergic reactions. But vaccines are not the cause of autism. None of this has convinced Ms. McCarthy and a fortunately small but unfortunately vociferous cadre of other parents.

Ms. McCarthy is a public figure, in large part because she has allowed herself to be photographed naked. Her campaign seems to have had an impact, however. Some parents have become convinced that vaccinating their children is risky, without seeming to understand the risk of not doing so. In fact, the risk of the diseases that the vaccinations prevent is far, far greater than the risk from the vaccinations.

Ms. McCarthy's notion that vaccines cause autism is not whimsical. Andrew Wakefield explicitly stated this in a research article published in a major medical journal. As shown on p. 231, the article has since been retracted by the journal. The assertions have been repudiated by Mr. Wakefield's coauthors. It turns out that the data he reported was generated via egregious scientific fraud.

Other Noteworthy Things to Know About Autism Spectrum Disorders

Autism spectrum disorder may affect as many as one in one hundred children. There are no racial or ethnic risk factors.

Some children with ASD display problems very early (practically from birth), whereas others seem to be developing normally when things begin to go wrong between 18 to 36 months. In most cases, problems become more apparent as the child fails to reach developmental milestones that other children the same age have reached. Some will lose language and social skills they had already acquired. ASD is generally diagnosed around age 3 (usually because the child has not learned to talk yet). Children with these disorders usually appear physically normal and have normal muscle control.

The revised diagnostic criteria, published in the DSM-5, have been somewhat controversial. They were motivated, in part, by the desire to identify children with the disorder as early as possible, since that would allow treatment to be more effective.

On rare occasions, a person with ASD will display remarkable abilities, such as precocious drawing or reading or musical ability (e.g., playing a song accurately after hearing it once).

Many children with autism are highly sensitive to certain sensations, including specific sounds, textures, or smells. Some will cover their ears in pain when they hear an airplane or a telephone. Some will find the feel of certain clothing excruciating. At the same time, stimuli that ought to cause pain and discomfort, such as extreme cold or a broken finger, may not bother the child with autism. Most unusually, the person with ASD seems to mix some sensory signals. One man heard sound when his chin was touched in a certain way. Another gagged whenever he felt wool.

The Face of Autism Spectrum Disorder

The spectrum of ASD is quite broad. In severe cases, a person diagnosed with ASD may be completely uncommunicative, have extremely limited intelligence, and be incapable of caring for himself as an adult. The disorder can be so severe that intervention is pointless and improvement is essentially impossible.

On the other hand, you are likely to meet some persons with ASD who have been in long-term treatment. Although the disorder is relatively severe, they have been taught basic skills of communication and socialization. During interactions, these persons may look as if they are acting. They recite niceties and go through the motions of social interaction, but it looks preplanned. In fact, it is. These persons have spent potentially years learning to be appropriate in social situations, and they are doing their best.

You are even more likely to meet persons with mild ASD. These men and women tend to be socially awkward. They may have difficulty talking about more than a few topics, and they might fail to notice both subtle and overt social cues (such as shifting feet or loud, long yawns).

I have worked with several individuals with mild ASD. They sought treatment because they were socially isolated, but they did not want to be. As a result, they were depressed. I learned two things about many persons with mild ASD. First, as much as anyone else, these individuals want to have friendships, spouses, and families. Second, they have sufficient insight to realize that others find them awkward, and this makes them anxious in social situations, which then enhances their awkwardness. I suggest that you respond to these persons with patience and kindness. If possible, ask them if you can offer them tips on how to do better in social situations, and then do so with kindness.

Distress and Impairment

Some children and adults with an ASD are not particularly distressed by their disorder. However, the impairment can cause secondary distress for others. Communication problems, especially not being able to relate to how another person is thinking and feeling, can cause relationship difficulties. They can cause problems making and keeping friends. It can be quite distressing, for example, for a high school or college age student with mild ASD to have few friends.

Impairment is part and parcel of the ASDs. The criteria to diagnose someone with an ASD are that the person be impaired with regard to communication and relationships. The severity of the impairment varies greatly from one person to another, but impairment is required for a diagnosis.

Hinted at by the term *spectrum,* there is a wide range of impairment severity within the ASDs. Some people with ASDs are relatively high functioning, and they are able to finish school, find work, and establish long-term relationships. At the other extreme, some persons with ASDs have severe cognitive deficits (and may in fact be diagnosed as having mental retardation) or have such profound language deficits that language communication is essentially absent.

A Complex Diagnosis

Although it is a brain problem, there are no medical tests (such as X-rays or CT scans) to detect ASD. Moreover, no two persons with the disorder present with the same behaviors and problems. Finally, several medical conditions can cause symptoms that resemble ASD, such as hearing loss, speech problems, and other neurological problems. If other causes such as these can be ruled out, an evaluation by a mental health professional (i.e., a pediatric psychiatrist, psychologist, or neurologist) who specializes in ASD is necessary. To be explicit, if a parent suspects that his or her child might have an ASD, the parent should consult with a mental health professional who has specific training and expertise in the ASDs. These professionals can be hard to find.

An ASD specialist should use a variety of methods, developed over the last decade or so, to diagnose the disorder. Methods include structured interviews with the parents about the child's early development (especially details about developmental milestones) and current behavior, as well as standardized ratings of the child's language and social behavior.

The Absolute Necessity of Early, Intensive Treatment

Parents will typically bring their child's problems to the attention of a medical doctor when he or she is fairly young. Whether and when this happens will be largely determined by the severity of the problems. The severity of the disorder likewise determines the need for treatment. To be more specific, treatment is needed by anyone with an ASD, but the intensity of treatment needed will vary according to severity.

The child with severe ASD will need a great deal of treatment and training if profound and lifelong psychosocial impairment is to be avoided. Treatment may be very intensive and last a very long time. There may be years of weekly (or more frequent) meetings. However, intensive and early treatment has been proven to improve the ability of children with autism to learn, to remain in school, and to communicate effectively.

On the other hand, children and adolescents with milder ASD would likely greatly benefit from social skills training so that they can better negotiate social situations in order to form friendships and collegial relationships. The treatment will be less intensive, but it is just as important.

In either case, parental involvement in treatment has proven to be essential for success. Parents help to identify problematic behaviors that need to be changed, as well as skills that need to be taught. Many programs train parents to conduct the therapy at home.

Behavioral Approaches to Severe ASD

Dr. O. Ivar Lovaas developed and evaluated the use of behavioral management methods for children with ASD in the 1980s. The treatment he developed was time-intensive, highly structured, and repetitive.

In its most basic form, the child is given a command, such as "sit down" or "look at me." If the child complies, he or she is rewarded. If the child doesn't comply, the behavior is "cued," such as a gentle nudge downward towards the chair when instructed to sit down. The reward is anything the child found reinforcing (rewarding), such as an M&M, a sip of juice, or a hug. The cue-response-reward process is repeated again and again over a period of up to two hours. If the child screams or otherwise tantrums, that behavior is ignored (i.e., not reinforced) and will eventually terminate. Eventually, the child learns to look when called and to sit when told, at which point more intensive training (e.g., speaking) is initiated.

Research suggests that the technique improves, at least to some extent, the behavior and functioning of most children with ASD. For some children, the Lovaas method works so dramatically that they can enter regular school. Similar behavioral treatments, modified and improved from the original, are used extensively.

Intellectual Disability

Intellectual disability (or intellectual developmental disorder) is the new and preferred term for mental retardation. Intellectual disability will be diagnosed if the person exhibits severe cognitive limitations and the attendant problems that come with it.

To be specific, intellectual disability is diagnosed after formal testing establishes that the person has an IQ of 70 or less. (The average IQ in the general population is 100, with a standard deviation of 15. This means that 95% of all persons have an IQ between 70 and 130.)

In addition to low IQ score, the person must exhibit severe psychosocial impairment, such as the inability to live independently by taking care of one's own basic needs (food and shelter).

Other Noteworthy Things to Know About Intellectual Disability

The prevalence of intellectual disability is estimated at between 1% and 3%.

The most common cause of intellectual disability is excessive alcohol use by mother while she is pregnant with the child. Fetal alcohol syndrome affects as many as 3 of every 1,000 babies born in the United States.

There is considerable overlap between ASD and intellectual disability. Most children with ASD have cognitive deficits that qualify for a secondary diagnosis of intellectual disability. (Most children with intellectual disability, on the other hand, do not also have ASD.) Similar to ASD, intellectual disability becomes evident in early childhood, as normal developmental milestones are not met.

Also similar to children with ASD, children with intellectual disability may exhibit tantrums, aggression, and self-injury.

Sometimes there are physical indications of disease processes that cause intellectual disability, such as the unique facial features exhibited by persons with Down syndrome.

Treatment Focuses on Reducing Impairment

As with all mental illnesses, persons with intellectual disability are quite variable. Some are profoundly impaired and will require lifelong care, whereas others may be capable of learning to live on their own.

Accordingly, interventions for intellectual disability attempt to maximize the functional capacity of the individual. Such training may include teaching the person to manage funds, purchase groceries and other necessities, use public transportation, and manage the demands of a job. As a result of such programs, relatively high functioning individuals with intellectual disability can live independently with only occasional assistance. Other persons with moderate intellectual disability can live semi-independently in what are termed "sheltered environments," wherein another adult is responsible for very complex tasks but the person can hold a job, manage money to some extent, and thereby live semi-independently.

Separation Anxiety Disorder

Separation anxiety is the only anxiety disorder that is unique to children. Children with this problem show excessive fear, anxiety, and even panic when not in the presence of their mother, father, or other primary attachment figure. In extreme cases children with separation anxiety disorder may even be unable to tolerate the attachment figure being in a different room.

Distress and Impairment

The distress and impairment that separation anxiety disorder generates are probably self-evident. The fear is extremely distressing and is accompanied by all of the symptoms of the fight-or-flight response (increased heart rate, uncontrollable shaking, panting and weeping, and nausea). Some children with this disorder get so anxious and upset that they vomit. Both younger and older children with separation anxiety disorder cannot enjoy social activities, which prevents them from making friends and makes it difficult to keep friends they might make. School-aged children will have great difficulty going to and doing well at school. Thus, this is the typical age at which parents will seek professional help.

Other Things to Note About Separation Anxiety Disorder

When asked why they are afraid, many children with the disorder say they are afraid of getting lost or of never finding their mothers again. Some may have exaggerated fears of animals, killers, monsters, or accidents.

As do others with anxiety problems, children with separation anxiety often express somatic complaints, such as stomachache, nausea, and headaches.

Treatment If Needed

Separation anxiety disorder usually disappears with age. However, if the child is intensely distressed and especially if the child's capacity to attend school is impacted, formal treatment may be necessary.

Treatment should be psychological. It should involve teaching the child techniques and strategies for managing and reducing anxiety. These include teaching the child relaxation strategies, correcting unrealistic fears, and gradual and accumulative exposure to feared situations, so that the child acclimates to increasingly anxiety-provoking situations.

Parents need to be involved in treatment. Many times, the primary attachment figure will inadvertently encourage excessive dependency on the part of the child. Alternatively, the parent may be excessively sympathetic with the child and may respond by giving in to the child's wishes to remain in close proximity (e.g., by letting the child skip school). These behaviors have the unfortunate and unintentional consequence of reinforcing both the anxiety-related behavior and the avoidance behavior on the part of the child. By meeting and observing the interactions between child and parent, mental health professionals can identify and modify behaviors, of both the parent and the child, eliminating the disorder.

Biological treatment involves giving a young child medication to reduce anxiety. Given the young age of the affected child and the proven effectiveness of psychologically-based treatments described above, in my estimation, such an approach would be difficult to justify.

Reactive Attachment Disorder

Attachment is the scientific term developed by psychologists to describe the normal and healthy emotional, loving bond between a young child and an adult or adults. For the most part, babies fairly quickly develop an attachment to their mothers and fathers. They want to be held by or at least be near parents, and they feel safe and comfortable in their presence. Also, for the most part, parents develop strong attachment bonds towards their children.

Reactive attachment disorder is a relatively new diagnosis created to describe severely dysfunctional social behavior on the part of very young children. A child may develop reactive attachment disorder if he or she never had the opportunity, as an infant, to attach to an adult because of severe neglect. That is, reactive attachment disorder would be the proper diagnosis for children who have never had an attachment figure (or who lost that person early) and who are emotionally withdrawn and inhibited. There have been news stories of the extreme problems that some adoptive parents have had with children from former Eastern bloc countries, where orphanages tended to be extremely impoverished and where, as a result, children may have been neglected for the first several years of their lives.

These children may be characterized as having an internalizing disorder, as they appear depressed, anxious, and lethargic. They either are extremely fearful of adults or they have had the natural instinct to want to be loved and cared for (i.e., to be attached to an adult) destroyed by reality.

Children with this disorder tend to be profoundly impaired. However, little is known about the prevalence of the disorder, and little is known about how it can be treated.

General Considerations in the Treatment of Childhood and Adolescent Disorders

The best treatments for disorders of children and adolescents are family-based and behavioral.

Family Involvement in Treatment

Families should be involved in order to learn from therapists how to implement techniques to help their child. Some therapists see children in one-on-one therapy, but they also usually meet with parents or guardians to teach them how to take a more effective approach with their child from one moment to the next. The parents and guardians are with the child every day. If teachers agree, it can also be very useful to meet with them to suggest new strategies for use at school.

Treatment should be family-based for other reasons as well. Children and adolescents sometimes lie. (Hard to believe, but true.) A mental health professional who sees a child or adolescent and asks, "So, how was your week?" will be told a lie: "It was great. Things at home are much, much better. I think I don't need treatment anymore." Family-based treatment or, at least, regular meetings with parents allows the parents to inform the counselor about how they see things.

Family-based therapy enables the counselor to evaluate and intervene in communication problems (which are extremely common between adolescents and parents especially) and other interpersonal disputes. Teaching parents to treat their child firmly but respectfully can be extremely effective in reducing conflict. Teaching children and adolescents that being respectful but assertive maximizes the likelihood that they will achieve their goals (such as going to a movie with friends). Both are needed to reduce problems.

The other reasons that families should be involved are the related issues of distress and motivation for treatment. As reviewed in previous chapters, most but not all mental illnesses cause considerable distress to the individual. If the person is distressed, he or she is motivated to change to reduce that distress. This is not the case with all children with disorders, especially ADHD, ODD, and CD. Children and adolescents with these disorders don't tend to experience distress, except the distress associated with getting in trouble. Parents and guardians are usually the ones distressed, and they are the ones motivated to change the situation. Hence, the parents or guardians (and hopefully teachers) are likely willing to be trained by the mental health professional to implement behavioral strategies.

Behavioral Treatment

In a very real way, it does not matter whatsoever whether the child wants to change. Behavioral strategies will change the behavior. Described briefly on pp. 261 and 262, behavioral treatments focus on cues and consequences. Cues are manipulated to reduce the likelihood that bad behavior will occur. For example, if a child often gets in trouble with certain peers, then restricting or eliminating contact with those peers (i.e., cues) will reduce the bad behavior. Consequences follow behaviors, and they are manipulated to increase desirable behavior (e.g., doing homework) and to eliminate undesirable behavior (e.g., swearing). For example, if a child breaks curfew, the consequence might be the loss of privileges (such as a cell phone) for a certain amount of time.

It sounds easy, but in general it is not. Consultation with a qualified mental health professional is necessary to alleviate the disorders described in this chapter.

Encouraging Treatment-Seeking and Treatment Persistence

Several things can be emphasized with parents and guardians whose child or adolescent is exhibiting a mental illness. The first is that treatment will help. Behavioral strategies can be difficult to implement, but they do work. Second, encourage parents and guardians not to blame themselves for the child's misbehavior. Third, relatedly, encourage them to try not to get overly upset. A corollary of this is not to act until your emotions are in check. Children and especially adolescents will sometimes attempt to discombobulate their parents by acting disrespectfully and being antagonizing. If parents respond with emotional upset, this allows the child control over the situation. Moreover, if a behavioral plan is to be implemented successfully, it must be done logically and rationally, not angrily. It can be impossible not to get angry, but it is always possible to pause to regain a sense of control over emotions and thus the situation.

Profiting From the Childhood Disorders, Part 3: Scientology

Much of the following is based on a 1993 article authored by John Weldon entitled "Scientology: From Science Fiction to Space-age Religion" published in the *Christian Research Journal,* as well as a 1996 article published by psychiatrists Abraham Halpern and Alfred Freedman entitled "A Response to Scientology" in *Psychiatry News.*

There is much misunderstanding about Scientology, and a great amount of underestimation about the damage the cult has caused. But information about Scientology is easy to find. It has been the subject of government investigations, descriptions by current and former members, and investigative reporting, including scathing reports in *Time* magazine (May 1991) and *Reader's Digest* (May 1980). The ultimate source is from Scientology itself in the book *Dianetics: The Modern Science of Mental Health,* authored by Lafayette Ronald Hubbard (1911–1986). Supposedly, *Dianetics* deals with issues of the mind and body, but its teachings are extended to spiritual issues.

Why Bother With Scientology?

There are two reasons to include Scientology in this book (and this particular chapter). The first is that some Christians are unknowingly falling prey to the falsehoods and heresies of Scientology. Scientology asserts that its beliefs are "not incompatible" with the Christian faith, but examining its teachings shows that this is a grotesque falsehood. A survey of over 3,000 members found that most Scientologists came from Christian backgrounds and that most of these members asserted that they were still Christian. Tragically, the response of Christian churches to the assault of Scientology has been almost nonexistent.

The second reason is more directly related to the topic of this book. Scientology has initiated and maintained an aggressive but covert assault on the cause and treatment of mental illness, which has caused uncountable suffering to individuals and families. Of course, disagreements about cause and treatment are good for science. If scientists didn't debate such things, we'd still treat depression by spinning people in chairs suspended from the ceiling. But Scientology is not interested in better care of persons with mental illness. They discredit the mental health profession for one reason: they want to make money.

Scientology negatively affects all persons with mental illness, but it is covered in this chapter because its damaging influence has been perhaps most profound on the disorders that affect children and adolescents.

Scientology Says Mental Illness Does Not Exist (But Thetans Do)

According to Scientology, each person on earth is a "thetan," an immortal spirit whose fundamental nature is good and divine. About 75 million years ago, some thetans were banished to earth by the cruel galactic ruler named Xenu. We thetans have been damaged by "engrams," which are mental representations of traumatic events. The original traumatic event was, obviously, being banished to earth by Xenu.

The problem is that engrams cause us to forget that we are in fact thetans, who are immortal, all-powerful, and perfect. We mistakenly think that the MEST (matter, energy, space, time) universe restrains us. Ironically, the MEST was actually created ("emanated") by us thetans trillions of years ago, because we were bored and wanted to amuse ourselves. Thus, in Scientology's reality, all aspects of the universe can be manipulated by a spiritually enlightened thetan. After all, we created it.

But we are not spiritually enlightened because of the MEST and the engrams (traumatic remembrances). Over the course of trillions of years, we thetans became more and more entranced with our own creation (MEST) until we lost all awareness of our true identity as thetans. Compounding the problem, when a body dies, the thetan in the dead body must enter another body. The death and the transfer are traumatic and create engrams. In this manner, we have accumulated many engrams.

We Thetans are thus enslaved to these engrams and to the material universe. According to Scientology, extreme examples of such enslavement are manifested as mental illness, such as depression, anxiety, and schizophrenia.

What Scientology Teaches About Proper Treatment

Fortunately for us all, thetan slavery to the MEST and to engrams has been defied by Hubbard's discovery of the true nature of humankind. He also developed a plan of salvation. The Scientology "auditing" process neutralizes engrams in order to make the thetan self-aware and "enlightened." Ultimately, the person will achieve self-realization and become an "Operating Thetan." By the way, the process can take years and is likely to be incredibly expensive.

In other words, for purposes of financial gain, Hubbard asserted that Scientology is the preferred approach to mental health problems. He claimed that Scientology's methods are 100% successful. The "Creed of the Church" holds that the healing of mental illness is a spiritual enterprise and "should not be condoned in nonreligious fields." While such a belief would be innocuous if it were restricted to a statement, in point of fact, leaders of Scientology have actively and aggressively worked to prevent people from getting treatment from mental health professionals.

Scientology's Surprising Success

Scientology has been alarmingly and surprisingly successful in discrediting psychiatry and psychology. This can be accounted for by three facts. First, they are subtle. They do not declare their intent nor do they disclose their name. They also do not widely publicize some of their more unusual beliefs. For example, Scientology claims that the psychiatric industry is controlled by creatures from outer space (the "Marcabs"), whose goal is to keep humanity enslaved to the MEST and to their engrams. (Scientology is therefore the only hope for humanity.) They also do not refer to Scientology in most of their documents. To be specific, the Citizens Commission on Human Rights (CCHR) is the guise that the Church of Scientology uses to broadcast and promote its agenda.

Second, as documented in the second volume, there are many instances of maltreatment of persons with mental illness throughout history, including by mental health professionals. Scientologists do not have to look far to find deeds to which anyone would object. For example, it is true that an unacceptably large portion (perhaps 20%) of prescribed ADHD medications end up being abused. Put a twist on that fact and you might convince some that most prescribed drugs are abused.

Finally, Scientology has been extremely persistent and pervasive. The CCHR has an ongoing mass media campaign entailing alarming and sensationalistic stories about mental health professionals.

What Scientology Teaches About the Mental Health Profession

Recognizing the opportunity to exploit parents of children with mental health problems, the CCHR promotes misinformation about ADHD. The CCHR selectively focuses on instances in which children had adverse reactions to medications and argues that there is vast overprescribing. It has organized pickets of scientific meetings and public conferences on ADHD and has distributed condemnatory pamphlets to students, parents, and teachers. Scientologists have written editorial letters to newspapers decrying psychostimulants and the "myth" of ADHD.

Some of the more flagrant falsehoods about psychostimulant medication made by Scientologists include that they are addictive; that they cause violence, depression, brain damage, and suicide; and that their use is controversial among psychiatrists. None of these claims have the slightest evidentiary base. Indeed, the CCHR does not even pretend that there is evidence, but it continues to make these claims. The CCHR has assisted parents in filing lawsuits against medical practitioners who prescribed psychostimulant medication, and it directly sued for fraud the American Psychiatric Association for establishing the criteria to diagnose ADHD. (The lawsuit was dismissed.)

Scientology encourages members to appear on TV to decry the myth of other mental illnesses as well, and some rich and famous members have taken the opportunity to do just that. Perhaps readers recall the televised interview between Matt Lauer and Tom Cruise wherein the latter, without mentioning Scientology, condemned the use of antidepressants and the field of psychiatry in general.

Scientology has made worldwide efforts as well. In 1986, the United Nations Subcommission on Prevention of Discrimination and Protection of Minorities submitted a report, to which Scientology's CCHR contributed greatly. The report's attack on psychiatry was unabashed and included the following statements: "Governments should start immediately to investigate psychiatry and the mental health field and get the real facts;" "An amnesty should be granted to all psychiatrists who admit to having engaged in abusive practices and human rights violations and who have ceased to do so;" "The use of all drugs, whether street drugs or psychopharmacological drugs, should be discontinued." Tellingly, the report also stated that "mental care [centers and] homes should be run by churches or other religious groups" and "the CCHR and others should provide governments with workable methods to handle the mentally ill."

A 1986 CCHR "report" submitted to the International Congress on Law and Psychiatry claimed that "most of the famous assassins and mass murderers are products of psychiatry and the mental health profession." In October 1995, Scientology's chairman of the board presented to Scientologists around the world several goals: "Objective One—place Scientology at the absolute forefront of Society. Objective Two—eliminate psychiatry in all its forms." Scientologists have lobbied to eliminate government funding of psychiatric treatment and research and have worked to defeat mental health parity laws (which seek to have mental illness covered by insurance companies in the same manner that physical illnesses are).

The Need for Vigilance

Christians need to recognize the threat of Scientology for what it is. It is not compatible with Christian faith.

Christians also need to recognize that Scientology threatens the health and well-being of persons and families struggling with mental health problems. One would be incredibly naïve to assert that Scientology is simply trying to improve the world and man's lot within it. Everyone should examine the evidence and realize that Scientologists believe there is a great deal of money to be made by coercing persons with mental illness to seek "treatment" from them alone.

Chapter 15

Child Abuse and Neglect

"See that you do not despise one of these little ones.
For I tell you that their angels in heaven
always see the face of my Father in heaven."
(Matthew 18:10)

Abuse and neglect are issues of particular concern for children and adolescents, since they are more vulnerable than adults who are usually more capable of self-care. These are topics about which anyone who works with children and adolescents needs to be both knowledgeable and competent to intervene.

In this chapter, the history of the notion that children need special protection is briefly reviewed, followed by a review of the history of child abuse laws. The current state of affairs with regard to the abuse and neglect of children and adolescents ends this section.

The Concept of Childhood

Christ recognized that children are different from adults. He called them "little ones," recognizing that they are smaller than adults. He appreciated their need for protection from falsehoods and mistreatment, warning of the dangers of leading little ones away from belief in him. He said, "If anyone causes one of these little ones—those who believe in me—to stumble, it would be better for them to have a large millstone hung around their neck and to be drowned in the depths of the sea" (Matthew 18:6). He also added, "Anyone who will not receive the kingdom of God like a little child will never enter it" (Luke 18:17), pointing out, in this nontheologian's opinion, that children, unlike adults, receive gifts without skepticism or concern about the giver's motives ("I wonder what he wants").

Christ recognized that children are different from adults, but most others did not. Into the Middle Ages, children were essentially treated as small-statured adults. Paintings from the time period show children dressed like adults. There were few schools, since children were needed to help sustain the family. (The exception to this were children of parents in the upper class. They were given an extended period of training and education to prepare them for positions of importance and authority.) At young ages, most children were expected to assist their mother or father with household tasks. As they grew larger, usually between ages 12 and 14, they did more intensive, adult-like work. In farm families, the work might be relatively safe and simple, and the parents or an older sibling probably supervised it. In other instances the work was away from home and enforced by adults who were not related. The work might be brutal and dangerous.

The concept of childhood as a distinct period of development took root in the early 1600s but required centuries to be fully realized. Historians suggest that the notion of childhood was the result of three historical events, each of which took hundreds of years to transpire.

The Industrial Revolution

The industrial revolution was enabled by the agricultural revolution of the 1600s, wherein farmers became more efficient in raising crops and animals, allowing a more abundant and predictable food supply. The industrial revolution began in the mid-1700s and profoundly altered nearly all areas of life by introducing factories and manufacturing. With factories came a dramatically increased need for coal, which led to changes in mining and an increase in railroad traffic to move the coal.

Most developing countries changed from commodities-based to cash-based economies. Thus, families needed cash to survive. Cash could be earned by anyone in the family. More mines and more factories meant more work opportunities, but the adult population was essentially tapped out. Children comprised as much as one-quarter to one-third of the entire population (recall that the average adult lifespan was fairly limited), and they became an important part of the workforce. Children, who formerly would have worked on the family farm, moved to mining camps to dig for coal or into cities to work at a factory, sometimes with their family and sometimes without. Instead of simply another mouth to feed, children became an economic asset to families. This happened more frequently in Europe, as America had more land and more farms, but child labor was highly prevalent on both sides of the Atlantic Ocean. For example, by the mid-1700s, about one in six workers in England were under the age of 14.

There were distinct advantages to having child laborers. First, children were neither particularly demanding nor particularly discerning. They were usually paid a fraction of what an adult would make. Whereas an adult would not do a dangerous job, since his family would starve if anything happened to him, children were inexperienced, not particularly wise, and easily deceived. A child could be convinced to do a dangerous task that an adult would refuse. Besides which, the child was relatively expendable (not to mention replaceable). Children were small, which meant they could work in the cramped veins of the coal mine or climb inside the factory machine to dislodge whatever was making it stick. Accidents that injured and killed children were commonplace.

Partly in response to concerns about their safety, but also in response to adults complaining that jobs were being taken by children, in 1833 the English Parliament passed the Factory Act, which limited the number of hours children could work. As with any law, details were necessary. The policy required a definition of the ages of childhood. So the Factory Act entirely disallowed paid labor by children under the age of 9 and declared that children ages 14 to 18 could not work more than 12 hours per day(!). This explains why, to this day, so many legal regulations define childhood as ending at age 18. Much later and for parallel reasons, in 1912 the United States established the Children's Bureau, which was to oversee children's working conditions.

By the early 1900s, then, across Europe and the United States, children and adolescents were being removed from the workforce. Technological advances speeded this process. Factories and mines became increasingly efficient, and improved efficiency always leads to less need for workers. Children were not as important of income earners as were adults, and child labor laws made it increasingly difficult to employ them. So as fewer workers were needed, children were usually the first to be let go.

So, what do we do with all these kids? Families had been moving to the cities, so there were no family farms for them to work. By then, the idea that educating children was a moral obligation had taken root.

The Protestant Reformation

The Protestant Reformation had a major impact on religious institutions, obviously. What is less widely known is the impact that the reformers had on the conceptualization of children. Martin Luther and others argued vociferously for the benefits of education for both an orderly civil society and for the understanding of the means of salvation.

As a result, Martin Luther taught. He translated the Bible so that nonclergy could read it. He proposed that monasteries be turned into schools. He founded a school in his hometown of Eisleben, Germany. He wrote his catechism for instruction in the faith. He entreated pastors and preachers in the preface to the catechism to "help us inculcate the Catechism upon the people, and especially upon the young."

In the late-1700s, Sunday school was formally implemented in England, and the practice soon spread to other parts of the world. In particular, perhaps paradoxically, the notion of moral instruction appealed to the bosses and foremen of the industrialized world. Factory owners wanted and sometimes required their child laborers to attend Sunday school. They wanted them to understand the ethic of hard work.

In short, as children were becoming less valuable as a labor resource, the value of educating children was taking hold. In testament to this, in many households, it was the children who read aloud the Bible (not to mention letters and the newspaper), as the parents were illiterate.

In 1867, the US Department of Education was created, and over the next century, mandatory education laws expanded. As with child protection laws regarding labor, child education regulations required a legal definition of childhood. The labor laws came first, and education laws simply followed suit. Mandatory education was thus defined, at least initially, as through the age of childhood, that is, through the age of 18.

The Emergence of a Middle Class

Improvements in education led to improvements in technology and vice versa. Improvements in education and technology greatly increased the complexity of work, and well-trained workers became more valuable. Productivity and efficiency increased, and wages increased. No longer was it necessary for factory workers to work 16-hour days for subsistence living. Many were able to earn enough to actually save money for cars and homes.

As a result, a middle class emerged between the wealthy and the poor. Factory workers could buy a modest home or one of those new Model T cars that were explicitly made for the everyday man. They could not pay off these purchases all at once, like the rich could, but their work was predictable and consistent, and banks were willing to loan money for purchases that could be paid off over several years.

Prior to the emergence of the middle class, the distinction between children of the wealthy and children of the poor was drastic. Children of the wealthy were treated better than children of the poor, but not because of less love or poorer parent character. Rather, the issues were resources and opportunity. The wealthy could afford education and leisure, on top of the costs of food and home. Unlike the poor, children of the upper classes did not join the workforce at an average age of seven. Instead, they were educated, groomed, and prepared for a privileged life. Thus it was understood and accepted, at both ends of the spectrum, that upper class children were better than lower class children. In contrast, the poor had to worry about food and home, and their children needed to work to help pay for these things.

The industrial revolution created a middle class, and it grew quite sizable. In addition to buying homes and cars, formerly the prerogative of the wealthy, the middle class also adopted the upper class attitude towards children. They had enough resources to insist that their children, too, were needful of education and protection.

◆ ◆ ◆ ◆ ◆

Thus did the concept of childhood emerge from the Protestant Reformation, the industrial revolution, and the emergence of the middle class. Without a concept of childhood, treating children as having different needs than adults would never have happened.

Child Abuse Becomes a Public Concern

Through much of antiquity, parents were allowed to treat their children as disposable resources. The vast majority did not, of course, but there were no laws preventing the mistreatment of children. In ancient Rome, fathers could rid themselves of children they did not want, such as a child born physically deformed or disabled. Until the late-1800s, English common law held that children were the property of their fathers, and the newly founded United States followed this tradition.

In the late-1800s, the international story of an abused child changed things around the civilized world.

The Case of Mary Ellen Wilson

Mary Ellen Wilson was born in 1864 to Francis and Thomas Wilson of New York City. Soon after she was born, her father died. Her mother got a job, but they nonetheless slipped further and further into poverty. Francis boarded her daughter with a woman named Mary Score, who turned two-year-old Mary Ellen over to the city's Department of Charities, which in turn placed the child into the home of Mary and Francis Connolly. They soon moved to an apartment in south Manhattan.

The foster parents badly mistreated Mary Ellen. Her plight was told to Etta Angell Wheeler, a mission worker who often visited to help the impoverished tenement dwellers. A neighbor told Mrs. Wheeler that over the previous years, a little girl had essentially been a prisoner of the apartment, rarely seen, often cruelly whipped, and frequently left alone the entire day, locked in an inner room of the darkened apartment. Many of the building's other occupants knew of the girl's plight, but they did not know what they could do.

Mrs. Wheeler decided to check on the child, which required tracking the family to yet another address. She talked with their neighbor, who reported that she often heard the cries of a child emanating from the apartment. Under the pretext of seeking assistance, Mrs. Wheeler chatted with Mary Connolly. The latter, in the course of the conversation, allowed her door to open. Mrs. Wheeler quickly slipped inside the residence and was able to see Mary Ellen. Mrs. Wheeler later wrote: "It was December and the weather bitterly cold. She was a tiny mite, the size of five years, though, as afterward appeared, she was then nine. . . . Across the table lay a brutal whip of twisted leather strands and the child's meager arms and legs bore many marks of its use." A black-and-white photograph of the child, which can be found online, shows that she had a scar that started at her left temple and carried down her entire face to end near her mouth. Mrs. Wheeler pretended not to notice the child nor did she speak to the child. When she left, however, she was determined to rescue her.

She reported the situation to city authorities. Although some jurisdictions in the United States, including the state of New York, had laws against excessive physical discipline of children, the authorities would not intervene. Mrs. Wheeler eventually turned to Henry Bergh, who was founder of the American Society for the Prevention of Cruelty to Animals (ASPCA), the precursor of the Humane Society. Mr. Bergh listened to the story of the little girl with interest. Given his activities with the ASPCA, he was quite familiar with both the court system and the strategy of arousing public sympathy through the use of newspaper stories.

Mrs. Wheeler brought him the written testimony of neighbors. Mr. Bergh sent one of his ASPCA investigators to the child's home, and he gained entrance to the dwelling by posing as a census worker. Mr. Bergh also had a court petition prepared, to have the police bring Mary Ellen to court. The child was carried into the courtroom, and her condition was testimony enough. The day prior, the caretaker had struck Mary Ellen with a pair of shears, leaving the above-noted gash on her eyebrow and cheek.

Mary Ellen told the judge that her parents were dead. She did not know how old she was and had no recollection of a time when she did not live with her foster parents. She reported, "Mamma has been in the habit of whipping and beating me almost every day. . . . I do not know for what I was whipped. Mamma never said anything to me when she whipped me." In response, Judge Lawrence placed the child under court control, essentially making himself her guardian.

Initially at the prodding of Mr. Bergh, but then because of the public's fascination, newspapers covered the case and the subsequent trial of Mary Connolly, who was found guilty of felonious assault and given a one-year sentence. More important, the extensive newspaper coverage raised public awareness and inspired states to pass laws to protect children. ASPCA attorneys argued before various state legislatures that laws protecting animals should not be greater than laws protecting children.

As a consequence, many (but not all) states and some foreign countries passed child abuse laws. The maltreatment of children and adolescents again gained national attention with the publication in 1962 of an article in the *Journal of the American Medical Association,* which detailed the short- and long-term effects of child abuse. It called for abuse to be recognized as a substantial health risk that should be routinely evaluated by pediatricians and others in regular contact with children. By the 1970s, every state had mandatory reporting laws (see pp. 233,234). A 1974 federal law provided funds for the establishment of Child Protective Services, including foster care and emergency shelters.

Defining Child Abuse and Neglect

Laws regarding child abuse need to distinguish between discipline and abuse. States seek to protect children from abuse, while at the same time allowing parents the right to raise and discipline their children as they see fit. The distinction can be difficult at times, but the distinction is made easier by focusing on the effect that the adult's behavior has on the child. If the effect is good, then it can be classified as discipline. If the effect is damaging, it can probably be classified as abuse.

Discipline is intended to teach children right from wrong. It establishes which behaviors on the part of the child are acceptable, or even commendable, versus those that are unacceptable and deserving of punishment. In other words, the child learns rules about behavior. If the child learns to distinguish good and bad behaviors, the child also learns to expect discipline when he misbehaves. Children need such predictability, structure, and clear boundaries, as well as the knowledge that their parents are looking out for their safety. Appropriate discipline provides these things. Abuse does not.

Abuse involves harm or injury to the child. It may be the result of a deliberate attempt to hurt the child, but not always. Alternatively, abuse can result from misguided severe discipline, such as using a belt on a child, or physical punishment that is inappropriate to the child's age or physical condition. Many physically abusive parents and caregivers insist that their actions are simply forms of discipline—ways to make children learn to behave. But the perspective of the parent might be overturned by the effect on the child. This effect determines whether the parent's behavior is appropriate or not.

Abuse does not teach a child the difference between right and wrong. Indeed, abuse teaches a child nothing about right and wrong but rather about the world and about herself. The child does not learn rules about behavior because such rules don't exist. Instead, abuse causes a child to live in fear, because abuse is unpredictable. The child never knows what is going to set the parent off. The child is constantly walking on eggshells, never sure what behavior will trigger a verbal, emotional, or physical assault. Abuse can severely damage a child's mental health and social development.

Abused children cannot predict how their parents will act. Their world is an unpredictable, frightening place. Whether the abuse is a slap, a harsh comment, stony silence, or not knowing if there will be dinner on the table tonight, the end result is a child who feels unsafe, uncared for, and alone. Abusive people can act out of anger or cruelty and not out of the motivation to properly teach a child.

Types of Abuse

Sadly, there are innumerable ways to abuse a child. Abuse can be categorized as neglect, verbal or emotional, physical, or sexual. Of course, these types of abuse are not mutually exclusive.

Neglect

Neglect entails failing to provide for a child's basic needs, whether it be sufficient food, clothing, or supervision. Sometimes neglect is due to hostile disregard, where the parent simply does not care about the child's welfare. Other times, it is unintentional and due to unfortunate circumstances. Neglect may be due to the demands of providing for the family, such as having to work excessively long hours and not being able to afford adequate child care. Sometimes a parent becomes physically unable to care for the child. Mental illness, alcohol misuse, and drug abuse may seriously impair judgment and the ability to keep a child safe.

Whether intentional or not, neglect is not always easy to spot. Shame and embarrassment will lead the child to hide or deny what is happening. Some children become adept at presenting a happy face to other children, teachers, and adults (especially if they crave attention). In some cases, the child, especially an older child, may take on the role of the caretaker of the parent and of other children.

Verbal and Physical Abuse

Verbal or emotional abuse includes screaming, threatening, name-calling, belittling, telling a child that he is "no good" or that she is "a mistake," bullying, or ignoring a child. It can also take the form of exposing the child to violence being inflicted on others, including his mother, a sibling, or a pet.

Physical abuse includes slapping, punching, poking, shoving, choking, kicking, and any other myriad of behaviors. It can be defined as aggressive bodily contact with the child in a manner that causes the child to experience fear and pain.

Sexual Abuse

Sexual abuse refers to forcing children to engage in sexual activities. (By definition, any sexual activity with a child is forcible, as the child cannot legally consent to it.) It might include sexualized kissing, fondling, and digital penetration of the vagina or anus, as well as oral-genital, genital-genital, and anal-genital contact. However, sexual abuse doesn't always involve body contact. Exposing a child to sexual situations or material is abuse, whether or not touching is involved. Noncontact activities also include exhibitionism on the part of the perpetrator and inappropriate observation of the child (such as while the child is dressing, using the toilet, or bathing).

Facts and Figures Regarding Child Abuse

The following information and statistics were compiled from various agencies, including the US Department of Health and Human Services, the US Government Accountability Office, the US Department of Justice, the National Council on Child Abuse and Family Violence, and the National Institute of Drug Abuse.

- Over three million reports of child abuse are made every year in the United States.
- Many of those reports include multiple children, so child abuse reports and allegations involve an estimated six million children annually.
- It is extremely likely that the vast majority of cases of child abuse go unreported.
- More than five children die every day as a result of abuse, and most of these children are under the age of four.
- Studies suggest that 30-70% of child maltreatment cases involve substance use on the part of the abuser.
- Children whose parents abuse alcohol or drugs are three times more likely to be abused and four times more likely to be neglected than other kids.
- Child abuse is associated with poverty, perhaps because the substance use disorders, environmental stress, and lack of education about proper parenting techniques are all more likely among poor populations.

The Enduring Effects of Abuse and Neglect

Child abuse and neglect leave lasting scars. Some of these scars are physical, but emotional scars also endure. Abuse "informs" children about themselves and about others. The knowledge absorbed is pathological (but they are too young to know that). Abuse and neglect thus damage a child's sense of self, ability to have healthy relationships, and ability to function at home, at work, and at school.

Knowledge About Self and Others

Regarding themselves, children who are abused learn that the emotional, physical, and sexual maltreatment is their fault. Most are told this over and over again. They are repeatedly informed that they are stupid and no good. This knowledge of such deep and abiding flaws causes educational and occupational under-attainment. They don't believe they can accomplish anything or that they are worth more than what they receive.

Regarding others, child abuse impairs the ability to trust easily and to love freely. The abused child learns in the most grotesque fashion that the person you most love cannot be trusted. They learn that their sense of love itself cannot be trusted. This leads to difficulty maintaining relationships due to fear of loving and being loved, which have been inexorably jumbled with being abused.

Emotional Impairment

Abused children learn quickly that it is unsafe to express emotions. They are typically punished even more if they express any fear, hurt, or confusion, so they learn to repress and ignore such emotions. As a result, adult survivors of child abuse often struggle with unexplainable anxiety, depression, or anger. They may turn to alcohol or drugs to numb out the painful feelings.

The long-term effects of abuse and neglect that might be attributed to emotional impairment have been documented repeatedly.

- About 80% of 21-year-olds who were abused as children met criteria for at least one mental illness. This is four times the base rate in the general population.
- As many as two-thirds of persons seeking treatment for a substance use disorder report that they were abused or neglected as children. (Keep in mind that most persons with an SUD do not seek treatment.)
- Children who experience child abuse or neglect are more likely to be arrested and more likely to commit violent crime. Thus, about one of every six men and one in every three women in prison in the United States were abused as children.
- Abused girls are more likely to become pregnant as teenagers, reflecting poor discernment, poor decision making, and a vulnerability to exploitation.

The Special Damage Inflicted by Sexual Abuse

Although it is never a good idea to compare suffering, most mental health professionals would probably agree that child sexual abuse leads to the most profound and far-reaching damage, including confusion, guilt, and shame. The sexual abuse and rape of children is almost always done by someone the child knows and should be able to trust. Most often, it is a close relative, specifically a parent, older sibling, or cousin. The sexual contact is an abuse of the person's power over and responsibility to the child.

The damage may be amplified by the "strategy" utilized by the predator. The predator knows perfectly well that the sexual contact is verboten, so he will take care to make discovery less likely. Child sexual predators who have been interviewed refer to this as "grooming" the child. The sequence of activities often progresses from private expressions of the specialness of the relationship with its unique love, trust, and caring. The special relationship will gradually become increasingly pseudo-romantic and sexualized, typically progressing from noncontact to mild (or "inadvertent") sexual contact to overt sexual activity over a period of time.

Whether they bother with such "grooming" or not, predators will invariably state to the child that the sexual activity was caused by or even wanted by the child. This is intended to make the child less likely to report the abuse. All children lack emotional maturity and discernment, and they rely on adults to help them to understand confusing situations. (Anyone who has ever comforted a child at a funeral knows this.) As preposterous as it sounds to an adult, the child will likely believe it when she is told, "This sexual activity that you loathe is actually your fault, because you are dirty and bad." As a result, sexually abused children are tormented by shame and guilt. Self-loathing leads to sexual problems as the child grows into an adult, including excessive promiscuity or an inability to have intimate relations. The shame of sexual abuse makes it very difficult for children to report the abuse. They may worry that others won't believe them, will be angry with them, or that it will split their family apart.

Responding to Child Abuse

It can be extremely difficult to respond to child abuse. I intentionally use the word *respond* rather than the phrase "know what to do," since almost everyone "knows" what they should do. Everyone knows that someone should do something. But it can be difficult to do.

It is perhaps made easier to do what is necessary by acknowledging that legal, moral, and ethical principles align perfectly with biblical teaching. All agree that child abuse is bad for the child and is bad for the person who does it. So what must be done is whatever it takes to stop it.

In the case of sexual abuse, the adult is engaging in extremely and grotesquely corrupt behavior that threatens the child's emotional well-being and even the child's salvation. This type of abuse can never be tolerated in any way, shape, or form.

In the case of other abuse, there are (at least) four things that should convince the reader that the thing to do is to report abuse to the proper authorities.

First, the behavior of the adult or caregiver abusing a child can be changed. The behavior is pathological. Like any pathological behavior, it can be unlearned and replaced by more healthy and effective behavior. This can happen *if and only if* the person wants to change. Moreover, it will almost certainly not happen unless the person obtains professional help.

Second, most persons who commit child abuse do not voluntarily seek treatment. Some will, because they are distressed at their own behavior and want to change it, but most will not. They will be distressed at their own behavior, but that distress will be overcome by shame and embarrassment. They will not want to admit what they are doing, so they will not seek help.

Third, there are mental health professionals who specialize in the treatment of adults who commit child abuse. They are trained to recognize minimization and denial, and they are trained to evaluate accurately the chronicity and severity of the abuse. They are trained in the appropriate and effective combination of confrontation, empathy, and instruction, as well as in evaluating whether or not intervention is making a difference.

Fourth, it is impossible for a nonprofessional to intervene in the abuse of a child. If a child is being abused by someone from whom separation can be effected, such as a cousin, neighbor, or babysitter, then obviously the parent or caregiver can intervene. Unfortunately, parents or caregivers commit most instances of child abuse, and intervening becomes very difficult. In fact, I would strongly caution that no reader attempt to intervene in abuse. The most likely outcome of such an effort is that the person who is abusing the child will deny what is happening or will express remorse and make a promise that it won't happen again. Then the reader will never see the person or the child ever again.

To summarize: with the exception of sexual abuse, the pathological behavior of child abuse can be changed. But the men and women who commit child abuse, although probably distressed by their own behavior, are too ashamed to seek help to stop it. There are mental health professionals who specialize in the treatment of men and women who commit child abuse, and they can effect behavioral change. In contrast, the chances that the reader can intervene successfully are incredibly slim.

Therefore, there is only one legitimate response. Child abuse must be reported to persons who have the authority, given them by state and local statutes, to require a person who commits child abuse to obtain treatment in order to change his or her behavior.

Two more points about reporting child abuse may help readers understand what will and will not happen. First, it is a priority of Child Protective Services to keep children in the home. Only in extreme cases of child abuse does a report result in a child being removed from the home. If the child is in clear and imminent danger, then the child must be removed to prevent injury or death. Second, reporting can be anonymous. In most states, reporters are not required to give their name when reporting child abuse.

Encouraging Treatment-Compliance

The person reported for child abuse and mandated to treatment will probably be feeling a mixture of shame and anger. It is important that the person stays with treatment and changes his or her behavior, and addressing these directly with them will help.

The reader invested in helping in these situations can take advantage of the feeling of distress and shame by encouraging the person who committed the abuse to recognize that the behavior is not what they want to do and that treatment can help them to change it. (See chapter 11 box on "motivational interviewing.") Be empathic and understanding, and try to reduce the shame that the person may be experiencing. Say things like, "You felt out of control of your anger, which is a bad feeling" and "You really love your children and really want to be a good parent."

Finally, be prepared to address anger. Acknowledge that the person is angry, and acknowledge that the situation is upsetting. Then encourage the person to realize that the authorities want what is best for both the child and them. The authorities are not interested in revenge or humiliation, nor are they forcing the issue because they enjoy doing it. They are doing what is best for everyone.

Postscript

More detailed information and training is available through the Gunderson National Child Protection Training Center (www.gundersonhealth.org/ncptc).

Gunderson is an internationally renowned organization that helps schools, churches, and child-oriented service organizations prevent and respond to child abuse.

Chapter 16

Mental Illness and the Elderly

"Do not cast me away when I am old;
do not forsake me when my strength is gone."
(Psalm 71:9)

People are living longer due to improved nutrition, better safety and sanitation practices, medical advances, and the adoption of healthier lifestyles. Older adults are the fastest growing segment of the United States population. According to the Census Bureau, at the turn of the 21st century persons 65 years of age and older accounted for one in eight persons of the population. They will constitute one in five persons by 2020 and one in four persons (25%) by 2050.

This chapter covers the mental illnesses that are particular to elderly persons (defined as over 65). It also reviews how the common disorders of adulthood may present somewhat differently in elderly persons. The typical presentation of an elderly person experiencing a mental illness is reviewed, as are recommendations for how to encourage him or her to seek and accept treatment. The chapter starts with a review of issues related to specific vulnerabilities of the elderly.

Special Considerations Related to Elder Populations

Regarding his more limited capacities, my grandfather used to say to me, "If you live long enough, you're going to get old." As he implied, the special considerations related to elderly populations are due to normal, inevitable age-related declines in physical capacity and mental abilities. Some but not all elderly persons also experience an increase in social isolation. This section also reviews the substantial stigma related to being old, which may be manifested in the way that elderly persons are treated by friends, family, and even health care professionals. All of these issues lead to greater vulnerability to abuse, neglect, and exploitation. As a result of increased vulnerability, there are mandated reporting laws, similar to the laws related to children and adolescents, and these are briefly discussed.

Physical and Cognitive Decline

Almost everyone will experience a decline in physical abilities as they age. For example, about one in five persons 65 years of age and older experiences some visual impairment, and almost one in two develops some hearing loss. Starting around age 40, bodies lose muscle tone and strength at the same time that tendons and other connective tissue become less flexible and bones become increasingly brittle. These lead to increased incidence of strains and sprains, as well as increased risk of balance problems and falling, all of which can limit physical mobility. Having lived more years, older persons are also more likely than younger persons to see the emergence of medical problems that can take years to develop, such as heart disease, arthritis, and cancer.

"I can't remember anything anymore!"

Elderly persons sometime believe that their memories are much worse than when they were younger. But studies have shown that their memories are only *slightly worse* than that of younger persons. The sense of being forgetful is largely due to the relatively large amount of information in the memory store of the typical older person. Being older means experiencing more events; learning more dates of importance, phone numbers, and directions; and meeting many more people than persons who are younger. In other words, the elderly have a lot more to remember and, thus, a lot more opportunity to experience forgetfulness. (This older versus younger contrast is the difference between forgetting the year Joe Namath led the Jets to the Super Bowl and not knowing who Joe Namath is.)

There is likewise normal cognitive decline as a person grows older. For example, memory capacity reduces somewhat with age. However, memory problems are usually not nearly as bad as the elderly person might suppose. Genuinely serious memory problems in an elderly person are not normal. Rather, they may be an indication of a brain disease that needs medical attention (reviewed beginning on p. 299).

Other cognitive declines are more normal and expected. Older adults do not process information as quickly as when they were younger. Put another way, older adults are able to understand and use information as well as younger persons (such as instructions for storing a number into a new smart phone), but it takes somewhat longer for them to do so. Related to this, as a person ages, he or she will probably realize a decrease in the ability to conduct efficient and effective information searches. This means, for example, that it will take an older person longer, compared to when he or she was younger, to find a new doctor who accepts his insurance, to find which library has the book needed for her book club, or to find directions to the new restaurant that opened downtown. By the way, this problem may seem worse than it is in our modern age where information searches can be conducted, by many members of younger generations, practically instantaneously (e.g., using Google).

All of these physical and cognitive declines are more likely to develop as one grows increasingly older, and once they start to develop they will be exacerbated with advancing years. For example, physical limitations that are bad at age 62 will likely be worse at age 72 and even worse at age 82.

Social Isolation

Elderly persons are more likely than younger adults to experience social isolation. Declining health will limit personal mobility, and both health problems and limited mobility will diminish public mobility (e.g., the capacity to drive or to use public transportation).

Social isolation can also increase as a result of fewer demands to get out of the house to go to work, to run errands, or to do the day-to-day tasks of raising a family (e.g., grocery shopping, taking a child to soccer practice). Retirement from work and from parenting duties may also lead to a loss of relationships with colleagues and with other parents. All of this may be compounded by fewer social opportunities as friends and loved ones pass away.

Social isolation is extremely bad for one's health regardless of age. Social isolation increases the likelihood of developing mental health problems, such as depression, anxiety, or a substance use disorder. Less obviously, social isolation also increases the likelihood of developing physical health problems, such as heart disease. In fact, researchers estimate that the health risks of social isolation are equivalent to smoking, which contributes to premature death for more than half a million people worldwide every year. Fortunately, in contrast to declining physical health, social isolation can be relatively easily mitigated.

The Stigma of Getting Old

Studies show that many people hold negative attitudes and beliefs about older adults. Older adults are often stereotyped as interpersonally and physically impaired. However, the most common stereotype is that elderly persons are mentally incompetent. These stigmatizing beliefs are widely held by persons of all ages, including the elderly themselves. Of course, the way one thinks greatly influences how one feels and behaves. As many an elderly person will attest, negative stereotypes thus lead others to feel negatively about elderly persons and to engage in obnoxious, insulting, and even discriminatory behavior toward them.

Vulnerability to Abuse, Neglect, Exploitation, and Poor Health Care

Age-related declines in physical and cognitive capacities will likely lead to increased reliance on others. As was seen in the chapter on child abuse and neglect, reliance on others leaves a person vulnerable to mistreatment, including abuse, neglect, and exploitation. Such vulnerability is even greater if the person is socially isolated. Stigmatizing stereotypes about the aged make it more difficult to identify and intervene when an elderly person is victimized. Moreover, when health care providers endorse stigmatizing stereotypes, the care provided to elderly persons can be not just less than adequate but potentially dangerous.

Abuse

Studies suggest that 3-10% of elderly persons are physically, emotionally, or sexually abused by persons on whom they rely for care. This figure may be an underestimate, as fear, embarrassment, and ignorance about what constitutes abusive behavior deter persons from reporting that they have been maltreated. Abuse is most likely to be committed by family members or friends, but it could also be committed by employees of or fellow patients at an institution (e.g., an assisted living facility).

Unfortunately, health care providers often fail to identify abuse (whether committed against an elderly adult, a child, or an adult victim of domestic abuse regardless of age). Although it is now recommended by health care provider organizations (such as the American Medical Association) and policy makers, many health care providers don't routinely inquire about abuse. Even though it means providing suboptimal care, research suggests that some providers are reluctant to ask questions that might be embarrassing to their patients.

A related issue that can make it difficult to identify abuse is that many elderly persons, by necessity, are accompanied to health care visits by others, such as an adult child. The older adult patient may have been proven insufficient at relating accurately pertinent recent events (e.g., recent falls), prior medical history, and current medications. Adult caregivers can help provide details, corroborate or correct information, and offer undisclosed information, all of which will make the health care visit more beneficial. Likewise, adult caregivers might better understand and ensure compliance with instructions and prescriptions. However, the presence of the other person may make it even more difficult for the provider to ask about or for the patient to admit unpleasant experiences, such as abuse. Most tragically, the person accompanying to the health care visit may be the person committing the abuse.

Neglect

Neglect is usually thought of as the failure of a caretaker to provide for a dependent person's basic needs. This definition easily fits with our impression of the vulnerabilities of children and adolescents. While it is obvious that children and adolescents need to be cared for until they reach an age when they become independent and assume their own care, the situation is not as clearcut with elderly persons.

The neglect of a child or adolescent, where needs are obvious, usually indicates a problem with the caregiver (e.g., an abusive parent, an alcoholic or addicted parent, a parent with severe mental illness). In contrast, the needs of an elderly person will probably develop very slowly over time, catching both the elderly person and their loved ones by surprise. Thus, for elderly persons, it is more likely that neglect is either unintended (e.g., not knowing that the elderly person was not eating regularly) or unrecognized (e.g., not realizing that the stairwell had gradually become unsafe for the person). Sometimes neglect is self-inflicted. Most older persons have spent a majority of their adult lives caring for themselves. As a result, they may compromise their own health and safety by refusing to acknowledge the need for help, by not asking for help, or by rejecting offered assistance due to pride, a sense of shame, or simple obliviousness.

In other words, many of the following examples of neglect of an elderly person can be remedied, and hopefully will be remedied, after the neglect of the need is discovered. (Of course, in the case of self-inflicted neglect, there may continue to be earnest disagreement between concerned loved ones and the elderly person regarding whether and when more intensive caregiving has become necessary.) The types of neglect are similar to those experienced by children and adolescents.

Emotional neglect occurs when a person is deprived, either purposefully or inadvertently, the basic emotional need of connectedness to other humans. For example, an older person is the victim of emotional neglect if he is left alone or ignored by others for extended periods. Neglect of *needs related to daily living* is also common for elderly persons. Age-related inabilities and incapacities can make previously simple tasks, such as bathing or making nutritious meals, difficult or impossible.

Unmet medical needs among elderly persons may be due to prohibitive costs or inadequate financial resources. Elderly persons are more likely than other age groups to have difficulty accessing providers and supplies due to limited mobility and inconvenient locations. Other health needs that may go unmet are related to normal age-related declines (e.g., proper eyeglasses, hearing aids, or dentures).

Unsafe living conditions is another common area of unintended neglect. Living quarters that were acceptable for the younger person may be dangerous to the now-elderly person. For example, most people negotiate stairwells with little thought for most of their lives, but climbing or descending stairwells can be an extraordinarily dangerous activity for an elderly person. Likewise, muscles that are somewhat weaker and less responsive make showers and bathtubs more difficult—and potentially dangerous—to get into and out of.

Financial Exploitation

Stealing from or defrauding elderly persons is extremely common. A former con artist admitted to the American Association of Retired Persons (AARP), "It is an article of faith in this business to go after the old folks." Exploitation may be committed by family members or friends, by professionals with whom they consult about financial matters, or by persons who merely pose as professionals.

Financial exploitation by family and friends may be as "simple" as stealing money or possessions, whereas more involved exploitation may include forcing or forging signatures on pension and social security checks, coercing the person to change her will, or convincing the person to assign power of attorney so that all decisions related to financial assets are placed under the control of another.

Since few people would claim they have complete and expert understanding of the financial world, nearly everyone is susceptible to deception and fraud. However, consumer advocates warn that elderly persons are particularly vulnerable to financial exploitation by strangers. Elderly persons are more likely to have burgeoning expenses but limited or fixed incomes, making them more eager to sign on for "can't miss" financial opportunities. Moreover, elderly persons have been found to be less likely to consult family, friends, or professionals to vet such "opportunities" in order to determine their legitimacy. Elderly persons are also less likely to report that they have been defrauded, making it impossible to seek restitution, because they may fear being considered incompetent or unintelligent.

Social isolation makes it more difficult for elderly persons to identify and respond effectively to attempts at fraud. Studies have found that older consumers are more receptive to both fraudulent schemes and honest but exploitative offers (e.g., telemarketers), because they have greater need of social interactions than the young. Simply put, older persons are more likely to be bored and lonely and thus are more likely to enjoy talking to strangers on the phone. Unfortunately, many strangers who call to talk are calling to talk them out of their money.

Stereotypes and Inappropriate Care

Medical and mental health professionals may endorse stereotypical beliefs about aging, which can interfere with appropriate care or lead to outright malpractice. For example, health care professionals who believe growing older is inherently a sad phenomenon will not evaluate an elderly patient for depression, be concerned about an elderly person who complains of depression, or think it appropriate to treat any evident depression. Mental illness that does not fit the usual stereotype towards aging may be misidentified. For example, an older adult complaining of increased fear around the home (perhaps related to increasingly unsafe living conditions) may be perceived as exhibiting cognitive impairment, which is the most frequent stigmatizing belief about aging. Likewise, pain in older adults may be mismanaged because of the incorrect belief that pain is an inevitable part of the normal aging process.

Health care professionals who exhibit patronizing attitudes and behavior will communicate to older adults that their opinions are no longer relevant, that their capabilities are no longer needed, that their choices are no longer respected, and that their complaints no longer matter. The consequence to the elderly adult is self-evident: decreased self-worth, embarrassment, humiliation, and a decline in self-efficacy (which is the sense of being able to accomplish what one attempts). All of this underscores the advice to seek out health care professionals with specialized training in working with geriatric patients.

The Proper Use of Elderspeak

Elderspeak is the term used for speech directed at elderly persons who have certain qualities. Elderspeak is slower than normal with shorter sentences, exaggerated intonation, higher pitch, simplified grammar, and a fairly limited vocabulary. Many older adults feel patronized when this style of speech is directed at them, and it is therefore sometimes pejoratively referred to as "secondary baby talk."

But research shows that elderspeak, when done properly, has some benefits. For example, one study found that using elderspeak to help elderly adults negotiate a location resulted in improved task performance (i.e., they were more likely to find the place). Another study found that communications between caregivers and older adults with Alzheimer's improved when the former used elderspeak.

So the question then becomes how to use elderspeak without being insulting.

In a series of fascinating studies, researchers "unpacked" elderspeak to differentiate its beneficial versus its patronizing aspects. The studies showed that using shorter sentences, a higher pitched voice, and slowed speech do *not* help and are seen as patronizing. However, the same studies found that using elaborations (such as paraphrasing and repeating) and using less complex sentences (that is, sentences with fewer subordinate clauses) both were helpful to and were not perceived as patronizing by the elderly subjects.

From Social Security to Adult Protective Services

Various protective mechanisms for elderly persons have been developed over the last 100 years. The most well-known is Social Security, but other formal protective mechanisms have also emerged.

Social Security

Social Security came into existence during the Great Depression of the 1930s as "social insurance" for elderly persons. The stock market crash of 1929 and subsequent bank failures had decimated private retirement and savings accounts, leaving many people, including more than half of the senior citizens, impoverished. Regular direct payments from the federal government were instituted to avert destitution and starvation.

Social Security steadily expanded in subsequent generations. For example, Social Security now covers persons who are disabled regardless of age. Improved finances meant improved nutrition and medical care (the latter was greatly enhanced with the institution of Medicare in the 1960s). Social Security, however, did and does not protect elderly persons against isolation and infirmity, nor has or will it protect them against abuse, neglect, and exploitation.

The Importance of Geriatric Specialists

To maximize the chance that elderly persons will receive effective, sensitive, and appropriate care for both physical and mental health, elderly persons should see health care providers who are geriatric specialists. These providers have expertise in issues specific to elderly populations. For example, geriatric psychiatrists and psychologists have special training in the diagnosis and treatment of mental illnesses that occur in older adults. They are more likely to recognize delirium and to differentiate types of neurocognitive disorder (see p. 299). They have special expertise in treating depression, anxiety, alcohol, and substance use disorders among elderly persons. They are expert at navigating issues related to physician-patient confidentiality that might arise when another person (e.g., an adult child) accompanies the patient to the visit. They are aware of mandated reporting requirements in cases of abuse and exploitation. Finally, health care providers who specialize in the treatment of geriatric populations are well prepared to help their patients navigate the health care system.

Special Legal Protections for Elderly Persons

In the early 1960s, the National Council on Aging petitioned Congress to establish programs to protect elderly persons. Congress did so, but it did not provide sufficient funding to implement any of the proposed programs. Finally, in 1974, Congress passed Title XX of the Social Security Act, which included permission for states to use Social Security Administration funds to provide services for the protection of both adults and children. By 1991, 41 states had passed legislation mandating that professionals (such as police and medical professionals) who suspected that an elderly person was being maltreated were required to file a report to state protective services.

However, almost immediately, there arose debate about balancing the needs for protection with the right to autonomy. Many advocates for older persons, such as AARP, expressed concern that adult protective services were overly paternalistic and, as a result, insulting towards elderly persons. As discussed earlier, children and adolescents are undeniably vulnerable, and laws related to their protection probably make sense to everyone. However, with elderly adults things are not nearly as clear. The basic issue is whether and when an elderly person becomes incapable of self-care, such that another should get involved to ensure his or her welfare. Unlike child maltreatment, problems are not always self-evident. Should protective services be called if a grandson steals regularly from his grandparents to buy drugs? Perhaps so. But what if they know about it and allow it to happen? Perhaps not. Then again, what if they know about it and allow it but as a result are unable to feed themselves properly?

Some have argued that the capacity to declare elderly adults legally incapable of caring for themselves may actually make them more vulnerable to exploitation. For example, some unscrupulous adult children have reported to state protective services that their elderly parent is incompetent in an effort to get the state to put them in charge of their parent's finances.

It is not always clear when adult protective services should be informed about situations. However, the reader should never hesitate to ask for a consultation. As with child protective services, these agencies are quite willing to consult and "think through" situations that are confounding to the children of elderly persons and to mandated reporters.

Mental Illness in Elderly Persons

The overall annual rate of mental illness for elderly adults is estimated to be about 26%, which is higher than for nonelderly adults. But this higher rate is largely due to the disorders that occur almost exclusively among elderly persons, such as dementia. If one eliminates disorders associated with the aging brain, the rate of mental illness for elderly adults is actually somewhat less than for nonelderly adults. The manner in which these disorders manifest or present in elderly persons, compared to younger persons, is often decidedly different.

Disorders particular to elderly persons and the different age-related presentations of depression, anxiety, and the substance use disorders are now reviewed.

Delirium

Delirium is an extremely serious condition that requires immediate attention. It comes on suddenly and is usually temporary. It is characterized by profound confusion, as it affects memory, orientation, attention span, and language. It can occur at any age, but occurs most frequently in persons who are elderly.

Symptoms of Delirium

A person in delirium will exhibit difficulty with short-term memory, meaning extreme forgetfulness about immediate events. Someone in delirium may forget that she turned on the faucet or stove, that she let the dog out, or what room she just entered. Attention is also seriously affected during a delirious state, such that the person may exhibit impairment in attending to basic surroundings. Consequently, the person will likely be disoriented, not knowing where he is or why he is there. Some persons in delirium even forget who they are. Some present with language problems, exhibiting difficulty making themselves understood and difficulty understanding others.

In some cases, the person experiencing delirium may experience visual hallucinations or persecutory or grandiose delusions. Persons experiencing delirium can become so disoriented that they threaten others or attempt to harm themselves.

Prevalence of Delirium

Delirium is a common presentation to emergency departments. It is likewise extremely common among residents of nursing homes. It frequently develops among elderly persons who are hospitalized, such that a sizeable portion of elderly persons hospitalized will develop it at some point during their hospital stay.

May Goes to the ER

May arose and took her medications, including her new medication for glaucoma. As she did every day, she then drove to her daughter's home to look after her two- and four-year-old granddaughters. Fortunately for May, the elder girl was quite bright and loved to talk on the phone. When Mom called from work to remind May that she was expecting an important package, Lisa answered. This was not unusual, but what was unusual was that Grandma was still in the bathroom. She'd been in there a long time, according to Lisa, and the baby needed changing and was crying (which Mom could hear). Directed by Mom, Lisa repeatedly knocked on the bathroom door and called for Grandma, but there was no response. Terrified, Mom called the neighbor and her husband and raced for home.

When she got home, the neighbor and May were sitting at the kitchen table, but they were not talking. The neighbor told Mom that she broke into the bathroom and found May looking out the window, saying nothing. She was unresponsive to questions. When May saw her daughter, she exclaimed, "Kristy. You're home. Your dad should be home soon and then we can eat." Dad had died 12 years earlier.

Kristy and her husband drove May to the emergency department. May could remember her name, but she could not relate the day or date or tell the doctor where she was or why she was there. After several hours, her son-in-law drove to May's home and retrieved all of the medication bottles on her sink. Soon thereafter, it was discovered that the new glaucoma medication had interacted with May's other medications to create the state of delirium. They were sent home and told to wait it out (and to dispose of the new medication). That evening, May started to respond appropriately but retired to bed early with a terrible headache. The next morning, she felt hung over but was otherwise herself.

Causes of Delirium

Delirium is typically caused by some sudden-onset disease process occurring in the brain. It occurs more commonly in persons who are elderly than in persons who are nonelderly, because these biological issues are more common in elderly persons. For example, infections are often more severe and dangerous in elderly persons due to the normal, age-related weakening of the immune system. Another issue making elderly adults more vulnerable to delirium is drug interactions. According to the American Society of Consultant Pharmacists, persons 65 to 69 years old take, on average, almost 14 prescriptions per year. Among adults who take five or more medications, over one-third will experience an adverse reaction, including delirium.

Delirium is an extremely serious condition indicating a dangerous medical emergency. Unfortunately, medical practitioners are not always well prepared to recognize it. It is estimated that as many as two in three cases of delirium go unrecognized by physicians. Substantial barriers to recognition are stereotypes about so-called normal aging. For example, someone with neurocognitive disorder (i.e., dementia, which is discussed next) can develop delirium, but the latter is often misdiagnosed as an aspect of dementia. It is vital to distinguish the two, however, as delirium indicates a dangerous, acute disease process that needs to be addressed. If proper treatment is initiated, delirium usually resolves as quickly as it arose.

Neurocognitive Disorder

Neurocognitive disorder entails a decline in cognitive functioning. (The condition was previously called dementia, but this was seen as pejorative and too nonspecific.) Memory problems and language impairment are the most easily observed cognitive declines, but other cognitive difficulties and personality changes are also seen.

Memory Problems

Memory has both short-term and long-term aspects, and neurocognitive disorder can affect both. Short-term memory problems include incapacity to track a conversation or to recall something just experienced. Everyone forgets things at times, of course, but the difference between normal forgetfulness and neurocognitive disorder is that effort does not help. For example, if the person with normal memory pays attention and attempts to remember, he usually can. In contrast, someone with neurocognitive disorder cannot remember information, regardless of effort. In another example, when a person with normal memory loses something, she can often retrace her steps to find it. A person with neurocognitive disorder will lose things and, because of short-term memory problems, be unable to recall where she was or what she was doing previously.

Neurocognitive disorder can impair long-term memories as well. Long-term memories include phone numbers, birthday dates, names of spouses and former colleagues, and other information that can be recalled—nearly instantly, nearly perfectly, and at essentially any time needed—from our storehouse of memories. The person with neurocognitive disorder may forget not just loved ones' names but even their faces and voices, leading to a failure to recognize even siblings, spouses, and children. Procedural memories, which are memories related to how things are done, will also be impacted. The person with neurocognitive disorder may forget how to dial a phone or use a television remote, the manner in which ingredients of a beloved recipe should be combined, or the rules to a favorite card game.

Language Problems

Language problems related to neurocognitive disorder may involve difficulty with expressive language, such as misusing words, trouble finding words, or relying on substitute words (e.g., calling a "phone" a "talking device"). Neurocognitive disorder may likewise affect receptive language, such that the person will have trouble following or joining a conversation. In severe cases, communication ability is completely disrupted.

Other Cognitive and Personality Changes

Unlike delirium, which by definition is a temporary condition, neurocognitive disorder is a permanent condition that will probably worsen over time. The person with neurocognitive disorder may exhibit extreme confusion, including disorientation to date, day, time, or place. Concentration may be impaired. As a result, the person may take much longer than previously to accomplish fairly simple tasks or he may lose the ability to follow simple directions.

Persons with neurocognitive disorder may also exhibit severely impaired judgment and sustained confusion. Impaired judgment might manifest as poor hygiene, giving away money to strangers, or inappropriate dress. Chronic confusion might be accompanied by depression, irritability, suspiciousness, anxiety, and fearfulness. Some may display delusional thinking (e.g., paranoia) or hallucinations, both of which are commonly seen with the psychotic disorders. Because of such cognitive problems, persons with neurocognitive disorder may start to exhibit severe behavioral disturbances, such as verbal or physical aggressiveness towards others, including loved ones and caregivers.

Dean Dries His Clothes

Dean was being taken care of by his daughter and her husband. One would visit in the morning, and the other would visit in the afternoon. They made sure he had meals and that he took his blood pressure and diabetes medications, and they helped him remember to consult his calendar (which listed his appointments, things he needed to do that day, and shows he wanted to watch). Three times a week, they took him to visit his wife, who had advanced Alzheimer's disease.

The daughter and husband decided to press the issue of assisted living when Dean started to complain that someone was coming into his condo and rearranging his furniture, which hadn't been moved in over a decade. He once tried to dry his wet clothes in the oven. However, he forgot that he had put them in there, and when his son-in-law arrived that evening, Dean was watching TV while several shirts and socks were smoldering in the oven.

They convinced him to move to the same living facility as his wife, just down the hall. For a while he visited her every day. After a year, the staff reported that the visits were becoming more sporadic. One day his daughter took him into her room, and he stood quietly away from the bed. Finally he said to his daughter, "Do you know her?"

Causes of Neurocognitive Decline

The cognitive decline leading ultimately to neurocognitive disorder may result from a variety of illnesses, including stroke, traumatic brain injury, Parkinson's disease, substance use, and Huntington's disease. In most cases, however, neurocognitive disorder is caused by Alzheimer's disease, which is an ongoing, degenerative process in the brain. The exact mechanisms are unknown, but evidence suggests that Alzheimer's disease is due to the excessive buildup of otherwise normally occurring proteins in the brain.

Prevalence of Neurocognitive Disorder

Neurocognitive disorder is uncommon before age 65, affecting less than 1 in 1000 persons in that age group. However, it is increasingly prevalent in each subsequent decade thereafter. Alzheimer's disease affects about 1 in 100 persons aged 65-74 and over 10% of those over age 80. In total, about 5 million Americans over age 65 are diagnosed with the disease.

It is estimated that one in three seniors will die with (but not necessarily due to) neurocognitive disorder. Alzheimer's disease is the cause of death for 100,000 people a year, and it is thus one of the leading causes of death in the United States. The damage to brain cells that causes neurocognitive decline also affects brain cells responsible for basic life functioning, such as breathing, heartbeat, and swallowing.

Care Issues: Costs and Challenges

There are drugs under investigation that will hopefully prove to inhibit the progress of neurocognitive disorder. Unfortunately, at present, there is neither effective treatment nor a cure. For this reason, the treatment of neurocognitive disorder entails intensive caregiving. It is estimated that in 2013, direct care costs were over $200 billion, and they are predicted to rise to over $1 trillion per year by the year 2050.

The person with neurocognitive disorder is entirely dependent on others for food, a habitable shelter, and moment-to-moment safety. The confusion inherent in neurocognitive disorder usually means that the person is inadvertently uncooperative with his or her own care. Likewise, unfortunately, the person with neurocognitive disorder often also exhibits personality changes, perhaps including extreme irritability.

The intense need, the unwitting resistance, and the potentially unpleasant behavior can be devastating to loved ones who are attempting to provide care. In short, caring for someone with neurocognitive disorder can be extremely difficult. Research has demonstrated that one of the better treatments of neurocognitive disorder entails providing intensive emotional support to caregivers. One program brings caregivers together so that they can share stories and sympathy, learn strategies, and vent their frustrations. The program has shown beneficial effects on not just the caregivers themselves but also on the persons with neurocognitive disorder.

The Anxiety and Depressive Disorders

The anxiety and depression disorders are presented together because they so often co-occur (i.e., are comorbid) in elderly persons. An elderly person with an anxiety disorder has about a 25% chance of also having a depression, and an elderly person with a depression has about a 50% chance of having an anxiety disorder. This seems to be largely related to the problem of undertreatment of both disorders. Not obtaining treatment for an anxiety disorder means that it will probably endure, which can lead to comorbid depression, and vice versa.

Prevalence of Depression and Anxiety Disorders

The overall rate of anxiety disorders in elderly persons is about half that in younger persons. Panic disorder, OCD, and PTSD all decrease in likelihood as persons grow older. On the other hand, generalized anxiety disorder (GAD), which is relatively uncommon (about 3%) in younger persons, increases threefold among elderly persons. This is likely related to increased social isolation and greater overall vulnerability to crime, exploitation, and physical health problems. The phobias do not seem to increase in likelihood with age, even though specific fears become more common. This is because fears that would be characterized as abnormal in young persons are often considered realistic for the elderly population. These include fears of living alone, dying, falling (which may incorporate fears of stairwells and of dogs that sometimes like to jump up in greeting), the dark, and strangers.

On the other hand, the depressive disorders (i.e., major depressive episode and dysthymic disorder) are more likely among elderly populations. One study estimated that 60% of elderly adults report some symptoms of depression, and as many as 20% meet criteria for a diagnosis of major depression (compared to 6-8% of the younger population). This is explained by increased likelihood of health problems and social isolation.

Depression, Anxiety, and Physical Health Problems

Research shows that depression and anxiety cause elderly adults to have considerably worse treatment outcomes for various health problems, including hip fractures, heart attacks, and cancer. For example, elderly adults battling cancer who develop either anxiety or depression experience greater rates of hospitalization, poorer physical capability (e.g., walking up stairs), a poorer quality of life, and greater experience of pain.

Thus do depression and anxiety exacerbate medical health problems. However, they are also often caused by medical health problems. For example, difficulty breathing, chronic joint or muscle pain, cancer, and heart disease, as well as the direct and interactive side effects of medications used to treat these issues, can cause depression. Research shows that depression and anxiety tend to improve when such medical health problems are eliminated or better managed.

The Face of Anxiety and Depression in Elderly Persons

Elderly adults are more likely to deny that they are experiencing emotional symptoms or to minimize the extent or severity of such symptoms. This is partly a generational issue of not believing it appropriate to talk about or express emotions. On the other hand, research has shown that older adults, compared to younger adults, experience negative emotions less strongly. That is, older adults tend to report lower levels of depression and anxiety, not to mention other negative emotions such as guilt, anger, and shyness.

Another reason that older adults may not complain about symptoms of anxiety and depression is because they may not experience them as anomalous. That is, older adults are more likely than younger adults to not recognize that what they are experiencing indicates a mental health problem. For example, some will have had such experiences for most of their lives and will therefore not perceive them as abnormal.

In related fashion, it is more likely for older adults than younger adults to attribute symptoms of anxiety and depression to physical illness and chronic medical conditions, which are both more common among elderly persons. Likewise, both patients and physicians may neglect symptoms of anxiety or depression because they misattribute them to medical conditions, to side effects of prescription drugs, or to a regrettable but natural aspect of growing older (which are stigmatizing stereotypes).

Finally, older adults may use language to describe symptoms of mental illness (e.g., "concerns" rather than "depression") that makes others suppose that the symptoms are not particularly distressing. Although they are not intentionally minimizing, the minimizing language usage and modest emphasis may cause caregivers and providers to miss the significance of the complaints.

Sleep Complaints in Older Adults

"How Much?" or "How Good?"

Sleep complaints are common among elderly persons. Therefore, it may be helpful for older adults with sleep complaints to understand that the need for sleep declines throughout the lifespan. Studies have shown that newborns sleep 16 to 20 hours per day, whereas children between the ages of one and four sleep about 11 or 12 hours per day, and an adolescent needs about 9 hours (although during the school year, many get much less). The average middle age adult needs about 7.5 hours, whereas the typical older adult needs less than 7 hours in order to function optimally. Some need even less.

If an older adult simply counts the number of hours asleep as an indicator of whether he is getting enough sleep, he may conclude he is "never sleeping enough." On the other hand, if he uses the methods sleep scientists use to gauge sleep need, he may realize that he is obtaining sufficient sleep, even if the amount is drastically less than when he was younger.

Sleep specialists don't count the number of hours slept as an indication of quality. People vary too much in how much they sleep. Sleep specialists gauge sleep quality in terms of how well the person does after sleep. If the person thinks, feels, and behaves okay (e.g., alert, rested, attentive, able to complete tasks successfully), then the person is obtaining enough sleep. So the question is not how many hours a person sleeps but rather how well the person does after sleep.

To Nap or Not to Nap

A previous chapter covered the sleep disorders, including a discussion of the unfortunate fact that the most common treatment for sleep problems is prescription medications. While sleep medications are an acceptable short-term solution, many people end up using these pills continuously for months or even years. The chapter strongly recommended behavioral (i.e., nonmedicine) strategies that have voluminous research supporting their effectiveness to improve sleep. Included in the recommendation is that someone with insomnia not take naps, to ensure that they are tired enough at bedtime to sleep.

However, older adults are much more likely than younger adults to not be able to obtain adequate hours of sleep in one period. For a variety of reasons, including medical issues and medications, older adults are more likely to experience difficulty staying asleep throughout the night.

Many older adults successfully incorporate naps into their schedule, to make up for interrupted sleep at nighttime. There are, however, some "napping rules" to follow. Naps should never be in the late afternoon, but rather in the early afternoon. Also, naps should be either about 20 minutes or about 90 minutes, but not in between. The typical "sleep cycle" is 90 minutes in length. The 20-minute nap doesn't allow one to get too deeply into the sleep cycle, whereas the 90-minute nap allows one to complete it. Research shows that either allows the person to wake from the nap feeling refreshed, whereas naps of in-between length disrupt the sleep cycle, resulting in grogginess and a sense of being sleep deprived.

Consequences of Different Presentations

As noted, older adults are less likely to recognize, acknowledge, or admit that they are experiencing anxiety or depression or both. The consequences are both predictable and unfortunate. Despite the existence of many effective treatments for both problems, older adults are less likely than other age groups to receive any treatment for either. Studies estimate that less than one in three older persons with a mental illness receives any treatment. Older adults are also less likely to receive adequate treatment if they do obtain it. Research suggests that of those older adults with mental illness who do get treatment, most obtain it from their general physician rather than from a mental health professional (i.e., a psychiatrist, psychologist, social worker, or master's level counselor). However, general physicians are generally poor at recognizing and adequately treating mental illness in patients of any age. Thus, older adults are more likely than other-age adults to be given treatment that is ineffective (e.g., insufficient dosage of a medication). They are also less likely to be treated with psychotherapy, which is a highly effective treatment for all age groups.

The dire consequences of inadequate treatment for mental illness are increased morbidity and mortality. Regarding the former, untreated mental illness does not tend to get better, and research shows that older adults are the least likely to recover from depression, anxiety, and other mental illnesses. Not adequately treating mental illness also increases mortality, as mental illness exacerbates physical illnesses and reduces the effectiveness of treatments for those illnesses.

In addition, untreated mental illness contributes to risk for suicide. Persons age 65 or older have the highest suicide rate of any age group. Older adults represent 13% of the population of the United States but account for 20% of all completed suicides. Persons over age 85 are twice as likely to die by suicide than younger persons, and the highest rate of suicide is among white males 85 and older. Underscoring the inadequacy of treatment, research has demonstrated that about three-in-four older males visited their primary care physician within one month of committing suicide (half saw their physician the week they killed themselves).

Substance Use Disorders

The substance use disorders look somewhat different in older adults than they do in younger adults. The largest issues are the reasons for use, the dangers of use, and the increased likelihood of unintentional misuse. Other important issues are the decreased likelihood that the older adult will be identified as having a substance use disorder and the increased likelihood that the older adult will reject the need for treatment.

Prevalence of Substance Use Disorders

The prevalence rate of substance use disorders among older persons is as difficult to estimate as for younger persons. Recall from chapter 11 that an alcohol or drug use problem is diagnosed when use causes a problem. Since epidemiological surveys of the substance use disorders rely on respondents admitting that use of alcohol or drugs is causing problems, the estimate of problems will inevitably be low. Estimates of prevalence rates have nonetheless been attempted.

Regarding alcohol, the 2011 National Survey on Drug Use and Health did not attempt to evaluate whether drinking was causing problems. Instead, the researchers determined rates of binge drinking, defined as having four drinks (for women) or five drinks (for men) within a relatively short period of time. Based on other research, survey researchers assumed that binge drinking was very likely to be problem drinking. The survey found that 8.3% of adults 65 and older reported binge drinking in the past month.

Compared to younger adults, the drug use disorders in older adults are much less likely to be related to illicit drug use. Nonetheless, the prevalence of drug use problems in older adults is higher than in other age groups. Older adults are prescribed medications approximately three times as frequently as other age groups, and their use of over-the-counter

(OTC or nonprescription) medications is even more extensive. Perhaps it is not surprising, then, that elderly individuals are much more likely than younger individuals to misuse both prescription and OTC drugs. Research suggests that as many as one in ten older adults misuse prescription drugs, such as benzodiazepines (often prescribed for the treatment of anxiety), sleeping pills, and painkillers. Older women are almost twice as likely as older men to misuse prescription medication.

In other words, most drug use disorders in older adults involves medications prescribed by physicians. Many physicians feel uncomfortable addressing this issue with older patients, and so they simply refill prescriptions in spite of clear contraindications and warnings on drug labels regarding excessively lengthy use. Some physicians may rationalize that there is little harm likely done, given the person's advanced years (another example of stereotyped thinking and discriminatory behavior and another example of the vital importance of seeing providers with specific training in working with older adults).

The Baby Boom Generation Enters Old Age

A generational issue is emerging with regard to illegal drugs, and it has mental health professionals somewhat concerned. "Baby boomers" is the phrase for the generation that reached young adulthood in the 1960s and 1970s, when there was increasing tolerance of experimenting with or regularly using illicit drugs, most especially cocaine and marijuana. Research has definitively shown that, despite the acclaim, these drugs are far from harmless. Nonetheless, some baby boomers are reaching older adulthood with many of these permissive attitudes and behaviors intact. According to a study by the Substance Abuse and Mental Health Services Administration, in 2011 about 6.3% of adults aged 50 to 59 admitted to recent use of illicit drugs compared to 2.7% in 2002. Given the size of the baby boom generation, some experts believe that a substance use crisis among older adults is imminent.

Different Risk Factors

Many older adults who misuse drugs or alcohol are merely continuing the bad habit from younger years. Some develop problems in later life, however. Younger adults with substance use problems report that they began using in order to feel positive effects (e.g., "to get high") and in order to improve the socialization experience (i.e., "to have a better time at the party"). Drug or alcohol use problems emerge in older adulthood for different reasons. Elderly persons diagnosed with a newly developed substance use disorder are more likely to report that they turned to alcohol (which many used without adverse effects for decades) or to illicit drugs in order to negate negative feelings. Risk factors for older adults, then, include onset of illness, physical pain, stress, social isolation, and grief from loss of loved ones. More general risk factors are boredom and low life satisfaction.

Different Dangers

Older adults, compared to younger adults, have a reduced ability to metabolize drugs and alcohol, with the result that a smaller amount of the substance goes a longer way. Other concerns about substance use among older persons, which are not as serious concerns for younger adults, include the increased risk of falling, the increased risk of serious injury due to accidents and falls, and the potential adverse interaction of alcohol and drugs with prescription medications.

The Hidden Face of Substance Use Problems in Elderly Persons

There are several reasons that substance use problems in elderly persons might go unrecognized, in which case there will be no opportunity for intervention.

As noted previously, substance use disorders are most readily diagnosed when substance use causes impairment. Being more limited in their social roles, older adults are less likely to exhibit such impairment. For example, older adults are less likely than younger adults to be working, raising children, or going out with friends, so that problems are going to be less evident in terms of occupational, family, and social impairment.

Another issue concerns the difficulty of diagnosing a problem with substance use when the person has been using for a long time without any previous indication of a problem. As a result, when problems do emerge, they may not be readily noticed or may be excused as anomalous (e.g., "Everyone drinks too much now and then").

As noted earlier, older adults who misuse prescription medications have, by definition, been prescribed those medications. They have the explicit permission and perhaps encouragement of their medical doctor to take the drugs. Older adults are often shocked, dismayed, and angry when told, perhaps by a new physician, that they have been misusing prescription medications. They may insist on consulting a different physician altogether if the medications are not prescribed again.

Finally, the stigma against having any mental illness is active at all ages, but it is particularly potent among older adults. Moreover, the stigma of having a mental illness is most extreme with the substance use disorders, which are typically seen as a failure of morality and of willpower.

As a result, older adults are more likely than younger adults (who are themselves extremely likely) to rebuff the suggestion that they are drinking too much or using drugs inappropriately.

Encouraging Elderly Persons to Seek Help

As noted numerous times in this volume, regardless of age group, most persons with mental illness do not obtain adequate treatment. This problem is even worse for elderly persons, with two caveats. First, the vast majority of elderly persons with delirium and neurocognitive disorder will be seen by and actively cared for by health care professionals. Hopefully, the health care professional is competent enough to diagnose and treat these issues, especially delirium, properly. Second, older adults with prior history of mental health problems and treatment are likely to continue that treatment.

However, proper diagnosis and treatment of *recently emerged* mental illness are far less certain for elderly persons than for younger persons, because diagnosis and treatment occur only if the person seeks help. Older adults are less likely to seek help for several reasons. First, seeking help requires acknowledging a problem. As noted previously, recognizing a mental health problem is much more likely if it causes distress or impairment. As noted, compared to those younger, older persons are less likely to admit distress and are less likely to exhibit impairment (since they are more likely to be retired from work, no longer actively parenting, and less socially active). Second, older persons are less likely to agree that mental health treatments can be beneficial. Finally, older adults are more likely to confront the "double stigma" of growing old and having a mental illness, both of which carry the stereotype of being perceived as mentally incompetent.

However, without some sort of intervention, the mental illness will compromise health, leading to more severe illnesses and more likelihood of dying from a treatable illness, and lead to greater rates of suicide. There are several strategies that can be used when encouraging elderly persons to seek help.

Usual Treatment Is Not Necessarily Needed

It is important to realize that the usual treatments for mental illness (medication and psychotherapy) are less likely to be needed by elderly persons with mental illness. A theme of this chapter has been comorbidity, meaning that many of the mental illnesses in elderly persons co-occur with or because of other problems. The common circumstances of being elderly include increased rates of physical health problems and limitations; greater vulnerability to abuse, neglect, and exploitation; greater risk of social isolation; and the ugly reality of considerable stigma for having lived so long. All of these increase the risk of depression, anxiety, and substance use disorders. Treating these disorders in elderly patients will often entail addressing these other issues, such as decreasing pain, increasing social opportunities, addressing financial concerns, and teaching them to cope with or simply ignore ignorant stereotypes.

Of course, for some older adults with mental illness, formal treatment may be necessary. The health care provider will determine this. If treatment is deemed necessary, emphasize its proven effectiveness. Researchers have developed and continue to develop efficient and effective psychiatric and psychological care specifically for mental health problems in older adults. It can likewise be useful to emphasize the range of treatments available, including different medications and different psychotherapeutic approaches. Also, emphasize both the widespread availability and the common use of formal treatment by many others, including probably many of his or her friends and colleagues. Both of these will suggest that formal treatment is much more acceptable to most people than perhaps realized. Emphasizing that Medicare covers the cost of treatment may make a similar impression.

Be Aware of Language

When discussing with an older adult concerns about his or her mental health, it is important to clarify what is and is not being said. Most older adults are quite familiar with the stereotype that the aged are cognitively impaired. The suggestion, no matter how well meaning, that they may have emotional problems may be perceived as a version of this stereotype. Clarify the difference between cognitive impairment and mental illness. Likewise, it may be useful to normalize their emotional state as an expectable reaction to their present situation.

A related strategy is to avoid using the term *mental illness* altogether. Instead, one can focus on individual symptoms without noting that, taken together, the combination of symptoms suggests the presence of a mental illness. Instead, focus on the sleep problems, the increased pain, the stress of the medical illness, and so forth.

Recruit Others

As with persons experiencing mental illness of any age, when you are trying to encourage an elderly person to recognize and seek help for a mental health problem, it can be useful to recruit the assistance of other persons. Be careful, though, to recruit those who agree with the point of the conversation. Recruit those who think that mental illness is not shameful, needs to be recognized, and can be successfully treated, but not those who think that getting old entails getting depressed, anxious, and addicted.

Be Persistent

For the reasons previously noted (less distress and impairment, less recognition of the value of treatment, more stigma), when encouraging an older adult to recognize that he or she has a mental illness, one should expect resistance. Recognize it as normal, try not to take it personally, and keep trying. One would not give up trying to get a younger person with a mental health problem to get appropriate treatment, and it would be immoral and unfair to forsake an older adult in such a way.

Chapter 17

Domestic Abuse

"People will be lovers of themselves, lovers of money, boastful, proud,
abusive, disobedient to their parents, ungrateful, unholy,
without love, unforgiving, slanderous, without self-control, brutal,
not lovers of the good, treacherous, rash, conceited, lovers of pleasure
rather than lovers of God—having a form of godliness
but denying its power. Have nothing to do with such people."
(2 Timothy 3:2-5)

"The acts of the flesh are . . . hatred, discord, jealousy, fits of rage . . .
Those who live like this will not inherit the kingdom of God."
(Galatians 5:19-21)

"Husbands, in the same way be considerate
as you live with your wives, and treat them with respect
as the weaker partner and as heirs with you of the gracious gift of life,
so that nothing will hinder your prayers."
(1 Peter 3:7)

Patrick and Sandra

When Patrick and Sandra sat down, I thought I was quite fortunate. They were in their early 20s, attractive, and friendly. They were seeking treatment for marital concerns, which delighted me since they had only been married for two years. Most couples wait many years, perhaps decades, before seeking needed marital counseling. They seemed to be on top of things, wanting to stop problems from growing worse and getting completely out of hand. They sat close and held hands on the couch. Patrick had a very good sense of humor. Although Sandra was quiet, she usually smiled or laughed politely at his japes. Patrick had a history at our clinic, as he had been seen for alcohol problems. He had lost his license and could no longer drive, but he proudly noted that he was coming up on his third year of sobriety.

After the first few sessions, things went slowly with them. There did not seem to be much to talk about nor much bothering them, but Sandra in particular seemed intent on returning each following week. I had not had much opportunity to do marital counseling up to that point, as I was still in training, so I was happy to keep scheduling them. Then one week, they did not show. My supervisor assured me that this was neither unusual nor unexpected. Some people in treatment take a while to realize that they don't need it anymore and, rather than terminate treatment, they simply stop showing. But later that week, Sandra called to reschedule. In what would have been our seventh session, Sandra came in alone.

Patrick could not make it because Sandra was no longer living with him. She had moved back home to her parents' house. It turned out that Patrick had been drinking and using drugs again, for the last several months. He was also regularly abusing Sandra. He never hit her in the face (even a novice trainee like myself might have noticed bruises and cuts on her face), but rather preferred to punch her in the stomach, arms, and breasts. The previous week, a few days after our most recent marital counseling session, she had left him and moved in with her mother.

When Sandra revealed this, I was stunned. At the same time, everything suddenly made sense: the lack of any real content in the session, Patrick's ongoing attempts to make light of things, Sandra's quiet insistence on another appointment.

Sandra disclosed that during our previous sessions, she kept hoping that I would somehow think to ask about abuse. She could not bring it up herself. Indeed, Patrick punished her if he felt she came too close to implying that he might be doing anything wrong. Sandra told me that while she was driving home from each of the last six sessions, Patrick would berate her for things she said during session that bordered on criticism of their relationship, emphasizing certain offenses with punches to her thigh.

So Sandra waited, week after week, hoping that I would ask any number of questions that might lead to a discussion of anger and violence. There are many ways to do so, such as:

"What is it like when you get mad at each other?"

"How do you resolve disputes?"

"Are there times when anger seems to get out of control?"

"Have there ever been instances, or maybe just one time, when one of you physically hurt the other?"

There are lots of ways to ask, but I failed to do so. So the abuse continued for all of the weeks they were in treatment with me.

Worst of all was that, during the most recent session, Sandra was not mad at me in the least. She did not seem disappointed in me, and she assured me that she didn't think I had done anything wrong. If she had gotten mad and cursed me for being a worthless therapist, I would have accepted and absorbed that criticism as just and appropriate. Indeed, I might feel less bad, to this day, if she had let me have it. Instead, Sandra was very nice throughout the whole session. She graciously accepted my apologies while insisting she knew that I had done all that I could.

She also accepted my referral to another therapist.

The Lesson Learned

That final session was excruciatingly painful for me. The best learning experiences usually are. I learned that domestic abuse does not announce itself. It does not paint its face orange and carry a sign in order to draw others' attention. The reality of domestic abuse is quite normal looking. It acts like you and me, and it looks like you and me.

Many mental health professionals have had similar painful experiences, and they learned, as did I, that in order to see domestic abuse, one has to look for it actively. The health care field and the justice system have come to realize this over the years. Both have developed a number of procedures to try to uncover what others try desperately to keep hidden. For example, emergency departments that treat females with injuries are expected to ask routinely, outside of the presence of any male who might be accompanying them, whether someone inflicted the injuries. Police departments have instituted training programs for recognition of and intervention with domestic abuse. Many have specialized units, comprising specially trained officers that almost always include a female officer, for responding to these situations.

Pastors and church workers will regularly come into contact with men who are abusive and women who are being abused. Most frequently, this will be revealed by her, probably after years of abuse, perhaps while it is still going on, but perhaps only after she was able to create and follow a plan for escaping the abuse. Understanding how to identify domestic abuse and how to help victims is essential for those working in the church.

This chapter reviews the issues related to domestic violence. This is an extremely important and very large topic, so this is one of the longest chapters. It starts by distinguishing stress-induced, situational violence from domestic abuse. The varieties of behavior constituting domestic abuse are reviewed, as are facts and statistics related to violence between men and women. The mentality of men who abuse is discussed, as are the extremely damaging effects that domestic abuse has on its victims (as well as the spiritual degradation it has on its perpetrators). The many internal and external factors that prevent victims from effectively responding to domestic abuse are presented. This leads into a discussion of what pastors and church workers should do (e.g., believe her, refer her to appropriate resources) and should not do (e.g., encourage her to act precipitously, which can put her in more danger) when domestic abuse is uncovered.

A Word About Word Choices

Before we proceed, some words about the word choices to follow.

Domestic Abuse

There are numerous terms that have been used to describe abuse within relationships, including *spousal abuse, domestic violence,* and *battering.* Most present-day textbooks and articles have adopted the term *intimate partner violence* (often abbreviated as IPV), reasoning that the word *domestic,* which derives from the Latin *domus,* or house, implies a marital relationship. IPV is thought to better indicate violence within dating relationships and long-term, nonmarital relationships.

In this chapter, however, the term *domestic abuse* will be used for several reasons. First, domestic abuse does not necessarily include physical violence. As will be seen, abuse has many varieties of behavior. In addition, IPV and other terms suggest that abuse entails discrete violent incidents separated by time. In contrast, as detailed below, domestic abuse is an ongoing situation from which the victim obtains no relief. Other advantages to the phrase are that the word *abuse* suggests that there is misuse of position or authority and that the term is likely familiar to most readers.

Victims and Survivors; Abusers and Perpetrators

The term *victim* is used in this chapter to describe a person presently enduring an abusive situation. The victim often needs help from others (i.e., trained professionals) to extricate herself and any children she may have from an awful situation. Victims become "survivors" when they extricate themselves from the situation of domestic abuse.

In this chapter, the person who commits abuse is referred to most commonly as the "abuser" but also occasionally as the "perpetrator." The words are harsh, but they are also useful and necessary. It is proper to speak of some actions harshly (e.g., "The evil person out of his evil treasure brings forth evil" [Matthew 12:35 ESV]). The words emphasize the responsibility of the person committing these acts, and they emphasize the seriousness of the issue. Finally, while not all abusive behavior is illegal, it is always a perpetration of wrong.

He, Him, His

Men commit the majority of domestic abuse and almost all serious violence. Therefore, consistent with previous chapters (e.g., using the female pronoun in the eating disorders chapter), this chapter will use male pronouns to describe perpetrators of domestic abuse.

Defining Domestic Abuse

This section distinguishes between situational violence and domestic abuse, which is defined in detail.

Stress-Induced Situational Violence

The majority of violent incidents that occur between men and women are spontaneous, stress-induced, and situational. This type of incident arises suddenly and unexpectedly, for example, while a couple is having a heated argument. Thus, this type of violence is most likely at the beginning or at the end of a relationship. A new couple may experience an episode of such spontaneous violence when confronted with their first major fight. It is also common in couples going through divorce, where tension is chronic and severe and where there are no longer efforts at mollification or reconciliation.

Stress-induced situational violence is equally likely to be committed by men and women (see box p. 320). Sometimes the violence is committed by one person against the other, and sometimes the violence is mutually inflicted. This type of violence is usually very short-lived. Although it can be serious, the violence is typically relatively minor (such as pushing, shoving, or grabbing). Consequently, it usually does not result in a need for either medical care or police intervention.

Stress-induced situational violence can occur if one or both partners have poor ability to control anger or to resolve conflicts. Incidents will be either singular or infrequent. Such violence will happen suddenly and will surprise both persons, either the one time it happens or each time it happens. Likewise, it will usually cause intense distress on the part of both partners. They will be alarmed at what happened and, as a result, they will likely be motivated to understand why it happened and to develop strategies for stopping it from happening again.

Couples who experience stress-induced situational violence could avoid future incidents by seeking help from a mental health professional to learn anger management and conflict resolution strategies, but many couples will not seek professional help due to embarrassment about the incident. Fortunately, they may be able to develop these skills on their own.

Are Men and Women Equally Violent in Relationships?

Readers might hear in the future, or perhaps some already have heard, the claim that women are as likely to be violent towards men as men are towards women. It that true?

In the 1960s and 1970s, related to the civil rights movement and the movement for women's rights, national attention was drawn to the issue of violence between men and women. Small studies were published on the experiences and observations of workers at women's shelters, in emergency departments, and in public safety. Various terms that are now familiar, such as *battered women* and *batterers,* were popularized during this time period. The impression from these anecdotal accounts was that violence was perpetrated almost exclusively by men.

However, as shown in the first part of this volume, research into the actual prevalence of problems, including violence, requires epidemiological surveys of the general population. When these were published, they indicated that men and women were about equally likely to report that they had been a victim of violence by an intimate partner. Many chose to ignore these results, asserting that the studies were flawed and the results were therefore misleading. Others attempted to use the findings to claim that men and women were equally likely to be victims (although men were even more unwilling to seek help). Therefore, it is sometimes argued that domestic abuse cannot be related to issues of male entitlement, the objectification of women, and so forth.

In fact the studies were *not flawed,* but the results must be carefully examined in order not to use them in *misleading* fashion.

In a 2008 article in *Family Court Review,* Joan Kelly and Michael Johnson published a review of studies of violence in intimate relationships. They distinguished "coercive controlling violence" from "situational couple violence" (and inspired me to do so in this chapter). Kelly and Johnson concluded that while women and men are equally likely to commit spontaneous acts of violence against their partner, this type of violence is qualitatively and categorically different than domestic abuse. Ongoing violence and other abusive behaviors against a partner that are committed with the intention of asserting power and achieving control entails domestic abuse. Kelly and Johnson concluded that between 85% and 95% of violence intended to coerce and control is perpetrated by males.

In addition, men commit the vast majority of serious violence; women are much more likely to be injured as the result of violence by a partner; domestic abuse is much more likely to result in severe physical and psychological damage to the person being abused; and violence within domestic abuse—but not situational violence—is associated with the subsequent murder of the victim by the perpetrator.

Domestic Abuse

Domestic abuse must be distinguished from stress-induced situational violence. Domestic abuse is not a single incident; it is a *pattern of behavior.* Domestic abuse is not situational, spontaneous, and pointless. Domestic abuse is *deliberate* with the goal of *intimidating* the partner in order to gain and then maintain *power and control* in the relationship.

Domestic Abuse Is a Pattern of Behavior

Abusive behavior is variable in terms of frequency. It may occur sporadically or continually. It may occur weekly, monthly, or twice a year. Regardless of the variability, it is domestic abuse because it occurs more than once. Each incident builds upon previous incidents, with the deliberate purpose of creating the expectation and anticipation on the part of the victim that more abuse could happen. In other words, domestic abuse describes a permanently fear-filled relationship.

Domestic Abuse Is Deliberate

Contrary to what many believe, domestic abuse is not a loss of control. Domestic abuse behavior is deliberate and intentional. It is carried out in order to gain and keep control over the victim. However, the abuser wants the victim to believe the contrary.

The abuser will insist that his behavior is beyond his control. He will insist that he does not want to act this way but that he simply loses control of his behavior. Perhaps immediately but more likely over time, as abusive incidents recur, he will assert that his abusive behavior occurs because of something she is doing. She causes him to lose control. This deception is intended to convince the victim that the only possibility of the abuse not happening in the future is if she changes. By the way, the notion that the abusive behavior is beyond control may add a useful element of randomness and unpredictability, which makes the abuse that much more frightening and, thus, more effective at creating an aura of intimidation in the relationship.

In fact, however, the abusive behavior is *entirely deliberate.* Anyone familiar with domestic abuse will easily observe that the abuser carefully chooses when, where, and against whom to perpetrate abuse. If it were truly out of the control of the abuser, the abusive behavior would be more commonplace and widespread. In fact, however, abusers do not act abusively any time they are stressed, such as at work with their boss or coworkers, in public, at stores, or towards neighbors. Also, abusers can stop the abuse in an instant when necessary or when it's to their advantage to do so (for example, when the police show up or the phone rings).

Abusers likewise are careful about where they commit domestic abuse. Like Patrick, they control themselves until no one else is around to see their abusive behavior. They may act like everything is fine in public but lash out instantly as soon as they are alone with the victim. Finally, abusers carefully choose whom they abuse. They don't insult, threaten, or beat up everyone in their life who aggravates them. If the police are called to the house, the man who was just engaged in violence against the victim will act calm, cool, and collected towards the officers. (The victim, in contrast, will usually be hysterical.)

Moreover, abusers are careful to conceal the abuse and its effects from others. Violent abusers usually direct their blows where they won't show. Rather than acting out in a mindless rage, many physically violent abusers carefully aim their kicks and punches where the bruises and marks won't show. They will pinch, poke, and strike stomachs, breasts, upper arms, and legs so that the bruises will not be easily evident.

Lisa

"He would punch me at the top of my arms where I could easily cover the bruises, and he always told me to keep them covered. He would kick me in the shins and legs and thighs, leaving bruises. He pulled my hair. Always he told me to not tell anyone and to cover up any bruises."

The Goals of Domestic Abuse: Intimidation, Power, and Control

To review, abusive incidents occur repeatedly, and the perpetrator will claim they occur because he loses control. In other words, from the victim's perspective, he keeps inflicting terrifying and painful experiences, and there is nothing he can do to stop them. This achieves the first goal, which is to create a situation teeming with fear and intimidation.

The perpetrator will ultimately assert that he has no control over his behavior because of some fault on her part. In other words, it is her fault that the abuse keeps happening. It happens because she causes him to lose control. Her only chance to avoid being further abused is to correct her faults, which will mean doing as he says, when he says, and how he says. Given the substantial, perhaps insurmountable constraints on her ability to respond otherwise (reviewed on pp. 327 and 342), many women are forced to comply with this assertion. At this point, he has achieved power and control.

Types of Domestic Abuse

Domestic abuse behavior varies greatly. It can be catalogued into six categories: physical violence; verbal abuse; psychological or emotional abuse, which can be aspects of "crazy-making behavior"; sexual abuse; abusive control over social and financial matters; and spiritual abuse.

Physical Violence

Physical violence is behavior that intentionally causes bodily harm to another person. It includes punching, hitting, slapping, backhanding, kicking, kneeing, choking, pushing, pulling, shoving, arm-twisting, pulling hair, biting, and burning the victim. It may involve restraining her, holding her down, or sitting on her. It may be not allowing her to leave a room or home (or locking her out of the room or home) or throwing objects. It can entail depriving her of medication, refusing to allow her to get medical attention, or forcing her to use substances (alcohol and/or drugs). Physical violence includes actions that deny or interfere with her basic physical needs, such as not allowing her enough to eat, interfering with her sleep, and not allowing her the opportunity to use the bathroom. Acts of physical violence may also be directed against children, friends, other family members, and pets.

The common understanding of domestic abuse is that it always involves physical violence. In fact, physical violence may be the least frequent type of abusive behavior. However, at least one or a few incidents of physical violence may be "necessary" to establish proper levels of intimidation. That is, physical violence will make subsequent threats and other forms of intimidation and abuse much more effective. Nonetheless, other behaviors besides physical violence are typically much more commonplace. Moreover, the other behaviors are committed on a regular basis, which is why domestic abuse is defined as a constant situation of intimidation.

Chelsea

"There were few nights that I got a full night's sleep. He would wake me up after I fell asleep, yelling, calling me names, and threatening to hurt me. After we had our first child, nights got worse. Some nights he would punch me in the neck or head to wake me. He held a pillow over my face until I woke up and then passed out."

Verbal Abuse

Verbal abuse is often as simple as screaming and name-calling. It includes other demeaning language, such as insulting her intelligence, criticizing her behavior, and belittling decisions that she makes. The abuser may make crude and offensive remarks about her body or appearance, such as calling her ugly or fat.

Psychological and Emotional Abuse, Including Crazy-Making Behavior

The problem with explicit verbal abuse is that it is explicit. It is hard to deny calling someone a profane term when the words were spoken aloud. The hurtfulness of cursing, name-calling, and derogatory insults cannot be denied. Many abusers therefore develop more subtle abusive behavior that can be denied and disavowed.

Related to this when domestic abuse started to become a focus of mental health professionals and policy makers, it soon became evident that the term *verbal abuse* was insufficient to describe the experience of many victims. Women would report what the man said or did and then say something to the effect of "It doesn't sound that bad, but it was awful." While not explicitly abusive with violence, nasty words, and threatening language, the behavior of the abusers was nonetheless clearly and incredibly impactful in both emotional and psychological ways. Hence the term *verbal abuse* was supplemented with the phrase "psychological and emotional abuse."

Psychological and emotional abuse may include unnecessary, unfair, or relentless criticism. The abuser will criticize or demean her in front of children, parents, other family members, friends, or even strangers. He may display disproportionate anger at her mistakes or irrationally blame her for problems at home, at his work, with the children, or for other things that are out of her control. The abuser may exhibit obsessive jealousy and make arbitrary accusations of infidelity or immodest behavior.

Psychological and emotional abuse is often—but not always—more subtle than verbal abuse (and it is certainly more subtle than physical abuse), and the abuser may try to further obscure its cruelty. It can be committed, and then it can be attributed as mere truth telling. He can make the comments and criticisms sound somewhat plausible. Its seriousness or intent can be disavowed, or it can be denied as a misunderstanding.

This is one example of a special form of psychological and emotional abuse sometimes called crazy-making behavior (or "gaslighting"—see box p. 326). The intent of crazy-making behavior is to make the victim question her grip on reality. This will hopefully cause her to doubt what she is thinking (e.g., that she is being treated unfairly) and what she is feeling (e.g., whether she is right to feel hurt). The abuser especially hopes that the victim will doubt that she has the capacity to do anything to end the abuse.

Crazy-making behaviors that all abusers will engage in are twofold. First, all abusers will either minimize the abuse ("It wasn't that bad;" "I didn't hit you that hard;" "It didn't last that long") or outright deny that abuse occurred ("You're crazy if that's what you think happened;" "That was an accident when that happened"). In addition, all abusers will deny responsibility for the abuse. He may blame his behavior on a bad day or, more remotely and more difficult to control, on a bad childhood. Eventually, all abusers blame the victim for their abusive behavior ("If you had not made me mad, I would not have *had* to do what I did"). In other words, the abusive behavior was a necessary response that any man would have made.

Threats are another important aspect of crazy-making behavior. *Implicit* threats are communicated with angry silence, body language, and threatening looks or gestures. A common implicit threat is driving recklessly and punching walls or doors. Other versions include smashing things and putting weapons on display. Implicit threats are easy to disavow or deny ("You misunderstood" or "That wasn't directed at you").

Shelley

"When he would get mad at me, he would get his handgun and start cleaning it. When I commented on that once, he said I was crazy, that a gun needed to be cleaned regularly. But he only did it when he was mad at me for something. He was sending a message, and I got it loud and clear."

Explicit threats include displaying one's fist, raising one's hand as if to strike, asking threatening questions ("How would you like another punch in the mouth?"), and making threatening statements ("Keep it up and you will pay"). The abuser may also threaten children or other family members. Another common tactic is to harm or threaten to harm or kill oneself. Abusers may threaten to file false charges against her or to report to authorities that she has abused the children. Not as easy to do as with implicit ones, explicit threats will nonetheless be disavowed ("You can't take a joke" or "I wasn't serious").

Other forms of crazy-making behavior include lying or otherwise confusing facts, denying that statements or promises were made, denying that certain things happened, telling tales and false stories (e.g., making up gossip about her that friends are supposedly spreading), and playing mind games (e.g., telling her there is not enough money for food).

"Gaslighting"

What this chapter refers to as crazy-making behavior, the National Domestic Violence Hotline and others refer to as "gaslighting." The term comes from the 1938 stage play *Gas Light* (also a 1944 movie), in which a husband attempts to convince his wife and others that she is crazy. One of his tactics was to turn down the gas supply to the lights in the house and then deny that the lights were dimming.

The Hotline's website states that gaslighting "is an extremely effective form of emotional abuse that causes a victim to question her own feelings, instincts, and sanity, which gives the abusive partner a lot of power. Once an abusive partner has broken down the victim's ability to trust her own perceptions, the victim is more likely to stay in the abusive relationship."

Sexual Abuse

Sexual abuse entails forcing or coercing one's partner into unwanted sexual contact or behavior. Common examples include unwanted touching, refusing to comply with the partner's request for safe sex, forcing or coercing the partner into sex with others, criticizing sexual performance or desirability, withholding sex as a punishment, forced or coerced intercourse or other sexual acts, rape, and rape with an object or other sadistic sexual acts. Some forms of sexual abuse are criminal. Of particular relevance to readers is that some abusers will use the victim's Christian faith to justify sexually abusive behavior.

Amy

"I never imagined he'd rape me, but he did. Twice. Each time he then said he'd done nothing wrong. He said it was his right as my husband and that I didn't understand what the Bible said about 'one flesh,' which meant that he could do what he wanted to me."

Abusive Control Over Social and Financial Matters

In order both to increase dependence on him and to prevent the victim from seeking support from others, the abuser will cut the victim off from meaningful contact with the outside world, such as family, friends, and grown children. He may require her to get his permission to do anything, go anywhere, or see anyone, or he may not allow her to have contact with other people unless he is present. The abuser may demand an accounting of her moment-to-moment activities, monitoring the mileage on her car, the minutes on her phone, and the activity on her email or social media pages (e.g., Facebook). Other behaviors used to impose social isolation include forbidding her employment or blaming her friends or family for relationship, child-rearing, and financial problems. The abuser will insult her friends or family, usually to her only, but perhaps directly to them with the intent of driving them away.

A powerful way to increase the victim's dependence on him is for an abuser to restrict her access to financial resources. Inadequate financial resources is the most common reason for victims to find it impossible to leave (see p. 346). As noted, many abusers will forbid their victims from having outside employment. The abuser may not allow the victim access to checking accounts (even if she has a job and is contributing to the family budget), credit cards, or other sources of money and potential financial independence. The abuser will insist on making all social and financial decisions, including vacations; spending on food, clothing, and other necessities; household repairs or upgrades; and all other purchases.

Lucia

"Even if I needed shampoo I had to ask him first, and when I got back from the store, he would check to make sure it was a cheap one or he'd make me return it. He used to come with me to the clothing store to pick things that were cheap or on sale. He wouldn't let me buy certain things. He'd say something like, 'That makes you look cheap' or 'You don't have the figure for that.' "

Spiritual Abuse

Spiritual abuse occurs when the abuser misuses religious beliefs, teachings, and Scripture—whether it is a shared faith or the faith of the victim only—to commit, justify, or excuse abusive behavior. Examples include unreasonable demands of obedience based on his "interpretation" of the Bible or of what they are being taught at church. An appallingly common version of spiritual abuse is the abuser insisting that the marital vows imply that the victim has consented or must consent to any and all sexual activity her husband desires. In other words, the abuser will insist that there is no such thing as sexual abuse between a husband and wife.

Other examples of spiritual abuse may include forcing the victim to violate her religious beliefs (e.g., forcing her to be complicit in thieving). Abusers may belittle the victim's religious beliefs and practices. He may simultaneously attempt to instill guilt in the victim when she supposedly violates those beliefs (e.g., "How can you call yourself a Christian if you don't forgive me?").

Abusers may refuse to allow children to attend religious services. Alternatively, he may make fun of children for doing so, or he may insist that children be allowed to choose whether to attend or not. Abusers may refuse to allow children to attend the parochial school or refuse to pay the school's tuition.

Spiritual abuse can devastate. The victim may begin to question the validity of her faith. Or she may come to believe that she must choose between her faith and the safety of herself and her children. If she believes the abuser is correct, she may think that she cannot be a Christian unless she tolerates the abuse, and she may then feel compelled to abandon her faith. In other words, domestic abuse threatens the salvation of the victim.

Bev

"When I prayed about our marriage, he would say to me, 'Why would God answer you? You're horrible. God wouldn't talk to you. God won't bless you.' For some time this destroyed my faith and my relationship with God. I stopped praying. I stopped asking God for help. I started to believe that I must deserve the abuse because I was a 'bad person' and needed to be punished."

• • • • •

To summarize, abusive behavior is variable. No two victims have had the same experience. Abuse might be individual behaviors, but it is most commonly multiple behaviors committed in combination (e.g., verbal and physical abuse). Abusive incidents might be sporadic and unpredictable, or they might be committed on an ongoing, continual basis. Either way, the incidents are repeated and, as a result, they will build upon each other to establish an atmosphere of fear and intimidation. The abuser may tell the victim that the behavior is not intentional but rather outside of his control. As it continues, the abuser will try to convince the victim that the abuse is her fault. To enhance the psychological damage, the abuser will try to persuade the victim that her perception of reality is faulty and that it is not what she thinks (i.e., it is not that bad, not that serious, or not even abuse at all).

Regardless of its type, combination, frequency or constancy, abuse is perpetrated for the same purpose: to establish and maintain power and control over the victim.

Statistics Concerning Domestic Abuse

National statistics about domestic abuse are readily available on the Internet and through other resources. This chapter does not provide all possible statistics but rather provides an overview. These facts and figures about domestic abuse come from federal government agencies charged with collecting and collating such information, including the Centers for Disease Control and Prevention and the US Department of Justice.

- Nine in ten persons who are abused are female.
- One in four women have experienced domestic abuse in her lifetime.
- About one in five female high school students reported being physically and/or sexually abused by a dating partner.

- Forty percent of girls ages 14 to 17 report knowing someone their age who has been hit or beaten by a boyfriend.
- One in four female college students report violence during a date.
- Women between the ages 20 and 24 are at the greatest risk.
- Those separated and divorced are at greater risk than married persons.
- Race and ethnicity are not related to the risk of domestic abuse.
- Persons who have lower income are more likely to experience domestic abuse than persons of higher income.
- About half of all females who experience domestic abuse suffer a serious injury. Approximately two million injuries occur each year as a result of domestic abuse.
- Soft tissue trauma, such as bruises and cuts, are most common, followed by injuries due to sexual assault, gunshot and stab wounds, and fractures.
- Only one in three persons assaulted seeks care.
- Women report to authorities only one in five rapes and one in four physical assaults perpetrated by intimate partners.
- Being pregnant is not a protective factor. As many as 8% of pregnant women are assaulted while pregnant.
- In 2002, approximately 11% of homicide victims were killed by an intimate partner. Males committed over 90% of these murders, and they were primarily committed using a firearm (as with murder in general).
- Half of homeless women and children have experienced domestic abuse.

The Mentality of Abusive Men

I write this section with hesitation, because I fear that it will be misconstrued as advice on how to help men cease their abusive behavior. It is not. As you read this section, please understand the following:

First, this section is in no way intended to excuse abuse, nor is it intended to garner sympathy for abusive men. Excuses and sympathy will encourage further abuse. Abusers justify their behavior—to themselves, to their victims, and to anyone who discovers their abuse—with a surfeit of excuses, and the excuses enable them to justify continuing the abusive behavior. Abusers thrive on sympathy. They fervently want others to believe they are victimized by their partner's misbehavior, meaning that their abuse is not something they want to do but are compelled to do.

Readers should therefore be extremely reluctant to extend excuses or to offer sympathy to abusers, because they will backfire.

Second and even more important, no reader should presume to be able to help an abuser change. Abusive men can learn not to be abusive, but it takes years (most experts assert at least two years) of genuine effort with a mental health professional trained in such work to do so. An abuser can change if and only if he understands and genuinely strives to change the attitudes and values that he holds and that justify the abuse. Very unfortunately, most do not.

Not only should no reader *ever* attempt to change an abuser, but no reader should *ever* even confront an abuser about his behavior. Confronting an abuser can be extremely dangerous to the female. As will be discussed, intervention in cases of domestic abuse comprises referring the victim, using extreme discretion in order to maintain her safety, to appropriate resources. Only after the victim and her children are clearly and permanently safe should any effort to get an abuser to repent (i.e., confession and absolution) and reform (meaning offering a referral to an appropriately trained mental health professional) be attempted.

The only concession that can be made to abusers is that they were created, not born. Abusers learned their attitudes from their families and from the culture within which they grew. As the following will show, abusers learned their attitudes of entitlement, narcissism, and superiority. They were taught to embrace mistaken notions about love and relationships; they were taught sexist and objectifying attitudes towards women; and they have become desensitized to committing abuse.

This section indirectly attempts to answer a frequent question about abusers: Do men enter relationships with the intention of becoming abusive? Do they know, going in, that they will abuse later on? The simple answer is, probably not. However, men who later abuse their partner enter the relationship with many or all of the attitudes and beliefs now reviewed. These both compel and justify later abusive behavior.

Beliefs of Superiority, Narcissism, and Entitlement

Abusers are lovers of themselves. They are narcissistic (although they do not necessarily meet criteria for narcissistic personality disorder). They have tremendous admiration for themselves. They look down on others, including anyone who does not agree with their attitudes and beliefs and especially anyone who may attempt to convince them to act or to think differently (includng you and me), with a mix of pity and scorn.

The belief in superiority lends to an attitude of entitlement. The abuser tends to be exclusively focused on his needs and wants, and he thinks he is owed satisfaction of those needs. He thinks himself entitled to continuous care from the victim, including having his meals made, his clothes washed, and his home cleaned, even if both he and she have jobs. He believes his emotional needs should always be understood and met (e.g., the need to be admired and deferred to as the authority) and his sexual desires anticipated and fulfilled. This belief justifies abusive behavior when he is not satisfied. He feels an obligation to himself to express his anger in a way that she will remember, so that she can correct her misbehavior. It also justifies his abusive behavior even when satisfied, in order to ensure that the victim continuously strives to meet his ever-changing, arbitrary needs.

The abuser thinks he is owed satisfaction while at the same time ignoring any needs of the victim. He has convinced himself that she does not or should not have any needs that are separate from his own. Mental health professionals sometimes refer to "boundaries" to describe the distinction a healthy person in a relationship makes between himself or herself and the other person. To have boundaries is to have a proper understanding that there exist differences in the way another person thinks and feels. Appropriate boundaries mean, for example, not getting angry at someone for not thinking exactly the way you think, for feeling happy when you are sad, or for not wanting to do something that you want to do. In contrast, the abuser believes that there is no distinction—or that there should be no distinction—between himself and his partner. Of particular interest to readers is that abusers either misunderstand or purposefully misinterpret the biblical reference to "one flesh" to justify their assertion that there should be no boundaries between him and his partner.

Audrey

"He'd come in and he'd wipe his finger on the furniture and say, 'This place is filthy. What have you been doing all day?' Of course, I was working, just like him, at the time. I was also pregnant with my daughter, and he's making me lift windows and clean them on both sides. I was absolutely petrified to stand up to him by that stage."

Mistaken Ideas About Love and Relationships

The abuser has a warped perspective on what love entails. He does not know how to act in a loving relationship. The abuser does not understand that love and relationships are mutual. His fantasy of her love and of what a loving relationship entails may include her always being kind, polite, attentive, adoring, and beautiful. He does not accept that these are qualities that don't perpetually exist in sinful human relationships that endure over time. He believes that they should continuously exist. With such unrealistic and unfair expectations, she will never be able to follow all of his rules or satisfy all of his needs. Inevitably, then, he will grow frustrated, and he will insist, through expressions of abuse, that she correct her behavior.

Objectifying Attitudes Toward Women

Abusers tend to endorse the idea that women are, as a general rule, inferior to men. This includes all women, not just their partner. They will degrade women as weak and stupid; as overly emotional, illogical, and irrational; and as less competent, capable, and intelligent. Abusers will therefore believe that, compared to men (and thus compared to them), women are less than fully human. They therefore do not deserve the rights and privileges accorded to human beings.

The obvious result to dehumanizing women is to view women as objects to be used, even if by force, for satisfaction of men's needs. The abuser will view the victim as his possession. Like any possession, he can do with her what he pleases. People possess objects, and this is the essence of what it means to "objectify" females.

Because he has objectified and dehumanized her, the abuser thinks nothing of acting disrespectfully toward his partner. He views her as less intelligent, less logical and rational, less capable and competent, and less worthy than he is. Her job is less important and, besides, it is easy to do. Any education she has attained in the past or hopes to achieve in the future is of no value. He will even suggest that his victim is less compassionate, caring, and sensitive than he is. She fails in her behaviors toward him, which is her most important obligation, and she must therefore fail in her behaviors toward everyone. This makes her not just a bad wife but also a bad daughter, a bad mother, and a bad friend. He will regularly highlight her inferiority to her, and he will use this to justify his abuse as a commendable effort, made for everyone's sake, to correct, control, and hopefully improve her as a person.

The attitude of objectification of females is, or course, strongly encouraged in present-day American society. Television shows, movies, and music encourage boys and men, as well as girls and women, to develop the attitude that women are challenges to be conquered in serial fashion.

The proliferation of pornography, which is appallingly easy to access by the Internet, takes objectification of women (and of the human body in general) to an extreme.

Isolation and Jealousy (and Perhaps Rage)

Attitudes of entitlement and possessiveness will lead to two abusive behaviors. First, the abuser will isolate the victim from friends and family or anyone who may potentially interfere with his ownership of her by entering a relationship with her. Second, the abuser will make jealous accusations that she has been unfaithful or is seeking to be unfaithful by dressing or acting provocatively with other men.

Attitudes of possession and ownership of the victim help explain why abusive men can become very dangerous if the victim attempts to end the relationship. ("If I can't have [own] her, no one can.") The danger to women who are attempting to move from victim to survivor cannot be overstated. Victims are in most danger of serious assault or even homicide when they take steps to end an abusive relationship.

Marsha

"The first time he ever slapped me we'd been out to a bar. We'd had a really good night, because lots of our friends were there too. It was a laugh. But when we got back home he said I'd been flirting with his friend. I couldn't believe it. He looked at me with this coldness in his eyes and said really quietly, 'You whore,' and slapped me."

Desensitized to Violence and Cruelty

One of the most difficult things for outsiders to understand about domestic abuse is that it happens at all. Most people recoil from the idea of violence and cruelty. If something cruel is said in anger, most persons feel ashamed or guilty, and apologies are usually quick to follow. It is nearly impossible for most to imagine being violent with someone they love.

Yet abusers abuse. They learn to express cruel words almost reflexively, and they learn to become violent with ease. This happens through the process of desensitization, wherein someone is so often exposed to an aversive event that they stop reacting to it with fear or revulsion. Desensitization is an essential process. For example, it enables emergency care workers, surgeons, dentists, and others to learn, over time and through repetition, not to become upset by the sight of wounds or blood. Desensitization is essential for them to learn to do their jobs. Becoming desensitized to committing abusive behavior, on the other hand, allows the behavior to be committed with greater and greater ease. Desensitization to abuse typically precedes the relationship, through cultural and especially family influences. But the process doesn't stop when the relationship begins. Rather, abusers become even more desensitized to their own cruel language and violent behavior through repetition.

The Desire for Control (Which Requires Intimidation)

It has been said repeatedly already, but it is worth repeating again. Abusers do not become abusive because they become angry and then lose control. In fact, the opposite is true. Anger does not lead to abusive behavior, rather abusive attitudes lead to inappropriate expressions of anger. As noted in Part 1 of this book, the way people think influences the way they feel and behave. Thus, these attitudes lead men to feel angry and to believe themselves justified in acting abusively when, for example, their needs are not met, when they are not always acknowledged as superior, when their loving relationship is not perfect, and so forth.

Abuse is not a lack of control, rather it is an effort to get his way. The abuser seeks to intimidate the victim, because intimidation enables him to control her feelings, thoughts, and behaviors. If he can achieve control, he hopes he will then be able to get her to act in a way that is consistent with his beliefs of entitlement and superiority and with his fantasies about love and relationships.

Abuse Is Not Due to Mental Illness

There is a myth that abuse is caused by mental illness or that abusers are mentally ill. This is not the case. Mental illness is not more common in abusers than in the general public, meaning about one in five abusers will experience a mental illness in any given year. (Note, however, that mental illness is *much* more common in victims of abuse.)

It should nonetheless be recognized that abusive behavior is more likely if the abuser is intoxicated. Someone with a substance use disorder is thus more likely to be abusive than someone without one. However, abuse is not caused by the substance use disorder. Instead, substance use lowers inhibitions, making an abusive man more likely to act abusively.

Why Some Men but Not Others

Obviously, not all men endorse the attitudes and fantasies that justify abuse. Moreover, some boys who were surrounded by these views growing up become men who reject them and who, instead, develop healthy and respectful attitudes toward women, love, and relationships. There have been decades of attempts to understand why similar experiences do not create similar people. For example, researchers have tried to explain why some persons develop schizophrenia or PTSD, whereas others with the same genetic makeup and family circumstances or the same traumatic experiences do not.

To summarize what has been found in the research: we have no idea. Since all human thinking and behavior is a product of both genetic predispositions and environmental influences, it is assumed by researchers that subtly dissimilar genetics and experiences account for differences between those who do and do not develop problems. However, these differences, if they exist, are apparently so subtle that they have yet to be uncovered. Researchers continue to investigate this question.

Luther's Lecture on Genesis 20:11-13

> Abraham replied, "I said to myself, 'There is surely no fear of God in this place, and they will kill me because of my wife.' Besides, she really is my sister, the daughter of my father though not of my mother; and she became my wife. And when God had me wander from my father's household, I said to her, 'This is how you can show your love to me: Everywhere we go, say of me, "He is my brother."' " (Genesis 20:11-13)

Here one should note that Abraham says that he spoke most respectfully to his wife. He did not give an order and did not say: "You must obey me; I compel you; I demand from you." No, he said "I beg you," and he does not consider her action obedience; he considers it a favor, as though by a superior person, in accordance with Peter's precept (1 Peter 3:7) "Bestow honor on the female sex." But why does Moses record this? Doubtless in order to present an example of a very fine marriage, something which is indeed a rarity on earth is most pleasing both to God and to men. Therefore by means of this very example Peter exhorts spouses to learn to love each other and to treat each other with respect and not as people are now in the habit of doing. Husbands generally are lions in their homes and are harsh towards wives and domestics. Similarly, the wives generally domineer everywhere and regard their husbands as servants. But it is foolish for a husband to want to display his manly courage and heroic valor by ruling his wife. On the other hand, it is also unbearable if wives want to dominate.

Such marriages—where both are capricious—are common, as the proverb has it, "Three things are rare, but they are pleasing to God: harmony among brothers, love among neighbors, and accord between spouses." The reason is that people generally enter into this kind of life without prayer, and like swine, regard only what is carnal. Therefore the wife does not see what is truly good in her husband. On the other hand, the husband sees in his wife only what displeases him. Since there is no mutual tolerance between them, quarrels and countless outbursts of anger arise.

Therefore this example deserves frequent attention from married people, in order that they may learn how to live together amicably. For one who is unwilling to overlook anything, but wants to go to extremes in all his demands, will lead a most wretched life. Besides he will be irksome to others; for, if I may say so, this life is truly scurvy, ulcerous, and full of troubles. Therefore one who lives in it will not find favorable conditions everywhere. "Where there is fire," they say, "there is bound to be smoke." Thus troubles are everywhere added to favorable conditions, but pious hearts will bear the troubles with patience and thank God for the favorable conditions.

The fact that Abraham gives Sarah the all-inclusive instruction: "In every place to which we come say that I am your brother" is evidence of his great weakness and inordinate fear; for it indicates that he is afraid not only of the people of Gerar but also of all other men. For this reason he did not have the courage anywhere to admit that Sarah was his wife. But why did Moses record this conduct, hardly creditable, about such a great man? He does this for our sakes, for the virtues of the saints should be praised in such a manner that we nevertheless conclude that they were human beings and that they both had and endured something human. (*Luther's Works,* American Edition, Vol. 3, pp. 353,354)

The Anatomy of Abuse

As difficult as it is to read about, it is useful to understand what domestic abuse looks like. The following descriptions of the initial and then the subsequent abusive incidents describe episodes of physical violence toward the victim. As previously noted, most incidents of domestic abuse do not involve violence. However, violence is almost always an essential aspect of creating intimidation. In almost all situations of domestic abuse, there has been at least one episode of violence or a credible threat of violence (such as threatening with a gun or knife, witnessing someone else become victim to the abuser's violence, or violence against children or pets). If there exists the credible threat of additional violence, then other types of abuse (such as screaming and name-calling) are much more intimidating and thus more effective at gaining the abuser control over the victim.

In the following, some readers will recognize the so-called cycle of abuse. This model was popularized years ago as a way to understand why domestic abuse was not typically continuous incidents of violence, but rather that it progressed through alternating stages of violence and relative calm. The cycle of abuse is a simplified and very useful version of domestic abuse, but it does not characterize all domestic abuse, so the following deviates somewhat from that model. To begin, however, it is important to understand what domestic abuse does not look like.

The Hidden Face of the Abuser

Abuse is not obvious. People who abuse their partners do not wear scarlet letters. They do not announce to their family, friends, business partners, colleagues, or ministers that they are abusive. As noted earlier, abusers are usually careful to commit abuse so that it leaves no evidence. They commit it behind closed doors, where no one can witness it, and they try to leave bruises and marks where the victim can conceal them. Many abusers will work very hard at being likeable, and others will react with surprise and even disbelief if they witness or otherwise learn of his abusive behavior. (While some abusers are prone to violence and outbursts of aggression in other places, they tend not to have a long-term, abusive relationship with anyone but the victim.)

In other words, there are many types of abusive men and many varieties of abusive behavior. But all abusive men work very hard at seeming otherwise normal, and all abusive men strive diligently to keep their abusive behavior hidden. As I learned with Patrick and Sandra, to see abuse, one has to look for it.

The First Attack

In situations of domestic abuse, there is always that first violent attack. Most initial violent attacks are preceded by incidents of verbal, emotional, and psychological abuse. The first attack will nonetheless surprise the victim, and it may also surprise the abuser.

After the first attack, and even after some subsequent attacks, the abuser will likely react with expressions of intense remorse. In the cycle of abuse, this is typically referred to as the "honeymoon phase." He may apologize repeatedly or he may try to minimize the seriousness of the incident. He may do both. He may try to explain what happened and why, asserting that he lost control. Some abusers apologize and try to overwhelm the victim with affection. Displays of remorse and affection can be coercive (i.e., he will insist that she forgive and insist she respond positively to affection). During this period of time, he may show no overt expressions of irritation or annoyance. He may promise that it will never happen again. Some abusers threaten self-harm or even suicide to assure the victim of their remorse, to gain her sympathy, and to discourage her from telling anyone what happened.

If the abuser accepts that his *attitudes* caused him to act abusively in both this incident and in the previous, nonviolent abusive behavior, then he may seek treatment to prevent future attacks. This is not likely, however.

Megan

"After we married, we agreed I would keep my job, which involved an hour commute. Soon, though, he began to complain about not seeing me enough, that I wasn't home to cook and was too tired. One evening, a storm caused me to get home late. He flew into a rage and accused me of having an affair. He took the glass he was holding and threw it across the room at me. When I ducked, he came across the room and grabbed me by the throat and pushed me against the wall. I was terrified. The next day, he bought me a bouquet of my favorite flowers and apologized for his behavior. He said that he just loved me so much. He was very sweet when he said he was sorry."

"But that was not the end. He criticized me all the time and started to grab me or push me or pinch me when he got mad. He stopped bringing flowers, and he stopped apologizing."

"One Sunday when I was supposed to meet my girlfriend whom I had not seen in months, he threw me across the kitchen and I fell into the pantry door. He was shouting, but I couldn't understand what he was saying. Then he slammed his fist into my jaw. I scrambled away from him, and he didn't follow. I locked myself in our bedroom and cried. Now he hits me almost every time he gets angry. Even if he doesn't, I get so scared that he will."

Subsequent Attacks

The "honeymoon phase" will yield to the "tension-building phase." Not expressing negativity and trying to behave lovingly (while harboring attitudes of entitlement and superiority) cause stress and tension in the abuser. This may happen slowly, over the course of months, or quickly, over the course of days. The tension-building phase is characterized by silent resentment, verbal aggression, emotional and psychological abuse, and perhaps even overt expressions of irritation, including indirect violence (e.g., breaking things). Over time, the nonviolent abusive behavior becomes more open, frequent, and intense.

Ultimately, the tension-building phase ends with another attack. Sometimes the tension is so unbearable that the woman will precipitate an attack, just to be done with it. When another attack occurs, the cycle of abuse (honeymoon phase, tension-building phase, another attack) begins again.

Stacy
"If I voiced my opinion I'd get a quick slap, or he'd get in my face and scream. He gets this look like he actually could kill me. I was terrified. I just lowered my head and did what he said."

The Familiarity of the Abominable

As noted, the cycle of abuse is a generalization. It does not define all situations of domestic abuse. In many domestic abuse relationships, there is no pretense of a return to normality. The first attack is followed in quick order by other attacks, some more severe than others. In other domestic abuse relationships, the pretense of a return to normality (i.e., the honeymoon phase) gets exhausted.

Whether the former or the latter, these situations result in naught but ongoing verbal, emotional, and psychological abuse; abusive control over social and financial matters; and occasional or frequent incidents of physical and sexual violence.

Effects on the Victim

According to survivors, the psychological damage caused by domestic abuse is worse than any physical effects (i.e., injuries). The psychological damage now described is related to the very different experiences of the abuser and the victim. Keep in mind the following:

The abuser is not exerting much effort to be abusive. He is simply acting consistently with his entitlement and narcissistic views, his negative attitudes toward women in general, and his presumption that it is the duty of his partner to satisfy his needs. For him, the abuse is easy.

In contrast, the victim must exert extraordinary mental effort to understand what is happening. She struggles to understand while being confronted with his crazy-making behavior. She will struggle to accept that she is in a dangerous and hurtful relationship of domestic abuse and that it is unlikely to change, which is in complete contradiction of what she wanted and to what she thought she was entering. Since in many ways his behavior will be consistent with the man with whom she fell in love, the victim will feel compelled to reconsider who he really is and, even more, how she thinks about herself. Finally, she will struggle with the need to stop the abuse even though the prospect of attempting to do so probably presents very real danger to her and to any children she may have.

The psychological damage done by abuse is enormous. Proof of this is that victims of domestic abuse are at much higher risk of developing depression, an anxiety disorder, or PTSD. Research likewise shows that victims of domestic abuse are at much higher risk of suicide.

Initial Reactions

The immediate effect of the first instance of abuse is fear and anxiety that the behavior will be repeated. This may give way to anger and being upset, as well as to a search for how best to respond. It is very likely, however, that her options for responding are limited (see p. 342).

One can assume that the relationship did not start with violence. The relationship most likely started well, and the victim probably loves the abuser. She does not want the relationship to end, she doesn't want to lose him, and she wants things to be right between them. She wants to believe his remorse and his promises that the behavior will not happen again. She may accept or at least pretend to accept the excuses he offers for the attack, with the ardent hope that it doesn't happen again. All of this may lead to accommodating behavior by her in an attempt to manage or handle the behavior of the abuser (that is, to make additional abuse less likely).

Gina

"Why did I stay? I used to believe what he told me: that I would lose my children and be penniless if I left him."

Long-Lasting Effects That Appear Quickly

As incidents of domestic abuse continue, the psychological effects on the victim start to emerge. The initial fear and anxiety become permanent aspects of her daily life. She is soon living in a constant state of intimidation and worry. In tragic irony, a common fear of victims is that the abuse will be uncovered. As detailed below, the perpetrator has likely assured the victim that, should anyone find out what he is doing, he will react with more severe abuse. He may threaten that if he is exposed, he will kill her, the children, and himself. Or he may threaten to divorce her and leave her and the children impoverished.

Given his efforts at crazy-making behavior, her self-esteem will likely plummet. She may start to believe his assertions that she deserves the mistreatment. She may start to accept that she is fat, stupid, ugly, and unworthy and, therefore, lucky to have him. These ideas may comingle with the thought that she is weak and pathetic for not standing up to him.

The materialization of low self-worth aligns perfectly with the desires of the abuser. From his perspective, the goal of domestic abuse is to cause the victim to develop a self-perception that she is weak, worthless, incapable, ugly, bad, stupid, and crazy. With such self-perception, she will come to believe that the mistreatment is deserved, and she thus will be less likely to complain about it; tell someone else, such as a sister or her pastor, about it; or to file a police report. Even better, she may come to accept that she is not worthy of better treatment from him. And, best of all, she will come to realize that she is lucky to have the abuser, who tolerates her despite all of her faults.

As reviewed next, the psychological damage of abuse contributes to the formidable, sometimes insurmountable, factors that keep victims from responding effectively to domestic abuse.

Bethany

"My husband told me that no one else was going to love me as much as he did. He said I would never be good enough for anyone else. Over the years, I started to believe I was really worthless. I cut my hair short and started wearing baseball caps and men's baggy clothing. Eventually, I did not leave the house at all."

Internal and External Factors That Constrain Victims' Responses

This section starts with an exposition of the harmfulness of the widely held belief that women can easily leave an abusive situation if they so choose. The numerous internal (psychological) and external (environmental) factors constraining women's capacity to respond effectively to domestic abuse are then detailed.

"How could she put up with that?"

This and similar questions are asked by many. "Why does she tolerate the abuse?" "Why doesn't she just leave?" "How can she put up with that?" "Why does she stay?"

Victims hear these questions all the time. Most times they overhear them in casual conversations at parties and gatherings. They even overhear these questions on the radio and television. Often the questions are abstract, such as, "Why would a woman stay in an abusive relationship? I certainly wouldn't!" Other times these questions are asked of them directly. Still other times the questions are explicitly asked about them. They may overhear them spoken by doctors and nurses when they go to the emergency room yet again. Some children ponder these questions. They may ask the victim these questions while the abuse is ongoing, or they may ask later, when they are grown and gone from the house. Many victims ask themselves these questions, causing them to doubt their own sanity.

The questions indicate a profound misunderstanding of domestic abuse. They imply that the victim has a choice, that is, that she can choose to end the abuse. Since it is a decision, it must be the case that, for some reason, the victim is deciding to tolerate the abuse. If everyone agrees that it is a choice, then the victim herself may come to believe that she is choosing to be abused. This will cause her to feel ashamed and embarrassed and to think she is incapable of good decisions, which in turn makes it difficult for her to ask for needed help and easy for her to suppose that, after all, she deserves the abuse.

In other words, these very questions help perpetuate the abuse. For years police departments around the country justified not intervening in domestic violence based on this notion that victims, for some reason, choose to stay when they could instead choose to leave. The questions imply that she could decide to leave or otherwise end the abuse. Or could she? This is simply not true.

Understanding the "Inexplicable"

Consider this statement: "I freeze, even though his fist is coming at me again." Many victims and survivors of physical abuse can relate to this remarkable statement. Many have held themselves perfectly still while they were being beaten. Have you ever kept perfectly still—as still as possible—while someone beat you? Can you picture yourself doing that? It's difficult to understand, but thousands of victims and survivors will tell you that is exactly what they did. On the surface, the behavior of freezing while being beaten seems like the "choice" to stay in an abusive relationship. On the surface, it seems inexplicable. Yet, it must be understood.

In the mental health profession, there are three principles to use when trying to understand the *seemingly* inexplicable. First, with the exception of behavior due to a psychotic disorder, all behavior can be understood. Second, if you do not understand someone's behavior, that is a failure of your imagination, not an indication that the behavior cannot be understood. Third, if you do not understand someone's behavior (or feelings or thoughts), then seek more information. Ask and listen, and you eventually will be able to understand.

Reject the idea that the victim of abuse is making the wrong choice. In fact, as reviewed next, there are many factors causing a victim to believe that she must endure abuse rather than act to end it. While considering these factors, keep in mind that they are compounded over time. For example, as abuse continues, low self-worth gets lower, fear gets more intense, having to care for children becomes more likely, financial dependence deepens, and the attitude of controlling, dominating entitlement on the part of the abuser gets worse.

Internal Factors

There are many internal or psychological factors within the woman that induce her tolerance of the intolerable. Many of these will predate the relationship, whereas others are either strengthened or created by the abuse.

Hope. One category of psychological factors that makes it difficult to end the abuse may be gathered under the term *hope.* She hopes that the abuser will return to being the affectionate, attentive man with whom she fell in love. In an insightful book entitled *Why Does He Do That?* (Berkley Books, 2002), Lundy Bancroft writes:

> The idyllic opening is part of almost every abusive relationship. How else would an abuser ever have a partner? Women aren't stupid. If you go out to a restaurant on a giddy first date and over dessert the man calls you a "selfish [expletive]" and sends your water glass flying

across the room, you don't say, "Hey, are you free again next weekend?" There has to be a hook. (p. 110)

Also making it difficult to end the abuse is the hope that the abuser is being honest when he says the abuse is not his fault but is rather the fault of his past experiences, the stress he is under, or the effects of the substances he was ingesting at the time. She hopes the abuse is due to issues that can be changed or will change, perhaps with her help. She likewise hopes he is being honest when he promises to change.

Moreover, the victim may also hope that no one else will find out about the abuse. Admitting to others that she entered a relationship with a man who became abusive is difficult. More difficult is acknowledging that she has long endured the abuse, when everyone, including her, knows how "simple" it is to leave (I speak as a fool). These various hopes will discourage the victim from reaching out for help.

Misinformation. Another category of psychological factors may be referred to as inexperience and ignorance. Although domestic abuse and violence are tragically common, most persons have little or no experience of them. When was the last news report you heard about domestic abuse? Given how common it is in relationships, there must be a lot of movies and television shows that depict domestic abuse. Did you take a high school or college course that covered it? In fact, while society and the media focus a great deal of attention on crimes committed by strangers, there is very little coverage of the crimes committed by abusive men.

As a result, victims along with everyone else tend to have little or no useful knowledge about laws related to domestic abuse or about resources available to help them. For example, many victims are unaware that many forms of abuse are illegal. Likewise, many are surprised to learn that many resources have been developed over the years for victims, including emergency shelters, free legal advice and representation, and even financial assistance. In related fashion, some victims may think, perhaps with the explicit encouragement of the abuser (or their family or even their church), that they have to tolerate abuse to show devotion to their religious faith.

Above all, there is fear. The primary category of psychological factors making it difficult for the victim to demand an end to the abuse or to leave the abusive relationship is *fear.* Many women fear that the abuser will retaliate with worse abuse if she tells anyone about his behavior. Research has shown that this fear is completely justified. If arrested and prosecuted, about half of men threaten retaliatory violence and more than 30% actually commit additional assaults, even if they are no longer living with the woman. In fact, women are most likely to be murdered when reporting abuse or attempting to leave an abusive relationship. (Thus no one should ever suggest to a woman in an abusive relationship that she leave unless and until there is extensive safety planning.)

A related fear is for the safety of children. Abusers will threaten to abduct children or even to kill children if she tells anyone about the abuse or if she tries to leave. Abusers will threaten that they will obtain full custody of the children by convincing the judge that the victim is insane or an unfit mother. Given the years of abuse she has tolerated and the terrible toll on her sense of self-worth, this outcome may seem very plausible to the victim. Likewise, abusers will threaten to leave the victim and her children homeless and penniless. Some abusers will threaten to quit their jobs, so that even if she obtains a favorable divorce settlement, he won't be able to fulfill its terms.

All of these factors are compounded by the extremely negative psychological damage done to the victim by abuse, including depression, anxiety, damage to her self-worth, and destruction of any sense of self-efficacy (i.e., the belief that she can act to make things different).

Kim
"Why don't we just leave? It's because our abusers are cruel and will punish us and our kids. We don't leave because we're afraid."

Environmental Factors

There are also numerous situational factors that make it difficult for women to either demand change or to leave.

Financial constraints. The first and foremost reason that victims endure abuse has to do with resources. Simply put, many victims are in situations where they rely almost entirely on the abuser for financial support. Food, housing, books, computers, clothing, gas in the car, taking children to the pediatrician, piano lessons, Christmas gifts, and everything else that one needs money to buy may all rely on his income and his beneficence. Many abusive men refuse to allow their wives to work. If she does, the man will insist on being the only one with access to the family finances, including denying her the use of a credit card or a debit card. She may therefore be convinced that there are few options but to stay and endure the abuse.

Children. Financial constraints on her behavior are much more powerful if the victim has children. A Department of Agriculture report estimated that in 2013 the average annual cost of raising a child (including housing, food, education, health care, transportation, and clothing) was over $12,000. In addition, many victims believe that it is better for children to have both parents in the home, even if there is abuse. (In contrast, research has repeatedly shown that children fare much worse in households where there is frequent conflict—especially violent conflict—than in single-parent households.) Finally, children may explicitly pressure the victim not to leave and even not to press the abuser to change. This will sometimes happen even if the children themselves are being abused.

Kelly

"With minimum wage, I can't pay both day care for my son and rent for our one bedroom apartment. Sometimes I think about going back, just to make sure my son has enough to eat. It hurts more to watch him eat macaroni with ketchup for the third night in a row than it ever did to get hit."

Lack of support. Another environmental factor is lack of support from others, including family and friends. If others were aware that the woman was being abused, they might help. They might give emotional support ("You are right to be upset, this isn't proper"), functional support ("You can stay here"), or advice ("You should talk to an abuse hotline").

That most victims do not seek support from others may be due to social isolation, as abusers tend to work very hard to cut off victims from close ties with others. Even if not socially isolated, shame will prevent victims from sharing with other people the fact that they are being abused.

However, many victims who do tell parents, siblings, or friends find the responses unhelpful or maybe even an extension of the abuse. (One victim told her husband's sister about his behavior, at which point "she grabbed me by the hair and snarled in my face that I better not tell anyone else.") Victims may encounter advice suggesting that the abuse is her fault, such as advice to try to do better. (One victim told her minister about her husband's behavior and "he suggested that I not make pasta so frequently.") Some women who enter what become violent relationships were raised in homes characterized by violence, and the abuser's abominable behavior may seem normal. For example, family members may advise the victim to stop complaining because that will only make it worse, or they might tell victims they must stay because ending the relationship would embarrass the family. More than one victim has been pressured to endure the abuse out of loyalty to the family's religious beliefs.

Finally, it is not uncommon for family members and friends to outright disbelieve the victim's experience. Convinced by his seemingly charming nature, their response may be to deny that anything bad is happening or to minimize the severity or impact of abuse.

In summary, the question, "Why does she stay?" is foolish. It attributes to the victim a decision that she is not willingly making. The question and the attitude underlying it cause more harm than good. The proper question is, "What are the factors keeping her from responding to the abuse in order to put an end to it?"

Bridget

"He called my graduate program and told them I had been hospitalized for trying to kill myself because of the stress of school. That led to me being suspended. He then sabotaged my job by calling them and telling them I was stealing. He did not allow me to have friends or family in my life. He got furious if I tried to talk to anyone outside of his presence."

The Effect on Abusers of Their Perpetrating Domestic Abuse

> "Everyone who does evil hates the light, and will not come into the light for fear that their deeds will be exposed." (John 3:20)

There are deleterious effects on the perpetrators of domestic abuse. In spite of his sense of entitlement and superiority, and in contrast to his excuses and justifications, abusers can experience intense shame about their abusive behavior. This is evident in the immediate remorse that is felt and expressed by most abusers. It is even more evident in the intense efforts to hide the abuse from others.

Shame and efforts at concealment may lead the abuser to become socially isolated, similar to how he isolates the victim. This can lead, unfortunately, to an even more dependent and enmeshed relationship with the victim. This in turn will increase the probability that he will become disappointed, frustrated, and irritated at her imperfect efforts to meet his needs, which in turn will justify further abuse.

With regard to the welfare of the victim, the most dangerous effect on the abuser is that he becomes habituated and desensitized to his behavior. As with so much sinful behavior, as he continues to commit abuse, abuse becomes easier and less shame-inducing. Eventually, abuse may become a habit toward which he devotes little conscious thought.

But the most dangerous effect of abuse on the abuser is the spiritual corruption that it causes in him. By definition, domestic abuse occurs repeatedly, despite the fact that the abuser knows it is wrong. Thus the abuser is living a life of unrepentant sin, thereby excluding himself from God's forgiveness. As Paul wrote to Timothy, "If anyone does not provide for his relatives, and especially for members of his household, he has denied the faith and is worse than an unbeliever" (1 Timothy 5:8 ESV). Peter warned husbands who mistreat their wives that their prayers will be hindered (1 Peter 3:7). Paul likewise taught the church at Galatia:

> The acts of the flesh are obvious: sexual immorality, impurity and debauchery; idolatry and witchcraft; hatred, discord, jealousy, fits of rage, selfish ambition, dissensions, factions and envy; drunkenness, orgies, and the like. I warn you, as I did before, that those who live like this will not inherit the kingdom of God. (Galatians 5:19-21)

Having said this, as was said previously, no one should confront an abuser in order to encourage him to repent unless and until the victim is safe from further abuse. Confronting an abuser will enrage the abuser, although he will not act out his rage against you. Indeed, he will either deny that he is abusive and act offended at the accusation or he will immediately repent and perhaps even thank you for showing him the error of his ways. Either way, he will then go home and punish, perhaps severely, the victim. After that, you will never hear from him again.

The Effect on Children

The effects of domestic abuse on children have been well documented. Children raised in violent homes have significantly more behavioral problems and mental illness than those who are not. They have significantly higher rates of aggressiveness toward others, delinquent behavior, truancy from school, and school problems. Not being exposed to appropriate conflict resolution strategies or relationship skills, they tend to have poor social skills, few friends, and problems with teachers. They are much more likely to meet criteria for conduct disorder, oppositional defiant disorder, depression, post-traumatic stress disorder, and separation anxiety disorder (in contrast to normal separation anxiety disorder, they fear separating from their mother out of fear for their mother's safety, not their own safety). Finally, keep in mind that there are higher rates of both child abuse and intersibling violence in homes where there is domestic abuse.

Laws Regarding Domestic Abuse

This section reviews historical and current laws regarding domestic abuse. Laws are established by states, so readers are encouraged to familiarize themselves with the pertinent laws in their area. A simple way to do this is to consult with a state-based agency that specializes in helping victims of domestic abuse.

Historical Protocols and Laws Related to Domestic Abuse

In 1871, Alabama became the first state to rewrite the law asserting a husband's right to beat his wife. The new law noted that the "wife had the right to the same protection of the law" as her husband. However, for the next one hundred years, there were few prosecutions of violence toward wives, as the principle of family privacy prevailed. If women being abused sought help, they did so from their families and from their church.

In the 1960s and 1970s, related to the civil rights and women's rights movements, there came increased attention in the media to domestic abuse. Statistics about violence against women and its effects caught the public's attention. Subsequent editorials and commentaries focused, in particular, on the inadequate response of the police called to domestic violence situations and on the inadequacy of laws related to the protection of victims.

Through the late 1970s, the protocol for police called to domestic abuse situations was to "calm and cruise." That is, officers were encouraged to attempt to calm down the male and female and then to leave as soon as possible. When the association between alcohol use and abuse was established, officers were further instructed to evaluate for intoxication (and perhaps suggests that the man go elsewhere to sober up), to mediate the conflict, and to make referrals for treatment. Many police training manuals specified that arrest be avoided if possible. In fact, arrest of the abuser was unlikely unless he acted belligerently toward the officers at the scene, which itself was unlikely if he was sober.

At the time, there was an accepted idea that domestic violence situations presented extraordinary risk for police officers. It was believed that attempting arrest could escalate the crisis and put police in danger. (Subsequent research proved this concern to be unwarranted.) Also during that less-informed era, arrest and prosecution was considered pointless because of the widespread, societal belief that domestic abuse was an intractable problem. That is, it was widely accepted that women being abused could leave if they wanted and, since they did not, there was nothing anyone could do. Thus the police often would not help beyond trying to calm the situation.

Research in the 1970s revealed the immediate and long-term effects of this protocol. Many abusers immediately resumed the attack after the police left. They would be enraged that the police were called, even if called by neighbors, and they would punish the victim. In other words, the effect of the usual police response was that domestic abuse continued.

The courts did not help either. Legal barriers that constrained victims' response to domestic abuse were numerous. For example, during this time period, a woman could not obtain a restraining order (or "order of protection") against a violent husband unless she was filing for divorce. Even when obtained, enforcement of the order was often nonexistent or weak, and penalties for violations were minor.

Scientific Studies of the Effect of Police Interventions

The Minneapolis Domestic Violence Experiment was conducted from 1981 to 1982. Police called to domestic violence situations responded in one of three ways. In the experimental design (which was needed to confirm the cause of observed effects), the police could not choose what to do. Instead, they had to follow one of three randomly assigned conditions: arrest the person suspected of committing violence; order one of the two persons involved in the violence out of the residence; or defuse the situation and make a referral for treatment. Note that this latter condition was most similar to the standard "calm and cruise" protocol. The effect of each of the three approaches was evaluated through follow-up interviews with victims and reviews of official records of subsequent police contact.

The results showed that subsequent offending was reduced by almost half when the suspect was arrested. These results were reported on all three major TV networks as well as in hundreds of newspapers across the United States. In 1984, the US attorney general recommended that state and local agencies adopt a "mandatory arrest" policy, which would require police to arrest suspected abusers when there was any evidence of domestic violence. Many states did so.

However, subsequent studies conducted in different states and jurisdictions failed to replicate the Minneapolis study findings. Also, evidence began to emerge that victims of abuse were less willing to report domestic violence if they knew that a mandatory arrest policy would be enforced, leading some to argue that the policy actually put victims at greater risk. Further, mandatory arrest policies, by definition, eliminate the discretion of the police officers at the scene. Police dislike having no chance to decide for themselves whether someone should be arrested, and many argued that eliminating their discretion created more problems than it solved. Relatedly, unlike when the Minneapolis study was conducted, police now undergo extensive training related to domestic abuse, and some have argued that they are therefore qualified to decide whether arrest is warranted.

The best police response to domestic abuse is still under debate, and studies are ongoing. Because of the lack of consensus, different jurisdictions have different policies.

Current Police Protocols and Laws

Currently (as of late 2014), 21 states have mandatory arrest policies. Nine states have adopted a "pro-arrest" policy, which encourages officers to make an arrest in cases of domestic violence, but ultimately leaves the officer with the discretion of whether or not to do so. The policy allows police to take into account the requests of the victim and other extenuating circumstances. It also gives officers the prerogative to make an arrest when, in the words of one such policy, "safety outweighs the wishes of the victim." Other states leave the decision of whether to arrest or not entirely to the officer's discretion.

These different arrest policies have been accompanied by improvements in police training, which helps officers become more aware of the issue (e.g., women do not "tolerate" abuse) and to intervene more effectively, regardless of their department's specific policy.

In addition, in most state, county, and city prosecuting attorney offices, specialized units have been formed to handle domestic violence cases. These attorney teams are specially trained in the various issues related to domestic abuse, such as safety planning and techniques for interviewing victims and abusers. Also, laws have been rewritten to allow immediate, emergency-based restraining orders, orders of protection, and no-contact orders. Enforcement of these orders was strengthened and penalties for violations have been made more substantial. Finally, treatment programs for domestic abuse perpetrators and victims are offered in many communities.

The federal government also got involved. The Violence Against Women Act (VAWA) was originally passed and signed into law in 1994, and it has been revised and reauthorized twice (2000 and 2005). Among other things, the VAWA provides funds to investigate and prosecute violent crimes against women, and it allows victims to sue in civil court if jurisdictions choose not to prosecute abusers.

How to Respond to Domestic Abuse

This section covers what to do when confronted with domestic abuse, as well as how to approach a woman when you suspect she may be a victim of abuse. Before discussing these important issues, let me suggest the following attitude towards victims.

A Dialectical Approach to Women in Abusive Relationships

When attempting to help victims of domestic abuse, a dialectical approach is recommended. (A dialectical approach can be considered the attempt to integrate seemingly contradictory thoughts or behaviors.) To summarize the approach, be empathic but encouraging. That is, be very *empathic* to her fear of attempting to end the abuse, but nonetheless *encourage* her to recognize that she can and must do something.

It is essential to be empathic. Empathy is both understanding and accepting *how* someone thinks and feels, including perhaps understanding the cause of the person's thoughts and feelings. The purpose of presenting detailed information about types of abuse, the mentality of abusers, and the effect of abuse on victims is to assist your empathic understanding. You now understand how internal and external factors may make it impossible—or at least seem impossible to the victim—to end the abuse. You understand that the victim is terrified and feels helpless to act. You realize that she may lack social support and financial resources. You accept that she may have low self-worth and may believe the abuse is justified. You understand that she probably has low self-efficacy and may believe she has no control over her life. Finally, you recognize that it will be difficult, or even dangerous, for her to do something.

The dialectic to empathic understanding of her fear, her sense of helplessness, and the environmental factors preventing her from action is the recognition that *she must do something.* You understand that the unfortunate reality is that, unless she does something to change the situation, the situation will not change. Why would it? The abusive man will not work to change it. The situation could not be more ideal for him. Thus, you gently encourage her to *realize* she must do something. You see her as a "victim" striving to become a "survivor," even if she does not.

Be very careful to understand what I am saying. You do not insist that she do anything. You simply recognize the reality that she must do something, and you encourage her also to recognize that reality. However, what she can and what she will do—what is within her capabilities to do—is entirely up to her. It is important to respect her thinking and her feelings, and it is crucial to respect the choices she makes. She understands better than anyone the potential danger that the abuser represents to her and her children.

Empathy for Domestic Abuse Victims: A Primer

Being empathic is extremely important. It communicates several things to the victim. It communicates that the way she is thinking, feeling, and behaving are "normal." If they were not normal, they could not be understood by you or anyone else. It communicates that anyone in her situation would think, feel, and act identically. It also communicates that you respect her, because you respect her perspective. Finally, empathy shows that you are striving to understand her experiences, which means that you care. Many victims have not experienced someone else's care in many years.

It seems odd to many, but observers, especially trained observers (i.e., mental health professionals), are often better at understanding the cause of someone's thoughts and feelings than the person experiencing them. For example, many persons do not understand why they are depressed, whereas the cause may seem obvious to others. Likewise, observers are often more accepting of someone's thoughts and feelings than the person experiencing them. For example, some victims of domestic abuse hesitate to express anger at the abuser or at unsupportive family members, whereas an observer can suggest, "That might make me angry if that were to happen to me."

You can use the information presented to great advantage when talking with victims of domestic abuse. Based on what you now know about the experiences of domestic abuse victims, you can empathize with her thoughts and feelings without requiring her to state them. (Such as, "I would guess that you are worried about finances" or "Maybe some people would not understand how scary that is, but it seems terrifying to me.") As most mental health professionals have experienced, doing so greatly enhances the empathic experience of the other person (i.e., the sense of being understood and accepted).

Having said all that, the dialectic of this recommended approach derives from the idea that being empathic does not necessarily mean agreeing entirely with the way she is thinking. For example, you don't agree that she is worthless or that she deserves the abuse. But never presume to disagree with her perception about the dangerousness of the abuser or the difficulty of her situation. Likewise, while we don't necessarily agree with someone's thinking, it never makes sense to disagree with the way someone feels. Of course, thinking influences feelings and behavior, and mental health professionals try to change the way people feel—e.g., less anxious or less depressed—by changing the way they think. Nonetheless, we never "disagree" with someone's feelings.

The Steps to Helping

When a victim discloses to you that she is being abused, there are several things you want to communicate to her. These are consistent with the dialectical approach suggested above. These are based on the internal and external factors, reviewed earlier, that are constraining her responding in a manner that will lead to an end to the abuse.

1. First, believe her. When a victim discloses that she is a victim, believe her. Have no hesitation whatsoever in believing her. Most women being abused wait years to disclose the abuse to someone else, and when they finally do so, it is essential that they be believed. The experience of domestic abuse has included constant harangues, by the abuser, that the abuse is not really happening, is not that bad, or is her fault. Simply put, to disbelieve a victim when she informs you that she is being abused will be a perpetration of abuse by you and almost certainly a guarantee that she will be further abused by her partner.

There is a mythology, motivated by the same attitude that argues that "women are as violent as men," that women commonly lie about being abused. While both women and men will lie about their partner being abusive, either because they have a mental illness (i.e., a personality disorder) or are being vindictive toward their partner, this happens so rarely that the chances can be effectively dismissed. Also bear in mind that a woman motivated to lie about her husband being abusive will almost always direct those lies to public safety officials or to the justice system (e.g., a judge or lawyer). Why would she bother to lie to you? You will have nothing to do with having him arrested or judging him to be at fault in the divorce. (In contrast, abusive men, who have had years of practice being cruel and deceitful, can practically be expected to file accusations of abuse against the victim in order to gain advantage in divorce and custody proceedings.)

So, believe her. Moreover, tell her you believe her. When a victim finally discloses to you that she is being abused, you should say something like, "I believe you," "I'm so sorry you are going through this," or "This is a terrible and terrifying situation for you."

2. *Attend to safety.* The safety of the victim and of her children is the paramount concern. (The following covers issues directly concerning safety.)

In cases of emergency, with actual current violence or certain future violence, public safety should be alerted. In other words, if you are actively witnessing violence or if the victim states she is in immediate danger of violence, call 911. Public safety personnel are the professionals trained to intervene in these situations, and they should be relied upon to do the job of securing someone's safety.

Most of the time when you learn of domestic abuse, the situation is not an active crisis. Instead, the victim will inform you of abuse during a meeting in your office or over the phone. However, safety concerns are still very much at issue, and one should keep in mind the following.

First, be aware that communicating with you (or anyone else) about the abuse may be dangerous for her. Her years-long unwillingness to tell others about the abuse is related to safety concerns and fear, and the factors contribuing to her fear still exist.

Second, as noted repeatedly, promoting the victim's safety likely means doing nothing and recommending nothing. She may be capable of doing nothing at the moment. Moreover, she cannot do anything without a safety plan. Attempting to extricate a victim from a situation of domestic abuse with no clear pathways to safety and security is a very bad idea. It will often be safer for a victim to stay in the predictable (albeit potentially violent) situation than to trigger a crisis.

Third, even if the victim is ready to leave a situation of domestic abuse, you should do and suggest nothing beyond referring her to professionals. They can offer her needed resources and consultation, and they have hard-won expertise in safety planning. To emphasize the complexity of this work and the need to refer to experts, see the box on safety planning.

Safety Planning Basics: An Incomplete List

The following is intended to dissuade any reader who imagines himself or herself capable of directly helping a victim of domestic abuse. Bear in mind, instead, that agencies and professionals who work with victims have earned their expertise in safety planning through numerous tragic experiences.

Hard learning over the decades has resulted in the following basic considerations of safety planning:

- Establish code words to communicate to others when in danger
- Use computers and phones safely, as it is likely that the abuser is monitoring both
- Develop and practice escape routes for future violent incidents
- Develop a realistic plan for protecting children
- Answer the following questions:
  - Where are safe places you can go?
  - Who are safe people who can and will help?
  - What is the best day and the best time to leave?
- Organize and hide (where the abuser cannot find it, even if he looks) an emergency "Grab and Go Bag" that will contain:
  - Survival necessities (e.g., money, medications and prescriptions, driver's license, phone numbers)
  - Needed documents (e.g., insurance cards, school records, medical records, welfare identification, car insurance, custody orders, rental contracts)
  - Precious possessions (e.g., pictures and photo albums, jewelry)

3. *Take your time, but be aware of her concerns about time.* When talking to a victim of domestic abuse, one of the most important things to give her is your time. Listening empathically will take time. She will need time to talk about the terrible things she has been experiencing. You will want to take the time to make sure she knows that you believe her, that you are trying to understand, that you respect her, and that you are concerned for her.

Having said that, be aware that the victim may be anxious to cut the meeting short. She may be fearful of being found out by the abuser, who may be monitoring her every move outside the home. If she abruptly expresses a need to leave, it is important to honor this. Alternativelly, she will likely feel bad for taking your time and for "burdening" you with her problems. If she expresses this concern, assure her that she is not. It will suffice to say something simple, such as, "I'm so glad you came in to talk about this" or "This is so important to talk about."

At the beginning of the meeting, it is a good idea to ask how much time she can spend with you. Knowing prior to beginning that she needs to leave at a certain time will be helpful. For similar reasons, it is important, at the beginning of the meeting, to inform her if you are limited in the amount of time that you have. Otherwise, she may mistakenly assume that you are ending the meeting because you don't believe her, don't care, or are repulsed by her.

4. Empathize. Empathy has been discussed repeatedly in this volume, because empathy is the key to helping another person. Empathy communicates many helpful things (see box on p. 354 and previous chapters). Expressing empathy helps the victim realize that you understand how she is thinking and feeling, why she does what she does, and why she doesn't do what she doesn't do.

Keep in mind that empathy is active. It is something you show her. Understanding the way someone thinks and feels is meaningless to that someone if he or she does not *know* that you understand. Empathize actively with victims of domestic abuse by using statements such as, "That sounds very frightening," "You must have been shocked," "It must be awful to be in your situation," "This is obviously very painful for you to talk about," and so forth.

5. Express concern. In addition to expressing empathy, which focuses on her feelings, express your feelings of concern for her. This will show that you do genuinely understand her dangerous situation. In contrast to what the abuser has stated to her repeatedly, it will communicate to her that abuse is an awful experience, the impact of which should not be minimized. It will also show that you care, which will be salutary in itself. As with empathy, you should demonstrate concern actively, saying things such as, "I'm really concerned about you" or "I'm worried about your welfare."

6. Follow up, maybe. At the end of the conversation, ask for another meeting. But don't be surprised if she declines. If she agrees, even tentatively, try to set up another time to meet. (Given the chaotic environment abusers create at home, this may not be possible. That is, she may not be able to fit another meeting into her regular schedule, because she does not have a regular schedule.) If she is willing to meet again but immediately scheduling another meeting is not possible, ask her to call you as soon as she can schedule one. If she is not willing at this time to have another meeting, express your wish that she call you or meet with you again at sometime in the future.

In contrast to the advice in previous chapters regarding the mental illnesses, do not suggest that you follow up with her. Doing so might greatly alarm her, because doing so could endanger her. On the other hand, if she asks you to initiate a follow-up phone call or visit, discuss with her a safe way for you to do so.

7. Communicate that abuse is sinful and illegal. Assuming that you have established that you understand and are concerned, that you are aware that action may be impossible for her at present due to safety concerns, and that you accept that she may be unable to do anything, communicate to the victim that domestic abuse is always wrong. Communicate that the Christian faith considers all forms of domestic abuse to be sinful. She may not realize this, and this is likely to be contrary to what she has previously heard from the abuser and perhaps others as well.

Also communicate that all violence and many other types of domestic abuse are unlawful and that the law (police, courts) is there to protect her from it. This information may also be unknown to her.

8. Communicate that she *decides what* you *will do.* During conversations, you will hopefully show empathy and concern. As noted above, you will hopefully express that abuse is sinful and unlawful. You are likely to communicate, as well, intentionally or not, that you are upset and alarmed at her situation. All of this is good, but all of this will inadvertently communicate to her that you want to do something. (By the way, you *will* want to do something.) This will, in turn, alarm her and make her worry that you will act precipitously, putting her in danger.

It will, therefore, be very important to *tell her explicitly* that you will do nothing without her permission. This communicates that you understand her potentially dangerous situation. It also communicates respect of her autonomy, which may be something she has not experienced in a long time. Say something like, "I hope it is obvious that I am concerned, but I want to assure you that I will do nothing at all unless you want me to" or "I will do nothing and say nothing to anyone until you ask me to do so."

9. Ask how you can help. Ask her if there is anything you can do to help. The best way for you to help is to inform her about resources and to refer her to professionals with expertise in domestic abuse. If she mentions other ways you might help, and if you are able to do so, then do so (so long as safety is not compromised).

The victim will not ask you for help unless you bring it up. Broach the topic directly by asking, "Is there anything I or the church can do to help you?" or by saying, "If there is anything I can do to help, please let me know, and I will if I can." (If she declines, remember to reassure her that you will not do anything without her permission.)

10. Tell her about resources. Victims of domestic abuse may or may not be aware of resources available to them at the national level and possibly at the local level as well. You should have a list of resources before any woman comes in to disclose that she is a victim of abuse. You won't know until she tells you, but you need to be ready when she does so.

The National Coalition Against Domestic Violence has a webpage listing the coalitions in all 50 states, the District of Columbia, and Puerto Rico. The web address is www.ncadv.org/learn/state-coalitions.

The best national resource is the National Domestic Violence Hotline, which can be reached by dialing 1-800-799-7233 or 1-800-787-3224 for TTY. The website is www.thehotline.org. Related to the paramount issue of safety, when one opens the web page, a small pop-up screen appears with the following message, and one must acknowledge the message for it to disappear so that the rest of the page can be viewed:

> Safety Alert: Computer use can be monitored and is impossible to completely clear. If you are afraid your Internet usage might be monitored, call the National Domestic Violence Hotline at 1-800-799-7233 or TTY 1-800-787-3224.

Her Need for Spiritual Consolation

Whether or not the victim attempts to end the abuse or whether or not she agrees to meet with you again, you should inform her that you are available for further conversations and support in the future. Whether she is a victim, a victim attempting to become a survivor, or a survivor of domestic abuse, she needs her church. She needs reassurance that God loves her, and she needs to hear that she is doing or has done the right thing by seeking to end the abuse. She especially needs the consolation of the gospel.

A Christian Perspective on Domestic Abuse

"Once you were alienated from God and were enemies in your minds because of your evil behavior. But now he has reconciled you by Christ's physical body through death to present you holy in his sight, without blemish and free from accusation . . . But now you must also rid yourselves of all such things as these: anger, rage, malice, slander, and filthy language. . . . And over all these virtues put on love."

(Paul to the Colossians, 1:21,22; 3:8,14)

The church is neither immune from nor exempt from domestic abuse. It will happen and you need to prepare yourself, in your mind's attitude and in your planned response, for how you will deal with it. The proper Christian perspective on domestic abuse can be summarized as follows.

First and foremost, from a Christian perspective, domestic abuse is absolutely unacceptable and should not be tolerated. For someone to intimidate, control, and abuse a spouse or partner is sinful and detestable. It violates man's law, and it violates God's law. It violates the vows the abuser exchanged with his bride before the eyes of God, family, and friends. It indicates treacherous behavior toward his wife and infidelity toward his faith (2 Timothy 3:2-6). One Christian should never enable another to continue in sin by ignoring the sin or by asserting that it is not sin (Isaiah 5:20). No woman should ever have to endure the evil of domestic abuse. The abuse endangers both the corporal safety and the eternal salvation of the abuser (Galatians 5:21; 1 Peter 3:7), the victim, and any children exposed to it.

Christians should recognize that domestic abuse can stop. However, repentance is not sufficient, and it is dangerous (to the victim) for anyone to assume otherwise. Keep in mind that the abuser has likely expressed repentance (remorse, regret, promises to stop) to the victim many times, only to abuse again. Reformation of one's attitudes and in one's habitual behavior is necessary. To reform and to change in order to stop being abusive requires that the abuser go through treatment to recognize that he has a sense of entitlement and superiority, as well as misconceptions about love and relationships. While this is doable, it takes serious commitment and a lot of work (i.e., at least two years of effort in counseling).

However, Christians should also recognize that, while it is possible for the abuser to reform, it is not very likely. The experiences of researchers and specialists who work in this area indicate that most abusers are unwilling to change. Many abusers will enter treatment expressing repentance, and they will do so in hope that going through the motions of reformation will suffice for her to forgive, forget, and stay. But they will not truly attempt to change. In a more honest style, when confronted about their behavior, many abusers will flat out refuse to acknowledge that abuse is wrong. They will continue the abusive behavior. Accordingly, divorce proceedings subsequent to domestic abuse are often initiated by the husband, after he realizes that his wife is insistent that he actually change or that she will not tolerate any more abuse.

What, then, is a proper Christian attitude about preserving a relationship that has been impacted by domestic abuse? The proper attitude takes into account the efforts at reformation on the part of the abuser but always defers to what is best for the victim/survivor.

Regarding the former, if the abuser does not truly repent and then make genuine efforts at change, then the abuser has sundered his promises to his spouse. It would be perverse for anyone to require the person being abused to uphold her promises to him despite his infidelity to his promises to her and his persistent sinful behavior. Likewise, it would be extremely harsh and unkind to instruct a woman being abused that she must stay and endure the abuse. To justify such instruction with the Bible or with Christian teachings would be iniquitous. Simply put, some women will find it necessary to divorce their husbands for their own safety and the well-being of their children, and because of his infidelity to his promises. To refuse to continue in a relationship that is corrupted by domestic abuse should not be considered sinful. Rather, it should be commended as just, good, and acceptable before the eyes of God, whose Son instructs us to ask the Father to deliver us from evil.

If the abuser demonstrates a commitment to reform his attitudes and behavior, the abuser and others may legitimately request or suggest that the victim maintain the relationship. However, it would not be legitimate to demand or require this. Abuse will always damage a relationship, and the damage may be irreparable. Abuse can be so destructive to her and her children's well-being that it may take years for them to recover. It is, of course, a Christian obligation to forgive others as we have been forgiven, but it would be presumptuous to demand that a survivor stay in a marital relationship with a man who terrified and hurt her.

Keep in mind, also, that some victims are desirous of maintaining the relationship, even if the abuser struggles to repent and reform. In these instances, it may be beneficial for the relationship if the victim were to separate from the abuser in order to force him to recognize that he must change. In any event, the victim should be encouraged to recognize that domestic abuse cannot be tolerated and that she must demand change—for her sake, for his sake, and for the sake of the children.

Couples Counseling for Domestic Abuse: A Very, Very Bad Idea

My experience with Sandra and Patrick, related at the beginning of this chapter, is not at all uncommon. It is, in fact, quite common. When a victim seeks to end the abuse, she may request of the abuser that she be allowed to seek counseling. In response, the abuser may insist that they seek it together (so that he can monitor and control what she says). Alternatively, the victim may herself suggest that they seek couples counseling, under the wrong (but commonplace) assumption that domestic abuse is caused by problems in the relationship, such as poor conflict resolution skills or inadequate anger management strategies.

While there are problems that may result in stress-induced situational violence (see beginning of chapter) and while couples counseling may be appropriate in these situations, domestic abuse is different. Domestic abuse is not a symptom of another problem. It is the result of neither anger management problems nor conflict resolution skill deficits. Domestic abuse is purposefully committed in order to terrorize and intimidate the victim. Domestic abuse by him is the problem.

If an abuser and victim enter couples counseling, a good mental health professional will ask the woman, in private (such as over the phone or in a one-on-one session), about domestic abuse. If it is uncovered during the private meeting, the competent mental health professional should then encourage the victim to contact appropriate resources. The competent mental health professional will then inform the couple that couples counseling is not appropriate for them, without attributing a reason.

Let me be as clear as possible. It is malpractice for a mental health professional to conduct couples counseling knowing that there is domestic abuse. The abuser will not allow the victim to talk openly about the abuse, or if she does, he will punish her severely afterwards. Conducting anger management will be a waste of time, since abuse is not committed in anger but rather with cold, ruthless calculation. Conflict resolution strategies are not needed and will never be implemented. There is not mutual conflict in their relationship; there is domestic abuse being committed by the abuser. In short, to conduct couples counseling in an attempt to end domestic abuse will assure that the victim will continue to be abused. Given that she sought counseling in order to stop the abuse, the opposite effect will be realized, with the assistance of the counselor.

Uncover Domestic Abuse by Looking for It

Domestic abuse is shameful to both persons. The shame drives both to try to hide the abuse from others. To uncover domestic abuse, then, one needs to search for it by asking directly about it.

When to Ask

There are two instances when you should ask a woman if she is a victim of domestic abuse. First, ask if she seeks your help for any reason. If she as an individual seeks your consultation about a mental health issue, then you should ask. Alternatively, if a couple seeks consultation with you about a relationship issue, you should insist on meeting with each of them individually (probably on separate nights). During the private meeting with her, ask about domestic abuse. (See previous section.)

Second, if you see warning signs of abuse, such as detailed in the box below, then you may decide to ask a woman if she is being abused. This latter instance requires great caution, however. Since she has not sought out your counsel, there is no excuse to offer the abuser to explain the private meeting with you. If you can do so safely, try to arrange a private appointment. Perhaps you could offer other reasons for the meeting, such as wanting to talk about joining choir or volunteering for Sunday school.

Signs That Someone May Be Being Abused

Domestic abuse is not necessarily obvious, so it will be necessary to perceive the signs and ask about the experience of abuse in order to uncover it. Based on the discussion of the effects of abuse on the victim, here are some of the behaviors and attitudes that may be exhibited by someone being abused.

- Seems afraid or excessively anxious to please her partner
- Goes along with everything her partner says or does
- Checks in unusually often with her partner
- Receives harassing or interruptive phone calls from her partner
- Talks about her partner's temper, jealousy, or possessiveness
- Has frequent injuries, perhaps excusing them as "accidents" or refusing to talk about them
- Frequently misses work, school, or social occasions without explanation
- Is restricted from seeing family and friends by herself or rarely goes out in public without her partner
- Has limited or no access to money or credit cards, to cars or other transportation, or to cell phones
- Has very low self-esteem
- Is depressed, anxious, or suicidal

Of all of the signs, fear is most pathognomonic (i.e., indicative of a problem). If you detect fear on the part of someone, then explore further. Fear is displayed in subtle facial expressions and body language. It may be displayed in ways that are not easily described but that are nonetheless sensed ("I'm not quite sure why I get this sense, but I am getting it").

How to Ask

There are some simple queries that can open up a discussion about possible domestic abuse with a woman you think may be being abused. It can be done in a way that will not offend.

Whether she has requested private counseling or you require a private meeting before seeing them as a couple, it is relatively easy to ask about the relationship ("How are things going with you and your husband?" "How are things between you?"). You can follow that up with questions about the universal couple experience of disagreements, such as "How often do you have disagreements?" or "How are disagreements resolved?"

Regardless of the answers, you should then ask specific questions about possible violence: "What is it like when you get really angry with each other?" "How is anger expressed?" "What is it like when you argue or fight?" "Are you ever afraid of each other when you get angry?" "Are you ever fearful of his anger?" (It has been repeatedly said that anger does not cause abuse, but anger is always an aspect of abuse. In this way, such questions invite a potential victim to disclose episodes of violence.) Finally, if it seems appropriate, you may ask explicitly about violence, such as "Has there ever been any physical violence between you two, either you towards him or him towards you?" or "Have things ever gotten so out of control that you hurt each other physically or one of you hurts the other?"

If you requested the private meeting because you observed signs that she may be being abused, start the meeting with another topic. Keep in mind that if she is being abused, she will need a legitimate excuse for your meeting with her. Likewise, be prepared to verify that reason to her partner, as he may ask (especially if there is domestic abuse occurring). At some point, acknowledge to her your concern about her. Share your observations of her with her, such as, "You seem really down lately" or "I cannot help but notice that there seems to be some tension between you and your husband." After opening with these observations, ask her if it would be okay to talk about these things.

If she states that she does not want to talk about these issues or if she states that she must leave, then immediately drop the subject. Nonetheless, you should mention that you are available and willing to meet or talk with her at any time in the future.

When There Is Not Abuse

If you ask these questions and there is not abuse happening, she will probably not be offended. At worst, asking will communicate to her that you take her welfare very seriously. You can simply state that these are questions you ask everyone in these circumstances.

If she tells her partner about your questions related to abuse, you should acknowledge to him that you asked them. You can apologize if necessary, but you should communicate to him that you have an obligation to ask about her, and his, welfare.

A Fervent Hope

This chapter was very difficult to write. I wrote and rewrote it several times, and I have edited and reedited it extensively. Domestic abuse is an extremely important issue. The topic lies near the heart of what it means to be a Christian, which is why the devil has worked so hard to corrupt God's Word in order to provide evil men with justification for committing abuse. Domestic abuse drives the victim away from God's kingdom by depriving her of trust in a loving, caring God. Domestic abuse drives the abuser away from God's kingdom by his unrepentant behavior.

I hope fervently that I have done the topic justice. I hope that any victims and survivors who read it will perceive it as fair, understanding, and charitable. I hope it helps pastors and other church workers to understand better and to deal more effectively with domestic abuse. I hope that any reader who is presently abusing his partner will recognize his sin and acknowledge his need for repentance and reformation.

A Primer on Effective Communication Within Intimate Relationships

To end this chapter, I present briefly a distinction between constructive and destructive anger in relationships. I start with the following supposition: Two people in a relationship will inevitably get upset at each other. Combining lives means sharing everything, including bank accounts, responsibilities (e.g., children) and stress, bedrooms and bathrooms, upsets and heartbreaks. Feelings will occasionally be hurt, and anger is likely to arise.

Since anger is inevitable, it is important that a couple be able to communicate anger effectively in order to resolve anger. Inappropriate expressions of anger can cause damage to marital relationships. I refer to this as destructive anger. (This is not the same as abuse, which is not a problem of angry feelings but of abusive behavior.)

Couples can learn to enable anger to be a constructive force in their relationship. Partners in any relationship, whether business, friendly, or romantic, will get mad at each other when things bother them. Anger is a sign that something needs to be talked about and perhaps changed. Resolving angry feelings will require resolving what is bothering them, which will be good for the relationship. Anger can thus be a constructive force in relationships if people think about anger properly and act appropriately when angry. The difference between destructive and constructive uses of anger is detailed in the following box.

Destructive and Constructive Anger in Relationships

A common problem for couples is that they *misunderstand* and mismanage their anger. They misunderstand and fear anger, perhaps because they were raised in a family that did not deal with anger appropriately. They allow anger to cause destruction to their relationship. But if people have a clear understanding of anger and a plan for how to behave when angry, it can become a constructive force in relationships.

Anger as a Destructive Force	Anger as a Constructive Force
Misunderstandings about anger	*Realistic thoughts about anger*
• "Anger is a choice."	• "Anger is not a choice; anger is a feeling."
• "Anger is always wrong."	• "Anger is not inherently wrong."
• "I should never have to feel angry."	• "Anger is an emotion that I will feel at times."
• "To make me angry is to do something bad or wrong."	• "Anger is a signal that something is bothering me."
• "If someone loves another, anger will never be felt; anger cannot coexist with love."	• "I will get angry at people I love; getting angry is not the same as not loving."
• "My anger is always sensible and rational."	• "My anger may often not make sense; there will be times when I am angry for no particular reason or for reasons I don't quite understand."
• "My anger is always reasonable and righteous; if I am angry, I am correct to be angry."	

Anger as a Destructive Force (continued)	**Anger as a Constructive Force** (continued)
• "My partner is responsible for making me angry."	• "I am responsible for my anger; my anger is mine."
Thoughts like these about anger cause secondary emotions, such as more anger, resentment, and fear, which exacerbate the original angry feeling, making it even harder to deal with appropriately.	Thoughts like these will enable the person not to feel secondary emotions. They will allow him or her to remain calm and to deal with anger appropriately.
Destructive behavior when angry • Anger isn't expressed at all • Anger is expressed with cold silences or by withdrawing • Anger is expressed by standing, stalking, screaming, yelling, name-calling, breaking things, throwing things	*Contructive behavior when angry* • If very angry, take "time-outs" to calm down • Wait for an appropriate time and place to discuss situation • Sit and talk • Express anger calmly, even if feeling upset • Use sentences that begin with "I," such as "I feel angry when . . . " • Make concrete suggestions as to how the situation may be corrected

Chapter 18

Concerning Suicide

"I eagerly expect and hope that I will in no way be ashamed,
but will have sufficient courage so that now as always
Christ will be exalted in my body, whether by life or by death.
For to me, to live is Christ and to die is gain.
If I am to go on living in the body, this will mean fruitful labor for me.
Yet what shall I choose? I do not know! I am torn between the two:
I desire to depart and be with Christ, which is better by far;
but it is more necessary for you that I remain in the body."
(Philippians 1:20-24)

The Beloved Elder

Mr. Anthony was popular at his church, where he had been a member for over 40 years. Over the years, he had served on various boards, including the finance board and the board of elders, but he was best known as a weekly fixture among the usher corps. He presented a very solemn facade when he ushered. When the occasional young child in the pews burst out "Hi, Mr. Anthony!" during offering, everyone in church smiled inwardly. Everybody was tickled to see Mr. Anthony act so dignified in his role as an usher, since he was so friendly and good-natured. After church, at Bible study, and at church functions, Mr. Anthony always remembered everyone's name and always greeted others with a big smile, probably a joke, and several questions about their family, whose names he also remembered. He was tall, and he still carried some of the physique he earned as a young man in the Marines. He always knelt on one knee when he talked to kids, so he wouldn't seem so big and scary. He insisted that everyone call him by his first name. "Mr. Parnisi is my brother. He's a lawyer, so don't call me that! Call me Anthony." But that did not seem respectful enough, so most people called him Mr. Anthony.

When Mr. Anthony died at age 73, the church grieved. He had not been to church in several months, and everyone knew he was sick. But the end came more suddenly than people expected. When word got around that Mr. Anthony had ended his own life, people reacted with shock. While his wife was at the drugstore getting a refill of the antinausea medications he took to help with the effects of the chemo, Mr. Anthony went out onto his back porch and shot himself with his favorite hunting rifle. Church members had difficulty understanding and accepting this. "How could he do that? How could he do that to his family? He seemed so strong in his faith, so how could he do such a thing? Did the medications do something to derange him? Was he out of his mind?"

The Pastor's Wife

In the neighboring state, at a different church, people likewise reacted with shock when the associate pastor's wife committed suicide. Some knew she had suffered from depression off and on for several years, but no one knew it was that bad. Even if he had wanted to, Pastor Jenkins could not have kept the cause of his wife's death a secret. The ambulance and police cars outside of the parsonage alerted everyone that something was wrong, and several church members were present when Mrs. Jenkins was put into the ambulance. That morning, he had told her that it was necessary, once again, for her to go to the hospital for another attempt to resolve her serious depression. She asked for time to shower, and she went into the bathroom. After 15 minutes of hearing the shower running, Pastor Jenkins broke through the bathroom door when she would not respond to his knocking. He found his wife in the shower. She had cut her wrists.

It was hard for church members to understand. Not only did she attend service every Sunday, but she had also been involved with the church. She was the substitute organist and the codirector of the choir. It was hard to understand. Mrs. Jenkins had a husband and four beautiful young children. Her youngest was less than a year old when she killed herself.

"How could she do that to them? Is there something about the family that isn't known? Had she lost her faith? What kind of an example is that for others? Surely things weren't that bad. Surely she knew what a good life she had."

The Troubled Teen

When Annie attempted to kill herself, her church did not react with shock. That's because her parents did not tell anyone. They did not tell the minister, any of Annie's teachers, or any of their friends or relatives. Annie was 17 and the eldest of three children. She was an honor student at her high school and had just begun the process of applying for college. She hoped to become a veterinarian.

Annie had a talent for fading into the woodwork. Those at church who would have recognized her, which was not many, would have known her as the "quiet, plump" girl. Annie had been treated for the eating disorder bulimia nervosa the previous year. She was no longer binge eating and purging, but she was still overweight and deeply ashamed of her body shape and weight. She had few friends, because she did not make them easily. She figured she was too strange and unattractive to have friends. Even when other girls acted nice towards her, she assumed they just felt sorry for her. Several times Annie had asked her mother if she could see a psychologist or a psychiatrist, but the idea that Annie might be depressed made her mother so upset that Annie stopped bringing it up. When she was caught forcing herself to throw up at school, the principal and the counselor insisted that her parents take her for treatment. She quickly stopped the behavior and, just as quickly, her parents withdrew her from treatment.

One Saturday afternoon, Annie ingested a bottle of Tylenol PM and lay down on her bed. Her determination to die lasted three minutes and thirty seconds. She knew this, as she told me later in one of our sessions, because she watched her bedroom clock the whole time she lay there. The clock seemed to go faster and faster as she got more and more frightened, imagining the poison working its way from her stomach into her bloodstream. Finally, she went downstairs and told her mother what she had done.

Her parents drove her to the emergency department, where they pumped her stomach and had her drink a charcoal mix. She overheard her parents say to one of the doctors, "We don't know why she does these things. She seems determined to be unhappy." She heard one staff person say to another, "I get so tired of these rich, spoiled kids begging for attention by pulling these stunts! I've got better things to do than mollycoddle an ungrateful teenager."

No one asked her if she was depressed. One of the doctors did recommend that she be taken to a psychiatrist, however. Her father talked to their pastor, who knew me and made a referral.

Put yourself front and center of these events. Imagine that you are the pastor at one of these churches. What would you say to your church about Mr. Anthony? How would you help people understand what happened to Mrs. Jenkins? What would you say to Annie if she came to see you?

Responding to Suicide With the One Thing Needful

Suicide is probably the saddest and most confusing event that a Christian will confront. Suicide has, does, and will happen within the Christian faith. Yet suicide seems to present an unsolvable conundrum that, unless it is solved, will actually increase the despair of those in distress and the anguish of those left to cope with a suicide tragedy. Those who work in the church need to be able to respond in a way that is helpful. You need to respond intelligently and compassionately—with understanding, with care, and with Christian assurance—to those considering suicide, those who have survived a suicide attempt, and the survivors of the suicide of a loved one.

The chapter starts with some basic information about suicide, beginning with definitions of the various types of suicidal behaviors. To help you recognize when someone may be in danger of attempting suicide, factors that put people at risk for suicide are reviewed. To help you react to try to prevent a suicide, the chapter presents explicit suggestions and instructions on how to talk with someone you believe may be in danger of suicide, as well as what to do if someone admits to being suicidal.

A Christian understanding of suicide is presented, followed by a discussion of a Christ-centered response to suicidal crises and suicidal tragedies. It is intended to help you understand, comfort, and counsel those who, like Paul, "desire to depart" or who have made an attempt to do so. Fortunately, you already have all that you need in order to do these things. A principal theme of this book is that the church is better equipped to deal with the depradations of mental illness than other institutions. Likewise, the church is optimally ready to deal with suicide. The church has "resources" that others do not, namely, the assurance of the atoning sacrifice and resurrection of Jesus Christ.

Definitions and Distinctions

It is important to distinguish between different types of suicidal behavior and different types of suicidal cognitions (thoughts).

Behavior

Suicide is defined as intentionally performing an act with the expectation that it will result in one's own death. Someone may *attempt* suicide, meaning he or she committed an intentionally self-destructive act that was interrupted (either by the actor or by some other person or event). For perhaps obvious reasons, mental health professionals do not use the term *successful suicide.* Instead, someone who actually kills himself is said to have completed suicide.

Cognitions

The distinction between thoughts about suicide, suicidal ideation, and suicide intent is extremely important.

Thoughts About Suicide

Many persons *occasionally think* about death and suicide. Survey research indicates that perhaps the majority of all persons, not just persons with a mental illness, have at some time in their life thought about what it would be like to be dead. For some, moreover, those thoughts about death included thoughts about committing suicide. Such thinking is most common in the late teens and early 20s, and it seems to be especially commonplace among college students. In the same way, many adolescents wonder what it would be like to have different parents or to be born in a different country. These abstract thoughts, including those about death and suicide, are entirely harmless. They are simply thoughts, meaning they are not associated with any mental illness or any intention to act.

Thoughts about death and suicide in someone with a mental illness are a different issue entirely, and this phenomenon is commonly called suicidal ideation. Suicide intent, but not suicidal ideation, indicates a crisis. It is thus important to distinguish between ideation and intent.

Suicidal Ideation and Suicide Intent

Some persons experiencing mental illness engage in *suicidal ideation,* which means they are contemplating their own death and perhaps thinking occasionally about acting to kill themselves. Thoughts about death and suicidal ideation are hallmark symptoms of depression, as well as some other mental illnesses (such as severe anxiety, substance use disorders, bipolar disorder, and schizophrenia). If someone reports suicidal ideation, the mental illness is probably fairly severe. Most persons with suicidal ideation will state, sometimes spontaneously but sometimes only if asked explicitly, that they do not harbor intent to kill themselves. Suicidal ideation can be extremely distressing to the person, but ideation is not an indication of future self-harm. Thus, in most cases, a person cannot and will not be hospitalized for suicidal ideation. A mental health professional will monitor closely someone with such ideation, because it could transform—especially if the mental illness worsens—into suicide intent.

Someone with suicidal ideation who is planning on acting on the thoughts is exhibiting suicide intent. That is, someone with *suicide intent* is making plans to kill himself. This indicates a suicidal crisis, and an immediate intervention must be implemented.

The Limited Usefulness of the Phrase "Suicide Gesture"

You may hear a mental health professional make reference to parasuicidal behavior, of which there are two types. A "suicide gesture" has the appearance of a suicide attempt, but is not intended to cause death. Examples include self-harming behavior, such as using a sharp instrument to cut one's arms or legs. It may also include very high-risk behavior, such as driving at high speeds, standing or walking along the edge of a steep drop, or other behavior that endangers one's life. A "suicide gamble" is when a person engages in behavior that will cause death over a period of time (such as taking sleeping pills) but actually hopes to be found and saved.

These terms imply that some suicidal behavior is less serious than other suicidal behavior. These phrases are thus sometimes used to reassure family, friends, and even mental health professionals that the behavior is not truly worrisome. More important, the distinction between severity of risk is useful to researchers. However, I think making a distinction between the "seriousness" of suicidal behavior has the potential to cause serious problems, and I strongly discourage people from making it.

First and foremost, these terms may make the suicidal behavior seem to be something less than what it is. Parasuicidal behavior is incredibly dangerous, and it sometimes results in unintentional death. For example, some persons ingest large amounts of acetaminophen (e.g., Tylenol) without the intention of actually dying, but large amounts of the drug cause irreparable liver damage, which will lead to a slow and painful death. Another example is the suicide gamble that is mistimed, so that there is no rescue.

Second, the distinction between "genuine" and "para-" suicidal behavior is sometimes impossible. It may be difficult to discern whether someone who committed suicide by drug overdose actually intended to be discovered and rescued, so the distinction may be in error.

Third, there is very good evidence that those who engage in parasuicidal behavior are at highly increased risk (perhaps 100 times the risk of the general population) for completed suicide. Researchers are concluding that parasuicidal behavior is a type of "practice." With enough practice, the behaviors get less scary and aversive, which enables the person to become more likely to complete the act.

Instead of typecasting them one way or another, any person who engages in suicidal behavior needs empathy and understanding. All suicidal behavior should be understood as a desperate and pathological attempt to end pain and suffering. With such understanding, help can be effectively offered. The person who engages in parasuicidal behavior wants help in ending the pain. The person who engages in parasuicidal behavior is starting to contemplate the idea that dying is the only way to end the pain.

Types of Suicidal Crises

Most suicidal actions can be categorized as one of three types. These vary in terms of severity.

Realistic and Fatalistic

Some persons commit suicide in order to end suffering that genuinely cannot be halted. Persons in this state who express suicidal ideation or intent are at very high risk. Thus are persons with painful and debilitating terminal illness at risk of suicide, as they are accurate in their belief that their suffering will not end. This partly explains why elderly persons have elevated risk. These persons can often be turned away from suicidal intention by relieving their pain or by treating underlying mental illness, especially depression.

Unreasonable Hopelessness

Most persons who attempt or commit suicide are in intense psychological distress, but they are not realistic in their fatalistic assessment of their future. They are convinced that their future is hopeless, but others see this assessment as unreasonably negative. The sense of hopelessness and pessimism, then, is an aspect of their mental illness, and it can hopefully be mitigated with proper treatment.

Pathological and Desperate Statement

Some persons who attempt suicide do not have the intention of ending their life. Instead, the action is a pathological and desperate attempt to communicate to others the level of their distress. The person may have no other means of getting others' attention. Either others are unsympathetic or emotionally unavailable, or the person inaccurately believes this to be the case. Such actions can be aggravating to witness or to hear about, and these behaviors are most commonly referred to as "parasuicidal." But they need to be understood empathically. The person engaged in an extremely dangerous, desperate, and pathological act, and he or she absolutely needs professional treatment (see box on p. 374).

Facts and Figures About Suicide

Studying Suicide

Accurate statistics about suicide are hard to obtain for several reasons. First, suicide is a *relatively* rare occurrence. Compare suicide to the mental illnesses. Depression and anxiety have annual prevalence rates of about 10 cases per 100 persons, whereas schizophrenia and bipolar disorder are relatively rare disorders with annual prevalence rates of about 1 in 100 people. All of these disorders are relatively easy to study. That is, it is not difficult to find persons with these disorders to study. In comparison, suicide is quite rare. In any given year only about 1 in 10,000 people will commit suicide.

Second, for obvious reasons, persons who commit suicide cannot be *directly studied.* It is only possible to interview and investigate directly any person who has attempted suicide or who has engaged in parasuicidal behavior. But researchers cannot be certain that such persons are similar to persons who actually complete suicide. Regarding the latter, researchers must study persons who have committed suicide retrospectively via *psychological autopsy.* Researchers will interview friends and relatives who knew the person, and they will try to find and interview health professionals who may have treated the person.

Finally, researchers are sometimes *uncertain whether a death was actually a suicide.* As noted previously, some persons who end up dead by suicide did not intend to die. They intended to communicate their distress via parasuicide, and so end up dying without intention. In contrast, many of those who commit suicide succeed in making their deaths look accidental. Researchers have estimated, for example, that at least 15% of all fatal automobile accidents are actually suicides. Likewise, there may be hesitation on the part of doctors and families to acknowledge that someone killed himself or herself in order to save the family from additional pain.

Despite this, there are many things known about suicidal behavior that are useful in trying to prevent it.

Suicide Statistics

The Centers for Disease Control and Prevention (CDC) is a federal agency tasked by Congress to protect public health and safety. It does so partly by tracking and compiling information about causes of illness and death, including suicide. According to the CDC, 36,909 people in the United States killed themselves in 2009. This makes suicide the tenth leading cause of death across all age groups. For reasons that are unclear, the suicide rate has increased every year from 2000 to 2009 (the last year for which statistics were available at the time of this writing).

For every suicide, between 8 and 20 people make a serious attempt but do not complete the act. In the United States, almost one million people attempt suicide in any given year.

Suicide Risk Factors

Suicide risk factors are characteristics of a person that have been found to be associated with greater risk of a suicide attempt or a suicide completion. For example, males are *more likely* than females to commit suicide, so being male is a risk factor for suicide.

Rish factors are important in several ways. Mental health professionals evaluate their patients for risk factors for suicide. If a patient has a relatively high number of risk factors (e.g., depressed, male, elderly, health problems) or a high intensity of one or two risk factors (e.g., very depressed), this will lead to increased vigilance on the part of the clinician. In addition, we evaluate risk factors because some of them can be mitigated (see p. 383). For example, schizophrenia is a risk factor. Persons with the disorder are at a higher risk for suicide than persons with other mental illnesses. But we can mitigate that risk by having a person diagnosed with schizophrenia take antipsychotic medications to reduce hallucinations and delusions.

Factors that have been found to be associated with suicide risk can be categorized as demographic, socio-environmental, and psychological.

Demographic Characteristics

Demographic risk factors for suicide include gender, age, health problems, ethnicity, and a family history of suicidal behavior.

Demographic Risk Factors for Suicide

- Gender (males at greater risk)
- Age (older at greater risk)
- Health problems (including chronic physical pain)
- Ethnicity (whites and American Indians at greater risk)
- Family history of suicidal behavior

Women are three times as likely as men to attempt suicide, but *men are four times as likely* as women to complete suicide. For example, in 2009 of the nearly 37,000 people who committed suicide in the United States, 79% were men. A simple reason for this is that men tend to choose more lethal and immediate means than women, such as using a gun versus using poison. The former method is instantly lethal, whereas the latter method usually gives the person some time to change her mind and get medical assistance.

Age is positively associated with suicide risk: *the older the person, the greater the risk.* This might surprise some. All of us have read stories about the tragic death of a teen suicide, whereas stories about the tragic suicide of a beloved elder are relatively rare. (Those stories don't sell as well.) This gives the impression that teen suicide is rampant. And, indeed, suicide is one of the top three causes of death in persons between the ages of 15 and 24 (the other two are motor vehicle accidents and homicide). But across age groups, persons under the age of 25 have the lowest rate of suicide. The group with the highest risk are those over 75. Age is associated with other risk factors as well, such as loss of social support, poor health, and increasing dependence on others that leads to a sense of being a burden.

Having severe or chronic *medical problems* is a risk factor for suicide. This is especially true if the problem causes pain or if the person is confronting an illness that can be neither cured nor improved. Illnesses that are progressively debilitating are especially dangerous. Medical problems that confer particularly elevated risk include cancer, acquired immunodeficiency syndrome (AIDS), quadriplegia, and multiple sclerosis. Some diseases are especially likely to afflict elderly persons, such as end-stage renal disease, chronic obstructive pulmonary disease (COPD), and chronic heart failure. The combination of old age and one of these diseases is especially dangerous.

Non-Hispanic whites and American Indians have approximately equivalent risk for suicide. Both have over twice the risk of African-Americans, Hispanic-Americans, and Asian-Americans/Pacific Islanders. There are no clear reasons for these *ethnic* differences, but several ideas have been put forth. With regard to American Indians, higher rates of poverty, crime, and substance dependence are well documented, and all of these factors increase risk of suicide. High relative rates of Christianity among both African-American and Hispanic-American subpopulations may account for their relatively lower risk. None of these explanations have been verified, however.

Finally, someone who has a *family history* of suicidal behavior is at greater risk for attempting or completing suicide. The reasons for this are not well understood. It may be that the example set by one's parent or uncle makes suicide seem less frightening and perhaps a more "legitimate" way to cope with problems.

Social and Environmental Factors

Social and environmental risk factors for suicide include occupation, employment, financial problems, loss of social supports, and the accessibility and lethality of means.

Social and Environmental Risk Factors for Suicide

- Loss of job, financial security, or status
- Employment problems
- Relationship losses/social isolation
- "Violent" occupation (e.g., physicians, police, military)
- Accessibility and lethality of means

Occupational problems may include increased stress and responsibility, a reduction in responsibilities, being put on probation, or the outright loss of one's job. Either may lead to increased financial stress or loss, not to mention the loss of status or social standing. Indeed, job loss may encompass all three (i.e., financial problems, the loss of important social relationships, and loss of status).

A person who is contemplating suicide is likely feeling isolated and perhaps alienated from others. Job loss may lead to isolation through the *loss of important relationships.* The loss of a relationship that had a lot of meaning is more traumatic than the loss of short-term, less-encompassing relationships (hence the loss of a spouse is one of the most traumatic events a person can endure), but the importance of a relationship is entirely subjective. Probably many readers have known a youth who attempted or committed suicide after the breakup of a relatively short-lasting relationship. Social alienation is likewise a serious risk factor for suicide.

Ironically and tragically, feeling despondent and suicidal can lead to a sense of alienation from others. It is not easy to talk to others about suicidal thoughts, because others will worry and become distressed. Implicit in the inability to talk openly with others about negative thoughts and feelings is that such thoughts and feelings are wrong and shameful.

Some *occupations* confer relatively greater risk for suicide. In particular, physicians and police officers are at greater risk for suicide. Both groups have highly stressful jobs, as they regularly encounter the worst that life deals out. Perhaps not surprisingly, both professions are renowned for high levels of alcohol use, as well as high prevalence of divorce. Both professions provoke very high expectations from others. Everyone expects doctors to be constantly at the top of their game, which is why they must carry malpractice insurance. Likewise, police are expected to be essentially flawless (polite, helpful, friendly, calm) in their labors. Given this expectation, both physicians and police are perhaps very reluctant to express a need for help with stress or depression. Finally, and perhaps most importantly, professionals in both occupations likely become desensitized to violence and death. What would make many of us cringe or nauseous, leading us to grow faint or be forced to turn away, may be everyday experiences for them. The notion of turning violent against oneself may be less intimidating for them.

Another reason that physicians and police have higher rates of suicide is likely related to easy access to means of killing (drugs and weapons), as well as expertise in knowing what kills. That is, research has shown that having *ready access* to a weapon or some other means of killing oneself is a risk factor. This is related to the fact that, although suicidal thoughts among persons with mental illness are common and for some may even be continuous, the act of attempting suicide tends to be impulsive. One researcher estimated that the average time between deciding to kill oneself and making an attempt is less than five minutes. (He interviewed one survivor who reported the time lapse to be approximately 10 seconds!) For someone at risk of suicide, getting beyond that impulsive moment is, literally, vital. Thus, an important aspect of suicide prevention is to eliminate access to such means (see following section on "Reducing Risk Factors").

Readers may notice that all of these factors affect military men and women. As of the writing of this chapter, the rate of suicide among our active service members and veterans is about one per day (see box).

Suicide and the Military

For reasons that are unclear, veterans of the wars in Iraq and Afghanistan have an unusually high rate of suicide. Several factors are likely involved.

Obviously, anyone who has deployed in a war zone has a greatly elevated risk of both post-traumatic stress disorder (PTSD) and traumatic brain injury (TBI), both of which cause intense psychological pain. (See chapter 10.)

Members of the military are pressured, as part of their job, to perform well regardless of the difficulty of the environment or their personal situations. As a result, many hesitate to admit that they are suffering emotional pain. If they did so, it could cause superiors to take away responsibilities. (To be fair, the issue is extraordinarily complicated. For example, if a soldier is distressed or impaired, offering help may require removing him or her from duties.) Moreover, impairment in these men and women is more often social and self-care, rather than occupational, making it less easily observed.

The can-do attitude necessary for military success tends to endure after discharge. The capacity to work well under stress makes former military men and women excellent people to hire. The hesitancy to acknowledge distress also remains. The end result is that ex-military men and women with mental illness do not get identified as needing help, and they likewise do not get referred to treatment that may help.

In addition, there are problems of post-deployment *readjustment* to civilian life. When the soldiers return home to the United States, they must reintegrate back into their careers, their marriages, their families, their neighborhoods, and their social lives. While they were deployed, spouses, children, employers, and friends learned to get along without them. Coming home and feeling unimportant and out of place can be highly distressing. Moreover, the vast majority of Americans have no idea what is actually happening in Iraq and Afghanistan. Veterans realize this, and they feel disconnected from their fellow citizens. The important, dangerous work they were doing in a foreign country is mysterious and unappreciated back home, which is a very discombobulating experience.

In summary, veterans and their families need special attention. They probably won't ask, but they and their families could probably use help in the adjustment back to home and church.

Psychological Issues

Psychological risk factors include mental illness, a sense of hopelessness, acute intoxication, previous suicide attempts, and feeling like a burden to others.

Psychological Risk Factors for Suicide

- Mental illness (especially depression and schizophrenia)
- A sense of hopelessness
- Intoxication
- Previous attempt
- Feeling like a burden to others

Researchers estimate that over 90% of those who commit suicide have a *mental illness* at the time of their death. In other words, if someone does not have a mental illness, it is highly unlikely that the person will be seriously contemplating suicide.

However, research suggests that the single best predictor of whether a person will attempt or complete suicide is the psychological state of *hopelessness.* This is the conviction that a dreadful situation will never end. It is the sense that things that are bad will never get better. It is the belief that the future holds more of the same badness and pain manifested in the present. The more convinced the person is that the situation is hopeless, the more the danger of suicide. A related notion is helplessness, which is the sense that a terrible situation is beyond one's capacity to change. Of course, helplessness contributes to the sense of hopelessness. If a bad situation is beyond one's ability to change, it will never end.

Combining these two major risk factors, that is, mental illness and a sense of hopelessness, one can understand why the mental illnesses that most endure (major depression, bipolar disorder, and schizophrenia) are those most associated with risk of suicide. Since these illnesses can be overwhelmingly difficult to resolve, some persons with them may conclude that they will never recover and that the pain will never end. That is, they will become hopeless about recovery from the illness, which greatly increases their risk of suicide. This may explain why 1 in 6 persons with major depression will attempt suicide, and as many as 1 in 100 persons with either major depression or bipolar disorder will kill themselves. Similarly, as many as 4 in 10 persons with schizophrenia will attempt suicide, and as many as 1 in 10 will be dead by suicide within 10 years of initial diagnosis.

Another major risk factor for suicide is a previous attempt. At the least, a prior attempt demonstrates that a person has the capacity to act in suicidal fashion. Also, appalling as it sounds, research suggests that prior attempts are a form of practice. Previous attempts may act to desensitize the person, so that he grows to fear the act of suicide less and less.

Finally, *feeling like a burden* ("burdensomeness") to others is a substantial risk factor. The person may believe, "My parents (children, spouse, family, friends) would be better off without me." She may believe she is a bother and a burden to others and that loved ones would otherwise have a good life if not for her. Virginia Woolf declared this explicitly in her suicide note to her husband Leopold: "I am doing what seems the best thing to do. . . . I know that I am spoiling your life". Probably this helps explain the relatively high risk of suicide among the elderly, who are no longer working ("no longer contributing"), who are perhaps sick (using up savings that could otherwise be left to loved ones), and who are using up the time of others who need to take them to doctors' appointments and so forth. They may feel like a burden, which may make them feel an obligation to end their own life.

Reducing Risk Factors

Some risk factors for suicide can be neither reduced nor eliminated. You cannot change someone's risk due to gender, nor can you givesomeone back years of his or her life. Other risk factors can be reduced, however.

For example, mental illness is a risk for suicide, especially if the person lacks confidence that the illness can be alleviated. Thus, it is essential that a person with a mental illness be in treatment with a mental health professional who is not only competent but who expresses *confidence* that things can get better. Competent care will reduce the distress attributable to the illness, and a confident attitude will also directly challenge the person's sense of hopelessness.

Another example of mitigating risk factors concerns access to means. As noted in the previous section, suicidal behavior is often impulsive, so eliminating or reducing access to means to commit suicide is an essential aspect of prevention. Partly for this reason, the serotonin-reuptake inhibitors (or SRIs, such as Prozac) were eagerly welcomed by psychiatrists. Ironically, the previous versions of antidepressants could actually be dangerous if taken in excess, whereas the SRIs do not carry this risk. Prior to the SRIs, psychiatrists had to balance the effort to alleviate the depression by prescribing antidepressants with the concern about giving the patient with severe depression the means to harm himself or herself. In a different example, mental health professionals routinely ask patients with whom they have concern of suicide whether they own a gun or other readily available means (such as sleeping pills) for committing suicide. If such means exist, the mental health professional may ask the patient to remove the gun or the sleeping pills (or whatever means is mentioned) from the household, such as by asking a friend, neighbor, or parent to keep it, until treatment has decreased their depression enough that suicide risk is reduced.

Asking About and Intervening in Suicidal Crises

The following section has recommendations for asking about suicide and for how to respond to suicidal crises. It begins with a discussion of when a pastor or church worker should ask about suicide risk and why they should do so.

When to Evaluate Suicide Risk

The answer to the question "When should I ask someone if he or she is considering suicide?" is different for mental health professionals than it is for pastors and church workers.

Different Situations

Someone who seeks a meeting with a mental health professional is either distressed, impaired, or both. If the person is highly distressed, she probably voluntarily sought professional help. If he is impaired but not particularly distressed, he was perhaps referred for professional help. Thus will most persons who come to see a mental health professional have one or more risk factors for suicide. It is thereby imperative that a mental health professional ask about suicide risk at some point in the first meeting and perhaps during later meetings as well.

Pastors and church workers will usually encounter different situations, such that they cannot assume that the person with whom they are meeting has suicide risk factors. For example, unlike mental health professionals, pastors and church workers may actively seek or request a meeting with a parishioner because they have observed something that concerns them. Likewise, parishioners will seek meetings with pastors for a variety of reasons, such as for spiritual counsel, to make complaints about the church, to make suggestions or recommendations, or to organize upcoming events (e.g., the marriage of a child). It would be odd indeed to incorporate into these meetings questions about suicide risk.

Myths and Realities About Suicide

Myth: People who talk about suicide will not attempt it. They are doing it to get attention.

Reality: Someone who talks about suicide is making an attempt to get help. He or she is in great distress and should be taken seriously.

Myth: A person who has attempted suicide will never attempt again.

Reality: A person who has attempted suicide is at much greater risk of another attempt or of suicide completion. Not only are future suicide attempts more probable, they are also likely to be much more serious.

Myth: Improvement following a suicidal crisis means that the suicide risk is over.

Reality: The months following a suicidal crisis can be the most dangerous time as the person may feel more conviction and have more emotional energy to follow through with a suicide attempt.

Myth: It is dangerous to disclose to others that someone has admitted to suicide risk (that is, you should respect his or her privacy).

Reality: If a person is suicidal, there cannot be absolute confidentiality. The primary duty is to protect his or her safety. If this requires breaking confidentiality, then you should do so. More typically, however, you can convince the person to tell others himself or herself (e.g., tell her therapist or psychiatrist so that he or she can be hospitalized).

Myth: A person intent on suicide cannot be stopped.

Reality: Suicide is preventable.

When to Ask

Nonetheless, pastors and church workers should ask about suicide risk in some situations. The reader will hopefully notice that these situations track closely with the risk factors identified earlier. The need to assess suicide risk is especially critical if the person is not in treatment with a mental health professional.

If there is any evidence of distress related to mental illness, ask about suicide risk. If the person seems depressed or anxious, is attempting to recover from a substance use disorder, has schizophrenia, or is otherwise highly distressed, you should ask about suicide. Likewise, if there are severe interpersonal problems or other stressors that put the person at risk, you should ask about suicide. These would include personal loss (e.g., recent divorce or widowhood), recent or worsening financial problems, feeling alienated from others, diagnosis of a terminal illness, or a physical illness that causes unremitting pain.

Finally, any time you have a sense that the person with whom you are interacting may be considering suicide, ask about it. In other words, never ignore your gut instinct. If during a meeting you develop the sense that the person is at risk of self-harm, he or she has somehow, in some subtle way, indicated to you that risk. You may not be able to articulate the reasons for your concern, but it is important that you follow your instinct in such a potentially serious situation. At worst, if you ask and your gut instinct is proven wrong, then you may be slightly embarrassed. However, you will have communicated to the person that you are trying to pay attention and that you care about his or her well-being.

The Reasons to Evaluate Suicide Risk

The reasons pastors and church workers should ask about suicide are more extensive than the reasons a mental health professional would ask. The obvious reason is to identify suicidal crises (i.e., someone in imminent danger) so that the crisis can be averted.

In addition, both mental health professionals and church workers should ask so that suicidal ideation (but not necessarily a crisis) can be uncovered. Suicidal ideation invariably indicates a fairly severe mental illness and high potential for future risk. If uncovered, referral to a mental health professional is necessary. If the person is already in treatment, then consultation with the treating professional may be necessary to alert him or her of the suicidal ideation. This is something that mental health professionals routinely do with each other. For example, if I am seeing someone for psychotherapy and the patient discloses suicidal ideation, I will communicate this to the treating psychiatrist. Ideally, you will alert a treating mental health professional after seeking and obtaining the person's permission. But keep in mind that you should alert the mental health professional even if the person hesitates or declines to give you such permission. The mental health professional, not you, is the expert in dealing with suicidal ideation, and you cannot keep this information to yourself. Also keep in mind, however, that it may not be necessary to alert the mental health professional at all if you can be reassured by the person that the clinician is already aware of the situation.

The other reasons that pastors and church workers should evaluate suicide risk are related to the assurances that you can offer, which a mental health professional cannot. These are discussed beginning on p. 400 in the section entitled "A Proper Christian Reaction to Suicidal Crises and Tragedies."

How to Ask About Suicide Risk

As detailed in the previous chapter, asking someone about domestic abuse can be complex and potentially fraught with danger to a victim. In contrast, it is neither difficult nor dangerous to ask about and identify a person at risk of suicide. In order to identify the person at risk of suicide, you need to look close and get close. You need to hear and accept, without judgment, the pain that the person is experiencing. Then you need to ask explicitly about suicide risk.

Look Closely

The typical exchange between people entails one blithely asking another, "How are you?" Most people reply equally mindlessly, "Fine, how are you?" Even someone with depression, being polite and socially appropriate, will lie and say "Fine," even though she is not.

In contrast, seeing that someone has a mental illness or is in some other way suffering requires looking close and seeing what is there. When you ask, "How are you?" mean what you ask and pay attention to the answer. It is fairly easy to see if someone is faking when she replies "Fine." She won't look fine. She will look sad and overwhelmed. She may look like she hopes you will ask more. Thus, looking closely may mean digging past the first answer. If someone doesn't look fine, you might gently respond, "You don't look well. Is there anything going on?" If the person is willing, follow up. In other words, getting close follows looking close.

Get Close

Getting close means approaching the individual and discussing that person's pain. Most people are not willing to do this, preferring a blithe response ("I'm fine") to a real dialogue about the pain life so regularly delivers. Getting close will require some privacy, obviously. Thus, if you are not in a place where you can talk bluntly and openly, arrange a private appointment. When doing this, moreover, be sure that there is enough time for a long talk.

In the private setting, ask again how the person is doing. For example, you might say, "I have been feeling concerned about you lately," "Recently, I have noticed some differences in you and wondered how you are doing," or "I wanted to check in with you because you haven't seemed yourself lately."

A similar approach might be to inquire about details of the person's life with which are are already familiar. Inquire especially about those things you know can be stressful, such as "How is the family? How is work? How is the job search going? Any update on the illness? How is treatment (for the mental illness) going?"

In other words, ask about the person's pain and be patient in waiting for a reply. Respond in a way that encourages him to tell you (versus the usual response of others, who communicate that they are not really interested). In other words, respond empathically.

Demonstrate Empathy and Acceptance

The most helpful thing to do with anyone experiencing intense distress, whether due to mental illness or not, is to be empathic (see p. 46 in chapter 5). Empathy means recognizing and accepting what the other person is experiencing. Keep in mind that you can be empathic without knowing the reasons behind someone's thinking or feeling. For example, you may not know why someone is depressed, but you can show that you realize she is and accept that she is. Likewise, you can be empathic while understanding why someone thinks or feels a certain way, while not agreeing with the reasons for those thoughts or feelings. For example, a woman may think that no one loves her and may therefore feel depressed. You might fervently disagree with the thought ("No one loves me") that is causing the depression, but you can nonetheless recognize and accept that the thought and feeling exist.

In other words, being empathic means recognizing and accepting the other person's thoughts and feelings without evaluating that person and, especially, without trying to correct that person. Empathy means being present and accepting. It means standing with the person in his or her pain, without feeling that pain. (Feeling someone else's pain is sympathy).

Empathy should be active. It does no good to be empathic with someone if that someone does not experience it. Empathy is something that should be communicated to the person in pain, such as "I can tell that you are in a lot of pain." Regardless of what the person is experiencing—whether they are terribly sad, in pain, stressed to their threshold of endurance, overwhelmed by anxiety, or in despair over their situation—communicate that you understand and that you accept what they are experiencing.

This is probably easier for Christians than for others. Christians don't look for sorrow and pain, but we don't flee in fear when we see it. Christians do not hold to the false idea that life should only be wonderful and joyous, and we reject the idea that to experience pain and sorrow is somehow pathetic and wrong. Christians understand that life can be tumultuous and difficult. We accept sorrow and anguish as part of this life, knowing that they are the inevitable result of sin. Christians take consolation in the redemptive sacrifice of our Savior, for "where sin increased, grace increased all the more, so that, just as sin reigned in death, so also grace might reign through righteousness to bring eternal life through Jesus Christ our Lord" (Romans 5:20,21).

Better than most, Christians can accept that the person in front of them is suffering. Indeed, we can accept that this person is suffering so greatly that he or she might be thinking what so many of the faithful through history have thought, that it would be better to depart this world to be with God.

Ask Directly

In summary, it is helpful to accept that someone might be considering suicide. But we also act however is necessary to stop the person from following through on that desire. To do so means asking explicitly about suicide risk, when necessary. On first reflection, the act of asking someone if he is suicidal seems difficult. It seemed to me that way when I began my career as a psychologist. After doing it a few times, I realized that, in practice, it is not particularly difficult. Let us walk through an imaginary scenario to demonstrate this.

Imagine that you and I are chatting during our first meeting. You sought my professional care because you have been depressed for a few months and your spouse finally insisted that you see someone. Over the course of our first meeting, you tell me about the pain of recently losing your parent, recent disappointments at work, feelings of alienation from your family, and the uncertainty about whether you have chosen the right career. You report that you have been depressed, that you have been having trouble sleeping and eating, and that you don't know what to do. At some point in the conversation, I will say the following: "Things are really not going too well for you right now. Sometimes when people are as down as you are, they may think about hurting themselves or killing themselves. Have you ever had thoughts like that?"

There are two possible scenarios. Either you have had such thoughts or you have not had such thoughts. Imagine you have indeed had thoughts about suicide. When I ask you if you have had them, your reaction will likely be one of immense relief. You probably haven't been able to tell anyone about these thoughts and weren't sure how to tell me. But I asked and gave you the opportunity to discuss them. The reason you haven't told anyone else about them is that you are ashamed about having them. (They are terrible thoughts! Who would have such thoughts?) But I just asked about them, and by doing so I reassured you that they are actually fairly common for people in great distress. What a relief. You are not abnormal after all. In response, you will likely say, "Yes, I have had those thoughts." You would then either reassure me that they have been thoughts only, or you and I would talk about how frequent and how serious the thoughts have been, so that I can determine your level of risk and take appropriate precautions.

The other possible scenario is very unlikely. That is, it is hard to imagine that a person who is not thinking about suicide will react with anger when asked if he is thinking about it. Instead, when I ask someone in distress whether he has had thoughts of suicide, but he has *not* had such thoughts, he reassures me that this is not the case and shows appreciation at my effort to understand. I have asked this question hundreds of times. The vast majority of people are not thinking about suicide, and they usually will say something like, "No, I'm not thinking like that. Things are bad, but I'm not thinking about suicide." In other words, at worst, the question will be seen as caring.

One more point about asking about suicide. Most students, including myself when I started my career, fear that asking about suicide will put the idea into the other person's head. In other words, they fear that the client will respond, "I had not been thinking about suicide, but now that you mention it, I realize what a great idea that is! I'm going to go kill myself! Thanks, Doc!" This is a very common fear, but it is also clearly absurd.

How to Ask About Suicide

There are several goals when asking someone about suicide. The primary goal is to get an honest answer. To get an honest answer, work toward the goal of normalizing the experience of suicidal thinking (and even intent), which serves the goal of getting the person to feel less ashamed.

This is how I ask. It works well, and I recommend you use this.

> "Sometimes when people are feeling as distressed as you have been feeling, they have thoughts of hurting themselves or even of killing themselves. Has this been your experience? Have you had any thoughts like that?"

I have asked the previous questions to hundreds of patients. I require my students to memorize the statement and questions before they begin working with their own patients. They are easy to memorize, and I strongly encourage you to do so.

The statement communicates that you *understand* that she is in great distress. This does not communicate that you understand why she is in distress, as you may not, but it does communicate, very importantly, that you recognize that the distress is there. It expresses appreciation of the pain and helps her feel she is not alone.

It also acknowledges that many people in distress think about suicide, which normalizes the experience. It does not encourage the experience, nor does it indicate that the experience is irrelevant or unimportant. It simply normalizes it, which will alleviate her shame and her sense of alienation from others.

The statement communicates that you have some expertise and understanding of the issue. It shows that you know something about her distress that she did not know (i.e., that suicidal thoughts are common).

Perhaps most importantly of all, it communicates that you are okay if she is having these thoughts—you are probably a person she admires, and you may be one of her ministers in her faith—and that you don't think she is weak, weird, bad, or stupid for having them.

If the person responds yes, then I proceed to ask whether they are thoughts only or whether they have actually planned a suicidal act. Follow-up questions might include the following:

"Can you tell me about those thoughts?"

"Have you actually made any plans on how you might do it?"

"Have you ever actually done anything to hurt or to try to kill yourself?"

The Advantages of Directly Asking About Suicide Risk

There are numerous reasons to ask directly about suicide risk. First and foremost, *most* persons who are suicidal will admit so if asked. (In the same way, those who are not suicidal will state that they are not.) If someone admits suicide risk, you can take action to reduce that risk.

Another advantage, however, is that directly asking someone about his or her risk of suicide reduces that very risk. By asking directly, expressing concern, and trying to understand, you have directly attacked the person's sense of isolation. By showing that you care, you make him feel cared for, and his sense of being alone and unlovable will be weakened. Relatedly, by talking about such important things, the person realizes that she can talk about important things. She will realize that how she is feeling is not something that needs to be hidden from others.

A third advantage of directly asking about suicide is that it potentially exposes irrational thinking, even to the person at risk, which also can reduce the risk. For example, someone may admit to suicide risk because "no one loves me." When patients have said that to me, I sometimes respond with a silent, quizzical look, to which they respond by saying, "Okay, that sounds ridiculous, I admit, but things are bad."

Related to this, recall that the vast majority of persons who are considering suicide are *ambivalent.* They are not certain that they want to die. (One report estimated that perhaps only 1 in 20 persons who attempt suicide are truly determined to die.) Directly asking about suicide risk encourages the person to be aware of the one-sided nature (so to speak) and definitiveness of suicide. In other words, asking directly about suicide encourages the person considering suicide to be aware that he is thinking that suicide is the only option. Mental health professionals refer to this as "tunnel vision," wherein a person is limited in what he or she can see. The simple act of asking directly about suicide puts that drastic option into stark focus, and it thereby encourages (but does not ensure) the person to see that his thinking is extremely limited.

How *Not* to Ask About Suicide

In addition to ways you should ask about suicide, there are ways that you should not ask about suicide.

Do not argue with the person who admits to contemplating suicide. To argue is to imply that the person is wrong. Likewise, do not lecture the person on the way he or she "should" be thinking. For example, do not say, "You have so much to live for," "Look on the bright side of things," or "You should not be feeling this way."

Do not promise the person that you will keep what he or she says confidential. Refuse to be sworn to secrecy. If necessary, you will break confidentiality to save his or her life by speaking to a mental health professional or by sending the person to the hospital.

You want to avoid anything that implies that only people who are weak, stupid, or bad have thoughts about suicide, such as:

- "You're not thinking of killing yourself, are you?" or "You're not going to do something stupid, are you?"

  (Implied: "Only an idiot would think like that. If you are thinking like that, then you are an idiot.")

- "It would be a real shame if you were thinking of killing yourself."

  (Implied: "You would be shameful if you were having suicidal thoughts. People, including me, will think badly of you if you are.")
- "I'm sure you're not thinking of killing yourself. That would be bad, and I know you wouldn't do that. You wouldn't do that to others. God doesn't want you to do that."

  (Implied: "You would be a horrible person who committed an unforgivable sin if you were to have these thoughts.")

How to Respond to Suicide Crises

There are three possible responses to the query, "Are you thinking about killing yourself?" The most likely response is "No, I have never thought about suicide." Unless there is contradictory evidence, you can believe the person and assume there is no risk.

The Need for Care Versus the Need for Hospitalization

The next most likely response is "Yes, I have had some thoughts about suicide, but I would never actually do it." Someone who says this is not in danger of suicide but is indicating that he is quite despondent. This person has admitted having suicidal ideation, which greatly enhances the risk of developing suicidal intent. As noted earlier, ideation and intent are distinct. While suicidal ideation is not a crisis, it is important that someone with ideation be referred for treatment. In these cases, express care and concern. Say something to the effect of "You are clearly in a lot of pain. I want you to get some help." Then refer the person to professional treatment.

The least likely response (by far) is some version of "Yes, I have thought about it, and I intend to do so." Someone who says this is in danger of suicide. This person has declared suicide intent, which means that the person has resolved to take his life. This indicates a suicidal crisis that needs to be addressed immediately. The person who intends to kill herself needs to be kept under careful watch, and she may actually need to be hospitalized.

If someone is at immediate suicide risk, you must turn the situation over to professionals. You cannot be the one to help. Inform the person of this, and see if he or she will willingly go to the hospital. In the vast majority of cases, he or she will be willing. (This is related to the person's ambivalence and to the desire to get better, both of which were discussed earlier.) If so, then make sure that this happens. You can drive with him or have someone take him (e.g., by calling a family member).

In those rare instances where the person is not willing to submit to voluntary hospitalization, inform him or her that you are forced to act in order to keep him or her safe. Then call 911.

To repeat, it is essential that readers understand that they are not to take responsibility for the person with suicidal ideation or suicide intent. The importance of referring to professional help has been repeated again and again in the suggestions above, as well as in other chapters. Unless you are a mental health professional, you are not qualified to treat someone with mental illness, much less suicidal ideation or suicide intent.

A Proper Christian Understanding of Suicidal Crises and Tragedies

This section starts with a brief tour of the history of Christian writings about suicide. A proper Christian understanding of suicide, based on the proper present-day understanding of mental illness and the proper theological understanding of the theology of the cross, is briefly presented. (A later chapter discusses a proper Christian understanding of mental illness in greater detail.) The section ends with a discussion of a Christ-centered response to suicidal crises and suicidal tragedies.

Much of the treatise in this section is derived from the excellent book by Reverend Peter Preus entitled *And She Was a Christian* (Northwestern Publishing House, 2011).

Augustine, Aquinas, and the Church Condemn Those Who Commit Suicide

There is a historical precedent of condemnation of suicide. Augustine of Hippo argued that suicide is expressly forbidden by the commandment against murder. Therefore, anyone who commits suicide has committed an unforgiveable sin and must be presumed to be damned. He nonetheless acknowledged some exceptions. He wrote that certain Christian women committed suicide rather than be raped, and he granted that they may have been right to do so. He also made an exception for Samson, who presumably received God's permission to kill himself when God returned to Samson his strength.

Thomas Aquinas concurred with Augustine. In his *Summa Theologica,* Aquinas stated, "Suicide is the most fatal of sins because it cannot be repented of" and "To bring death upon oneself in order to escape the other afflictions of this life is to adopt a greater evil in order to avoid a lesser."

In other words, Augustine and Aquinas were two of the original rationalists. They thus assumed that suicide was a knowing, rational, and reasoned act to end one's suffering. They taught that suicide was an act of unbelief since, at the very least, it is a usurpation of God's authority over life and death. The teachings of these two dominated the church for centuries. Because of these and related teachings, those who committed the unforgivable sin of suicide were not buried with Catholic rites and were not permitted interment in consecrated cemeteries.

Of course, many today are unaware of the historical treatment of suicide by the church. More relevant to most are the typical reactions to suicide of fear and horror.

Fear, Horror, and Other Reactions to Suicide

Confronting suicide generates many emotions and thoughts. Very rarely is the emotion compassion. Instead, usually the emotions are horror, anger, and sadness. People are frightened by suicide. This is at least partly because our society does not talk about death in general, and it especially does not talk about death by suicide. Death and suicide are frightening, and suicide can be difficult to understand, making it even more frightening. When something is scary and mystifying, it tends to make people angry and upset.

Thus, when confronted by suicide, very rarely is the thought, "Somehow this made sense to the person." Usually the thoughts are some version of deprecation and denunciation. In order to create a sense of distance and, thus, safety from suicide, people will try to explain it in ways that allow them to feel confidence that they and the people they know and love are not vulnerable. Thus, people tend to condemn suicidal behavior as a sign of weak character and flawed morals. The person who considers, attempts, or ultimately commits suicide is or was immoral, weak, and selfish.

Misunderstanding Faith and Misunderstanding Suicide

The most difficult aspect regarding suicidal behavior in a Christian is resolving the contradiction between the Christian's faith that God loves and blesses him and the Christian's contemplation about, attempt at, or completion of suicide. A common way to resolve this contradiction is to condemn the person for having weak faith, as did Augustine and Aquinas. The person is or was clearly not a "good Christian" or a "strong Christian." Perhaps the person was not actually a Christian at all. Of course, this might be correct, for no one can really know what another person believes. In the same fashion, by the way, we *could* doubt that a paragon of faith who died recently—someone who attended weekly, was involved in all aspects of the church, was a generous donor, an elder, a good father, and a faithful husband—actually did not believe and actually was not a Christian. Of course, we never hold or profess such doubts about any such person with so many obvious manifestations of faith. We could, but we don't. Somehow, however, we think it is fair to do so with the Christian who considers, attempts, or completes suicide.

The Causes and Consequences of Such Attitudes

Unfortunately, these usual reactions to suicide and suicidal behavior are almost perfectly unhelpful. The family struggling to understand and cope with the suicide of a loved one is not helped by explicit expressions of criticism ("She should not have done that to you!"). They are also not helped by implicit expressions of suspicion ("Were there any warning signs? If there were, you obviously missed them, which means you are obviously not a good spouse/parent.").

The consequences of such attitudes are that persons who contemplate suicide or who survive a suicide attempt, or the family members of the person who completes suicide, are looked at with pity, derision, and suspicion. There are no words of consolation offered. Instead, they are avoided. These Christians are treated as aliens to the Christian faith. Of course, this compounds their distress, putting those at risk of suicide at even greater risk and putting all at risk of rejecting, in turn, the faith of the church that rejected them.

A More Enlightened Attitude Toward Mental Illness

Instead of being reactive and reflexive in our reaction to suicide, we can be reflective and intelligent. We have scientific research that informs us about suicide. We agree with Augustine and Aquinas that the person who contemplates, attempts, or completes suicide is in profound distress. However, unlike those patriarchs, we have scientific knowledge to inform us about that distress. (They had very little by way of scientific research and indeed did not even have the term *mental illness* to guide their thinking.) We understand that the distress is due to some highly painful situation, most commonly from mental illness but due to other causes as well (e.g., terrible loss, painful illness, intense loneliness). We also now know that the person contemplating suicide forced to conclude that the situation will not improve. The sense of hopelessness about ever escaping the pain leads to despondency and despair, for which suicide is the only seeming option. In sum, we agree with Augustine and Aquinas that suicide is an act intended to end suffering, but we now know that most persons who commit suicide have a mental illness that deprives them of rationality and reason.

A Proper Christian Understanding of Suicide

In this section, I presume to remind readers what they already know, what they have been taught, and probably what they themselves teach. It is a necessary thing, as we can be removed from what we know in the face of the horrifying, such as in suicide crises. The horrifying can leave us looking around, at ourselves and at the world, for an explanation, so that we can reassure ourselves that the horrifying is an anomaly, something that should not have happened, something that won't happen again, and therefore something that we need not fear. The strength given to us by our Christian faith enables us to confront the horrifying.

The question is, can faith coexist with thoughts about suicide, attempts at suicide, or suicide tragedies? A proper scriptural understanding of faith leads to a proper understanding of God's grace and forgiveness, and both will help resolve this question.

Luther and Suicide

To begin, let us recall that Martin Luther did not automatically consign suicide tragedies to hell. He wrote, "I don't share the opinion that suicides are certainly to be damned. My reason is that they do not wish to kill themselves but are overcome by the power of the devil. They are like a man who is murdered in the woods by a robber. . . . They are examples by which our Lord God wishes to show that the devil is powerful and also that we should be diligent in prayer. But for these examples we would not fear God" ("Table Talk," *Luther's Works,* American Edition, Vol. 54, p. 29).

Luther was not afraid to acknowledge the reality of sin, which captures us all. Luther preached the objective reality of Christ's saving work, which cannot be deprived of believers regardless of their particular sin. Luther was admonishing us, as he often did, to be clear about what we profess and believe. In his statement about suicide, Luther reminds us that faith is nothing more and nothing less than trust that Christ has died for the forgiveness of our sins.

Tragically, there are many false teachings about faith that directly affect how Christians, if they fall prey to such false teachings, may react to suicide. If we believe in the inevitability of sin, and if we believe in the saving work of Jesus Christ, then these false teachings must be rejected.

False Teachings

Many have heard the false teaching that faith produces a wonderful feeling. Those who do not feel wonderful are left to question whether they truly have faith. This is a pernicious and vicious teaching. A related false teaching is that faith will always in certain ways show itself. We are instructed that we should feel good about our faith if, but only if, we display certain behaviors. For example, we are told that the faithful will always choose good and reject evil. We are told that a faithful Christian will never break any of God's commands. Christians would never commit murder, engage in adultery, or steal. "True Christians" love God's commandments; always conform their thoughts, feelings, and behaviors to those commandments; always feel enthusiastic about life regardless of what must be endured; and are always optimistic about the future. In short, a Christian would never contemplate, attempt, or commit suicide.

Another false teaching is that we are responsible for the strength of our faith. But faith has nothing to do with human agency. Faith is from the Holy Spirit who, through the words of the gospel, enables us to trust in the saving work of Christ. Faith does not look to itself in judgment, and faith does not have faith as its object. Faith does not praise itself as sufficient nor condemn itself as inadequate. Coming to and remaining in faith has nothing to do with our ability or strength. Faith looks only to Christ, having Christ alone as its object. This could not be any clearer in the Bible (e.g., Romans 3:28; Romans 10:17; 1 Corinthians 12:3).

A related false teaching about faith is that it comes from our own reasoning. Although this idea would never be expressed in such stark terms, we may nevertheless say and hear that a Christian never loses the capacity for reason and that reason always leads to faith. A true believer is always reasonable, it is asserted, and will never come to the conclusion that "God hates me and I'd be better off dead."

The true teaching is that faith is not about thinking clearly and reasonably or understanding why God did as he did and does as he does. Human intellect does not help us in our faith. It is not those who "understand" God's Word who are saved; it is those who "hear" God's Word. Christian faith does not depend on reason. Indeed, faith must often oppose reason. What reasonable person believes that we eat and drink the body and blood of Jesus; that Jesus died, was buried, and rose again;

that Jesus ascended into heaven; and that there is life after death? Reason tells us that God's Word makes no sense. As Peter Preus writes, "Faith is not the same thing as [our ability to reason properly]. [By the grace of God], a sick mind does not represent a sick faith" (46,51).

Another false teaching, which might be both the most popular and the most pernicious, is that Christians should never despair but should always be happy and optimistic. The true teaching is that faith is not the same thing as being happy, having hope about one's future, or maintaining a positive view of life. Faith in Christ does not preclude being convinced that things will not become the way we want them to be. Faith in Christ does not exclude the knowledge that God allows us to be in pain. Paul could not be any clearer about this when he wrote, "I was given a thorn in my flesh, a messenger of Satan, to torment me. Three times I pleaded with the Lord to take it away from me. But he said to me, 'My grace is sufficient for you, for my power is made perfect in weakness' " (2 Corinthians 12:7-9). Faithful Christians on occasion, or perhaps more often than that, will experience despair.

Proper Teaching

Ultimately, these false teachings reject the reality of sin. They reject the biblical teaching upon which all of Christianity rests: we are conceived in sin. These false teachings fail to acknowledge that creation was corrupted by sin and that therefore sin manifests itself in corruption. For some, this means physical illness, such as heart disease, diabetes, cancer, or chronic pain. For others it means mental illness, such as depression, schizophrenia, or other chronic emotional pain. These illnesses can lead to despair, which can lead to suicide. Therefore, with regard to suicide, faithful Christians must think and say, "This is awful. This is tragic. This is sin. This is no life." In other words, Christians should respond to suicide by seeking refuge in the saving work of Jesus Christ.

In short, we are saved through the forgiveness of our sins. This and only this is the source of our salvation. We are not saved because our faith is "strong enough." To quote Preus, "Faith does not save because it is particularly trusting, because it is exceptionally uncompromising, or because it is so strong or secure. Faith saves solely because of what it possesses, Christ and his forgiveness."

The true teaching is that faith is not about feeling good and doing good. Human emotions and behavior are not indicators of our faith. Both St. Paul and Martin Luther explicitly reject the false teaching. Paul wrote to the Romans, "I do not understand what I do. For what I want to do I do not do, but what I hate I do. And if I do what I do not want to do, I agree that the law is good. As it is, it is no longer I myself who do it, but it is sin living in me. For I know that good itself does not dwell in me, that is, in my sinful nature. For I have the desire to do what is good, but I cannot carry it out. For I do not do the good I want to do, but the evil I do not want to do—this I keep on doing. Now if I do what I do not want to do, it is no longer I who do it, but it is sin living in me that does it" (Romans 7:15-20). Martin Luther had to remind Christians that believing that they can actually fulfill God's commandments is heresy. In his catechism he reminds us, for example, that hateful thoughts are murder, impure thoughts are adultery, and jealousy of another's possessions is theft. These points are elaborated on in the next section.

A Proper Christian Reaction to Suicidal Crises and Tragedies

Christians should contend with suicide and suicidal behavior in all ways possible. All thoughts and behaviors related to suicide are the product of hopelessness and despair that the pain of life will never end. This thinking is most commonly due to mental illness. Thus, suicidal ideation should be viewed as serious and dangerous, and every effort should be made to get the person to change that thinking. Likewise, suicide attempts must be averted, and suicidal crises must be halted. God gave mental health professionals for these purposes. They are trained to deal with these issues in order to preserve life.

The role of pastors and other church workers in regard to suicidal thinking, suicide attempts, and suicide tragedies is to preserve eternal life, that is, to preserve the person's faith and salvation.

To comfort those contemplating suicide, those who have attempted suicide, and those who are left to cope with the death by suicide of a loved one, preach Christ crucified. Preach that it is wrong to believe that suicidal thinking and suicide attempts occur only in those who have lost faith. That is, never let anyone presume a lack of faith in the gospel on the part of the person considering suicide, the one who acts on these thoughts, or the one who ultimately ends his own life.

Words of Consolation to Those Experiencing Despair

The Christian experiencing suicidal ideation or the one who attempted suicide, like Annie from the beginning of this chapter, needs to be comforted with the gospel. As noted above, you must refer them to a mental health professional or you should encourage them to stay in treatment. (That is, you have recognized the limitation of your expertise and have turned them over to a professional trained in the cure of their dangerous illness.) At the same time, you should stay involved in order to give them what the mental health professional cannot, which is words of consolation from the Bible.

They need to hear two things from you, lest their despair be magnified by guilty concern that, as many have misled them, their faith is weak. First, they need to hear that their suffering is awful and needs to be addressed but that it does not mean a lack of faith. Neither they nor the widow nor the man dying of heart disease nor the child succumbing to leukemia are suffering because of a lack of faith. Second, they need to know that they are not alone, which is to say that God and you (and others) both see and care about their suffering.

Preach that suffering is not a sign of weak faith. Preach that suffering and faith are not incompatible. Remind the despairing what Jesus Christ told us, "In this world you will have trouble. But take heart! I have overcome the world" (John 16:33). As Christ intended, let this be a source of peace to Christians. In other words, preach that suicidal thoughts and attempts are perhaps the most tragic of all tragic results of the corruption of the world caused by sin, but they are not the result of a lack of faith.

Luther said about suffering, "Every Christian must be aware that suffering will not fail to come. That in fact God has appointed that we should suffer and it cannot be otherwise." And, "Our suffering conforms us to our Lord, that we may become like him here in suffering and there in life to come in honor and glory." Luther knew the Bible, where this is stated again and again and again (e.g., Psalm 34:19; 2 Timothy 3:12; 1 Peter 4:12-19; Philippians 1:29).

Thus, we dare not transform or misconstrue the gospel as law, lest we drive the sufferer away from faith. Do not presume that Paul, Peter, James, and others were criticizing those overwhelmed by suffering (e.g., Romans 5:3-5; 1 Peter 4:12,13; James 1:2-4). Do not interpret the words of the gospel as an admonition to be happy about being in despair. The saints were speaking of salvation, not current happiness (Psalm 34:19; 126:6; Romans 8:17,18; Hebrews 10:36; 2 Timothy 2:12; 1 Peter 5:10; Revelation 21:4).

Just as God informs us that we should expect suffering, are we also assured that God sees our suffering? For his reasons, he allows us to endure suffering. But our suffering does not mean he has turned away from us. God did that only to his Son, the sacrificial Lamb who was forsaken on the cross to pay for the sin of the world. God is with us in our suffering.

It is extremely important to reassure the person experiencing despair, which has led him to consider or attempt ending his life, that you and others do not reject him or consider him an alien to the faith. Empathize with his pain. Do not argue about whether it should exist or not, simply empathize with it and accept that it is so. Empathy means understanding the way someone is thinking or feeling but not necessarily thinking or feeling the same way; it means not judging as wrong the thinking or feeling of the individual. As has been repeated throughout this volume, empathy assures the person that he is not a monster, freak, or alien. If you demonstrate that you understand, then what he is thinking or feeling must, by definition, be understandable. The relief provided by this alone cannot be overstated.

Show that you understand the pain the person is or was experiencing. The person who contemplates or attempts suicide despairs of this life. The despair may be due to illness. The despair may be irrational or otherwise difficult to understand. Comfort those despairing that they should not doubt the corruption of this world and of our flesh. Remind them of the power of Satan, who never rests to overcome and destroy even those who have faith.

Words of Consolation to Those Who Have Lost a Loved One to Suicide

The most important thing to tell those grieving the death of a loved one by suicide is that they can be assured their loved one is in heaven, because he or she died in the faith. At least, they should be told not to assume that suicide meant falling away from the faith.

The consolation to the living is that their loved one was baptized and made a child of God and an heir to his kingdom, regardless of what they did. Remind them that Baptism is not a work of man, dependent on the goodness of men. Instead, as Luther reminds us, Baptism is a work of the Lord God, who "is able to save and help from sin, death, devil, and hell with a little drop of water." For we know that "we were therefore buried with him through baptism into death in order that, just as Christ was raised from the dead through the glory of the Father, we too may live a new life" (Romans 6:4).

Reassure the living that suicide is simply one of the many ways that sin and death find their way into the lives of believers. That is, offer the same consolation you would to anyone else mourning the death (also caused by the corruption of this world and of our flesh) of a loved one.

Remind them that we are all conceived in sin, and all of us sin perpetually. Just so, God forgives perpetually. We may be sure every Christian loved one who precedes us in faith is in heaven. Suicide is one sin of many that may find their way into the lives of believers in the final moments of their lives. Having been conceived in sin, all of us sin perpetually. By God's grace, however, we are also forgiven perpetually.

Reassure the grieving by preaching Christ crucified. Reassure that their loved one is in heaven, despite what they did, because God chose them as one of his own, and God does not forsake his children.

Lord, If You Had Been Here, My Loved One Would Not Have Died

Many people wonder "Where was God?" when a loved one dies. It is probably fair to state that this question resonates even louder for those who lose a loved one to suicide. With his permission, I reprint part of the text of a sermon Reverend Jeremy Mills gave at the funeral of my nephew, Max, who died tragically in 2011, at the young age of 23. The consolation of these words can be used to comfort survivors of suicide tragedies.

Max's Funeral Sermon

> *"'Lord,' Martha said to Jesus, 'if you had been here, my brother would not have died.'"* (John 11:21)

Jesus arrived in Bethany and found a group of mourners just like us. The question on Martha's lips aimed at Jesus that day has been asked I'm sure by all of us at some point in these past few days: "Lord, if you would have only been here . . . my brother, my son, my grandson, my friend would not have died. You could have prevented it."

Some say death is a natural process of life, but we know better. Death is the most unnatural thing. Eternity has been placed into our very beings so that when someone dies the pain and anguish felt is like nothing that can be described in words. And the response to death is anger. Anger directed at this broken world we live in, anger directed at ourselves for not being there or doing more, anger directed at God over the sin and suffering we experience in our short lives here on earth. We can understand Martha's question because it's a good question: "Why God? Why now? Why him? Why me? Lord, if you'd only been there to stop it or at the very least let me stop it—if only I would have driven him to work, kept him on the phone but a few more minutes, hugged him a little longer—he would still be here today." This way of thinking is torturous to our minds.

To Martha and to us, Jesus speaks words of release and words of hope: "[He] will rise again" (John 11:23). We must let go of the idea that we are in control of our lives. Control is an illusion and we must trust that God is in control. We must heed the words of God when he says, "My thoughts are not your thoughts, neither are your ways my ways" (Isaiah 55:8). We must pray as Jesus prayed, "Thy will be done," no matter how hard it is.

Jesus' response to Martha was no flippant answer to death but was rather a heartfelt message from God. The Word made flesh, bearing the sins of the world—carrying the pain of Martha and Mary and the pains of all the world, even ours—spoke real comfort: "I am the resurrection and the life" (John 11:25).

As he stared upon the grave of Lazarus, Jesus wept. In that moment, he gives us a glimpse into the compassion of God. God weeps over death. When Max died, God wept. He wept because he knew Max. He created him, knit him in his mother's womb, numbered his hairs and his days. He knew Max. He saved him through the waters of Holy Baptism. He knew Max. All of his idiosyncrasies, his gentle and humble heart, his sense of humor, his artistic side. He knew his sorrows and struggles. He still knows him today as they share eternal company with each other. God weeps because it was never meant to be this way. It was never God's will that any of us should die. God weeps over the brokenness of his creation, over the deaths of his saints, over sin and its consequences. Although it's not God's will that Max died, God knew the date and time he would take his servant. And this past Wednesday, Max attained the number of days on this earth that God had appointed for him.

And so we mourn. But we do so with hope knowing that Jesus mourns too and he will not stand idly by and watch his children suffer. God is a God of life. God in Christ joined himself to human misery and death to bring an end to suffering, to bring an end to grief, to wipe away every tear from our eyes, and to crush once and for all the sting and penalty of death. Christ shared our mortal life so that he might share his immortality with Max and with us. Through his death on the cross, he conquered death. Through his resurrection, he imparted life.

Jesus wept that day at the grave of Lazarus, but he also spoke: "Lazarus, come out" (John 11:43). What he did that day in Bethany was small and personal. He will do it again, large and universal. On that final day the trumpets will sound and Christ our Lord will call to his children, including Max: "Come out."

And just like Lazarus, we too will be raised, not just for a little while, but for all eternity: "So will it be with the resurrection of the dead. The body that is sown is perishable, it is raised imperishable; it is sown in dishonor, it is raised in glory; it is sown in weakness, it is raised in power" (1 Corinthians 15:42,43). So says the Lord of life.

THREE

PART 3

THE PROPER WAY FOR A CHRISTIAN TO UNDERSTAND AND ADDRESS MENTAL ILLNESS

Preview of Part 3

The last part of this volume provides an argument for the proper way in which Christians should understand mental illness. Chapter 19 presents some of the misunderstandings many people have about mental illness. Some of this misunderstanding has been generated by misguided individuals, but some is directly attributable to corrupt and malignant organizations. Some of this misunderstanding is due to a misunderstanding of the Bible. For example, some Christians believe that if a person's faith is strong enough, then a person will not suffer anxiety, depression, or any other mental health issue. As will be shown in Chapter 20, this is contradictory to the Old and New Testaments, to the teachings of Jesus Christ, to the writings of St. Paul and other epistle authors, and to the interpretation of all of these by numerous theologians from antiquity to today.

Based on this, chapter 21 addresses the proper way that individual Christians should react when they experience a mental illness or, more likely, are faced with the sacred task of helping a fellow believer who is suffering from the effects of mental illness.

Chapter 19

Common Misunderstandings About Mental Illness

"As [Jesus] went along, he saw a man blind from birth. His disciples asked him, 'Rabbi, who sinned, this man or his parents, that he was born blind?' "
(John 9:1,2)

Human nature desires that bad things be understandable and predictable so that they can be controlled and avoided. If a bad thing, such as blindness, can be explained, then its occurrence in the future can be prevented and the bad thing is less frightening. Examples of this are easy to find. The days and weeks following a plane crash are filled with efforts to explain how it happened. When others hear that Joe was badly injured in a car accident, they immediately wonder if he did something to cause it ("Was he driving too fast?"). When Nina is diagnosed with cancer, others might be dismayed to observe that there is no identifiable cause ("And she didn't even smoke!"). We want terrible things to have a cause, so that those causes (faulty planes, driving too fast, smoking) can be eliminated or avoided so that the bad thing won't happen to us.

A corollary of wanting to understand why bad things happen is a strong preference for simple explanations and solutions. Simple explanations are easy to understand, and simple solutions are easy to implement.

Mental illnesses are bad things, and human beings want simple explanations and fixes. This is not easy, however. First, mental illnesses tend to be complex. There are many versions of mental illness and, as often as not, the same person may have more than one mental illness (called comorbidity). Also, mental illnesses seldom have simple causes or explanations. There are current and past causes. There are biological causes and environmental causes. Sometimes the environment changes biology, leading to mental illness. Finally, mental illnesses rarely have simple solutions. Unlike infections, there are no pills to eliminate them. Unlike broken bones, stabilizing a mental illness and giving it time to heal doesn't work.

Despite all of this, there has been an astonishing proliferation of simplistic notions about the various mental illnesses, including how a person with mental illness will usually look and act, what causes mental illness, and how the mental illnesses should be treated. Some of these ideas can be charitably dismissed as misguided. Others can be shown to be purposeful in obfuscation and malignant in intent.

Both this chapter and the following chapter review various misunderstandings regarding the what and the why of mental illness. This chapter starts with a discussion of the sources of commonly accepted information (and misinformation) about mental illness. This is followed by a review of the most commonplace misunderstandings about mental illness, such as the idea that persons with mental illness are dangerous and unpredictable and that mental health treatment is ineffective. Also reviewed is the preposterous, corrupt, and tragically commonplace notion that mental illness does not exist, a notion that is promoted most assiduously by Scientology. The terrible effect that these ideas have on persons with mental illness is also presented. The chapter ends with an attempt to summarize correct information about the manifestations, causes, and treatment of mental illness.

Socially-Endorsed Stigma Toward Mental Illness

America's attitudes toward mental illness are intensely negative and stigmatizing. Such attitudes are so normative and ubiquitous that they largely go unnoticed and unappreciated. To be sure, however, those suffering from mental illness frequently notice them. Moreover, stigmatizing attitudes have extremely damaging effects.

Simplistic Ideas About Autism

Severe autism is a terrible disorder that begins in childhood and causes profound impairment in social functioning. There have been several simple explanations, with easy-to-implement solutions, for autism. One example of this is Andrew Wakefield's (chapter 14). Another is "facilitated communication."

In the early 1990s, "facilitated communication" (FC) was promoted across the United States and Canada as a miracle approach to autism. Advocates claimed that many persons with severe autism, despite their apparent profound intellectual and social impairment, actually possessed normal levels of intelligence and the capacity for meaningful communication. They claimed that physical incapacity for spoken language, not autism, caused problems with communication and, thus, the appearance of limited intellect. By "facilitating" communication, previously uncommunicative persons with autism (and other disorders) could express themselves. FC involved trained facilitators holding and steadying the hands of persons with autism (and others) while they typed or pointed to keys. The results were astonishing. Children and adults who had been mute their whole lives were suddenly, finally able to communicate. They could now tell others what they were thinking, how they were feeling, and what they did and did not like to do. Parents learned that their child didn't really like strawberry jam or preferred Mr. Rogers to Sesame Street. Some with severe autism wrote vivid essays and composed beautiful poetry. Others expressed loneliness in their writing, saying they were sad that others ignored them on the assumption they had nothing to say. Shockingly, some described experiences of abuse, and some parents and caregivers faced criminal prosecution.

Proponents of FC did (and still do) assert that the complex problems of autism and mental retardation actually had a simple cause and an equally simple solution. FC thereby caused great excitement. The procedure was fervently embraced by some parents in the hope that their children were, in actuality, normal.

Unfortunately, when researchers conducted controlled studies, FC was shown to be completely useless. For example, when researchers posed simple questions to the children with severe autism, the test revealed that the children could only provide the correct answer when the facilitator knew the answer. If the facilitator could not see an object that the child was asked to name, the child could not name it. It was concluded that facilitators were helping, unintentionally, persons with severe autism to answer questions.

Based on the findings of such studies, the American Psychiatric Association, the American Psychological Association, and the Autism National Committee have declared that FC has no validity. Facilitated communication was promoted as a very simple solution to a terrible and complex problem, and it turned out to be untrue.

Sources of Stigma

The easiest explanation for the source of stigmatizing ideas about mental illness is that everyone is raised with those ideas. Stigma against mental illness, in other words, is an American social norm.

Social norms are ideas and expectations about how to think and behave that are generally agreed upon by those in a certain group or culture. Simple examples of American norms, which are not necessarily shared by other cultures, include greeting each other with a handshake, eating three meals per day (usually while sitting), making eye contact when engaged in conversation, and maintaining "personal space" (Americans prefer about four feet of distance, which is double the preference of some European countries).

Social norms are learned over the course of a lifetime in a variety of ways. Some are explicitly taught, such as teaching children to say "please" and "thank you." Others are taught implicitly. They are learned by observing others or by experiencing the reactions of others. They are also learned through everyday interactions and conversations with others, including family, friends, teachers, and colleagues. Examples of implicitly taught social norms may include dressing nicely for church service or becoming a fan of the local team. Many older readers were probably raised in families where racism was the norm. (Fortunately, norms can be unlearned.) Norms are reinforced by national conversations conducted in news reports on television, in newspapers, and in magazines, and also by the stories told through books, television shows, and movies.

Some norms are so widely and readily accepted that they go unnoticed and thus unappreciated. For example, a generally underappreciated social norm in America is generosity. Never in human history has there been a country as compassionate and generous as the United States, not just in the instances of disasters but moment-to-moment and day-to-day. Similarly, some norms are so pervasive it is difficult to pinpoint how they came to be normative. For example, the "norm" for female beauty started to change in the 1960s toward, among other things, a requirement to be unrealistically thin, but the reason for the change is unclear.

As these last two examples illustrate, some social norms are positive (such as the American norm of generosity), whereas others are negative (such as the norm of unrealistic thinness). Social norms toward mental illness are most definitely negative.

Personal Experience

Social norms about mental illness may either be reinforced or challenged by additional exposure to mental illness. Media stories tend to reinforce stigmatizing attitudes. For example, when news stories describe how a person with a mental illness attacked a stranger, then the commonly accepted idea "Persons with mental illness are dangerous" will be reinforced. In contrast, personal experience with and exposure to persons who have a mental illness tend to challenge stigmatizing ideas about mental illness.

For example, interacting with the typical person suffering from anxiety, depression, schizophrenia, or any other mental illness usually demonstrates that the person is, in fact, quite similar to everyone else. It can be surprising to realize that persons with mental illness are most often simply distressed, slightly or greatly ashamed, and generally quite anxious about what others may think of them.

A common challenge to stigmatizing attitudes is to be newly informed that a long-time friend or acquaintance has a history of mental illness. This happens fairly frequently, since most persons with mental illness are successfully able to hide that fact.

The most intense challenge to negative attitudes toward mental illness happens when someone develops a mental illness, which one in five persons in any given year will do.

Unfortunately, regardless of their personal experiences with others, some will continue to endorse stigmatizing beliefs about mental illness. Family members may accuse the person with mental illness of being manipulative (e.g., pretending the illness is worse than it is). Others may gossip about or avoid interacting with the ill person. Most sadly of all, many persons with mental illness endorse highly negative attitudes toward mental illness and, thus, toward themselves.

A Variety of Stigmatizing Beliefs About Mental Illness

There are a variety of commonly accepted ideas about mental illness, about persons with mental illness, and about those related to someone with a mental illness.

Mental Illness Happens to Those of Weak Character

A dominant American social norm is that we shape our own destiny. Americans are taught to believe that we can control the things that are essential to personal success. We are obsessed with personal control. We praise extreme ambition, fortitude in the face of adversity, and unwavering dedication to personal progress. We likewise collectively believe there is no reason that someone cannot continually improve one's self and one's life. That is, if we try hard enough, we will succeed. Relatedly, if we are doing things correctly, we will never suffer.

Extending this to mental illness, it follows that persons who develop a mental illness are at fault. All emotional disorders comprise problems in the way a person thinks, feels, and behaves. As we are taught to believe that the way we think, feel, and act is always and entirely under our control, the idea that mental illness is due to weakness is inevitable. The person with depression needs not think in such depressing fashion, the person with anxiety needs to lighten up, the person with a substance use disorder needs to stop behaving that way, and so forth. In short, the most common stigma agaist mental illness is that there is some weakness of character that led the person to develop it.

Some Christians even extend this faulty notion to faith, believing that anyone who has a strong enough faith will not develop a mental illness. This odious and dangerous idea is addressed in the following chapter.

Mental Illness Is Voluntary

Some people endorse the idea that some embrace mental illness purposefully. The idea is that the person's thinking or behavior is voluntary and self-inflicted. This stigmatizing attitude has been applied to all of the disorders, including depression ("He just needs to stop feeling sorry for himself!"), anxiety ("She needs to stop looking for things to upset her!"), and even the psychotic disorders ("He needs to take better care of himself"). It is especially applied to the substance use disorders and the eating disorders, as these are principally disorders of behavior, which is seen as more controllable than thinking and feeling.

A related stigmatizing attitude is that the person is only pretending to have a mental illness or that the person "enjoys" having the mental illness. This attitude is exhibited when people describe the person with anxiety as "a worry wart" or the person with depression as "reveling in her misery." Pretending to have a mental illness does happen, of course, but it happens only rarely. (See box.)

Malingering and Factitious Disorder

The notion that mental illness is voluntary has a weak but real basis in reality. Persons who pretend to be ill are "malingering" or can be diagnosed with "factitious disorder" (from the Latin word for "artificial").

Persons who malinger do not have a mental illness. They are lying. A malingerer pretends to have a mental illness because he wants to be relieved of having to work, to qualify for disability, or to receive an insurance settlement. Malingering is fairly difficult to pull off with physical problems, as doctors have scanning technology (X-rays, etc.) and objective tests to evaluate physical health. On the other hand, malingering a mental illness can be fairly simple. All mental health professionals rely almost entirely on self-report to determine whether a person has the symptoms of a mental illness, such as depressed mood, hallucinations, nightmares, excessive worries, and so forth. That said, it is believed that malingering a mental illness is uncommon, but if it is suspected, a properly trained professional can recognize malingering for what it is.

Someone with factitious disorder also is pretending to have an illness, including a mental illness. However, he or she pretends in order to gain attention for being sick, in contrast to the malingerer who pretends in hopes of some external gain.

Persons With Mental Illness Are Unpredictable and Dangerous

The most widespread belief about persons with mental illness is that they are unpredictably dangerous. The belief is as old as the origins of Western civilization.

Antiquity and into the Middle Ages. According to Plato, when a friend observed to Socrates that many citizens of Athens were "mad," the philosopher contradicted this by stating, "How could we live in safety with so many crazy people? Should we not long ago . . . have been struck and beaten and endured every other form of ill usage which madmen are wont to inflict?" Likewise, the ancient playwright Plautus had a character explain why a maid took up a sword and was threatening everyone: "She's gone crazy." In ancient Greece and Rome and into the Middle Ages and the Renaissance, persons caring for persons with mental illness were explicitly instructed by authorities to restrain them, if necessary, to prevent violence against others.

To be fair, this socially normative belief was probably based on firsthand experience or on stories from others with firsthand experience. It is likely that many persons of the day who were profoundly mentally ill were indeed out of control (unpredictable) and potentially dangerous. For example, imagine that the only knowledge you had of air travel was based on airplane accidents. You might reasonably conclude that air travel is dangerous. Constantly pairing two things that don't necessarily always occur together creates the appearance that they do always occur together. That is, it creates an "illusory correlation." It would have taken an astute observer to realize that many persons who were not out of control might nonetheless have a mental illness.

Even Socrates, who has a reputation for being a fairly smart guy, fell prey to illusory correlation. When he considered mental illness, in his memory he had many instances of mentally ill persons who were violent, and he concluded that the one goes with the other. Socrates did not consider that those who were unobtrusively depressed, anxious, or terrified (e.g., of their own hallucinations) might also have a mental illness.

Unfortunately, stories about safe air travel and stories about persons with mental illness who are not dangerous are boring. They don't make for good stories about Socrates, and they don't make good scenes in plays. They also don't attract the attention of the media.

Early media. The Gutenberg printing press made the production of the Bible and other books relatively inexpensive. Lower cost, in turn, allowed more people to buy reading material, which increased the literacy of the population and the demand for more reading material. The printing press ultimately enabled the emergence of popular media, such as magazines and newspapers. (The colloquial expression for newspapers, "the press," derives directly from the printing press.)

Newspapers and magazines did and do need good stories to sell, and they quickly caught on to the appeal of random, unpredictable acts of violence. In 1843, the *London Times* published the following editorial ditty the day after Daniel McNaughten was acquitted by reason of insanity after he murdered the secretary to the prime minister: "Ye people of England exult and be glad, For ye're now at the mercy of the merciless mad!" Again, to be fair, there probably seemed a high co-occurrence of insanity and violence, since the former term was reserved for persons with severe mental illness.

Since then, of course, scientific research has greatly expanded our understanding of the causes, treatment, and management of mental illness. As a result, serious, disruptive mental illness is unlikely to be confronted personally. Thus, the illusory correlation between mental illness and dangerousness, as well as other socially normative negative attitudes toward mental illness, could be reasonably expected to abate. But they have not. To the contrary, evidence suggests that things keep getting worse.

Current media. More than ever, today's media inform us about mental illness. Mental illness is portrayed on TV shows and in movies, and it is described in newspaper and magazine stories. Unfortunately, the mental illnesses are usually presented with some shocking event (violence, mass murder), and illusory correlation is the result. It is widely believed, as in the days of Socrates, that persons with mental illness are dangerous.

An analysis of prime-time American television programs, sponsored by the National Institute of Mental Health, found that almost one in five dramas depicted a character as having a mental illness. Of these characters, 75% were portrayed as violent (compared to 40% of the other characters) and 25% were shown to be homicidal (compared to 10% of other characters). An analysis of movies released between 1990 and 2010 in which a character was said to have schizophrenia found that most of these characters were violent, one in three were homicidal, and one in four committed suicide. Analysis of stories from the United Press International database found that 86% of all stories that included a person with a mental illness focused on a violent crime, which was usually either murder or mass murder.

Ironically, then, as our understanding of the causes and treatments of mental illness have improved over the last five decades, normative attitudes toward mental illness have gotten worse. For instance, people are twice as likely today than they were in 1950 to believe that mentally ill people are prone to violence.

Seeing the Stigma Against Mental Illness

As I sat in the airport on November 15, 2013, working on this chapter, Headline News (HLN) was blaring from a TV near my gate. The news program had a brief report about a 12-year-old boy who had had a fight with his dad, took the family car, and smashed it into some other cars, injuring four people. The report ended with, "Police say the boy was off his medications." HLN then went on with another report.

This is a small but telling example of the casual way in which most Americans think about mental illness. It is a singular example of uncountable instances that occur everyday that tell us what America understands (the social norm) about mental illness. The statement "The boy was off his medications" ended the report. Nothing more needed to be said. The program clearly understood that the sentence would provide some explanation as to what happened. There was no mention, since it would be readily assumed by viewers, that the medications were for a mental illness. There was no need to mention, since it would be assumed, that the dangerous action was the result of mental illness.

Start listening for these offensive statements, and you will realize that they are all around you. Start to hear them, and you will understand their effect on those who have a mental illness.

The Effects of Socially Endorsed Stigma

Recall that the way a person thinks affects how that person feels and behaves. For example, if you think you are in danger, you will feel fear and will attempt to act to increase your safety. Likewise, if someone holds stigmatizing attitudes about mental illness, those attitudes will influence the way that person feels about and behaves toward persons with a mental illness. Stigma against mental illness is keenly experienced. Three in four persons with a mental illness report they have experienced it from others. Perhaps sadder still is when a person turns stigmatizing attitudes, feelings, and behaviors against himself after developing a mental illness.

Stigmatizing Attitudes Lead to Negative Emotional Reactions

The stigmatizing beliefs that persons with mental illness are dangerous, weak, and weird lead to predictable feelings toward persons with mental illness.

The belief that someone with a mental illness is dangerous leads to a feeling of fear. This is evinced in the large percentage of people who readily declare that they do not want to live near someone with a mental illness, that they would worry about someone who dated or married a person with a mental illness, and that they support the idea that persons with mental illness should be forcibly hospitalized in order to protect others.

The belief that mental illness is due to weakness on the part of the person or failure on the part of the family leads to feelings that are a combination of scorn and revulsion. Others might harbor a sense of superiority or, at the least, a sense of differentness from those with mental illness. This allows the person to feel less fearful that mental illness may afflict him or his loved ones (e.g., "He was weak and developed PTSD, but I and my loved ones are not, so this will not happen to us").

Stigmatizing Attitudes Lead to Discrimination

The behaviors that result from stigmatizing attitudes toward mental illness are also predictable. All of the following have been found in research studies.

Persons with mental illness are often deprived of educational and occupational opportunities afforded others. For example, a study of human resource personnel found that one-quarter of respondents attributed mental illness to personal weakness, which in turn led them to assert that they would not hire someone with a mental illness if they were to discover it.

The person with mental illness will be avoided romantically and socially. Around 7 in 10 Americans assert that they do not want someone with a mental illness marrying into their family, and 6 in 10 do not want someone with mental illness in their workplaces. Most persons with mental illness report that they experienced friendship loss when others learned of their condition. Such discrimination starts early, as one in three adolescents with a mental illness reported that teachers and school staff acted fearful and unfriendly toward them, made obvious attempts to avoid them, and regularly underestimated their abilities.

There is an appalling amount of institutional discrimination directed at persons with mental illness. If medical providers learn that a patient has a mental illness, the care provided is demonstrably inferior. Until the passage of the 2008 Mental Health Parity Act, health insurance policies regularly discriminated against mental illness by offering less coverage for treatment. That now-forbidden practice was based on the notion that persons with mental illness are not in real treatment but rather simply like going to the doctor. Some states still ask about mental illness history when couples apply for adoption, related to the idea that persons with mental illness are irresponsible, unpredictable, and dangerous.

Stigma Directed at the Family

Families are also affected by stigma toward mental illness. For example, many persons hold parents responsible for their child's mental illness. In fact, in the past, some mental health professionals actively promoted this idea. Parents, and especially mothers, have at various times been blamed when their child grew up to develop a mental illness. Both autism and schizophrenia, for example, were blamed on inadequately attentive parents. You can still detect such attitudes in writings about depression, anorexia nervosa, and borderline personality disorder.

In like fashion, children of a parent with mental illness are expected to either be very strange or to become mentally ill themselves. "Being raised by crazies makes you crazy," after all, but there is also the inevitability of genetics. At the least, these persons who are related to a person with mental illness are looked upon with suspicion and fear. The same stigmatizing attitudes are accorded to siblings of persons with mental illness. These entail what researchers call courtesy stigma, which means that simply being related to a person with mental illness garners a person some of the stigmatized attitudes.

Spouses confront the greatest level of stigma, as others are confounded that someone would willingly marry someone with a mental illness. It is often thought that these persons obviously lack discernment (about their spouse's character). At the least, spouses are pitied or, perhaps worst, looked upon as "heroic" for their "sacrifice."

Thus are families of a person with mental illness treated to with fear and suspicion. These lead to strained and distant relationships with others, including extended family, as well as fewer social invitations and opportunities. One study found that stigma reduced marriage opportunities not only for the individual but also for the person's family members. Another study showed that families of someone with a mental illness reported feeling less accepted within their religious communities.

Public Stigma Becomes Self-Stigma

Most people hold stigmatizing beliefs about mental illness. For most, however, holding these beliefs does not matter to them or to those they love. Most people do not have a mental illness, and most are not related to someone with a mental illness. In fact, most assume they don't know anyone with one either. (This is highly unlikely, of course, but that is what they believe.) Thus, believing that persons with a mental illness are dangerous, unpredictable, weak, and weird holds no consequences for them.

These beliefs matter, on the other hand, when someone is confronted with mental illness either in themselves or in someone they love. As described earlier, some persons change their beliefs when they are forced to confront mental illness personally. They will end up with a more enlightened view as they learn more accurate information about mental illness in their effort to deal with it. Others, on the other hand, cannot overcome their negative attitudes, which they now turn on themselves or their loved one, making the development of a mental illness doubly dreadful.

The Process of Recognizing Mental Illness

The process of recognizing that one has a mental illness comprises numerous steps. The first step is no step at all. When someone is personally confronted with mental illness, the first reaction is usually denial. This may last a very long time. (My own research documented a patient, seeking treatment at age 72, who indicated that the problem for which she was seeking help had lasted 45 years.) If some type of problem cannot be denied any longer, there usually follows an anxious search for alternative explanations (besides mental illness), such as "I must have the flu" or "It's someone else's fault."

Most persons will discuss their difficulties with others. Some are approached by others, who have noticed the distress or the impairment. These others may suggest seeking help from a mental health professional. More frequently, the person will seek out the counsel of friends or loved ones, their physician, or perhaps someone from church. Again, the fortunate ones will be encouraged to seek the help of a mental health professional.

The person then *may* come to recognize and accept that he or she has a situation or a condition that may benefit from consultation with a mental health professional, but this is not certain by any means. Consulting a mental health professional could result in being diagnosed with a mental illness, which would then require that he or she apply to himself or herself all of the stigmatizing attitudes (dangerousness, badness, and weakness) and feelings that accompany that label. Many refuse to seek the help of a mental health professional for that reason alone.

Nonetheless, some will decide to seek help from someone like me. Do not imagine that she does so happily or readily, however. As these persons formerly applied all the negative implications entailing mental illness to others, they must now potentially apply them to themselves. Let me summarize this as follows: in my experience as a provider of psychological services for almost three decades, I have been involved in the care of thousands of patients (many directly but most indirectly through supervision of trainees) and have yet to meet or hear about a patient who was not *ashamed* of having a mental illness. (See chapter 5 for more discussion of the shame associated with mental illness.)

Mental illness is unique in such "self-stigma." Moreover, such self-stigma can be extremely damaging.

The Effects of Self-Stigma

As noted, one of the effects of the potential of self-stigma is to avoid admitting the experience of a mental illness. The person will deny or minimize the thoughts, feelings, and behaviors that indicate a mental illness. Alternatively, the person may admit to himself the existence of mental illness, but he will refuse to acknowledge this to others, such as friends and family. He will also refuse to seek treatment, which would entail acknowledging that something is wrong. He will thus live in fear of being exposed as having a mental illness, and he will be embarrassed and humiliated if others find out.

Self-stigmatizing attributions lead to predictable self-directed feelings, of which shame predominates. Other feelings include a sense of worthlessness, of weakness, and of incapacity. Moreover, self-stigmatizing attitudes and self-directed negative feelings lead to *self-directed discrimination.* The person will not apply to certain schools or for certain jobs due to the belief that she is not worthy of being hired. She will stop calling friends and turn down social invitations out of the belief that she is not worth having as a friend. This will lead to isolation, as well as an exacerbation of feelings of weirdness and perceptions of being avoided. For example, of persons with schizophrenia discovered that half endorsed the belief that former psychiatric patients are less trustworthy than others. Those who believed this tended to isolate themselves from social support.

Many persons with mental illness will develop a sense of hopelessness that the illness will ever get better. This sense of hopelessness may emerge early, based on stigmatizing beliefs that mental illness is always permanent. This attitude of permanence and this feeling of hopelessness will contribute to a reluctance to seek help.

In summary, the person who turns stigmatizing attitudes about mental illness inwardly will act in ways that deprive himself or herself of opportunities for improvement. Treatment can help or even cure mental illness, but only if treatment is sought. Many individuals who avoid disclosing their mental illness may instead adopt unhealthy coping behaviors to manage the distress, such as smoking, drugs, or using alcohol excessively. Most people with serious mental illness can be helped to obtain and retain employment through job training, employer training, and peer-support networks. However, most do not seek such assistance and remain unemployed, which consigns them to life below the poverty line.

Self-Stigma

In a booklet published in New Zealand in 2006, called *Fighting Shadows,* people with mental illness describe the effects of self-stigma.

- "People are told that someone is worthless because he or she is crazy, and these stereotypes and perceptions are being portrayed by the media, so now that I experience mental illness, I must be like that too."

- "When I was told I was a schizophrenic and would be on medication for the rest of my life, that killed me. It was a death sentence."
- "Should I tell, will they stay, did they break up with me because of it?"
- "Mental illness kills your dreams. It killed my dreams of having children."
- "That inner voice, that inner doubt. It's that repetitive skipping record that constantly reinforces your own inability and lack of worth."
- "After being told what you have, you begin to feel shame, fear, confusion. . . . You don't know how this is going to impact your life, afraid other people might find out. You start to isolate yourself from others and eventually from society."
- "I'm afraid my friends might find out about my illness. I begin to avoid social events, because you are feeling insecure about what happens when they find out that you are crazy."
- "You have doubts about how people are going to react when they find out. Also, sometimes you might have [a] fear of letting new friends know about your mental illness."

Misinformation About Mental Illness That Is Actively Promoted

Not all stigmatizing attitudes and misinformation about mental illness are due to social norms and, to a lesser degree, personal experiences. Unknown to probably most readers is that some of the most dangerous ideas about mental illness are actively promoted. These include the idea that mental illness is not real but rather an invention of the psychiatric and pharmaceutical industries. A related idea is that mental health treatment does not work.

Mental Illness Is Not Real

Some persons, including some Christians, insist that mental illness is not real. A corollary of this notion is that drug companies, psychiatrists, psychologists, and other mental health professionals are getting rich by convincing people that they have a mental illness.

This notion is completely absurd, of course, but it nonetheless endures. The reason for this can be laid at the feet of a thoroughly discredited but unfortunately prolific psychiatrist who allowed himself to be exploited by the rapacious, ever-active, pseudo-religion called Scientology.

Thomas Szasz

In contradiction to evidence from the entire history of humankind, the notion that mental illness is not real was created in the 20th century. It was developed and promoted by a psychiatrist named Thomas Szasz (1920–2012), who became famous for this idea and for this idea only. This explains why he clung to it despite advancements in science that completely undermined it.

Szasz took Cartesian duality to an extreme misinterpretation by arguing that mental illness does not exist because, unlike other diseases, there is no physical manifestation. According to Szasz, anything that cannot be observed, such as feelings of anxiety, depressed mood, euphoria (in the manic state of bipolar disorder), hallucinations, and delusions, cannot be part of a disease process. In other words, Szasz asserted that genuine illnesses and diseases must be characterized by tissue pathology or other objective findings. Since doctors can objectively see and measure broken bones, cancer cells, fevers, and diseased hearts and vascular systems, these can be called diseases. Subjective complaints, according to Szasz, cannot.

According to Szasz, thoughts, feelings, and behaviors are products of the brain. Since they are by definition subjective, others cannot judge the quality of the thoughts, feelings, and behaviors. To do so is to impose an incorrect perspective. Szasz argued that those improperly diagnosed with a mental illness were merely reporting feelings and thoughts and acting in ways that do not conform to what society wants or expects.

When Szasz initially expressed this opinion in 1960, there was indeed limited measurable, objective evidence of mental illness. In 1960, there were no sophisticated brain-imaging techniques, such as CT scans and MRI machines. There are now, and there were when Szasz died in 2012. But reams of evidence of physical abnormality ("not typical or normal") in mental illnesses such as schizophrenia, ADHD, drug addiction, bipolar disorder, and depression, to name a few, did nothing to persuade Szasz to abandon this position. In a bizarre tautology, he asserted that any physical evidence underlying symptoms of mental illness demonstrated that the illness was not mental but physical. Again, he argued, the mental aspects of the so-called mental illnesses, that is, the irrational thinking, the excruciatingly painful emotions, and the maladaptive behavior, were irrelevant to diagnosis. If they co-occur with these physical manifestations of disease, it does not matter, as only the physical manifestations are germane.

Szasz was sort of correct in his criticism of the subjective underpinnings of the mental health field. Medical doctors and mental health professionals have always relied on subjective reports of feelings, thoughts, and behaviors. As noted earlier, people seek help from a mental health professional only when thoughts, feelings, and behaviors are either distressing or when they interfere with functioning. These subjective complaints are a major, unfortunate, but unavoidable limitation of mental health care. (There is not now and never will be an X-ray that can show whether someone is depressed or not.)

But Szasz was not satisfied with simply reminding mental health professionals to be skeptical about subjective reports. Instead, Szasz argued that what mental health professionals called symptoms of mental illness were not symptoms of illness at all. He argued that they were completely normal and entirely voluntary, regardless of their association with distress and impairment. He stated this about all mental illnesses. Regarding the person with schizophrenia describing auditory hallucinations, Szasz said that the person was "choosing" to describe his own thoughts as coming from outside of his head. Paranoia is likewise the choice, on the part of the person, to believe that others are trying to hurt him. Depressed mood, panic attacks, frightening nightmares about a traumatic event, extreme euphoria, feelings of worthlessness because of abuse as a child, and all other symptoms of mental illness are simply choices, according to Szasz.

He took this perspective to a loathsome, despicable, and shameful extreme. In 2005, he commented on efforts by colleges to reach out to students who were suicidal, in order to prevent them from killing themselves: "Preventing suicide—like preventing drunkenness—is the responsibility of the college student, not the college administration."

It may be surprising to readers that anyone still talks about Szasz. Candidly, I regret the need to mention him. I have no respect whatsoever for his perspective, and I hope that over time his ideas are consigned to the same pile of historical oddities in which can be found trephination and phrenology. But it is necessary to discuss him because the idea that mental illness does not actually exist endures. It endures not because of him, but because Scientology used Szasz to promulgate their own ideas.

Scientology

The Citizens Commission on Human Rights (CCHR) was founded in 1969 by Scientology in collaboration with Szasz. The purpose was to create a legitimate-seeming front for Scientology's war on psychiatry. (The CCHR leaves off its publications any hint that they are Scientology.) CCHR openly asserts, nearly verbatim, Szasz's opinion about mental illness: "Psychiatric disorders are not medical diseases. There are no lab tests, brain scans, X-rays, or chemical imbalance tests that can verify any mental disorder is a physical condition." CCHR also asserts openly and repeatedly that mental health treatment is "torture or cruel and inhuman or degrading treatment" from which everyone should be protected.

In 1995, David Miscavige, the organization's leader, addressed the International Association of Scientologists in Copenhagen. As reported in *International Scientology News,* he told the members that the second main objective for their organization, going into the new millennium, was to "eliminate psychiatry in all its forms." (Objective number one? "Place Scientology at the absolute center of society.")

Scientologists are quite open about their motivation. They seek to destroy anyone, including psychiatrists, psychologists, social workers, and pharmaceutical companies, who stands in the way of profit that they can make with their own version of "treatment" (see chapter 14 for more details). They want the money that would otherwise go to mental health professionals. For example, it has become standard practice within Scientology to require members to sign lengthy legal contracts and waivers that explicitly acknowledge its perspective on the mental health profession. These were examined in a series of media reports in 2003, and a typical contract asserts: "I disagree, as a matter of religious principle, with the use of psychiatric treatment for anyone" and "Should I get into a situation in the future where others may think that I need psychiatric treatment of any kind, that I instead desire to receive Scientology spiritual assistance." The spiritual assistance, by the way, may include the "Introspection Rundown . . . an intensive, rigorous religious service that includes being isolated from all sources of potential spiritual upset, including but not limited to family members, friends, or others with whom I might normally interact."

The whole scheme would be laughable, as are the religious beliefs of Scientology in general, if not for the very real influence that their ideas exert in the United States. For example, Scientologists promoted legislation in Florida that would have prevented schoolteachers from recommending mental health consultations, such as an evaluation for a possible learning disorder or ADHD, to parents of children that are struggling in school. Thanks in part to the advocacy of famous actors (such as Tom Cruise and John Travolta) who openly promote Scientology, the bill passed, only to be vetoed later by Governor Jeb Bush. A similar bill passed in Utah and was vetoed by Governor Jon Huntsman Jr.

In summary, Scientology latched on to the singular and discreditable ideas of Szasz to legitimize their attempt to profit from mental illness. In other words, any Christian who believes or states "mental illness does not exist" should acknowledge, and should feel obligated to inform those who hear the pronouncement, that he or she is repeating an idea started and promoted by Scientology.

Stigmatizing Ideas About Mental Health Treatment

There are two incorrect but commonplace ideas about mental health treatment. The first and most common is that it is ineffective. The second is related to the idea that mental illness does not actually exist, which leads to the idea that treatment is unnecessary.

Mental Health Treatment Does Not Help

The idea that mental health treatment is ineffective can be partly laid at the feet of Scientology, which has actively, surreptitiously, and unceasingly promoted this notion for decades. (Okay, Tom Cruise was not particularly surreptitious when talking to Matt Lauer in June 2005, but most of the time Scientology is very secretive about its beliefs.) To be more accurate, Scientology has promoted the idea that mental health treatments are not just ineffective but are dangerous to the recipient.

Above and beyond these despicable lies of Scientology (but not entirely due to it), there is widespread belief that mental health treatment is ineffective. As reviewed in the second volume, in fact, the treatment of persons with mental illness improved dramatically in the 19th century and has been improving ever since. A variety of effective treatments for mental illness have existed for a long time, although they have not been and are not always either available or applied. Treatment of mental illness has been shown in thousands of studies to be highly effective, and it continues to improve on an almost weekly basis.

Mental Health Treatment Is Not Necessary

An indirect version of stigma against mental health treatment follows from the idea that mental illness is due to character flaw. In this version of stigma, mental health treatment is meaningless since there is nothing that can be done except to become a stronger person. The many corollaries of this are versions of the thematic idea that mental illness is merely a version of defeatism in the face of difficulty. Versions of this idea are encapsulated in advice to persons with mental illness to "pick yourself up," "pull yourself together," and "stop feeling sorry for yourself."

Correcting Misinformation About Mental Illness

Despite the fact that simple explanations and simple solutions to complex problems rarely work out, some achieve a type of immortality. For example, Socrates and his contemporaries expressed the idea that persons with mental illness are dangerous. Likewise, facilitated communication is still practiced, and the thoroughly discredited idea that vaccinations cause autism (and a host of other problems) remains entrenched in some corners of society.

It is hoped that accurate information about mental illness, such as is presented in this book and available at countless resources, will affect the attitudes, feelings, and behaviors of readers. In particular, this section presents the evidence for and against the negative attitudes most persons hold toward mental illness and the millions affected by it.

Causes and Treatments of Mental Illness: A Brief Review

As discussed throughout the chapters on the specific mental illnesses (chapters 6 through 18), there are three primary causes of mental illness. The factors that contribute to a person developing a specific mental illness were covered previously in the chapters devoted to those illnesses. A more detailed examination of causal factors, including genetics, prior experiences, and environmental stress, is provided in the second volume. What follows is a brief review.

Biological Factors

Research proves that biology has a large influence on the likelihood of developing a mental illness. The evidence is both direct and indirect.

Indirect evidence comes from genetic and medication studies. Research shows that most mental illnesses are more likely to develop in persons who have a family member with that mental illness, which implicates biological or genetic determinants. Also, medications that change the biological composition of someone's brain, for example, by increasing or decreasing the activity of neurotransmitters, have been proven to have profoundly beneficial effects on various mental illnesses.

Direct evidence comes from biomedical and imaging studies. Biomedical evidence confirms a direct relationship between certain biological factors and specific mental illnesses. For example, some persons are born with trisomy-21, which is a defect in the genetic code (the person has three rather than two copies of chromosome 21). Trisomy-21 inevitably causes the development of Down syndrome, which is characterized by physical abnormalities and severe cognitive impairment. Also, research with various imaging (e.g., MRI) methods clearly implicates biology. For example, persons with schizophrenia have been shown to have a different brain structure than peers who do not have schizophrenia.

Psychological Factors

Psychological factors have also been demonstrated to have a great influence on the likelihood of developing a mental illness. Research has shown, for example, that habits of thinking and behaving are learned as a young child and tend to endure into adolescence and adulthood. Habitual ways of thinking and behaving affect how persons think about, feel about, and behave toward themselves and other people. If thinking is overly negative, then emotions will be overly negative (depressed, anxious), which may cause someone to develop a mental illness. Likewise, the way someone thinks about himself and others will affect his behavior toward himself (e.g., poor self-care, excessive drinking, social isolation) and toward others (e.g., paranoid, aggressive, unfriendly, excessively trusting). These behaviors can lead to profound social impairment, which is a hallmark of mental illness.

Consider the example of love. Perhaps the most important knowledge someone gains, knowledge that is the most influential to mental health and potential mental illness, is whether or not he or she is loveable. Everybody learns this from the way that parents, and to a lesser extent other adults and other children, behave toward him or her. If someone is treated lovingly, then someone learns he is loveable. If someone is treated neglectfully, disdainfully, or abusively, someone will learn he is not loveable. Unless this learning is corrected later, it will remain. To believe one is unlovable makes someone vulnerable to serious relationship problems later in life, as well as to serious mental health problems.

Environmental Factors

Some mental illnesses are entirely determined by environment. For example, as detailed in the chapter covering post-traumatic stress disorder, traumatic experiences can cause mental illness. Other environmental factors that can cause mental illness include chronic stress and deprivation. For example, research shows that persons coping with chronic life-threatening illness, such as cancer or heart disease, are at high risk of developing depression or anxiety.

The Diathesis-Stress Model

To repeat, research has clearly implicated biological, psychological, and environmental influences on the development of mental illness. Their relative influences vary according to the particular mental illness. Some mental illnesses are primarily or entirely due to biological factors, including autism and schizophrenia. Other mental illnesses are due primarily or entirely to past learning, such as anorexia nervosa. Some are due entirely to environmental events, such as PTSD. Research has further shown that not everyone exposed to the same trauma develops PTSD, that not all children who are unloved grow into adults with mental illness, and that not all persons who inherit a biological predisposition toward schizophrenia develop the illness. For this reason, most researchers endorse the diathesis-stress model of mental illness.

In medicine, a diathesis (from the Greek *diathe* or "to dispose") is a predisposition, tendency, or risk to develop an illness. Stress, of course, is emotional strain or tension due to aversive environmental conditions. The diathesis-stress model asserts that biological factors and early childhood experiences *predispose* some people to develop mental illness, which will actually develop if the environment presents sufficient *stress.*

In other words, some persons born with a genetic predisposition towards schizophrenia will not develop it because the environment is not sufficiently stressful. Of two persons exposed to the same environmental trauma, only the one with a predisposition to anxiety will develop PTSD. If an abused child enters a loving, supportive environment as an adolescent or adult, then she may not develop a mental illness.

Dangerousness and Mental Illness

Research shows that the association between mental illness and dangerousness is true only to a small extent. Let's start with some facts.

Fact one, the vast majority of people with mental illness do not exhibit any violence whatsoever (not including violence toward oneself). Fact two, persons with mental illness are more likely to be victims of violence than to commit violence, and they are twice as likely to be victims of violence than persons without a mental illness. Fact three, persons who are not mentally ill commit the vast majority of violent crime. They commit crimes because of avarice, jealousy, and anger, not mental illness.

Nonetheless, there is a small association between mental illness and violence. However, the association disappears when controlling for other factors (see box). Persons with severe mental illness who also have comorbid problems, including substance use problems or a history of victimization, are more likely than other persons to be violent. Persons with mental illness without a comorbid substance use problem, however, are not more likely to commit acts of violence.

Studying Violence and Mental Illness

Studying the link between mental illness and violence is difficult. Most studies are conducted by doing retrospective analyses of persons who have committed violence, but retrospective studies are limited. What is needed is a prospective study, which means finding persons with mental illness and then following them over a period of time. That very study has been done. An epidemiological survey (such as described in chapter 4) called the National Epidemiological Survey on Alcohol and Related Conditions interviewed people about their mental health, and then 12 months later interviewed them again. The survey specifically asked about violent behavior during the time period between the first and second interviews. It then compared the responses of those with to those without mental illness.

The survey found that persons with severe mental illness, such as schizophrenia and bipolar disorder, were more likely to be violent than those without a mental illness, but only if they also had a substance use disorder. Mental illness by itself was not predictive of violence.

Scientific Research on the Effectiveness of Treatments for Mental Illness

Mental health treatments, which include psychiatric medications and psychotherapy, have been more thoroughly researched than any other health treatment in history. The research indisputably shows that mental health treatment works to induce positive changes in the way people feel, behave, and act. A meta-study published in 1993 summarized over 9,000 studies of psychotherapy that, in total, included over one million patients. The meta-study concluded that the typical psychotherapy studied benefitted two in three persons who obtained it. Since 1993, thousands more studies have been conducted, focused less on *whether* psychotherapy works and primarily on making psychotherapy even more effective and efficient. (This research will be reviewed in more detail in the second volume.)

Chapter 20

A Proper Christian Understanding of Mental Illness

"We are hard pressed on every side, but not crushed; perplexed,
but not in despair; persecuted, but not abandoned;
struck down, but not destroyed.
We always carry around in our body the death of Jesus,
so that the life of Jesus may also be revealed in our body."
(2 Corinthians 4:8-10)

"Jesus answered, 'I am the way and the truth and the life.
No one comes to the Father except through me.'"
(John 14:6)

Some Christians may believe that mental illness, unlike other illnesses, is something that a person can avoid if he or she has a strong enough faith or is a good enough person. Related notions are that mental illness is either punishment from God or abandonment by God because of sin.

This chapter starts with a discussion of the theology of glory from which these ideas derive. The injurious effects of these ideas on Christians who are afflicted, directly or indirectly, by mental illness are also presented. The chapter concludes by presenting the proper Christian understanding of mental illness, which is identical to the proper Christian understanding of any other illness, tragedy, or misfortune.

The Theology of Glory

Martin Luther coined the phrase "theology of glory" in the Heidelberg Disputation in 1518. The history of the church, however, is replete with examples of the dispute between this false teaching and the biblical, Christ-centered theology of the cross.

Paul, Augustine, and Luther Warn Against the Theology of Glory

Paul wrote to the church at Galatia, "I am astonished that you are so quickly deserting the one who called you to live in the grace of Christ and are turning to a different gospel—which is really no gospel at all. Evidently some people are throwing you into confusion and are trying to pervert the gospel of Christ" (Galatians 1:6,7).

A few centuries later, St. Augustine spoke of *"incurvatus in se"* ("turned inward on oneself") to describe the preference, being exhibited by some Christians, to look inward for evidence of God's approval rather than focusing outward on the saving work of God through the sacrificial death of Jesus Christ.

Martin Luther expanded on both when he stated that the theologian of glory "does not know God hidden in suffering . . . (preferring) works to suffering, glory to the cross, strength to weakness, wisdom to folly, and, in general, good to evil." Theologians of glory will acknowledge that Christ died on the cross, but they will deny that the purpose was the necessary sacrifice of the innocent Son of God for the salvation of humankind. Instead, according to this theology, the act was a necessary, if regrettable, way for God to transform humanity in order to establish a kingdom of glory on earth. That kingdom will include wealth, prosperity, happiness, and joy for those who believe appropriately and sufficiently. In other words, the theology of glory asserts that faith in God secures happiness during life.

Present-Day Applications of the Theology of Glory

A present-day extension of the theology of glory is that the "strength" of one's faith in God will be directly proportional to one's quality of life. The stronger one's faith, the better one's life. For this reason, the theology of glory is seductive. Indeed, many present-day preachers have found it to be highly profitable, and mega churches around the United States have flourished by peddling this idea. As one pastor of a very large church in Texas puts it, "He wants us to live our lives happy. He wants us not to endure [our lives] but to enjoy them." Prosperity preachers can, of course, point to their own lives for evidence that what they preach is true. Many theologians of glory have very good and prosperous lives. They are admired and adored, living in gigantic mansions, packing stadiums with worshipers, and making millions selling books and TV shows.

Present-day theologians of glory have distinguished affective, behavioral, and cognitive ways of feeling, showing, or proving your love for God and, in turn, God's love for you. (Compare this to the ABCs of life in chapter 2.) *Mysticism* is the notion that sufficient faith allows us to feel God's love and presence. *Moralism* incorporates our outward works of goodness and out-loud expressions of piety and faithfulness as demonstrations of our faith. *Rationalism* uses human logic and intelligence to reassure our belief that God exists and loves us. In other words, according to the theology of glory, anyone who has strong enough faith will feel wonderful about God's love, will *behave* in a way consistent with the wonderful feeling that God's love gives, and will have thoughts and beliefs that are consistent with these wonderful feelings and behaviors.

While seeming to be innocuous and perhaps appearing clever, the theology of glory must be roundly and soundly condemned by right-thinking Christians who believe what the Bible says. The theology of glory must be condemned because it makes understanding and dealing with the tragic reality of mental illness, which is difficult for anyone, even more difficult for Christians.

The Effect of the Theology of Glory on Those Who Suffer

The effects of these ideas on persons who suffer mental illness are devastating.

Practicing a Theology of Glory

What happens when sorrow in life occurs? What happens when bad things happen? What happens when the Christian loses his job, when her child is killed in an accident, when schizophrenia stalks her adult son, when flood destroys his farm, or when suicide takes her mother? Where is the comfort of the theology of glory? "Woe to you who are well fed now, for you will go hungry. Woe to you who laugh now, for you will mourn and weep" (Luke 6:25).

What would the theologian of glory say to Mark (chapter 6), who has experienced depression on and off since age 13? What would he say to Michelle (chapter 7), who is assailed by anxiety about what others think of her? What would the theologian of glory say to Melanie (chapter 8), who was diagnosed with schizoaffective disorder, or to Ryan the Marine (chapter 8), who was so traumatized that he developed psychosis? What would the theologian of glory say to a young wife who is raped and develops PTSD (chapter 10) or to Marjorie who is diagnosed with bipolar disorder (chapter 11)? According to the theology of glory, one can look at a person's life and discover the relative strength or weakness of the person's faith. How a person thinks, feels, and acts directly reflects his or her strength of faith. Likewise, strength of faith determines how much God loves and provides. It is a short, logical, ineluctable conclusion that suffering from mental illness, as do Mark, Michelle, Melanie, Ryan, and the young mother, is an indication of weakness of faith.

The theologian of glory must likewise blame a lack of faith for Kathryn's anorexia nervosa (chapter 11) and Corporal Patten's loss of contact with reality (chapter 12). The same lack of faith must be blamed for children and adolescents who are abused, wives who are beaten, and elderly parents who are neglected. The theologian of glory teaches that God "wants us to live our lives happy." If they truly believed in their hearts, their lives would be happy.

In a twist of the knife that they have plunged into the heart of sufferers, the theology of glory also asserts that if someone strengthens his or her faith, then his or her life will improve accordingly. In other words, someone who is suffering does not have to suffer. To be more explicit with regard to mental illness, the theology of glory asserts that someone who is suffering due to mental illness is someone who has insufficient faith and is someone who can choose, by increasing his faith, not to suffer from the mental illness. Therefore, the person who suffers does so willingly. He might be pitied, but only somewhat. Because, after all, the illness is his fault.

Living Under a Theology of Glory

Of course, not even the most perverted theologian of glory would publicly state any of these things. But he or she does not have to do so directly. Teaching the theology of glory has already accomplished magnification of misery. Recall from the previous chapter the difference between public stigma and self-stigma. Public stigma is experienced when others think badly of someone for having a mental illness, and it is terrible to endure. Public stigma causes embarrassment and leads people with mental illness, and their families, to try to hide the illness. As bad as that is, self-stigma is much worse. Self-stigma is applying those stigmatizing attitudes, emotions, and behaviors toward oneself when mental illness develops. Self-stigma leads to shame of oneself. Self-stigma is made worse by the theology of glory.

Those who fall victim to the theology of glory must come to believe that "the reason for my suffering is my lack of faith." And their suffering is magnified. Their depression is aggravated by guilt and shame that they are not good enough Christians. Their anxiety is compounded if they believe that God is displeased with them more than with those who do not suffer dread. Their feelings of despair about the depredations caused by a loved one's addiction are augmented and exacerbated by the teaching that God, obviously, has turned his back on them. They may go to church and they may pray, but they wonder if they should not bother, since they are obviously doing something wrong.

In Rejecting the Theology of Glory, Some Lose Salvation

Mental illness tends to endure. Any person who must deal with debilitating depression or anxiety (or any other mental illness) must deal with the public stigma of embarrassment and the self-stigma of shame. Since mental illness tends to endure, this struggle may last for a long time.

As a result, many persons coping with serious and chronic mental illness, such as schizophrenia and serious depression, learn to fight the sense of stigma. They educate themselves and learn that the person with mental illness is not dangerous or weak. Ideally, they reject the stigma of mental illness. The entire reason for the founding and success of the National Alliance for Mental Illness (NAMI) is to provide accurate information about mental illness in order to reduce stigma.

What will the Christian who must endure a mental illness do? It was clear to my client Joyce (chapter 5), who was well trained in the theology of glory, what she should conclude: "I hate God. *It's quite obvious that he hates me,* so why shouldn't I hate him back?"

For the Christian who only knows the theology of glory, the distress and impairment of the mental illness, the embarrassment from public stigma, and the shame of self-stigma are compounded by feelings of failure with regard to his or her faith. This must happen to any Christian who adheres to the theology of glory, regardless of whether he or she is a new convert or a lifelong church member. (It is self-evident, but worth repeating, that Christians adhere to this false theology because they have been taught it.)

In the same way that persons with mental illness must confront and hopefully reject public stigma and self-stigma, Christians who fall prey to the theology of glory might reject it. Tragically, these persons are more likely to reject their faith altogether than to adopt a proper theology.

Encouraging Stigma From the Pulpit

Theologians of glory tend to need to portray themselves and their ministry as happy. Happiness is a central notion of God's kingdom of glory. However, some ministers preach a more mean-spirited version of the theology of glory. There are many examples of ministers who publicly denounce mental illness as evidence of the devil's work combined with the weakness of faith of the victim who falls prey to the devil. As these examples show, it takes unusually capable and strong people to resist such teaching. We must mourn for those who hear these messages and are unable to defend themselves.

- Joan Houghton spent five weeks in a hospital following a psychotic episode. She recovered completely and took a job at the National Institute of Mental Health (NIMH). In 1989, she wrote about her experience with mental illness, including a visit to church after being discharged recently from the hospital. "The minister (who knew of my history, faith, and strong belief in God) began his sermon with reference to the devil. He said, 'If you ever want to be convinced of the existence of the devil, you should visit a mental institution.' To illustrate his point, he described people who had lost control of their bodily functions, who screamed out obscenities. . . . I drove home vowing to never return . . . but maybe I had misunderstood. I invited the minister to my home. His visit was our last encounter. Not only did he see evil in mental illness, but he conveyed an unforgiving attitude to those who have the misfortune of residing in mental hospitals."
- During his sermon, Joanne Kelly heard the minister say, "If you are diligent enough in your spiritual practice, you don't need psychotropic medications." Kelly was happy that her adult son, who has a serious mental illness, had skipped church that day. After the service she said to her minister, "What you said was extremely irresponsible." Leaning close to her and clearly angry, he replied, "When I give a sermon, I am channeling God." Neither Joanne nor her son ever returned to that church. She found a new one. She later got involved in the National Alliance on Mental Illness (NAMI), serving as president of both her local and state chapters. She has since been involved in forming the Interfaith Network on Mental illness, which has a goal to educate the clergy about mental illnesses.

A Christian Understanding of Mental Illness

The theologian of glory teaches that it is proper and, indeed, virtuous to seek satisfaction, fame, wealth, justice, and peace in this world. As

Luther states, the world "does not want to suffer hunger, trouble, disgrace, contempt, injustice, and violence, and those who can be free from all this it counts blessed."

A proper Christian understanding of mental illness rejects the theology of glory as the theology of a ravenous beast that wants to kill and devour us. A proper Christian understanding of mental illness rejects the theology of glory as contrary to what Christ said and to practically every word of the Bible. A proper Christian understanding of mental illness, instead, begins and ends with the three articles faith expressed in the Apostles' Creed, which are the foundation of the Christian faith.

The Kingdom of Earth and the Kingdom of Heaven

> *"I believe in God the Father almighty, maker of heaven and earth."* (First Article of the Apostles' Creed)
>
> *"Again, the devil took him to a very high mountain and showed him all the kingdoms of the world and their splendor. 'All this I will give you," he said, "if you will bow down and worship me.' "* (Matthew 4:8,9)

A proper Christian understanding of mental illness rejects the theology of glory as contrary to the First Article of the Apostles' Creed, which holds that God's kingdom is not of this world, that God ordains all things that happen on earth, and that the world suffers because of its fallen nature.

The theology of glory asserts that humans can exalt themselves into a state where there is no suffering, hunger, trouble, disgrace, contempt, injustice, or violence. A proper Christian understanding of mental illness rejects this theology as no theology at all. The Christian, rather, recognizes these teachings as those of the devil, who tried to lure Jesus Christ away from his saving work by offering him just such a world.

Comfort Those With Mental Illness by Preaching the Theology of the Cross

On the contrary, the theology of the cross receives Christ's words that the lives of believers will include suffering: "Whoever does not bear his own cross and come after me cannot be my disciple" (Luke 14:27 ESV).

A proper Christian understanding of mental illness embraces the theology of the cross. A proper Christian understanding acknowledges that mental illness reflects the sinful human condition in the same way that death, cancer, accidents, droughts, floods, violence, pain, and all other sources of heartache do, and it rejects the idea that mental illness is somehow a special category of suffering that God specifically inflicts on those who are "especially" sinful.

Faith and Suffering

It is baffling to confront the idea that faith protects one from suffering, such as with mental illness. It is baffling because the Bible is replete with examples of the exact opposite. Consider all of the biblical characters who are considered exemplars or "fathers" of faith who suffered.

Immediately after the Lord informed Abraham—who is certainly an exemplar of great faith—that he would be the father of many nations and of many descendants, the Lord also informed Abraham that he should "know for certain that for four hundred years your descendants will be strangers in a country not their own and that they will be enslaved and mistreated there" (Genesis 15:13). Faith did not preclude Abraham's suffering.

Faith does not preclude sin, nor does it preclude fear, depression, and suffering. God directed Jonah to go to Nineveh, and Jonah was so afraid he promptly fled in the opposite direction, saying at one point, "It is better for me to die than to live" (Jonah 4:3). Fearing that he would be killed because Abimelek desired his wife, Abraham told everyone, "She is my sister" (Genesis 20:2). Moses grew so weary of the Israelites that he requested of God to kill him at once if God intended the burden to continue (Numbers 11:15).

Samuel was directed by God to choose Saul as king and, at his life's end, Saul was a violent, jealous, irrational drunkard who fell on his own sword. Yet, King David commended the men who buried Saul. King David was a man of faith and a man after God's own heart. David committed adultery and then had the woman's husband killed so that he could take her to be his own wife. He wrote in various psalms that his soul was in anguish, the troubles of his heart had multiplied, his eyes were weak with sorrow, the terrors of death assailed him, and his spirit grew faint. Job questioned why he did not "perish at birth" (Job 3:11). Faith does not preclude suffering.

Peter declared Christ to be the Son of God, yet he later tried to prevent Christ from going to the cross, and later still he denied knowing Christ out of fear. Paul said explicitly to the Thessalonians, early in his second epistle to them, that their faith was increasing despite the afflictions they were enduring, meaning that faith does not preclude suffering were unrelated (although we endure suffering easier if we have faith). To the church in Rome he similarly asserted, "Indeed we share in his sufferings in order that we may also share in his glory. I consider that our present sufferings are not worth comparing with the glory that will be revealed in us" (Romans 8:17,18).

Paul directly assaults the theology of glory in his letter to the Hebrews. He observed the ancients, who were commended for their faith and were not protected from the hardships that must be endured in life. "All these people were still living by faith when they died. They did not receive the things promised; they only saw them and welcomed them from a distance. . . . They were longing for a better country—a heavenly one" (Hebrews 11:13,16). Moses endured mistreatment "because he was looking ahead to his reward" (Hebrews 11:26). In addition to the women who received back their dead through faith, "There were others who were tortured, refusing to be released so that they might gain an even better resurrection. Some faced jeers and flogging, and even chains and imprisonment. They were put to death by stoning; they were sawed in two; they were killed by the sword. They went about in sheepskins and goatskins, destitute, persecuted and mistreated—the world was not worthy of them. They wandered in deserts and mountains, living in caves and in holes in the ground. These were all commended for their faith, yet none of them received what had been promised, since God had planned something better for us so that only together with us would they be made perfect" (Hebrews 11:35-40). Again and again, Paul points out that faith did not and does not preclude suffering.

In summary, the Bible is replete with examples of persons of faith who suffered. Christ praises those who believe without seeing, but many of our fathers and mothers spoke directly with God. These men and women of great faith nonetheless became fearful, depressed, and resentful. And God loved them anyway. He sometimes discussed his decisions with the complainer, and he sometimes forced the wayward person to do what was right (e.g., sending a giant fish). But God never condemned them for their emotional reactions of fear, despondency, and anger. Fear, despondency, and anger are normal in the earthly realm. For that reason, we look toward our heavenly home.

The theologian of the cross is a theologian of eternal glory. In contrast to the theologian of temporary, worldly glory, the theologian of the cross believes Christ when he stated in the Sermon on the Mount, "Blessed are those who mourn, for they will be comforted" (Matthew 5:4). The theologian of the cross takes comfort in Paul's declaration that faith means having confidence in what has been promised, which is eternal salvation. The Christian who suffers mental illness can take comfort in the knowledge that "our light and momentary troubles are achieving for us an eternal glory that far outweighs them all. So we fix our eyes not on what is seen, but on what is unseen, since what is seen is temporary, but what is unseen is eternal" (2 Corinthians 4:17,18).

C. F. W. Walther on Faith and Suffering

In *The Proper Distinction Between Law and Gospel,* Walther warned young pastors not to preach a false picture of what it means to be a Christian. He pointed out that all Christians are at times confused and weak in faith but that they should never conclude that they are not under grace. He states, "The Word of God is not rightly divided when a description is given of faith, both as regards its strength and the consciousness and productiveness of it, that does not fit all believers at all times." Walther noted that pastors, like all Christians, may be underachieving, guilt-ridden, uncertain of their salvation, lazy, despondent, and unhappy. Nonetheless, they are still believers in the saving work of Christ and are thus saved.

God Punished His Son for Our Sin

"I believe in Jesus Christ, his only Son, our Lord, who was conceived by the Holy Spirit, born of the virgin Mary, suffered under Pontius Pilate, was crucified, died, and was buried. He descended into hell. The third day he rose again from the dead. He ascended into heaven and is seated at the right hand of God the Father almighty. From there he will come to judge the living and the dead." (Second Article of the Apostles' Creed)

"Now there were some present at that time who told Jesus about the Galileans whose blood Pilate had mixed with their sacrifices. Jesus answered, 'Do you think that these Galileans were worse sinners than all the other Galileans because they suffered this way? I tell you, no! But unless you repent, you too will all perish. Or those eighteen who died when the tower in Siloam fell on them—do you think they were more guilty than all the others living in Jerusalem? I tell you, no! But unless you repent, you too will all perish.'" (Luke 13:1-5)

Some Christians, including some clergy, believe and teach that mental illness is God's punishment for sin. Mental illness certainly feels like a punishment. Then again, all serious illness, such as blindness, and all serious misfortune, such as the degrading death experienced by the Galileans, seems like punishment. This is an age-old idea that was directly asked of Jesus Christ.

When asked whether God was punishing "worse sinners," Jesus replied emphatically, "I tell you, no!" Jesus Christ firmly, clearly, and explicitly rejects the idea that suffering is always God's punishment for sin. Likewise, the disciples asked him, "Who sinned, this man or his parents, that he was born blind?" (John 9:2). Jesus replied that the blindness was not caused by the sin of either.

Can We Say Mental Illness Is Punishment for Sin?

So should a Christian assert that mental illness is due to a lack of faith or, at the least, weak faith? The Christian certainly can, as long as the Christian is willing to ignore what the Bible says. However, that Christian should be fair and not single out mental illness, persons with mental illness, or their families as somehow especially bad and sinful and in need of punishment. To be fair, the Christian who claims mental illness is punishment for sin should also state, in the same way, that cancer only afflicts those who don't live good, sinless lives. To be fair, that Christian should also then say that being mugged or sexually assaulted or beaten up or otherwise victimized is merely a reflection of God's justice, a punishment inflicted on a sinner. It would be necessary for a Christian who attributes mental illness to punishment from God also to assert that childhood leukemia, heart disease, being on the top floor of one of the World Trade Center buildings the morning of 9/11, losing one's job, having an unfaithful spouse, and all other misfortunes are God's punishment of sin. (To paraphrase Paul, I am, of course, speaking like a fool.)

The Fallen World Decays

A proper Christian understanding of mental illness rejects the notion that persons with mental illness are more "bad" than others because they suffer. It scorns the idea that mental illness is a form of punishment from God, recognizing that all have fallen short and that all deserve such punishment but that, by the grace and mercy of God, we do not receive what we deserve.

A proper Christian understanding of mental illness asserts that persons with mental illness are sinners (like us), that they are suffering (like us now or like us eventually), and that they can be comforted by the Holy Spirit through hearing the Word of God.

In other words, a proper Christian understanding of mental illness recognizes that persons with mental illness are the persons Christ identified, over and over again in his direct ministrations and in his parables, as those most in need of his comfort. A proper Christian understanding of mental illness thus recognizes that the church is uniquely qualified—because it is perfectly qualified—to help those with it.

Those who cling to the Bible as God's Word must reject the idea that mental illness is punishment for sin. For "the Lord is compassionate and gracious, slow to anger, abounding in love. He will not always accuse, nor will he harbor his anger forever; he does not treat us as our sins deserve or repay us according to our iniquities. For as high as the heavens are above the earth, so great is his love for those who fear him; as far as the east is from the west, so far has he removed our transgressions from us" (Psalm 103:8-12).

Preach Christ Crucified to Comfort Those With Mental Illness

The theology of glory must hold that mental illness is punishment. It must assert that punishment is necessary for correction. It must assert that the correction will lead to a more God-pleasing life. The theology of glory, in other words, is about self-saving acts.

A trademark of the theology of glory is refusal to acknowledge that "all have sinned and fall short of the glory of God" and, relatedly, that God sent his beloved Son to die for the world, including theologians of glory. To be specific, theologians of glory refuse to acknowledge that it is impossible for them to fall short of God's approving benediction. Theologians of glory claim that their love for God is so thorough and that their faith in God is so great that they have justly earned God's favor and blessing.

The theology of the cross preaches Christ crucified. The theology of the cross preaches the consummate act of Christ, who declared "It is finished" before he expired. The theology of the cross knows that Christ completed the work of salvation by taking onto himself the sins of the world, which were expiated by his innocent suffering and death, thereby removing all enmity between sinful people and God and bringing peace on earth.

The theology of glory is about our works that earn God's approval and blessing. It rejects the necessity of the saving work of Jesus Christ. The theology of the cross accepts the reality of God's work for us without any assumption of merit or worth.

Martin Luther on Mental Illness

Martin Luther famously admonished his colleague who was despondent that his faith did not keep him from sinning, "Sin boldly!" In this way, Luther tried to remind him that no Christian can avoid sinning, nor should any Christian tell himself that such a thing is possible. In this way, he directly attacks the theology of glory by reference to the Second Article.

Moreover, an examination of his other writings shows that Luther had personal, familial, and professional (i.e., pastoral) experience dealing with mental illness. He was very clear that faith *should* cause all suffering to cease but equally clear that this was not possible. In one of his sermons on Matthew, Martin Luther stated, "The life of Christians should properly be sheer joy and bliss, but there are few who truly experience this joy. . . . But even the great saints do not feel joy and strength at all times, and the rest of us cannot attain to such great comfort and strength because of our unbelief."

Luther had a very good, almost modern understanding of the roles of both thoughts and behaviors in mental illness. Regarding cognitions he said, "You know the proverb, 'Imagination produces misfortune.' Therefore you ought to take pains to divert rather than entertain such notions. I too must do this. For our adversary, the devil . . . knows our physical health depends in large measure on the thoughts of our minds." In this regard, Luther admonished persons struggling with mental illness not to trust their own thoughts but rather to trust the comforting words of others, saying, "Cease relying on and pursuing your own thoughts. Listen to other people who are not subject to this temptation" (that is, the temptation to depression under the assault of Satan's accusations) but rather "give the closest attention to what we say, and let our words penetrate to your heart. Thus God will strengthen and comfort you by means of our words."

Elsewhere he wrote, "Solitude produces melancholy. When we are alone the worst and saddest things come to mind." Thus, Luther counseled those in despair to seek out the company of others, both for encouragement and for the purpose of keeping them from acting on suicidal thinking (see especially his letter to Mrs. Jonas Von Stockhausen). Luther stressed the importance of the comfort of the gospel, which contrasts distinctly beliefs about ourselves as terrible and unlovable with the reminder that God loves us as his own children.

Faith Is a Gift From God

"I believe in the Holy Spirit; the holy Christian church, the communion of saints; the forgiveness of sins; the resurrection of the body; and the life everlasting." (Third Article of the Apostles' Creed)

"The person without the Spirit does not accept the things that come from the Spirit of God but considers them foolishness, and cannot

understand them because they are discerned only through the Spirit." (1 Corinthians 2:14)

The theology of glory asserts that Christians are responsible for their faith. This theology usually directly states, and at the least always implies, that humans come to faith as an act of their own good work. In this way, the theologian of glory wants to share in the glory of God by making himself a co-redeemer of himself. According to him, the act of coming to faith is a demonstration of our love for God, and faith thereby brings God's blessing upon us. Since the act of faith comes from the person, an absence of faith or inadequate faith is an indication of weakness and badness in the person. Likewise, since faith brings a good life, the absence of goodness in life, or the insufficiency of the good life, is an indication of weak faith. In this way, the theology of glory condemns the suffering Christian as having weak faith.

The theologian of glory wants it both ways. He will declare that God is all-powerful. At the same time, he will assert that God needs our help, as God cannot bring us to faith on his own. Apparently, God's limitless power needs to be activated by our act of faith.

A proper Christian understanding of mental illness rejects the idea that inadequate faith leads to mental illness. A proper Christian understanding rejects this as a violation of the Third Article of the Apostles' Creed. Instead, Christians properly acknowledge that faith is a gift from God received through the Holy Spirit.

Comfort Those With Mental Illness by Preaching That Faith Is a Gift From God (Not a Work of Man)

Jesus Christ declares repeatedly that faith is a gift from his Father in heaven. He says, "No one can come to me unless the Father who sent me draws them" (John 6:44), and later in the same chapter he says, "This is why I told you that no one can come to me unless the Father has enabled them" (John 6:65). In the same way, Jesus ascribes righteousness to Simon Peter after the latter declared, "You are the Messiah, the Son of the living God." Specifically, Jesus stated that the faith Simon Peter declared was given to him by God: "Blessed are you, Simon son of Jonah, for this was not revealed to you by flesh and blood, but by my Father in heaven" (Matthew 16:16,17).

Since faith comes from God, not of our own accord, Jesus later comforts Peter, who will deny knowing Jesus, "But I have prayed for you,

Simon, that your faith may not fail. And when you have turned back, strengthen your brothers" (Luke 22:32). For this reason, "The apostles said to the Lord, 'Increase our faith!'" (Luke 17:5).

Paul, the persecutor of so many Christians, knew firsthand the requirement that people be saved by God. He informs us again and again that faith is a gift. To the Romans he wrote, "There is no one who seeks God" (3:11), because "the mind governed by the flesh is hostile to God; it does not submit to God's law, nor can it do so" (8:7).

In his letter to the Ephesians, Paul remonstrates believers that we should not boast about how wonderful we are in our acts. No more should we boast about our "act" of coming to faith. To the contrary, good acts are the result of faith, and faith is a gift from God: "It is by grace you have been saved, through faith—and this is not from yourselves, it is the gift of God—not by works, so that no one can boast" (Ephesians 2:8,9).

To the other churches Paul made similar statements more simple: "No one can say, 'Jesus is Lord,' except by the Holy Spirit" (1 Corinthians 12:3) and "It has been granted to you on behalf of Christ not only to believe in him, but also to suffer for him" (Philippians 1:29).

To his young pastor friend, Paul wrote, "Opponents must be gently instructed, in the hope that God will grant them repentance leading them to a knowledge of the truth" (2 Timothy 2:25).

The Bible assures us that faith is a gift from God. How then can someone say that if faith is strong enough, then one will not have to endure mental illness? To say that is to claim that God does not give strong enough faith, that his gift is insufficient.

A proper Christian understanding of mental illness is that mental illness is not due to weak faith. Mental illness has the same cause as physical illness, maladies, misfortune, regrets, troubles, adversity, accidents, betrayals, trials, tribulations, suffering, pain, and death. The cause of all these is the sinful condition of the world.

The theologian of glory wants nothing to do with this world, believing it possible to create a perfect world and preaching, contrary to every word of the Bible, that God expects us to create a perfect world.

The theology of the cross properly looks to the unfathomable love of God, who sent his only Son as the crucified Redeemer of the fallen world and who sends his Holy Spirit to bring us into faith in God's Son.

Robert D. Preus on Mental Health

In an article entitled "Clergy Mental Health and the Doctrine of Justification," Dr. Robert D. Preus spoke of the fallacy of taking emotional comfort in the strength of one's faith, falsely believing that feeling good is an indication of one's own good work. "The troubled sinner (ought) not look inwardly to feelings, experiences, or quality of faith to gain assurance that he or she is right with God. . . . Of course, justified sinners feel joy and at peace with God, but these emotions are the results, not the criteria, of their justification." The life of any believer will contain pain, suffering, stress, affliction, and sorrow. He wrote, "Pastors who suffer stress and affliction, like any Christian in similar circumstances, may be tempted to look to their faith as a reason for self-esteem and assurance, rather than to the only object of faith, Christ and His pardoning Word. They conclude that failure and inability to cope are due to weak faith or the lack of faith altogether. They are viewing faith as their act rather than as their reception of God's mercy."

Preus points to the example of Luther, who had periods of severe depression and "was often given to anger and impatience," as well as "the inability or unwillingness to cope and to suffer adversities and afflictions and wrong with calmness and love and without complaint." Likewise, St. Paul boasted of his infirmities, persecutions, and frustrations. Thus did Preus conclude, "It is perfectly possible for pastors who know they are forgiven, are certain of their salvation, and live in the grace of God, to suffer burnout and mental exhaustion."

Conclusion

The theologian of glory declares that sufficient faith will make a person happy, healthy, and wealthy. This is contrary to the First Article of the Apostles' Creed. The theologian of glory asserts that God needs our help to accomplish his saving work. This is a violation of the Second Article of the Apostles' Creed. The theologian of glory asserts that we come to faith of our own accord and that, as a result, some have insufficient faith. This violates the Third Article of the Apostles' Creed.

A proper Christian theology holds to the articles of the Apostles' Creed. God made heaven and earth. God is in heaven, and the world is corrupt with sin and suffering, which leads to universal suffering. Christians therefore look to eternal salvation in "a better country—a heavenly one." Christians look forward to heaven because of the saving, sacrificial act of Jesus Christ, who kept all of God's commandments perfectly. He suffered and died for our sins and gave to us his righteousness. Christians know that they come to faith in Jesus Christ and the Father in heaven through the work of the Holy Spirit, who convinces us that our sins are forgiven and that we will be resurrected to life eternal.

Chapter 21

The Essential Role of the Church

"Do you not know? Have you not heard?
The LORD is the everlasting God,
the Creator of the ends of the earth.
He will not grow tired or weary,
and his understanding no one can fathom.
He gives strength to the weary and increases the power of the weak.
Even youths grow tired and weary, and young men stumble and fall;
but those who hope in the LORD will renew their strength.
They will soar on wings like eagles;
they will run and not grow weary,
they will walk and not be faint."
(Isaiah 40:28-31)

This chapter briefly reviews the previous chapters, including the prevalence of mental illness and the many barriers that discourage people with mental illness from seeking effective care. Included is a review of the challenges faced in particular by some Christians to accept, understand, and respond to mental illness effectively.

The primary aim of this final chapter is to describe the essential role of the church in aiding persons suffering with mental illness. Persons with mental illness and their families will seek the comfort that the church and only the church is uniquely qualified to provide. Likewise, the church is well placed to provide guidance to appropriate treatment. The "how to" of this last topic is examined in great detail in the second volume.

Mental Illness in the Church

This section reviews the prevalence of mental illness, the effectiveness of treatment, and the reasons persons do not seek treatment despite its effectiveness.

The Inevitability of Mental Illness

In any given year, one in five persons will experience a mental illness. For most, the mental illness will be some version of a depressive disorder, an anxiety disorder, or a substance use disorder. But for 2 of every 100 persons, it will be one of the serious and persistent mental illnesses, such as bipolar disorder or schizophrenia. Children may be struggling at school due to ADHD; adolescents (especially females) may be dealing with an eating disorder; and older adults may be exhibiting one of the age-related disorders, such as dementia. Children, adolescents, and older adults are also particularly vulnerable to abuse. Couples may be caught in a cycle of domestic abuse, which is almost always directed at the female. Regardless of the type, mental illness is profoundly distressing and debilitating, leading some to contemplate or even carry through with suicide.

It would be wonderful to believe the theology of glory and allow ourselves to be convinced that having Christian faith protects us from suffering. But right-thinking Christians must confess that this is not true. Christians are just as likely as anyone else to develop cancer, heart disease, diabetes, or other medical illness; to suffer mishap, misfortune, or tragedy; or to fall prey to other depredations of this fallen, sinful world. Christians are just as likely as anyone else to develop mental illness, to grow desperate for release like Moses or Paul, to quail in meek fear like Noah and Abraham, or to feel poor in spirit and mourn like King David.

The Effectiveness of Treatment

Over the last 100 years, doctors and researchers around the world have created numerous effective treatments for mental illness (reviewed in detail in the next volume). Treatments for particularly difficult problems, such as severe depression, PTSD, and schizophrenia, stand alongside treatments for less severe problems, such as for children struggling with separation anxiety, students adjusting to college, or couples struggling with conflict. There are treatments designed with specific populations in mind, such as the psychotherapy designed for the special needs of the elderly, children, adolescents, families, or couples. There are effective treatments designed for each particular disorder, such as cognitive therapy for depression, cognitive processing therapy for PTSD, panic control therapy for panic disorder, motivational interviewing for alcohol-related problems, and behavioral therapy for sexual dysfunction. In most instances, these treatments cure, but at the least they reduce the distress and impairment associated with the mental illness.

Underutilization of Treatment

Treatment of the mental illnesses is highly effective. Comparatively, treatment for mental illness is as or more effective than many widely used medical treatments, such as medication for high blood pressure. However, only about one in four persons with mental illness receives proper treatment. Less than half of persons with mental illness will seek any treatment at all, and less than half of those who do will obtain help from a qualified mental health professional. The reasons for this are evident.

Ignorance About Mental Illness

Persons with mental illness do not seek care or, if they do seek it, may not benefit from care because of ignorance and misunderstanding. Our society does not openly discuss mental illness and its varieties, except to belittle it and those with it. As a result, many persons with mental illness and their family members are unaware that the misery they are experiencing and the impairment they are exhibiting are signs of a mental illness. Instead of recognizing the signs of mental illness, they cannot explain why they feel the way they do. As a result, they do not seek treatment.

Stigma of Mental Illness

The greater and more common reason readily available and effective treatments are underutilized is the stigma our society attaches to mental illness. Our society foists on those with mental illness a sense of profound shame, as it moralizes that mental illness only happens to those who are weak or bad. As a result, many persons refuse to admit to themselves or to others that they or a loved one are experiencing a mental illness. Spouses, parents, siblings, and other family members will also discourage such an admission, as they don't want the embarrassment of having someone in the family with a mental illness. The stigma associated with having a mental illness prevents people from getting appropriate care. As a result, people suffer more and longer than they need, and some die from suicide.

The Essential Roles of the Church

If one in five persons will experience a mental illness in any given year, it is inevitable that there are persons in your church who are experiencing mental illness. In any given year, probably every other person in your church is either experiencing a mental illness or has a family member (or members) struggling with mental illness.

The church has three essential roles in the care of persons with mental illness. These roles are familiar to all church workers, but they have special significance and application to those with mental illness. First, the church offers comfort to those who suffer, whether from mental illness or any other problem encountered. Second, the church seeks out and corrects those who are lost, meaning those who believe or fear that God has stopped loving them. Third, the church points those with mental illness to the proper care of trained mental health professionals. All of these roles rely on a proper Christian understanding of mental illness.

Comfort, Comfort My People

Persons with mental illness and their families are in profound distress. They are very likely to seek care and comfort from their church. They may or may not understand or recognize that they have a mental illness, and they may or may not be in treatment with a health professional. But they will probably come to their church when in distress. (If not, you will need to seek them out, as explained in the next section.)

Of course many persons with mental illness turn to their church! The church is the messenger of God's love and care. To seek solace and comfort from the church makes perfect sense and is entirely appropriate. Unlike the present world and those wretched theologians of glory, the church that preaches the theology of the cross does not flee from the sorrows and burdens of life.

The church offers comfort to the ill because it does not try to deny the existence of illness. The Bible is replete with stories that are familiar and relevant to those coping with mental illness. Jesus, Moses, David, Paul, and all of the prophets speak of weariness and burden; of the need for rest; of confusion, fear, and despair.

The Church as the First Resource

Surveys show that people confronted by mental illness will usually first seek help from their church. In fact, many will prefer to get care only from their church. This cannot be allowed, since professional treatment is necessary, but it points to the centrality of the church in people's lives.

To those with illness, including mental illness, the church says, "Welcome! Welcome and be of good cheer. We do not think you are weak, sinful, or damaged just because you are sick. Because here we know that we are all sick and dying."

The church preaches that all illness comes from our fallen nature, and that all of us have that fallen nature. "All have sinned and fall short of the glory of God" (Romans 3:23). Thus do Christians stand and proclaim at every worship service, in words and in songs, to God and to one another, that we are all poor and miserable, that we are all weak, sinful, unclean, and unworthy. We confess that we do not love God with our whole hearts and that we justly deserve punishment. We confess that it is not because of our own good works, but only because of God's grace that we are spared from tragedy, sickness, and death. What a comfort to the person with mental illness to know that the members of his church do not look down upon him, but rather look at him as a fellow Christian, that is, an unworthy, sinful, loved child of God who has been redeemed by the sacrifice of Jesus Christ.

Having a firm foundation in the Christian faith and the theology of the cross bestows a tremendous advantage in understanding and accepting mental illness. The church thereby offers a comfort to those who struggle with mental illness that they cannot obtain anywhere else. The church is the sanctuary where persons who are suffering are offered compassionate understanding for, and forgiveness of, their weak and sinful human nature.

The comfort in this knowledge is of course the comfort of our ultimate triumph over this great affliction. Paul's words to the Romans summarize our comfort: "This righteousness from God comes through faith in Jesus Christ to all who believe. There is no difference, for all have sinned and fall short of the glory of God, and are justified freely by his grace through the redemption that came by Christ Jesus" (Romans 3:22-24 NIV 1984).

The church comforts by preaching Christ crucified. We proclaim that God loves us despite our sinful nature. We proclaim that God sent his

Son as an atoning sacrifice through which believers gain eternal salvation. We proclaim that God brings us to and sustains us in our faith.

Of all the ways that Christians can help other persons with mental illness, preaching the theology of the cross is the most worthy. The church declares to those dealing with mental illness that the world is full of hardship, tragedy, and despair for all of us. But we preach Christ crucified, and through the Holy Spirit, who gives us faith, we can look forward to that which we do not yet see.

To Seek and to Save What Is Lost

The second essential role of the church with regard to mental illness is to seek out and save lost souls. We tend to think of "the lost" mostly in terms of "those outside the church," those who don't know Jesus as their Savior. That certainly is correct. But it may be helpful also to think of "the lost" in your church. That includes those who believe that their mental illness or the mental illness of their loved one is proof that God has abandoned them. "The lost" also include those who refuse to admit that they have a mental illness, out of fear that this proves they are weak and bad and, thus, deserving to suffer in this manner. "The lost" are those who are struggling to cope with mental illness but who do not seek the comfort of their church out of shame and fear.

These lost may not communicate their problems and struggles to others in their church because they are encumbered by the profound shame that our society places on mental illness. They may feel isolated from and abandoned by all communities, including the community of their church. They may have fallen victim to the depredations of the theology of glory, which falsely asserts that people of sufficient faith obtain God's earthly blessings and will not be afflicted by mental illness. This apostasy says that God would not give a good person bipolar disorder, an unfaithful spouse, or a child with schizophrenia. It asserts that a good person would never develop a drug or alcohol problem. It says that anyone afflicted with mental illness must be either weak in faith or bad in character, thereby deserving of God's punishment in the form of the mental illness. It would be quite normal for someone with mental illness who is exposed to this to not seek the comfort offered by the church, presuming that God is mad at them and that church leaders and other church members would be disgusted by them.

In short, it is likely that some of the members of your church who struggle with mental illness are faltering in their faith in a loving God.

They avoid church because they believe that there is nothing there for them.

The proper Christian response to those with mental illness who do not come to the church for comfort flows directly from the proper Christian understanding of mental illness, which is the same as understanding any human suffering. The proper response is to seek out and to reassure them that mental illness is not some special version of suffering or of punishment that is somehow proper and just. Reassure them that mental illness, like any other human suffering, is due to the fallen state of the world. These souls must be sought out and saved. Find them and declare to them, "Come back to church. You are welcome here, as are all sinners and all who suffer. Come back and be comforted by the Word."

Take Care of My Sheep

The third essential role of the church is to refer those with mental illness to proper treatment. The pastor and other church workers have, above all, concern for the spiritual needs of members. However, the Bible clearly teaches that caring for the corporal well-being of members is part of the duties of the office of the keys (for example, see Acts 6:1ff; 11:29,30; 24:17; Romans 12:8,13; Galatians 2:9,10; 1 Timothy 5:10; 1 Thessalonians 4:11,12).

Church workers must help those with mental illness by referring to a competent mental health professional. Mental health professionals offer what the church cannot, which is safe, scientifically based, effective treatments for mental illness. God has bestowed on his creation many gifts, including plentiful harvests, natural resources, and health care professionals. The church does not pretend that believers can live without food or can drive their cars without fuel, nor does the church eschew health care. Another essential role of the church, then, is to encourage persons with mental illness to seek such treatment and to assist them in obtaining maximum benefit from such treatment.

Church members with mental illness and their families will fall into one of four categories.

Those Doing Well (or Mostly Well) in Treatment

The first group includes those in treatment who are doing well or mostly well. In other words, some persons in your church who have a mental illness will be receiving proper treatment. Some of these will be intent on continuing treatment, and some may be planning on ceasing treatment because it has helped and is no longer needed. Some are currently being treated by a mental health professional, but others are being treated by a provider without special expertise in mental illness. Some have been in treatment for a long time, for a long-standing mental illness such as schizophrenia, major depression, bipolar disorder, or a substance use disorder. Some are in a treatment episode that started fairly recently. Some have just begun treatment. Others are wrapping up successful treatment.

If you become aware of these persons, they (or their families) should be congratulated, encouraged, and admired. They should be assured that mental illness is nothing special. They should be encouraged to recognize, as you do, that mental illness is merely one variation of the suffering that all Christians endure as part of the fallen world. As with any person dealing with a serious illness, they should be offered the comfort of the gospel.

Those in Need but Who Falter in Their Commitment to Treatment

The second group includes those who are in treatment that is helping (possibly helping immensely) but who may refuse to acknowledge that treatment is helping. They may be faltering somewhat in their commitment to it, and they may be wondering whether to stop treatment, which they view as unnecessary. They may be struggling with accepting that they have a mental illness, or they may be struggling to accept that treatment is necessary.

This doubt about the need for treatment may very well be because of the illness itself. For example, some persons with depression contemplate quitting treatment because progress is slow and they grow doubtful that it will ever help. Likewise, some persons with bipolar disorder want to quit treatment because they are feeling really good as part of the manic phase of the illness. Some persons with schizophrenia may come to doubt that they actually have an illness, even though they have been in treatment for the illness for many years.

The family members of these persons may come to see you, out of concern that the person is not cooperating with treatment. Both the family members and the person with the illness should be assured that mental illness is similar to other illnesses, meaning it is not some special indication of weakness of faith or badness of character. In other words, offer them the comfort of the gospel. In addition, the family members may need your support in reminding the person with mental illness that all illnesses need to be treated by a qualified health professional. These persons need to be strongly encouraged to stay in treatment. The family may need assistance in dealing with the person if they do indeed quit treatment.

Details about dealing with this situation, as well as other situations in which a person or family dealing with mental illness needs referral for proper treatment, are provided in the second volume.

Those in Need but Who Are Receiving Inadequate Treatment

The third group will be in treatment, but they are genuinely not being helped. They may be tempted to stop treatment altogether, which they need, rather than find an effective alternative treatment. If treatment is not helping, they may grow despondent. Not knowing that there are more effective options, they may drop out of treatment altogether. Inadequate treatment might be because the care is being provided by a medical doctor without adequate understanding of mental illness. It might be being provided by a mental health professional who is simply not helping, either because they are not generally competent or because they are not particularly competent with this specific problem.

These persons should be encouraged to talk with their treatment provider about a referral for either alternative or adjunctive (additional) treatment, such as adding psychotherapy to medication or vice versa. The treatment provider *should* be amenable to a discussion about the inadequacy of treatment. If he or she is not, this indicates a lack of professional objectivity. In that case, it would be appropriate for you to suggest that the person seek the opinion of a different mental health professional.

The second volume will have extensive discussion about evaluating the effectiveness and appropriateness of treatment being provided. It will also contain information about how to find a well-qualified mental health professional and how to provide a referral to church members.

Those With Mental Illness Not Receiving Treatment

The fourth group will likely be the largest group, which is those with mental illness who are not in any treatment whatsoever. You now know that persons with mental illness eschew treatment for reasons related to ignorance and misunderstanding (i.e., not realizing that they have a mental illness) and to stigma and shame (i.e., feeling ashamed and embarrassed that they have a mental illness or need mental health treatment). In your church, these persons may be fearful about their salvation, possibly believing, as corrupt theologians have taught them, that mental illness means that God has abandoned them.

These persons need encouragement and comfort from their church. They need the comfort of the gospel and the reassurance that having a mental illness does not mean they have inadequate faith or that God is punishing them. They need encouragement to recognize that mental health treatment can help greatly, that their distress can be alleviated, and that their impairment can be rectified.

The second volume provides extensive discussion of how to approach someone in your church who you believe may have a mental illness that is not being treated. It will discuss how to start the conversation, how to express concern, and how to make a referral.

Pray, Praise, and Give Thanks

With regard to caring for those with mental illness and their families, your church can do something during the next worship service. I invite all readers to incorporate prayers for those suffering from mental illness. Prayers may ask God to grant those with mental illness, and their families, both the comforting knowledge of eternal salvation and the courage to seek and persist in treatment. A prayer of thanks for the benefits of treatment would also be appropriate. It might be best to do this within the prayers for the sick, which will explicitly acknowledge that mental illness and physical illness are both due to the same thing. Probably few prayers would include the names of people who are in psychiatric hospitals, out of respect for confidentiality and privacy.

A Preview of Volume 2

This book and this final chapter hopefully demonstrate that the church and its workers have a central, vital, essential role in helping those with mental illness. My prayer is that this book will help you understand the experiences of persons with mental illness. Such understanding will help you to comfort and console them.

The next volume focuses on four things. It covers the causes of mental illness. It also reviews scientifically valid treatments for the various mental illnesses. Additionally, it discusses the mental health treatment system (e.g., the difference between psychiatry, psychology, and social work) and how you, the church worker, can encourage your church members dealing with mental illness to seek proper treatment.

The next volume also provides information and advice for church workers regarding how to help their church members to access and benefit from treatment, including how to start the conversation about needed care, how to find good mental health professionals to whom they can refer (in particular, mental health professionals who will respect Christian faith), and how to evaluate whether treatment is helping or not.

• • •

Soli Deo Gloria

Subject Index

E

F

G

H

N

O

P

R

S

T

V

W